AF469334

LONDON

THE PANORAMAS

MARK DENTON

CONSTABLE · LONDON

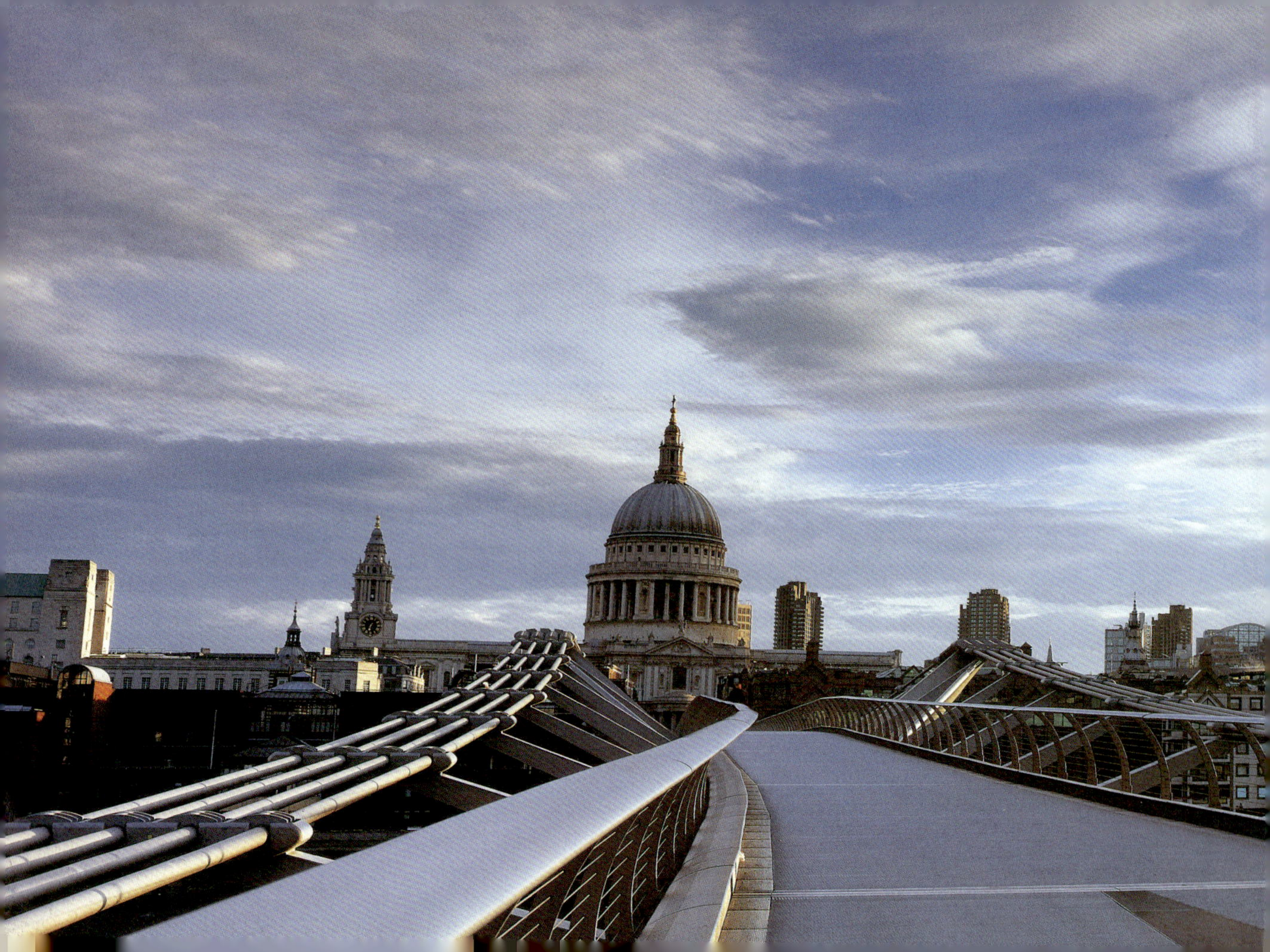

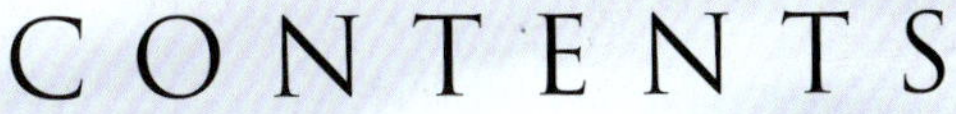

CONTENTS

INTRODUCTION

London is a city of panoramas – geographical, social, and historical. Europe's largest conurbation covers 600 square miles (1,555 sq km) and is home to over eight million people, speaking around 300 different languages. A far cry from the day in AD43 when the Romans founded a storage depot on the marshy banks of the Thames and called it Londinium.

London gained pre-eminence among English cities when William the Conqueror became the first king of England to be crowned in Westminster Abbey, on Christmas Day 1066. Soon after, he built the White Tower that is now the centrepiece of the Tower of London. Sadly, more than 13,000 mediaeval and Tudor buildings were destroyed in the Great Fire of London in 1666 – ending a cycle of devastation begun when the Great Plague decimated the city's population.

Then, as now with the 2012 Olympics around the corner, London's energy spurred on a reinvention of the city, under the guidance of the architect of St Paul's Cathedral, Sir Christopher Wren. Another burst of building during the nineteenth century reflected London's role as hub of a British Empire spanning the globe. Hitler's Luftwaffe wrought fresh havoc on the city during the Second World War, and in the years after the war swathes of mediocre architecture were thrown up as an impoverished Britain struggled to rebuild its capital. From the 1980s London began to show renewed care for its architectural character with a string of iconic buildings – the London Eye, Tate Modern, the new Wembley Stadium and a remodelled South Bank Centre.

Throughout its history, London has maintained an antipathy towards the sort of

PAGES 2-3: ST PAUL'S CATHEDRAL AND MILLENNIUM BRIDGE

planning that moulded cities such as Paris and New York. Instead London is bonded together with the help of its villages. Unlike American cities with their clear divisions into downtown and suburbia, London's heart – the City of London and the West End – is complemented by outlying former villages gradually absorbed by the city's sprawl, while still maintaining their own identity and structure. Hampstead in the north, Blackheath to the south-east and Richmond in the west are just three featured here.

To truly get a feel for London, therefore, visitors should go beyond the most familiar places on the tourist map. So, as well as Covent Garden market, visit Brick Lane and Spitalfield in the East End. If in search of historic houses, discover the marvellous Elizabethan-meets-Art Deco hideaway that is Eltham Palace. Sample the eclectic watering holes of Hoxton. The same applies in the centre of the city, too. There's a local saying that tourists walk along Oxford Street, while Londoners cut across it, heading into Soho to the south or Fitzrovia to the north.

Around 700 of the city's buildings bear blue plaques (www.blueplaque.com) telling us about famous past occupants. There's even one for the fictional detective Sherlock Holmes at 221b Baker Street. As inhabitants of the most cosmopolitan city in Europe, London's people are as much a part of its character and appeal as its historic buildings, wonderful shops or beautiful parks, and all around the city, certain areas take on the flavour of specific communities – Portuguese around Vauxhall, Caribbean in Brixton, Jewish in Golders Green, Bangladeshi in Brick Lane.

Like the city's architecture, variety triumphs over homogeneity in its population. Tolerance is a London trademark – a crucial one with so many people crammed so close together. What may be branded English aloofness is often simply a respect for privacy in a city where space, both physical and personal, can sometimes be at a premium. But don't be fooled. London is a friendly city as well as a big one: expansive in every sense.

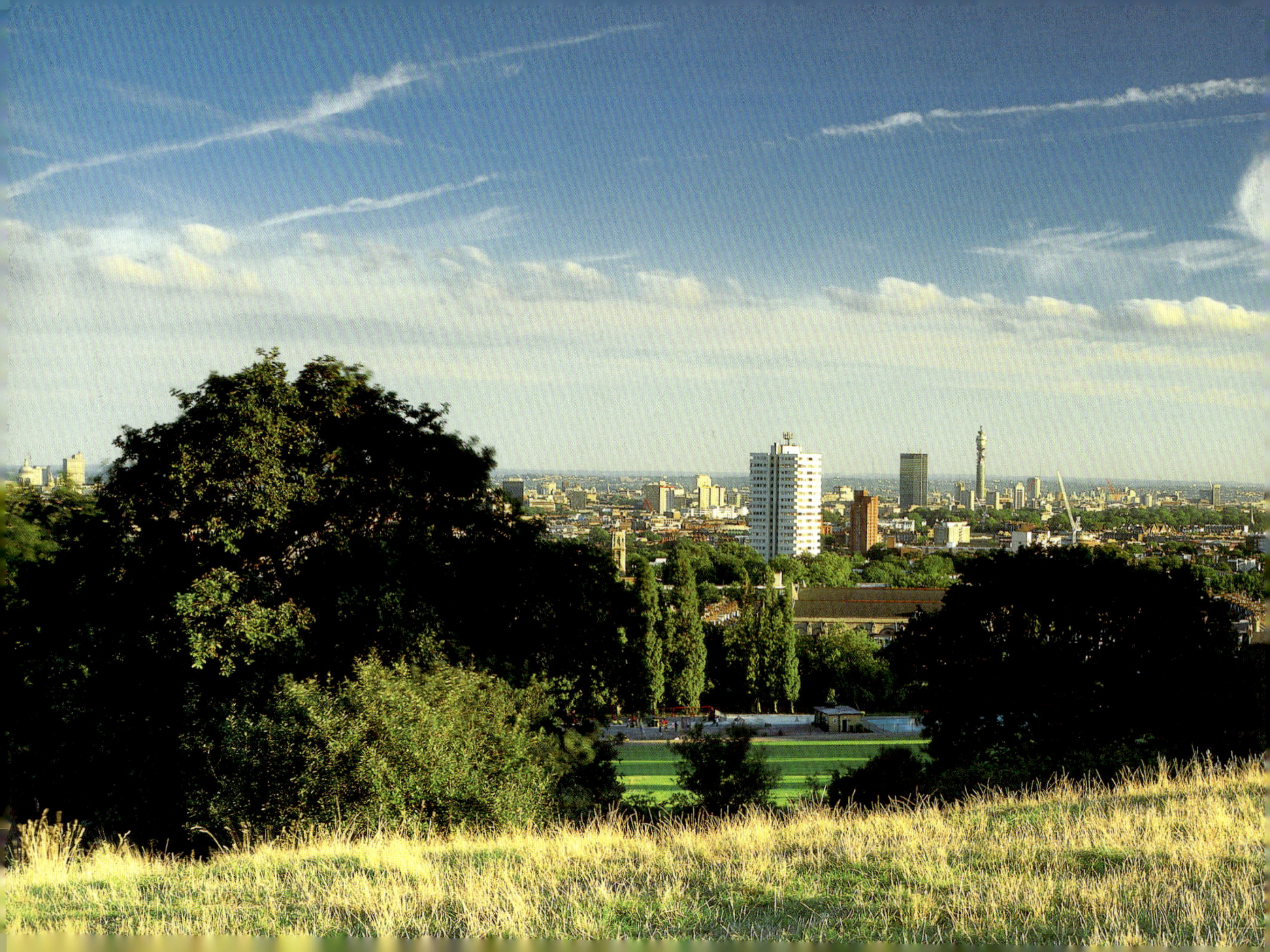

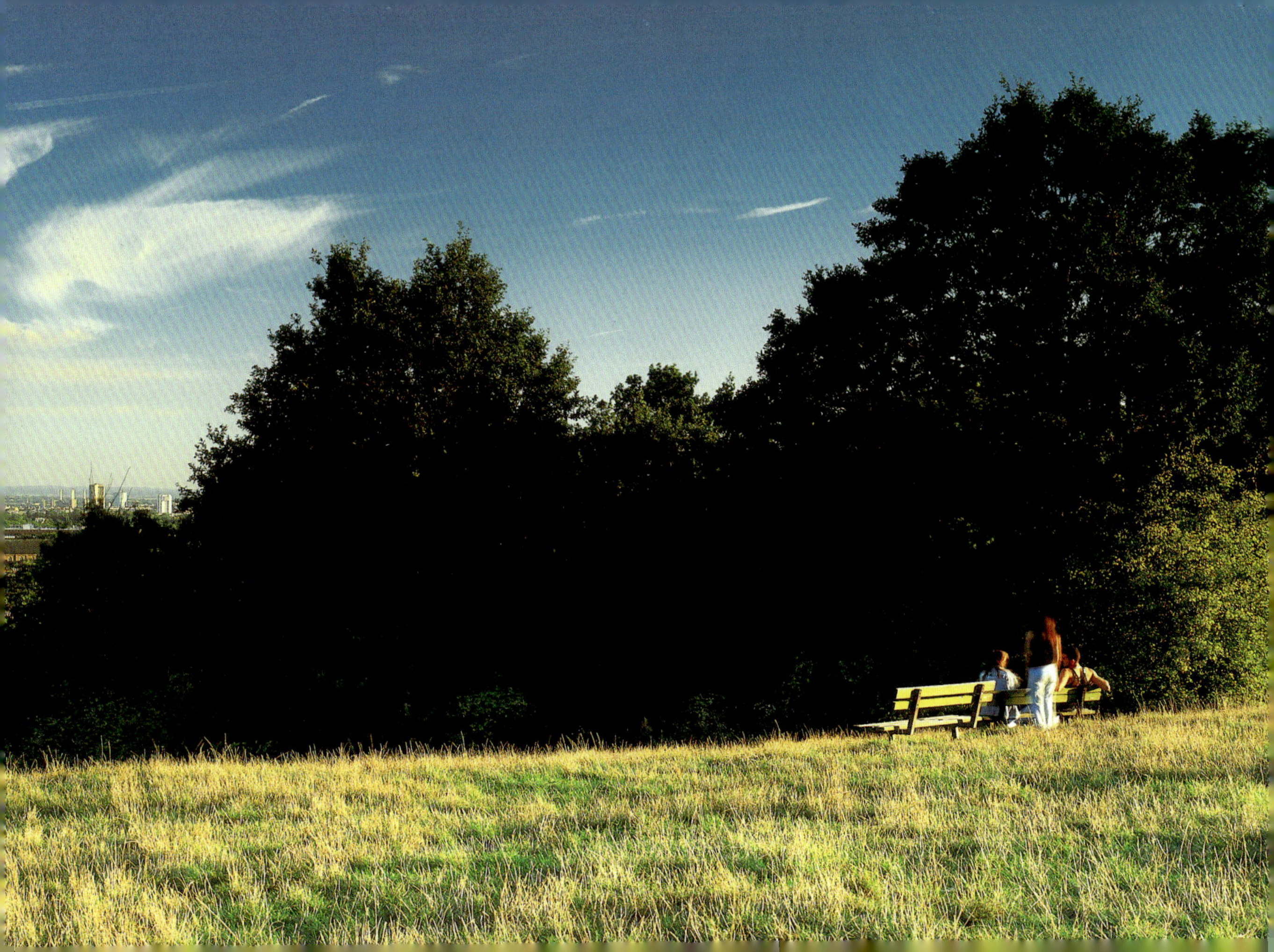

WESTMINSTER AND THE WEST END

Like the Eiffel Tower in Paris, the London Eye was intended to be a temporary structure. London, like Paris, saw sense, leaving the Eye to imprint its beautiful circle on the rectangular urban skyline.

Across the river, the famous honey-coloured stones of the Palace of Westminster have stood for nearly a thousand years. The Mother of Parliaments is one of London's most famous icons – almost as familiar as the sound of Big Ben which marks the passing of the day across London and, via BBC radio, across the world. Big Ben, of course, is the name of the bell not the clock tower, made by the Whitechapel Bell Foundry. Founded in 1570 and still at work today, it's one of the oldest companies in the world, forging not only Big Ben (1858) but also the original of America's famous Liberty Bell (1752).

While the Victoria Embankment running along the north bank of the Thames cries out for a purpose other than the snarl of traffic, Trafalgar Square a few hundred yards to the north-west is an example of London renewing a key space to great effect. For decades, this magnificent square was reduced to little more than a giant roundabout. Nelson's Column, a towering monument to England's greatest admiral, and Edward Landseer's magnificent bronze lions brooded over a pigeon-filled space which came alive only for occasional protest rallies and as a rowdy gathering place on New Year's Eve.

Recently Trafalgar Square has been reborn as a place for people rather than cars. A sweeping expanse of white stone now frames the twin buildings of the National Gallery – the 1820s original and the modern Sainsbury Wing, famously denounced by Prince Charles in 1991 as 'a monstrous carbuncle on the face of a much-loved and elegant friend'! In the

PAGES 6-7: SUMMER, HAMPSTEAD HEATH

square's north-west corner is the Fourth Plinth, a site for a rotating series of thought-provoking sculptures and installations.

London's parks, of course, welcome everyone. Green Park is one of the largest of the city's central parks, bordering Piccadilly with its famous hotels such as The Ritz, and luxury shopping spots such as Burlington Arcade and the Royal Academy art gallery. First recorded in 1554, Green Park's name refers to its relative lack of flowers. For its first two centuries, it was best known as the site of frequent duels rather than relaxation. Though now devoid of buildings, the Park once contained a Temple of Peace and a Temple of Concord, both destroyed during firework displays – the former in 1749, the latter in 1814. The park was opened to the public in 1826.

For many Londoners, though, St James's Park has a greater appeal. The oldest of the city's Royal Parks, it is surrounded by three palaces – Westminster (Parliament), St James's Palace and Buckingham Palace, the latter at the end of arguably London's most beautiful stretch of road, The Mall. Once a marshy water meadow, St James's Park took its name from a leper hospital founded here in the thirteenth century. In 1532 Henry VIII acquired the site to satisfy his passion for hunting, and built the Palace of St James. Elizabeth I used the park for frequent fêtes, though it had a more sordid reputation as a meeting place for sexual encounters, chronicled by the rakish aristocrat John Wilmot, the Earl of Rochester – subject of the 2005 film *The Libertine*.

Horse Guards Parade stands on the east side of the park, home to the Queen's traditional corps of soldiers, within a short horse ride from the monarch's famous residence at the western end of the Mall. Outside Buckingham Palace is the Queen Victoria Memorial, including not only a statue of England's longest-reigning monarch but also figures of Victory, Courage and Constancy, and ornamental gates given by three of Britain's former Dominions – Australia, South Africa and Canada.

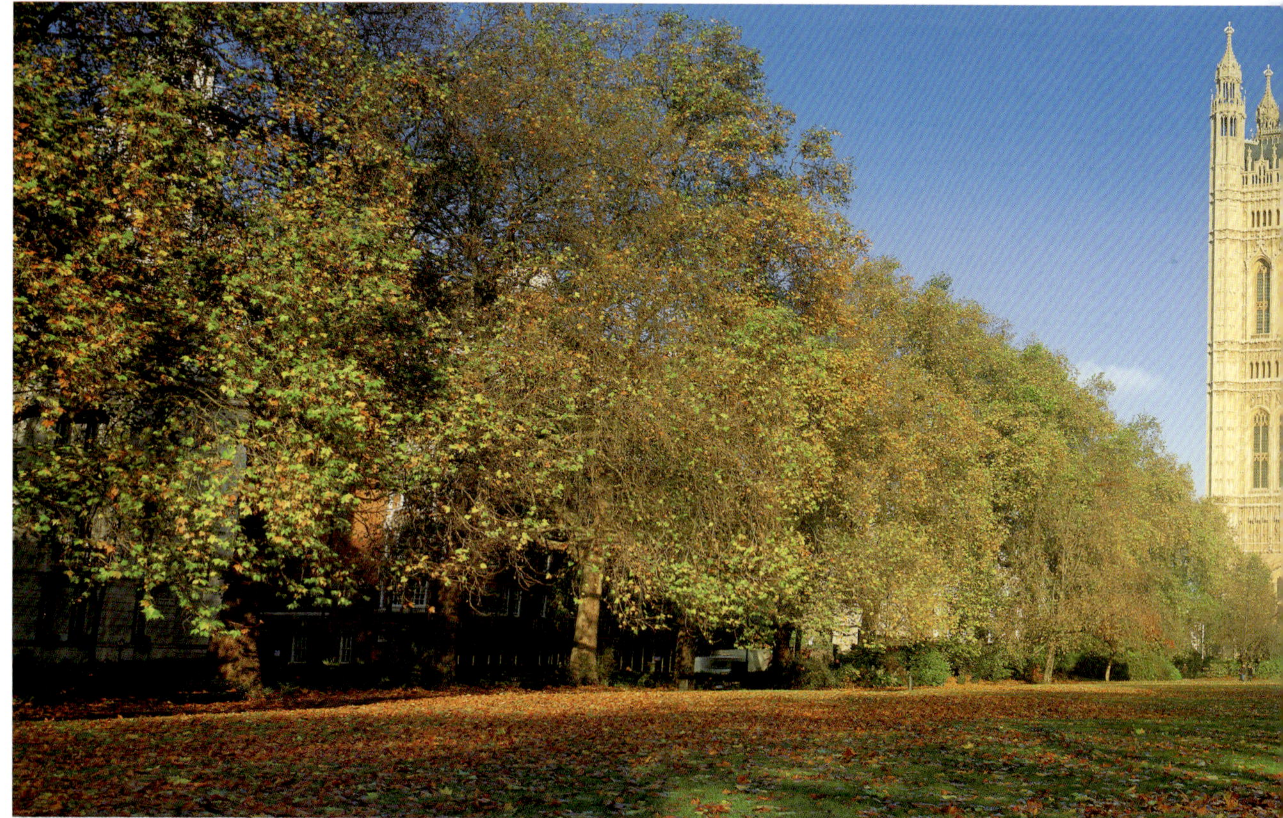

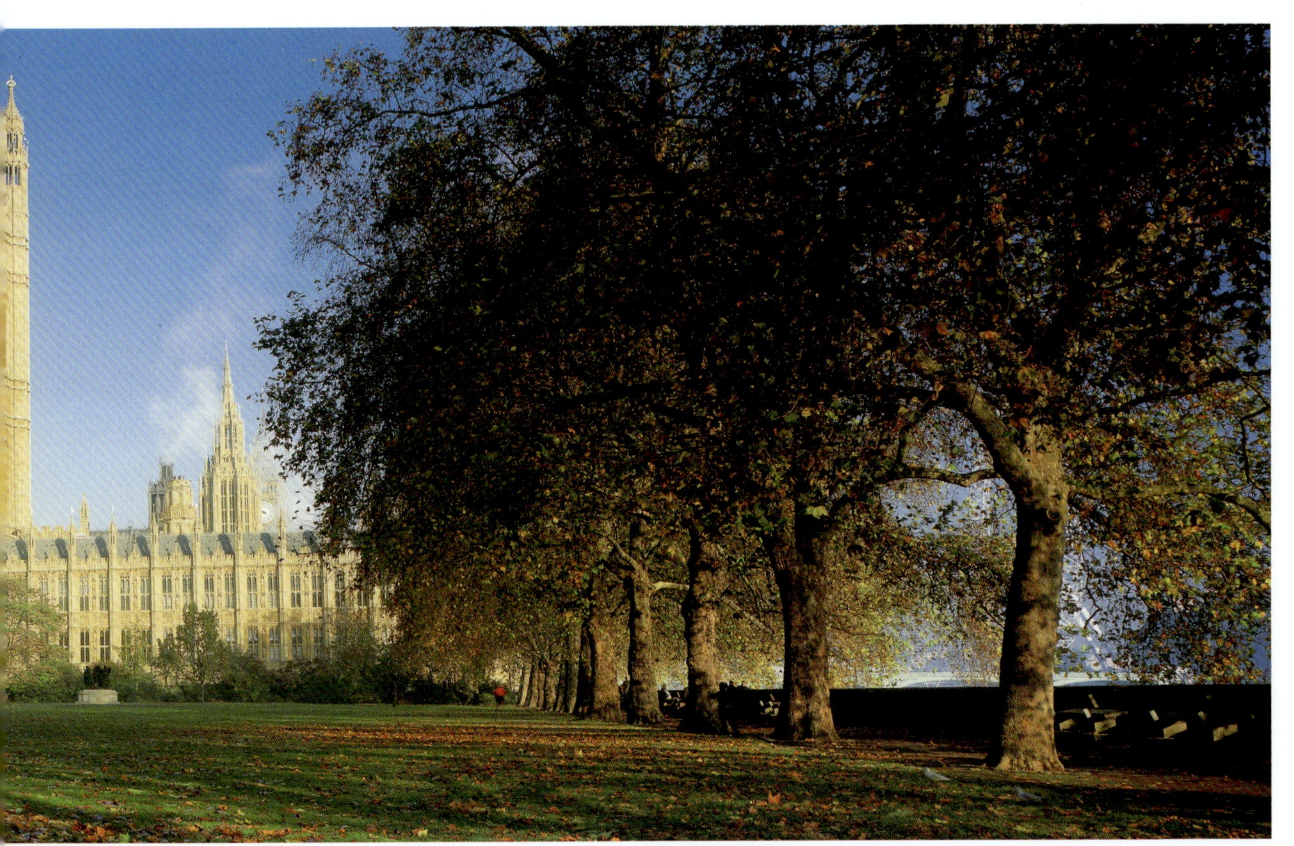

VICTORIA TOWER IN AUTUMN, PALACE OF WESTMINSTER

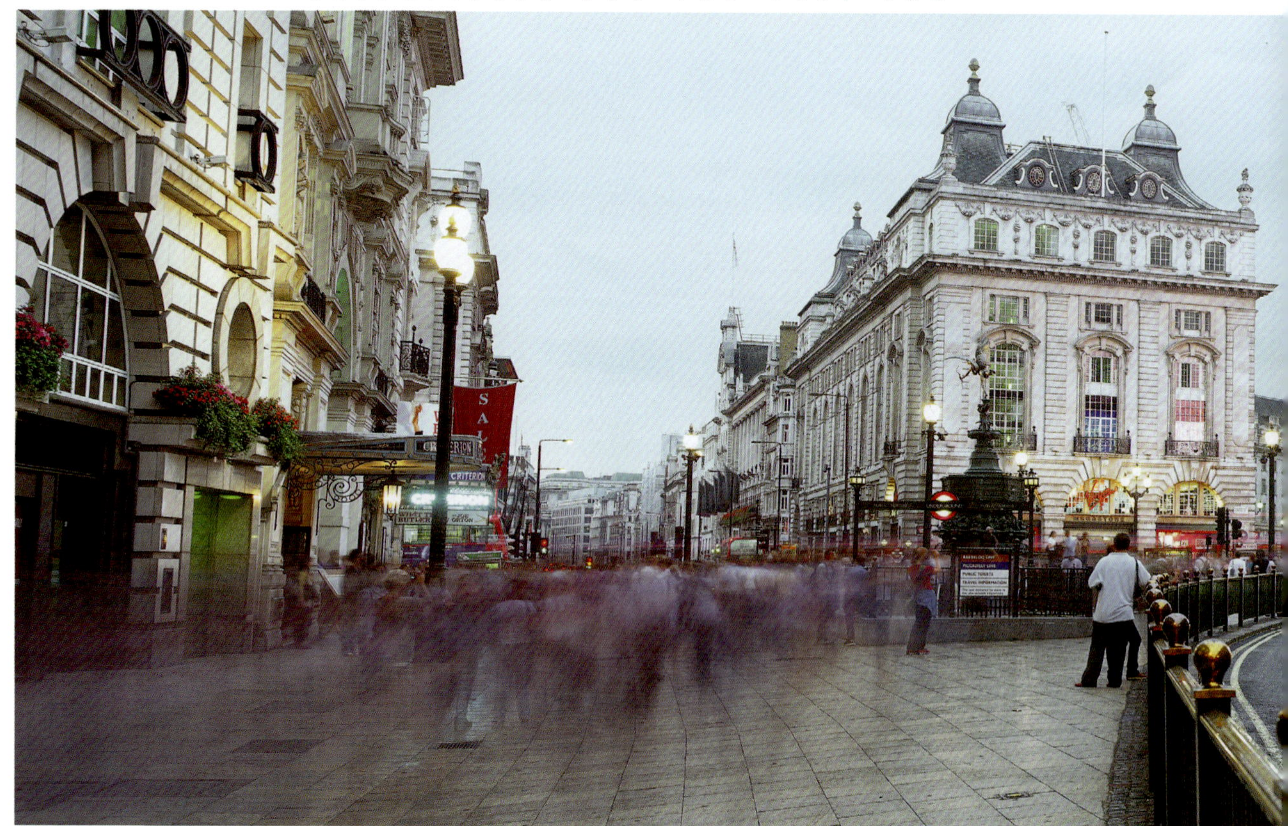
CRITERION

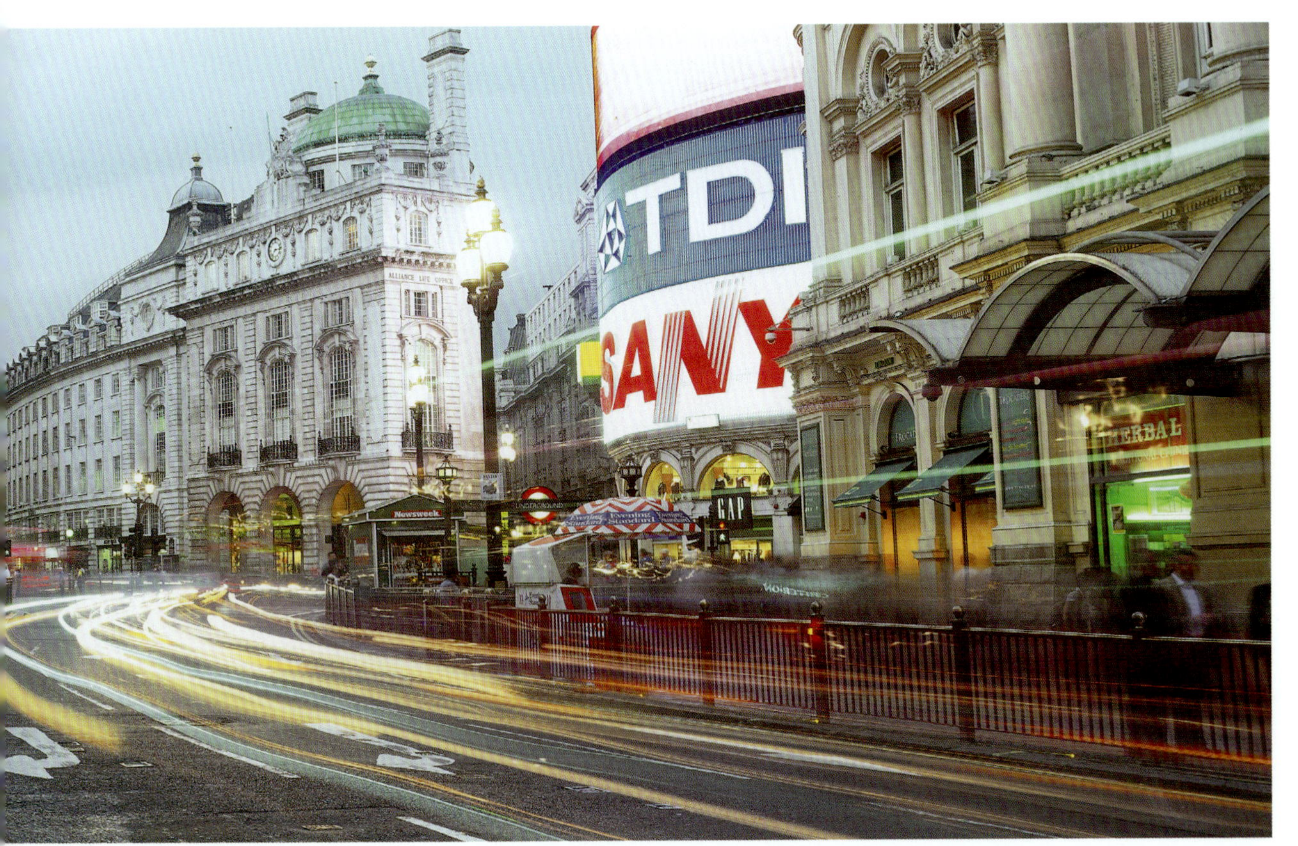

TRAFFIC TRAILS, PICCADILLY CIRCUS

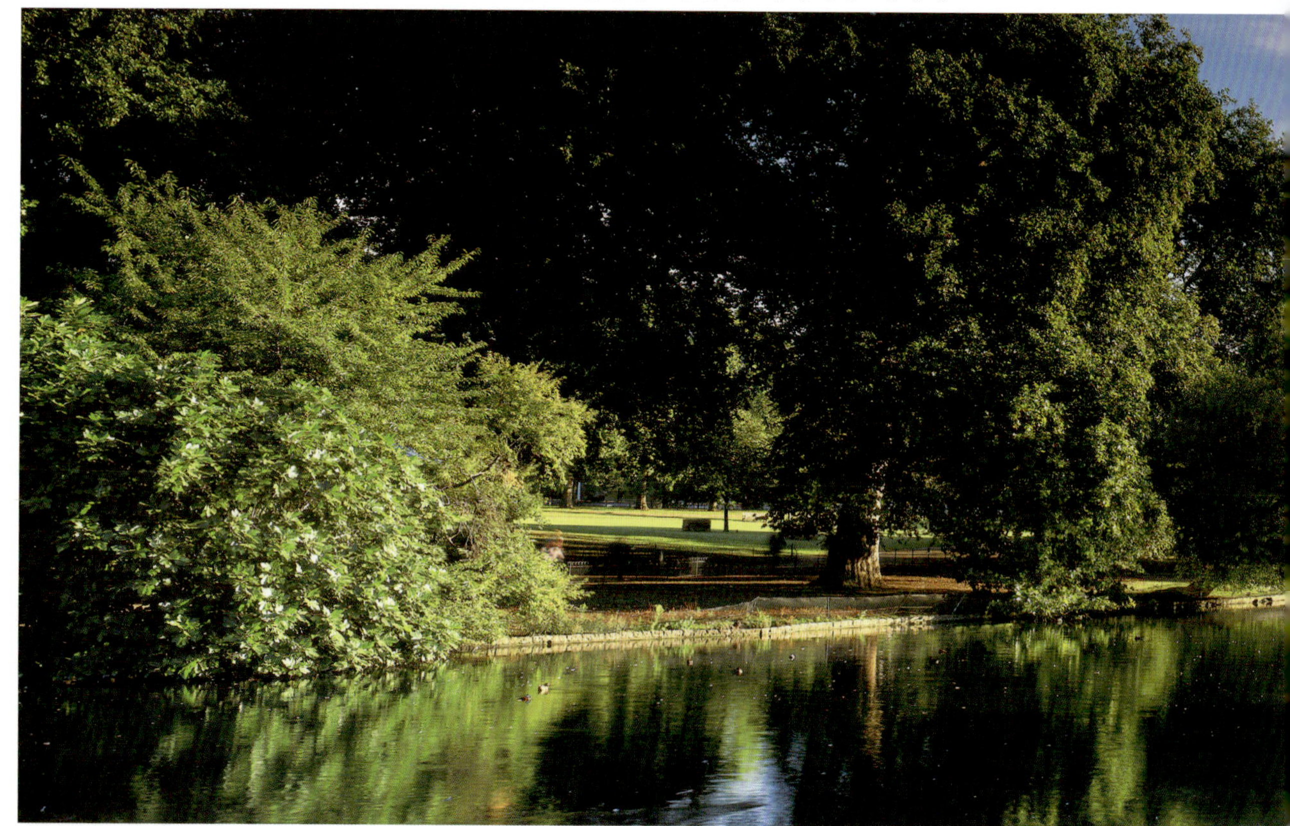

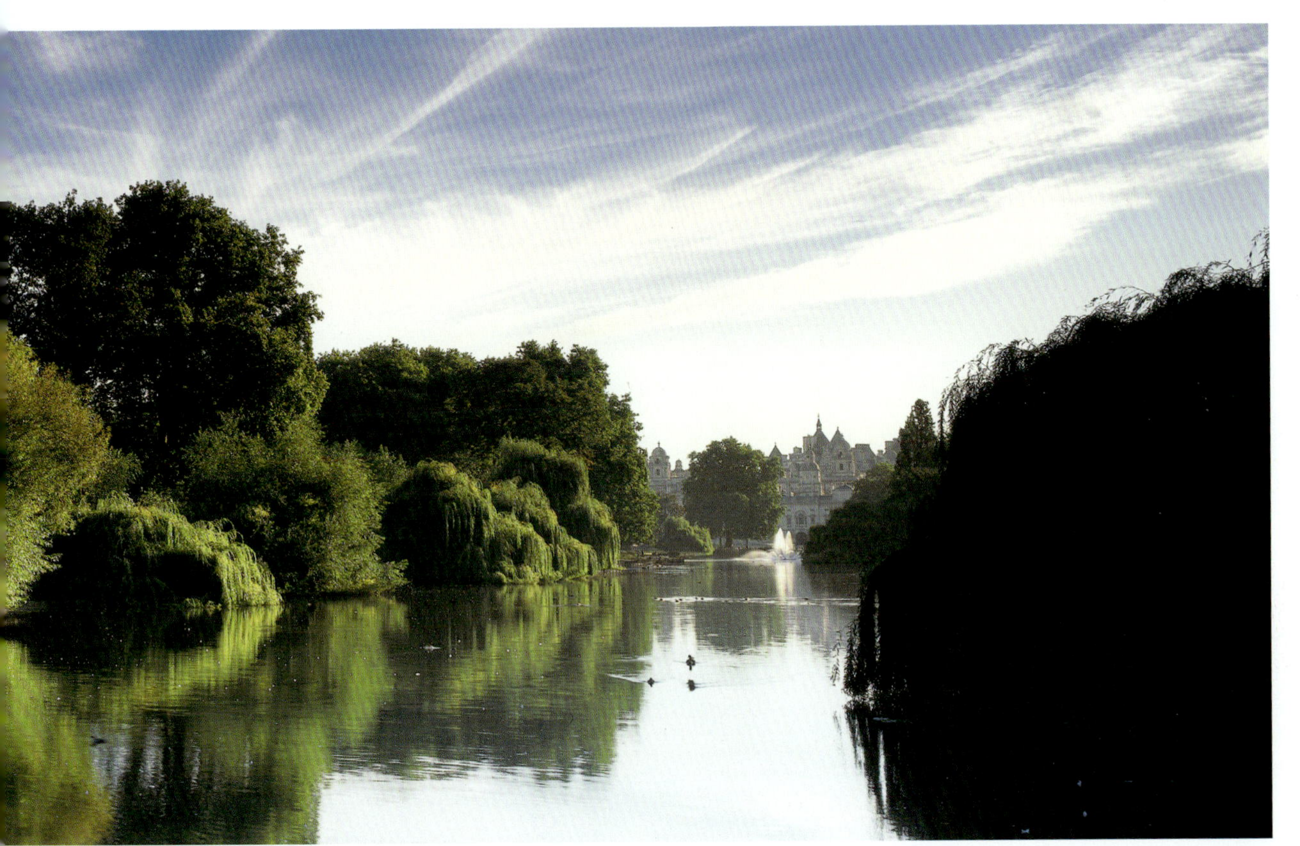

DAWN, ST JAMES'S PARK

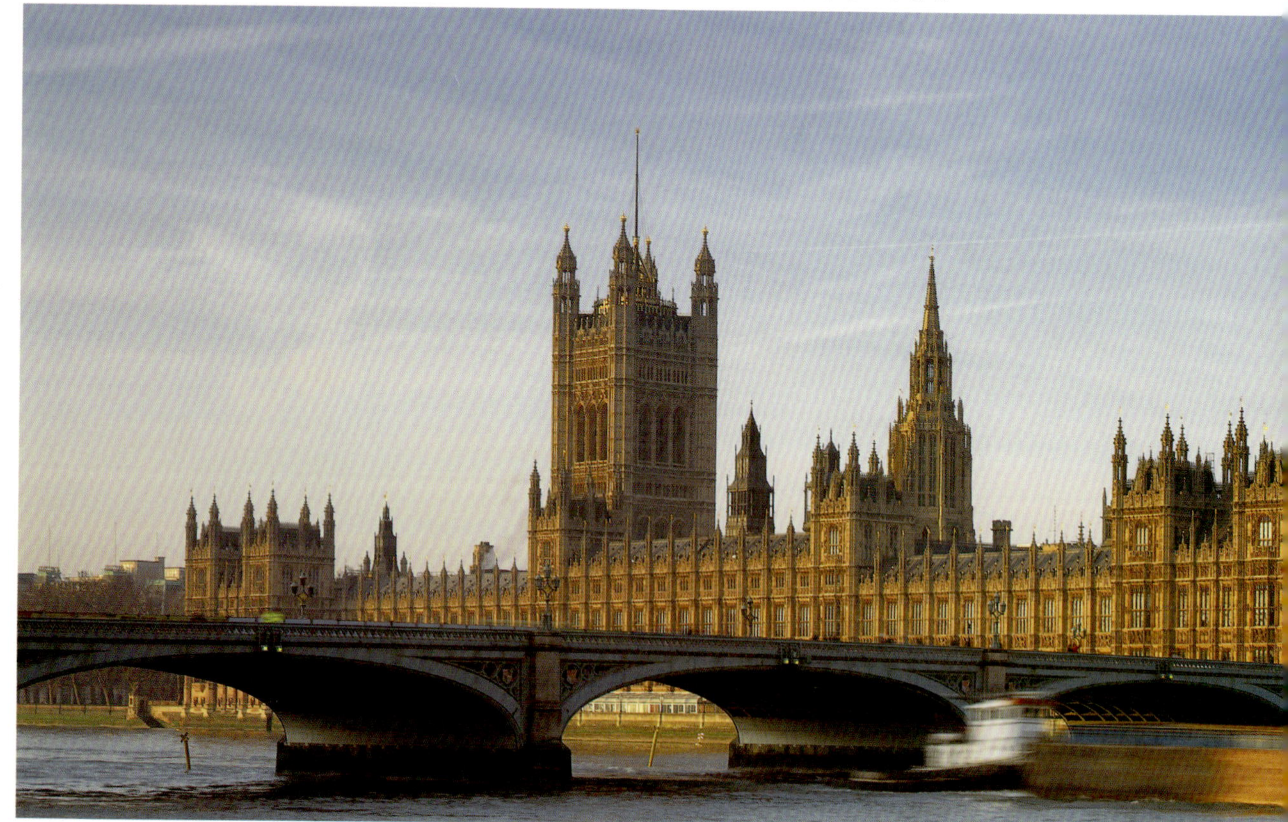

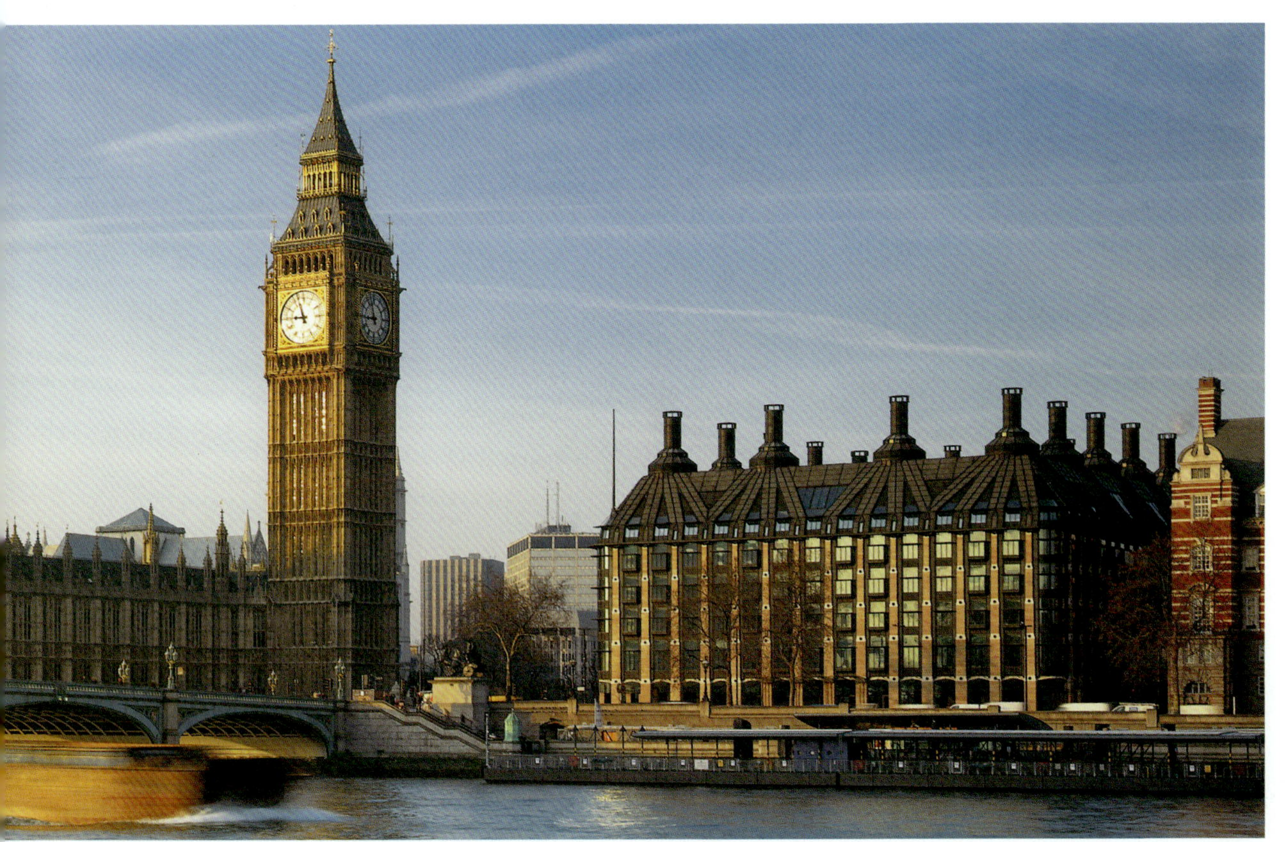

MORNING SUNSHINE, PALACE OF WESTMINSTER

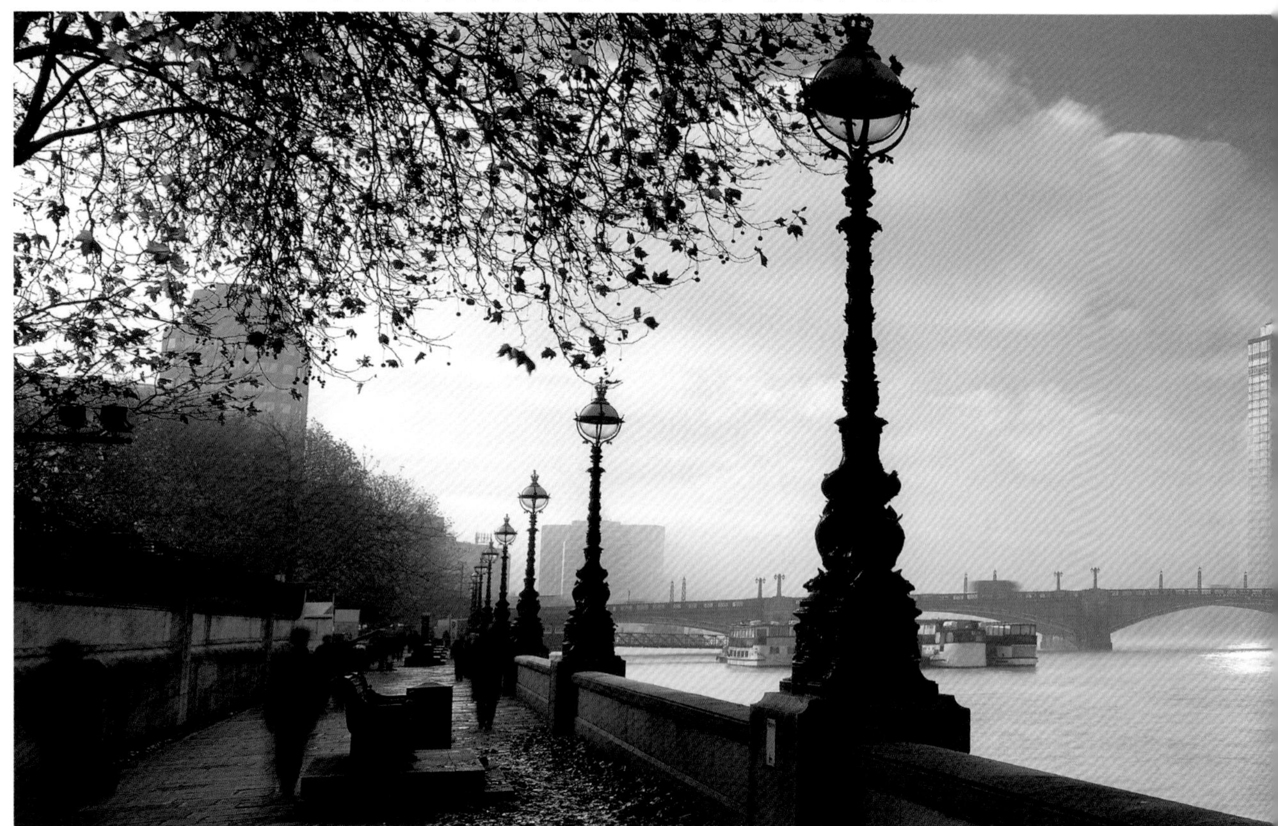

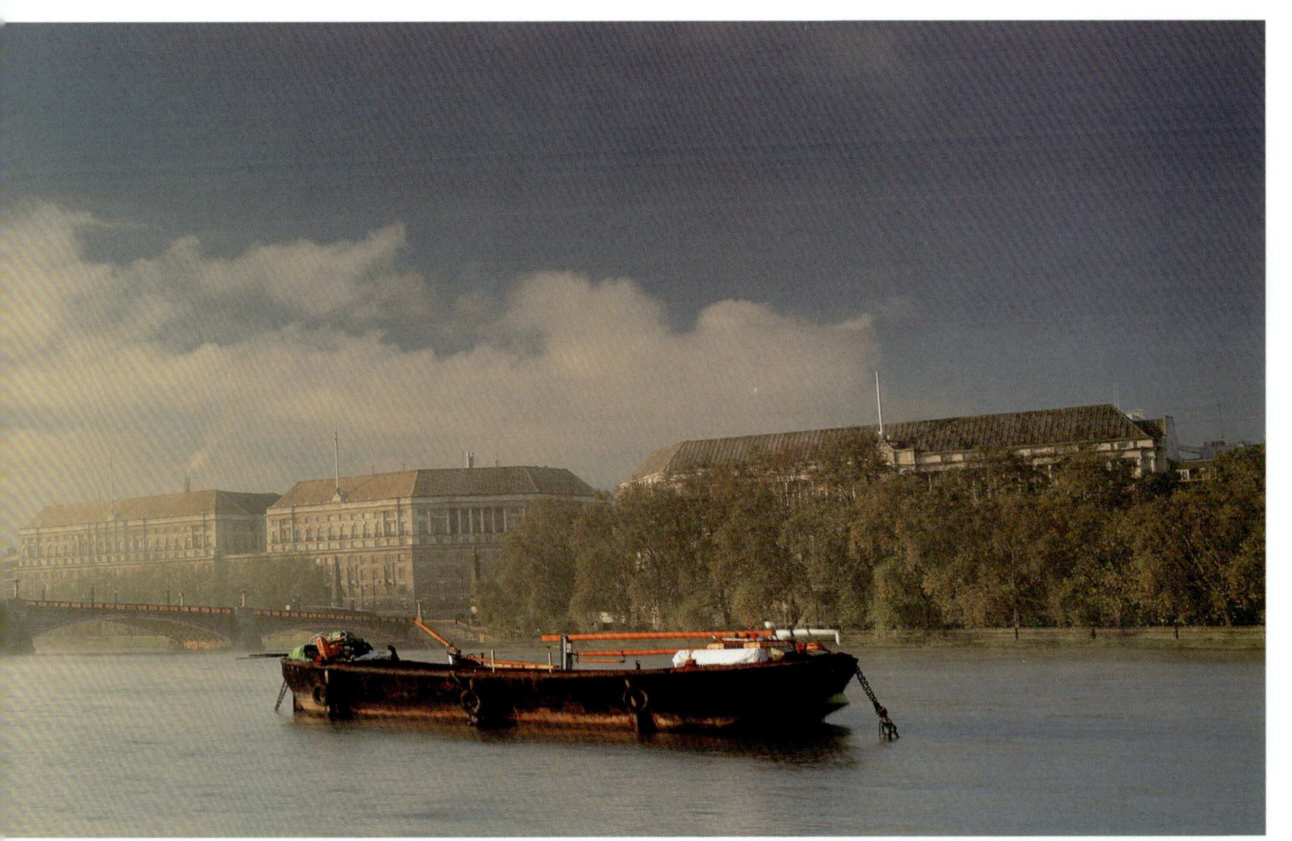

MILLBANK TOWER IN MIST

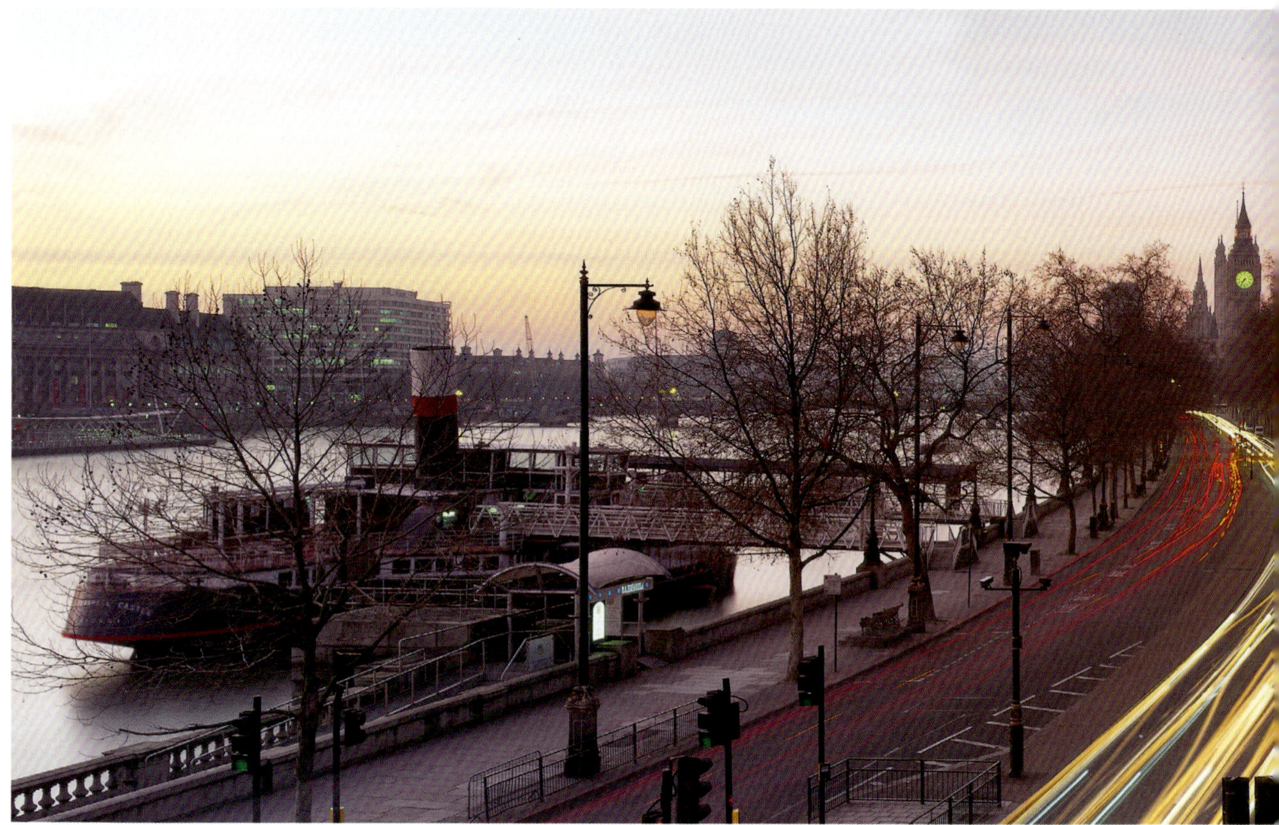

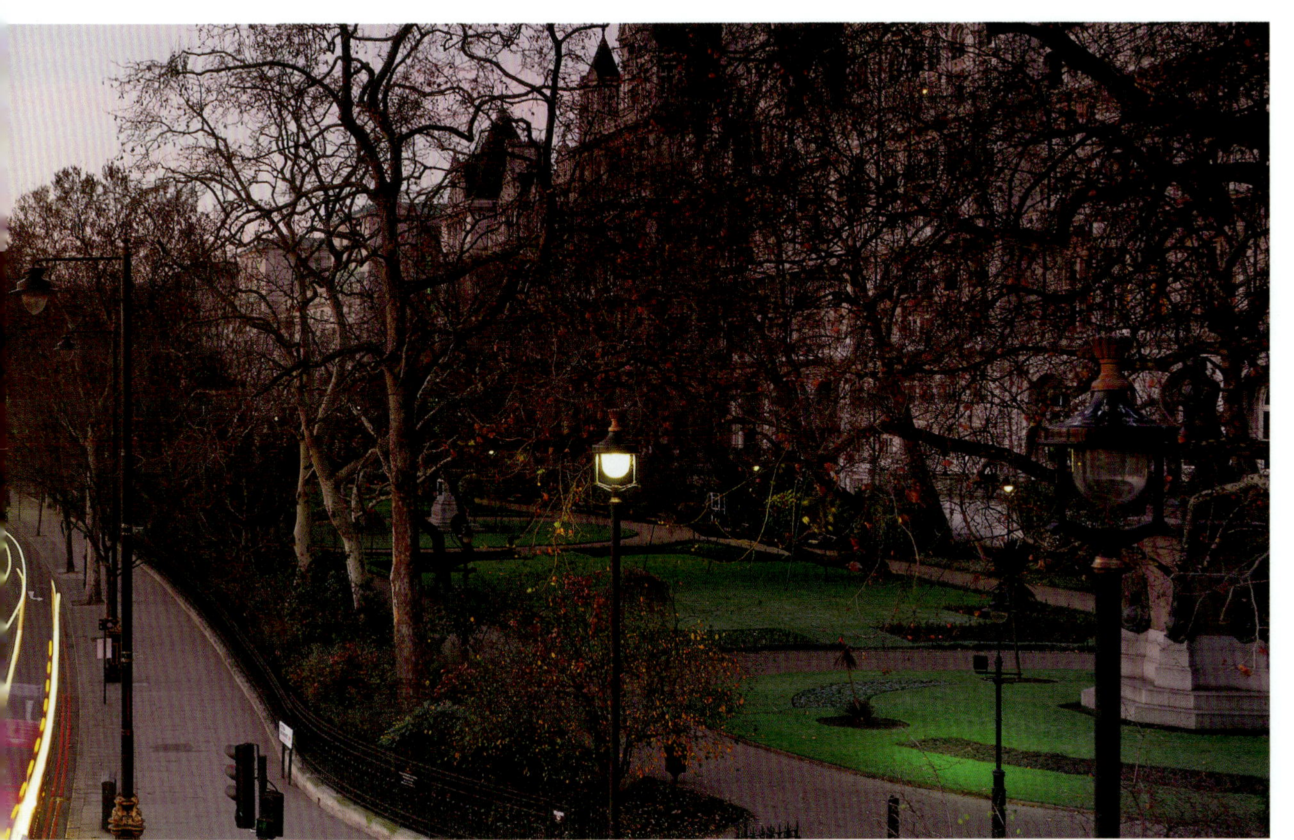

MORNING DASH, VICTORIA EMBANKMENT

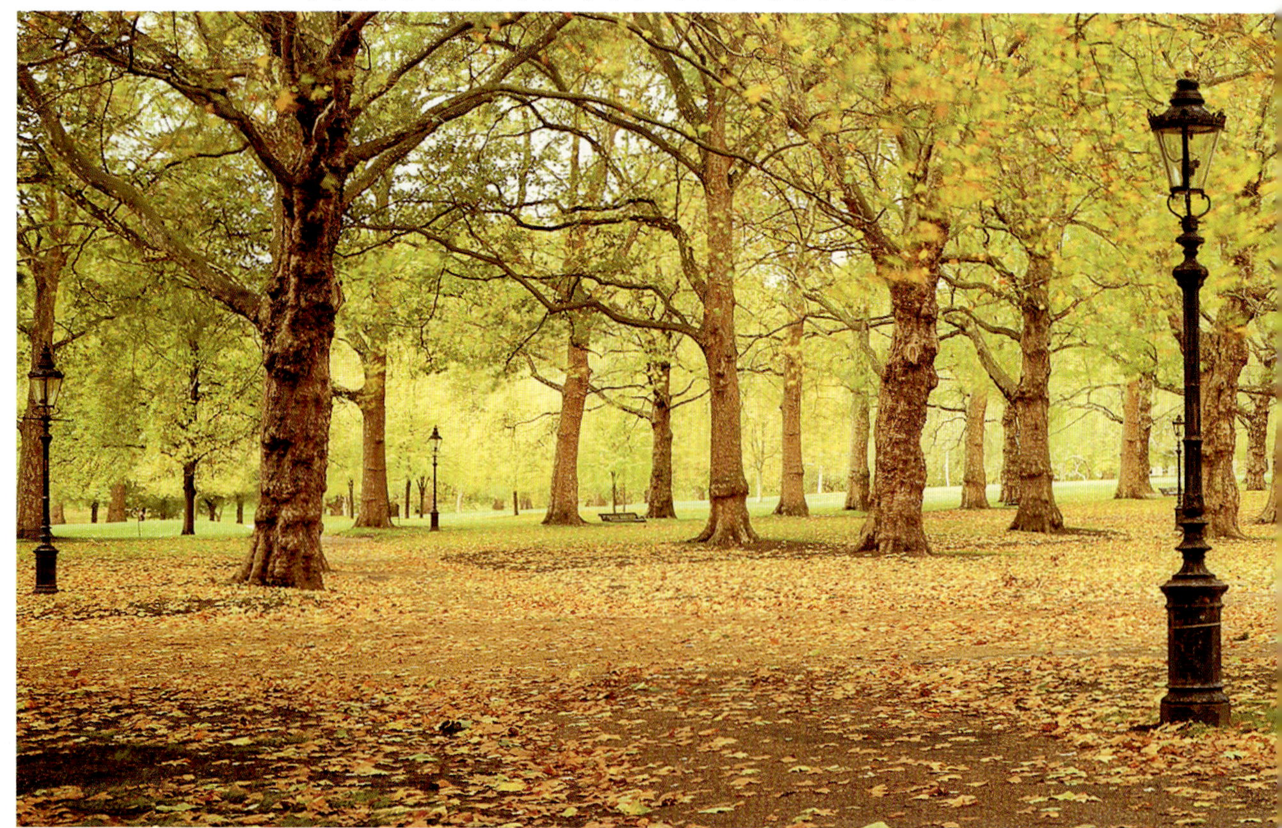

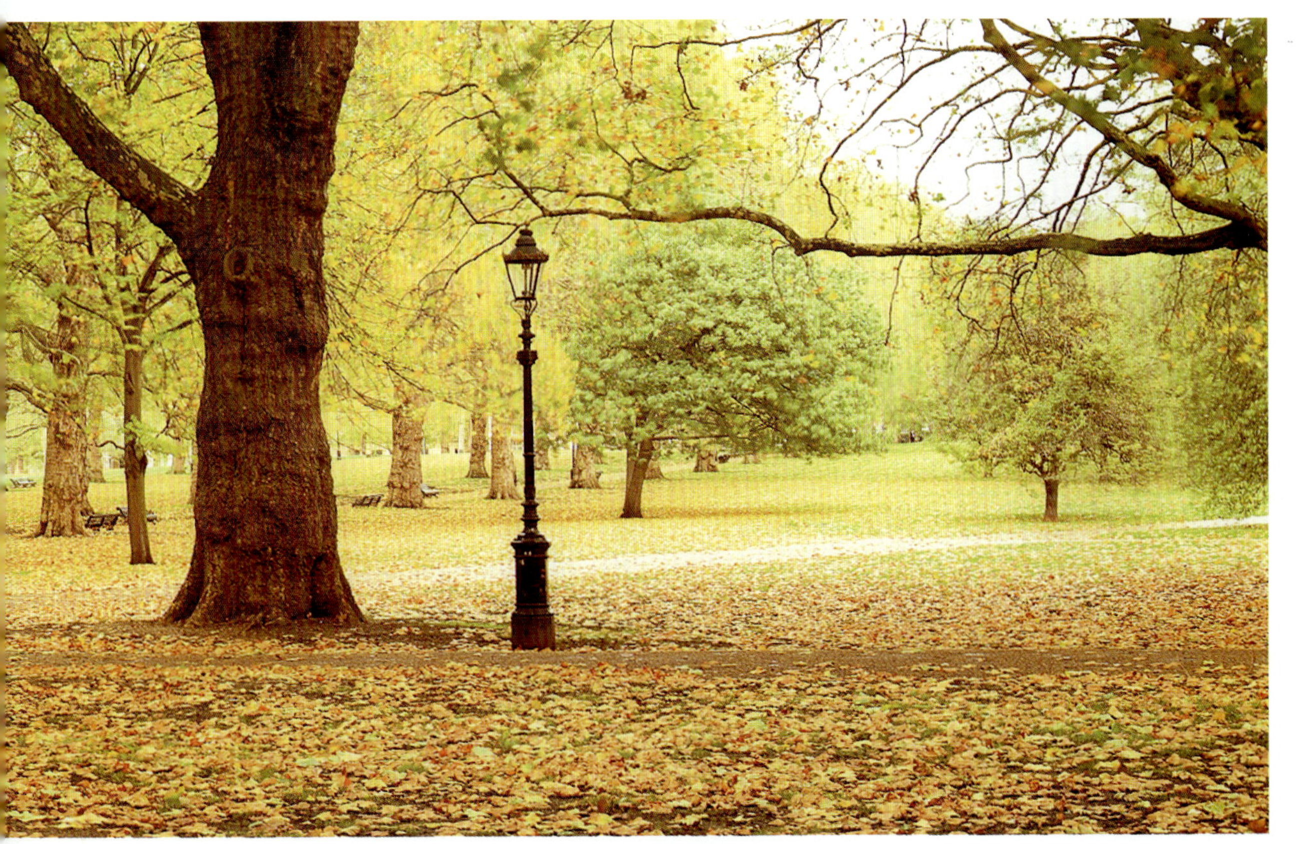

NARNIA LAMPS, GREEN PARK

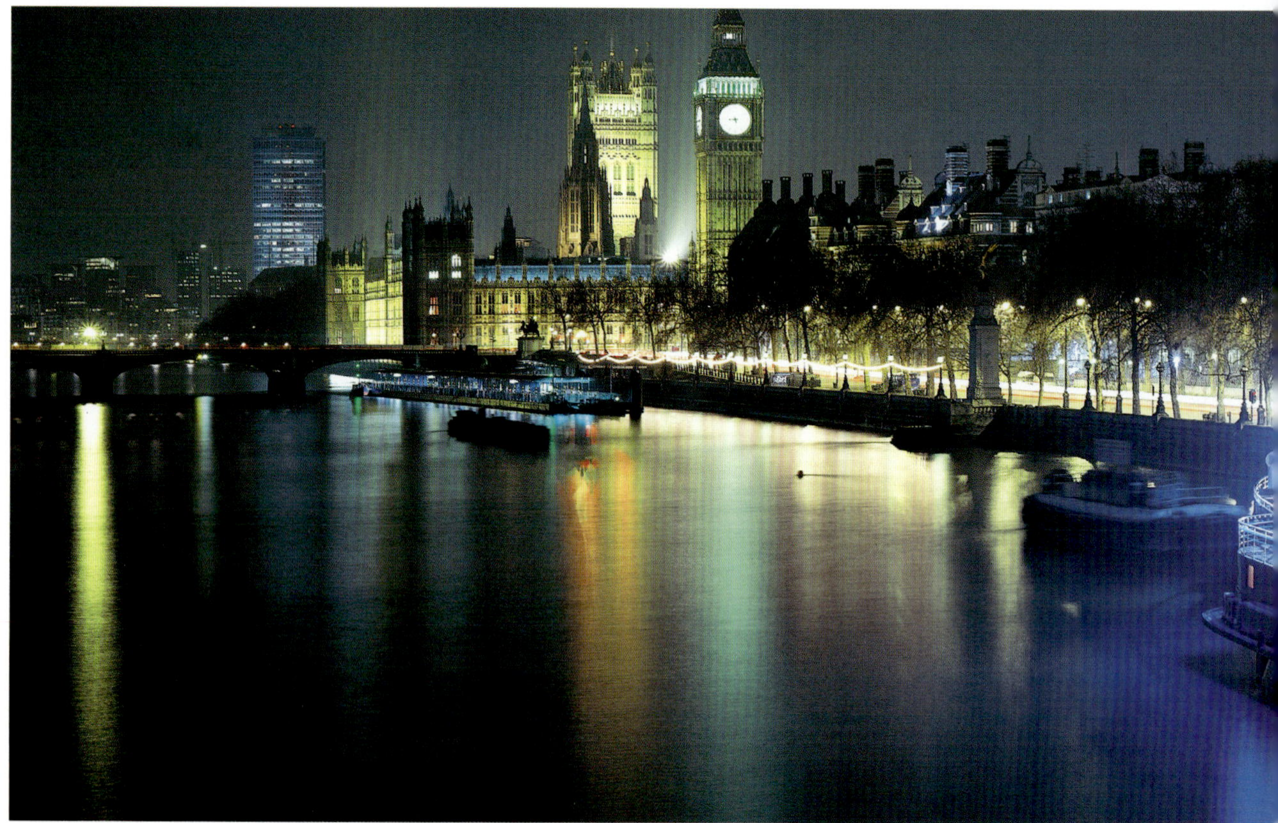

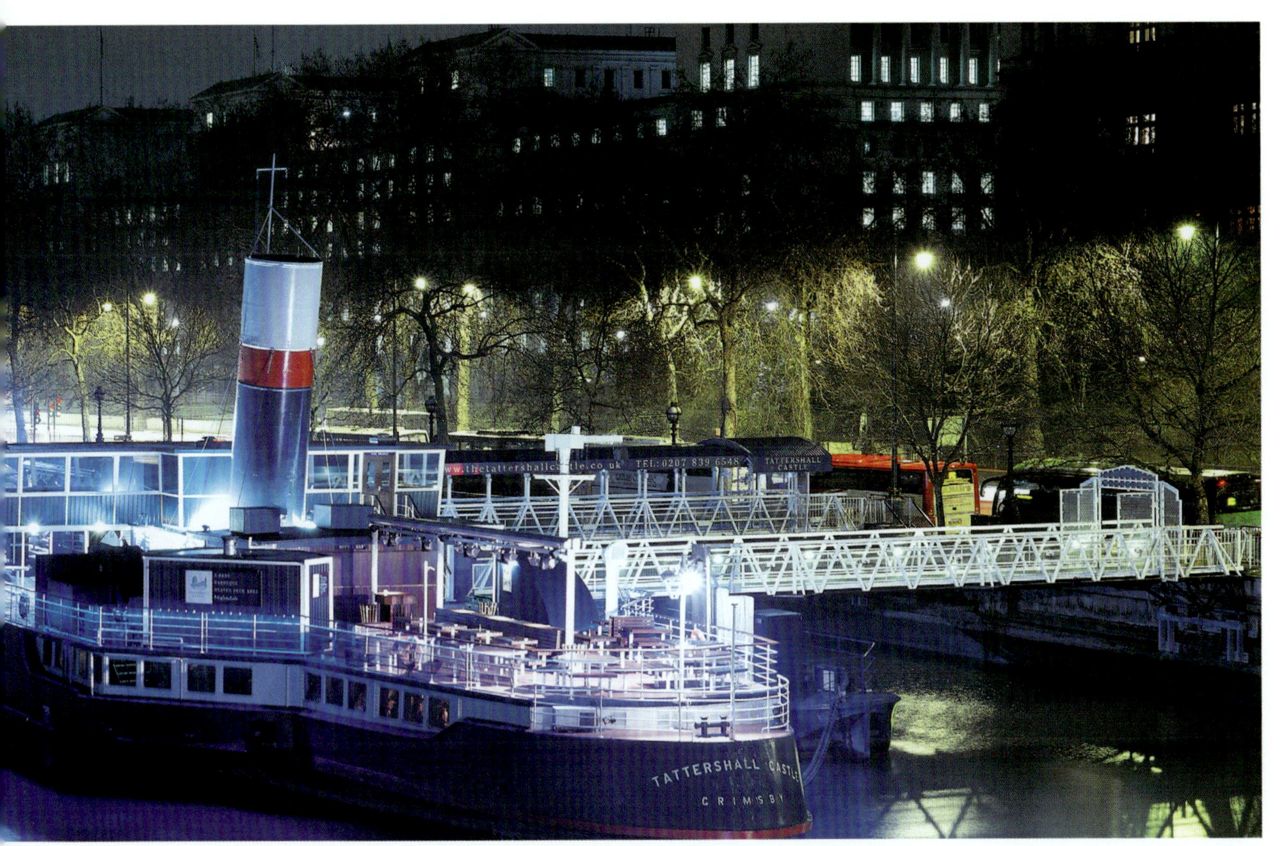

TATTERSHALL CASTLE AND WESTMINSTER FROM THAMES

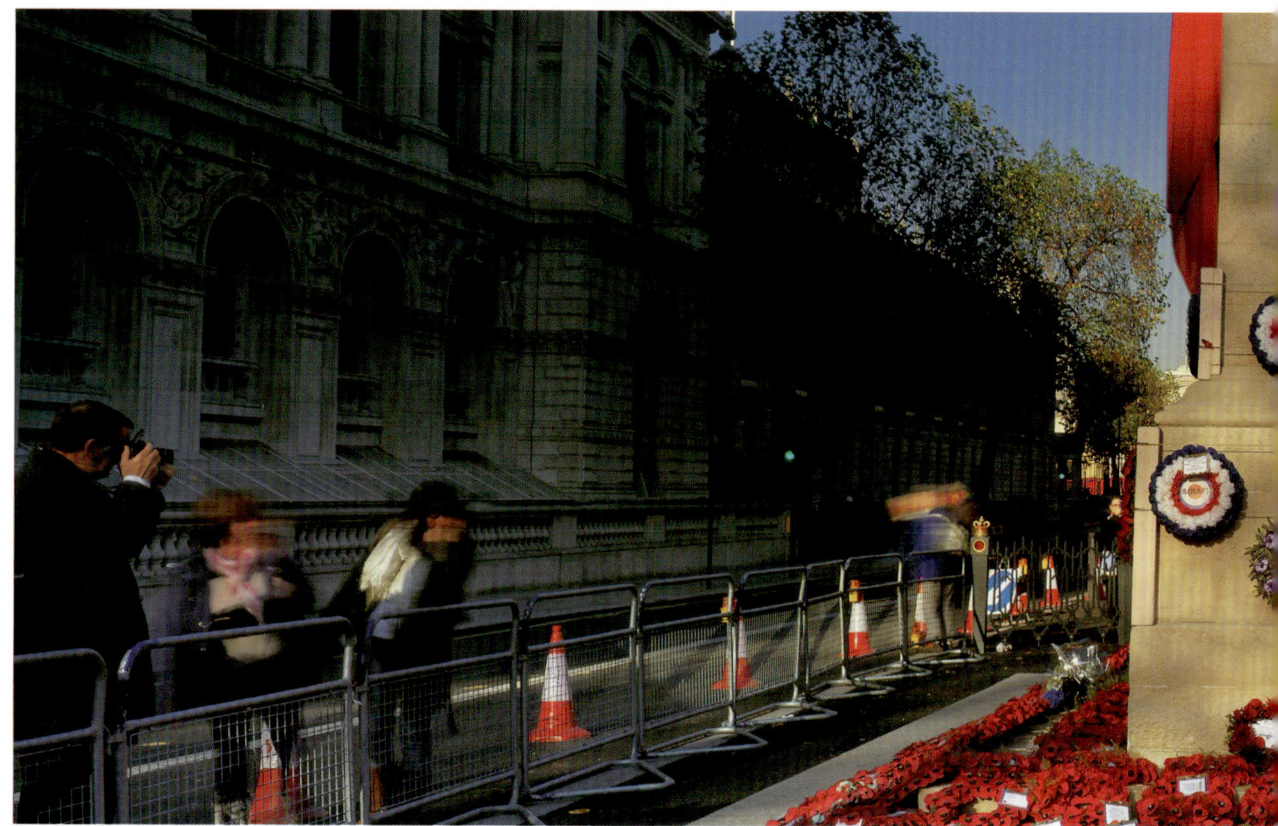

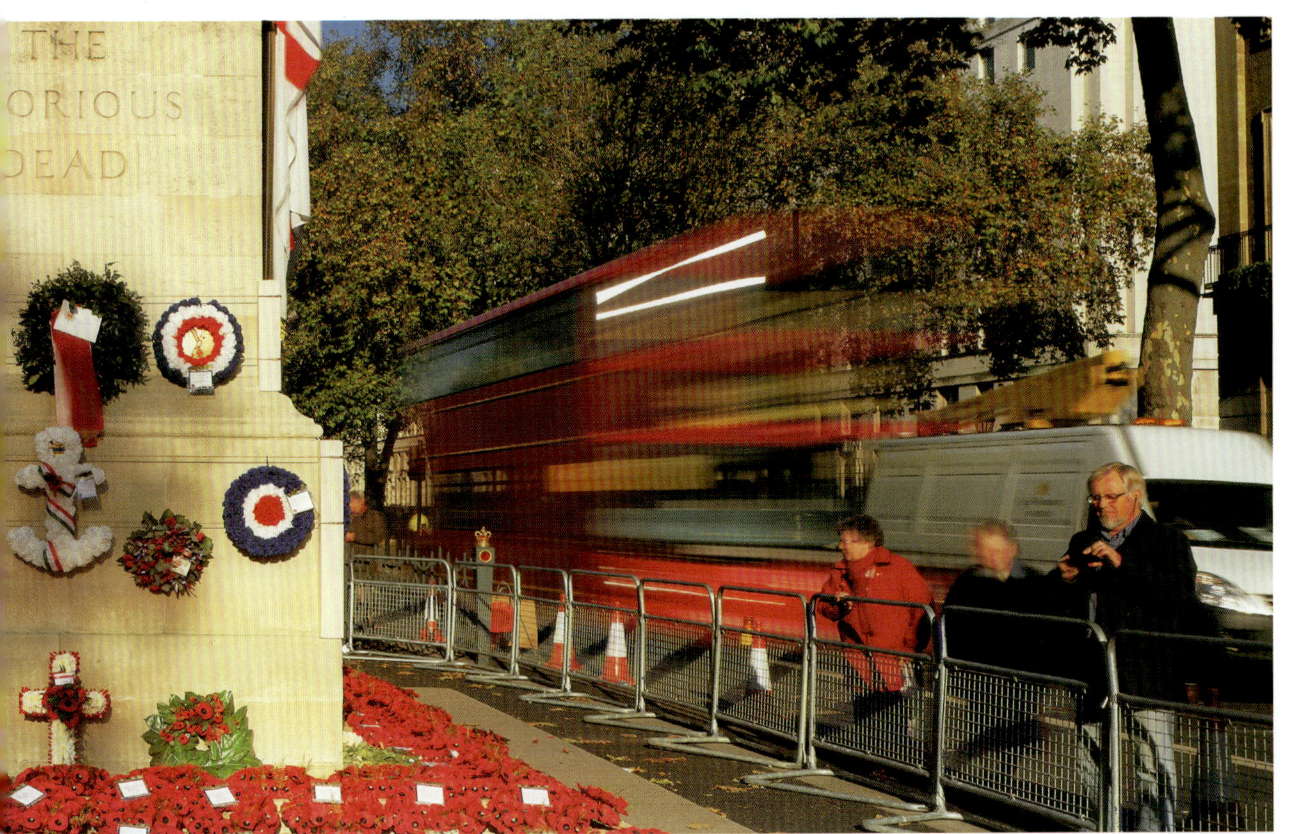

THE GLORIOUS DEAD, THE CENOTAPH, WHITEHALL

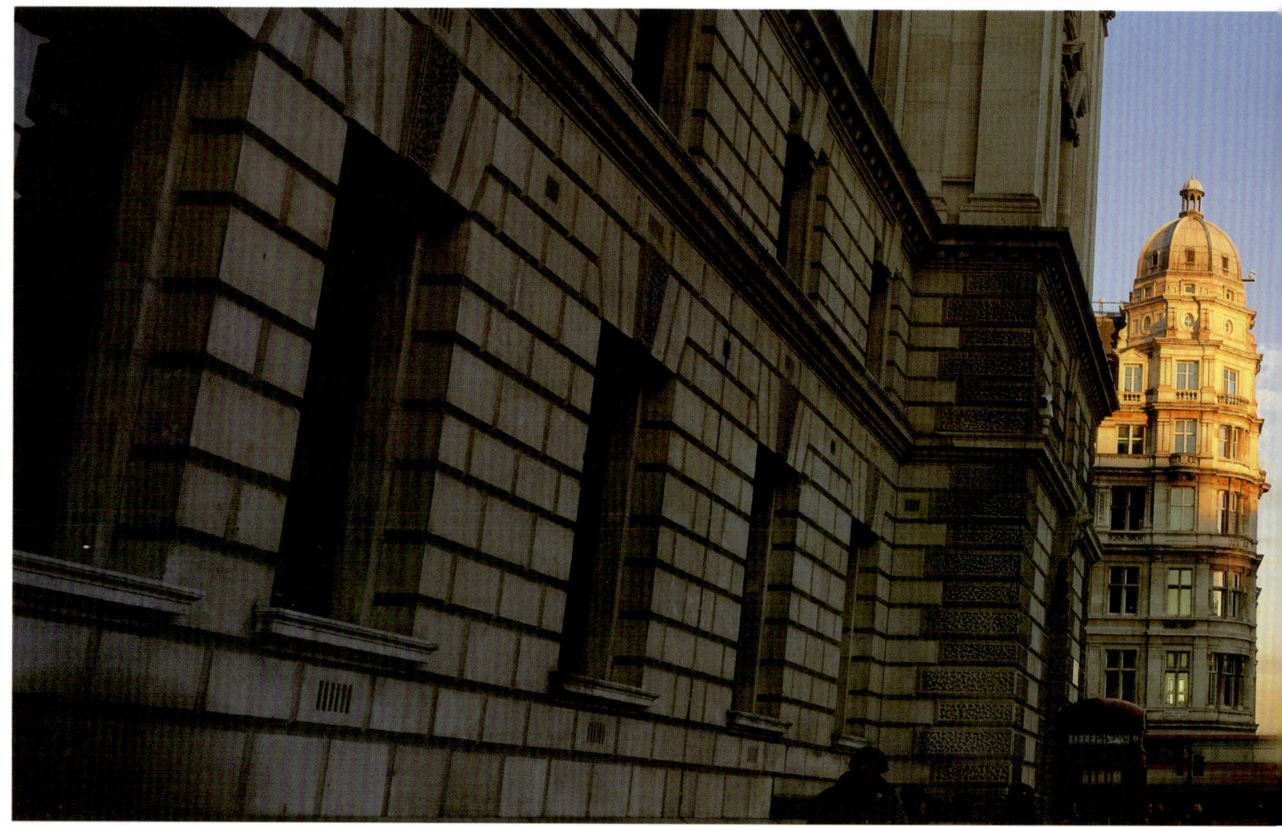

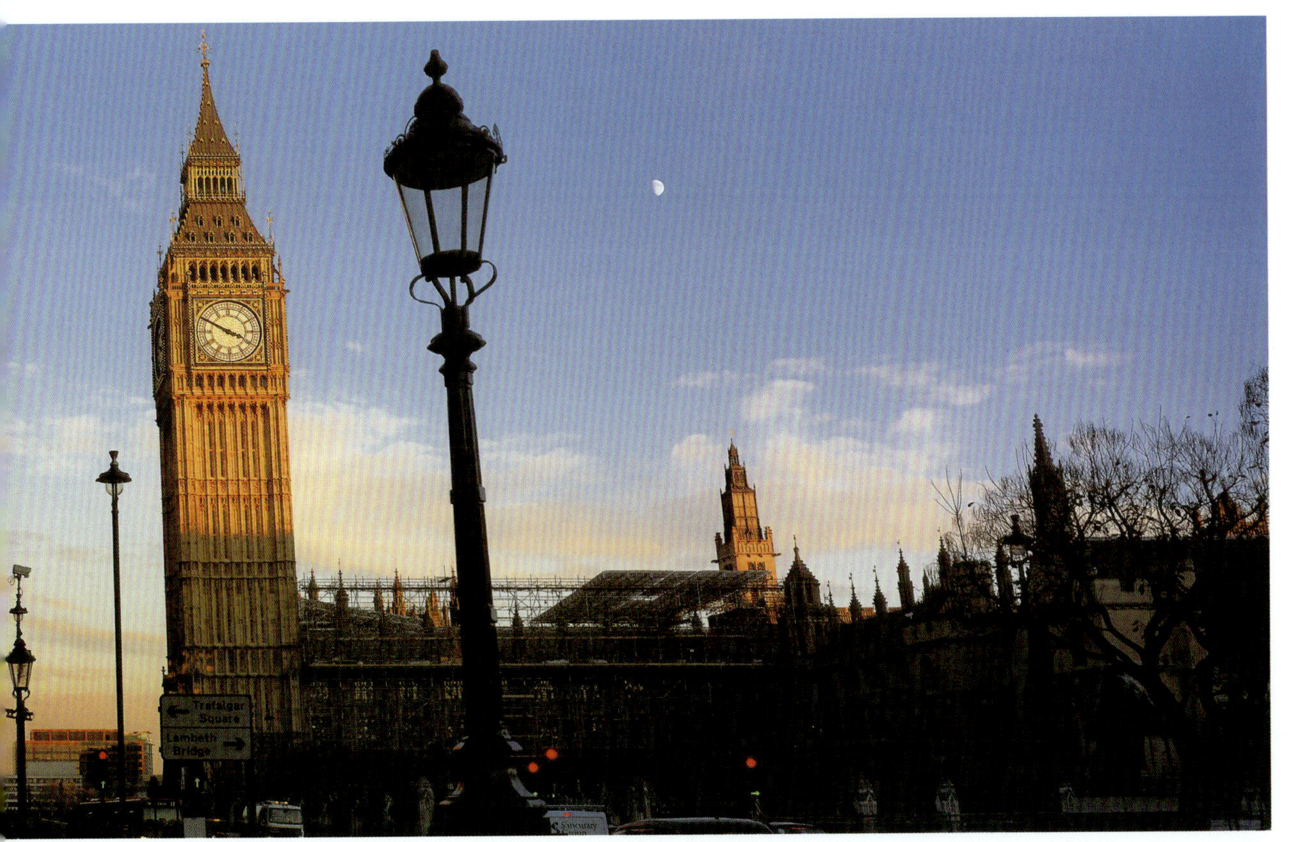

THE MOON BEYOND BIG BEN

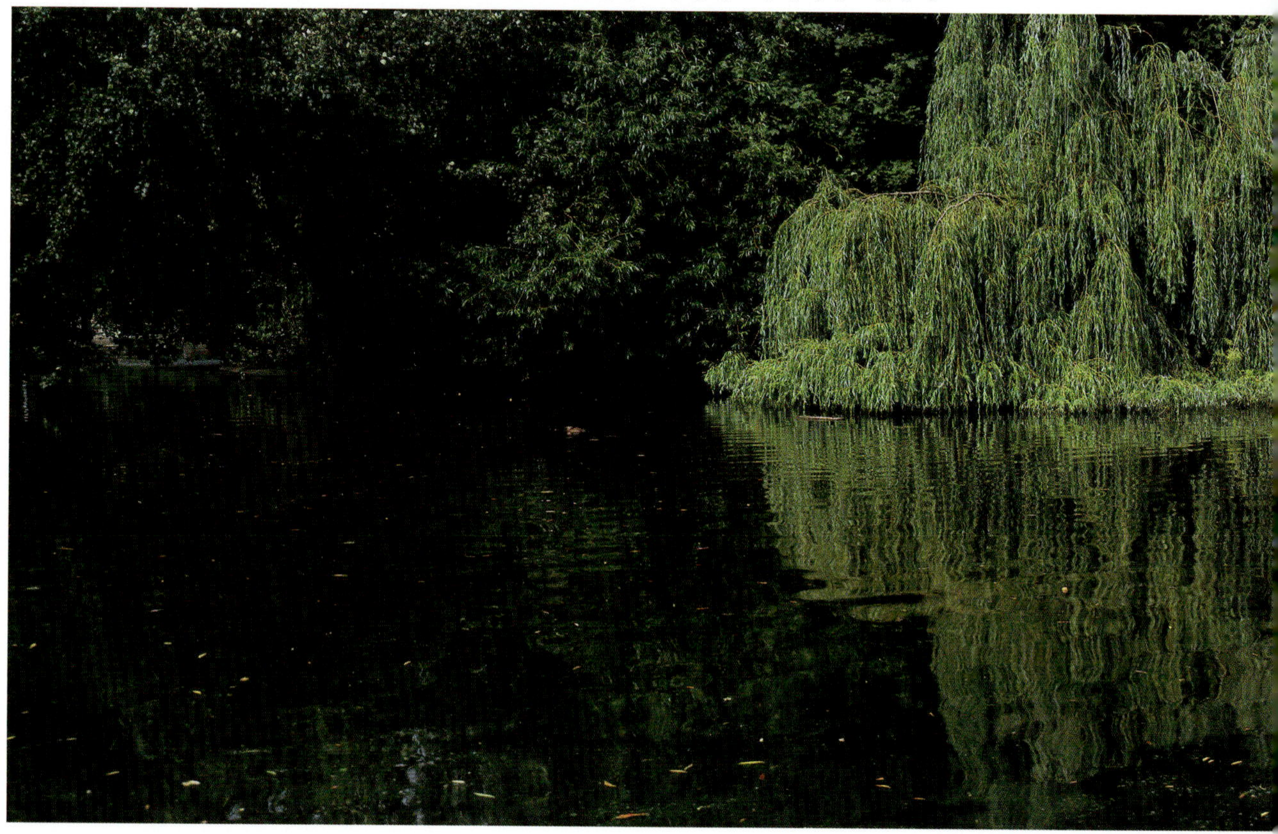

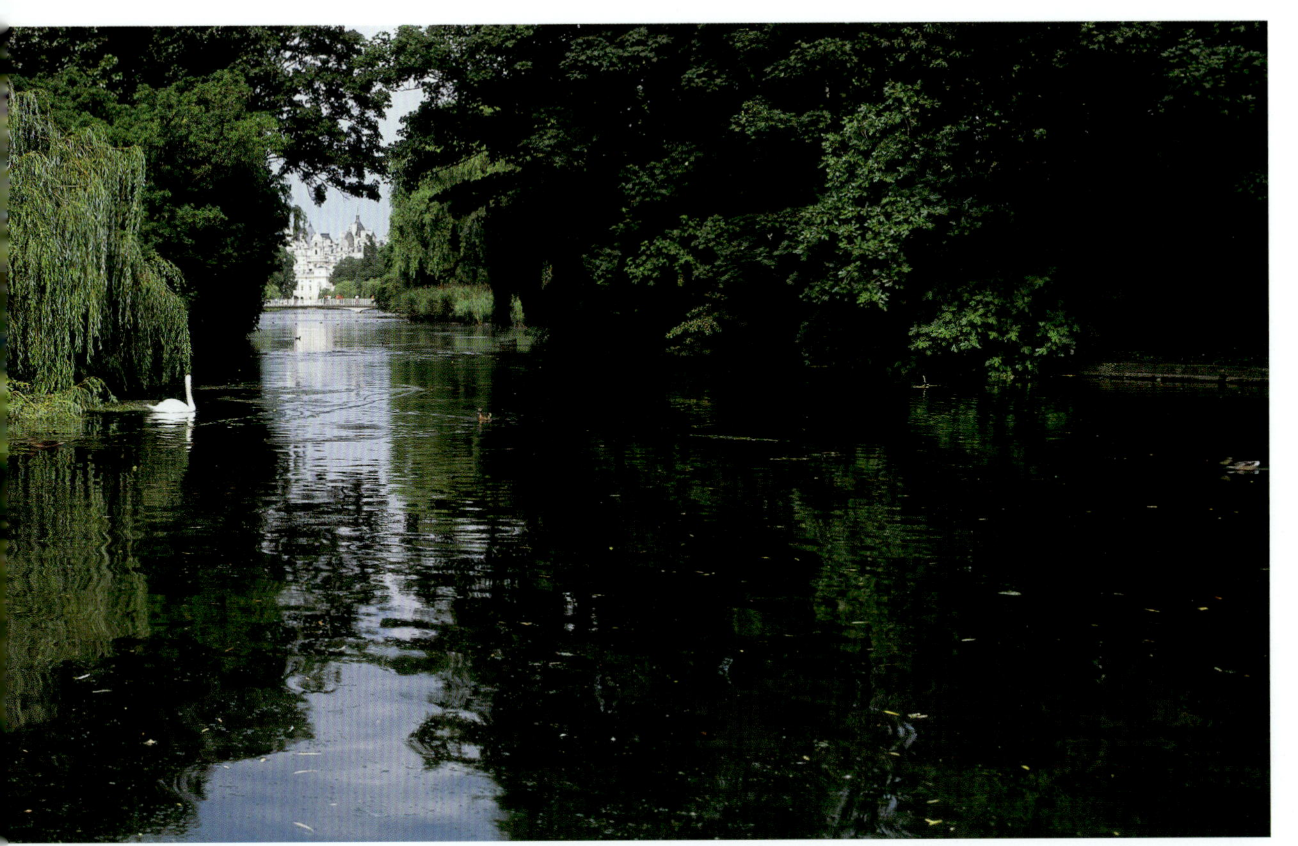

LONE SWAN, ST JAMES'S PARK

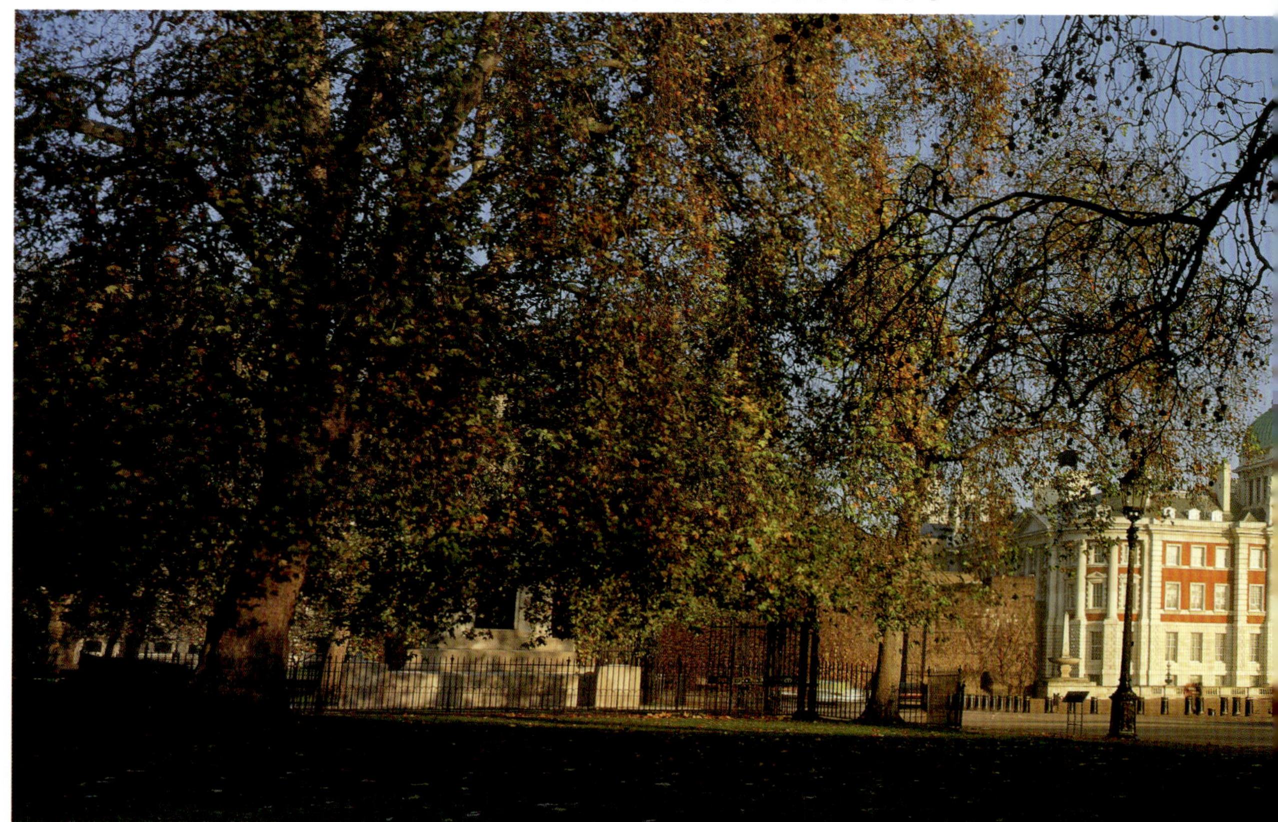

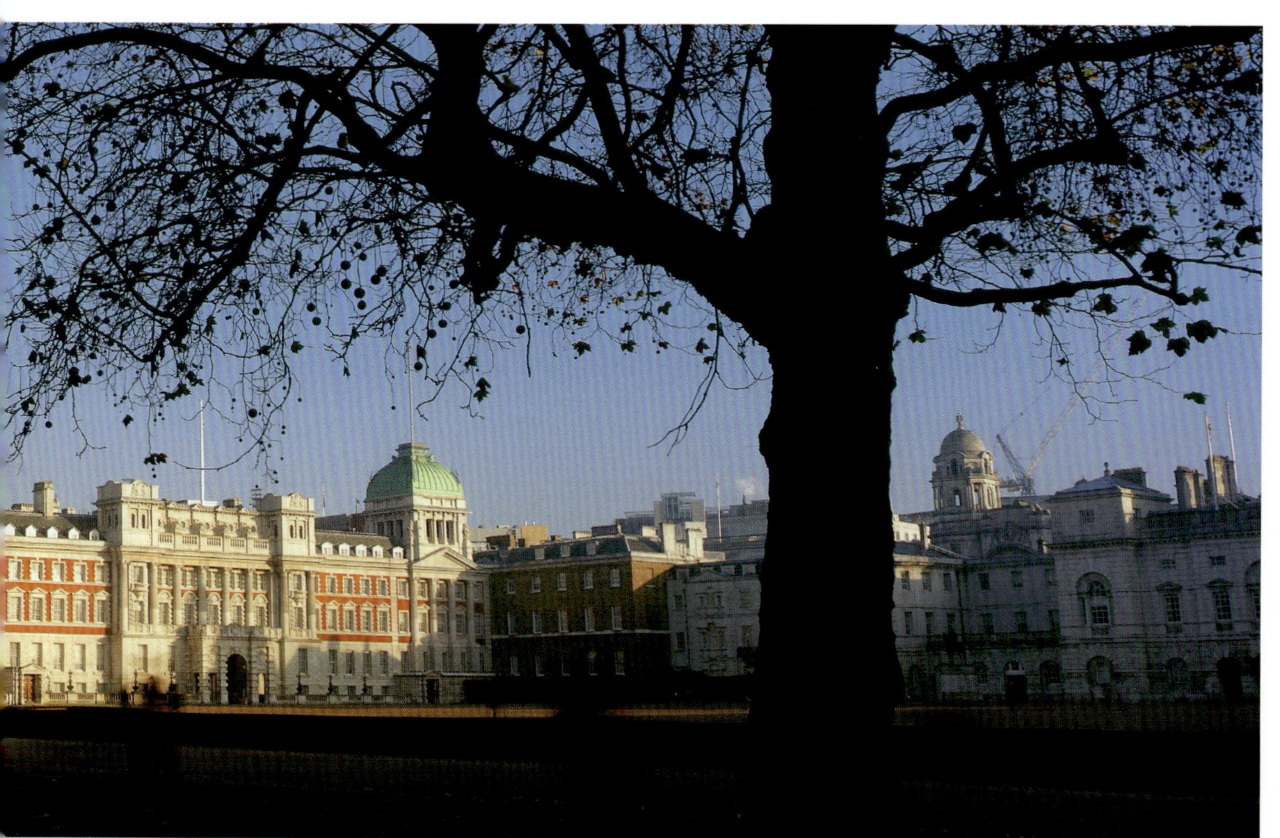

THE OLD ADMIRALTY BUILDING, HORSE GUARDS PARADE

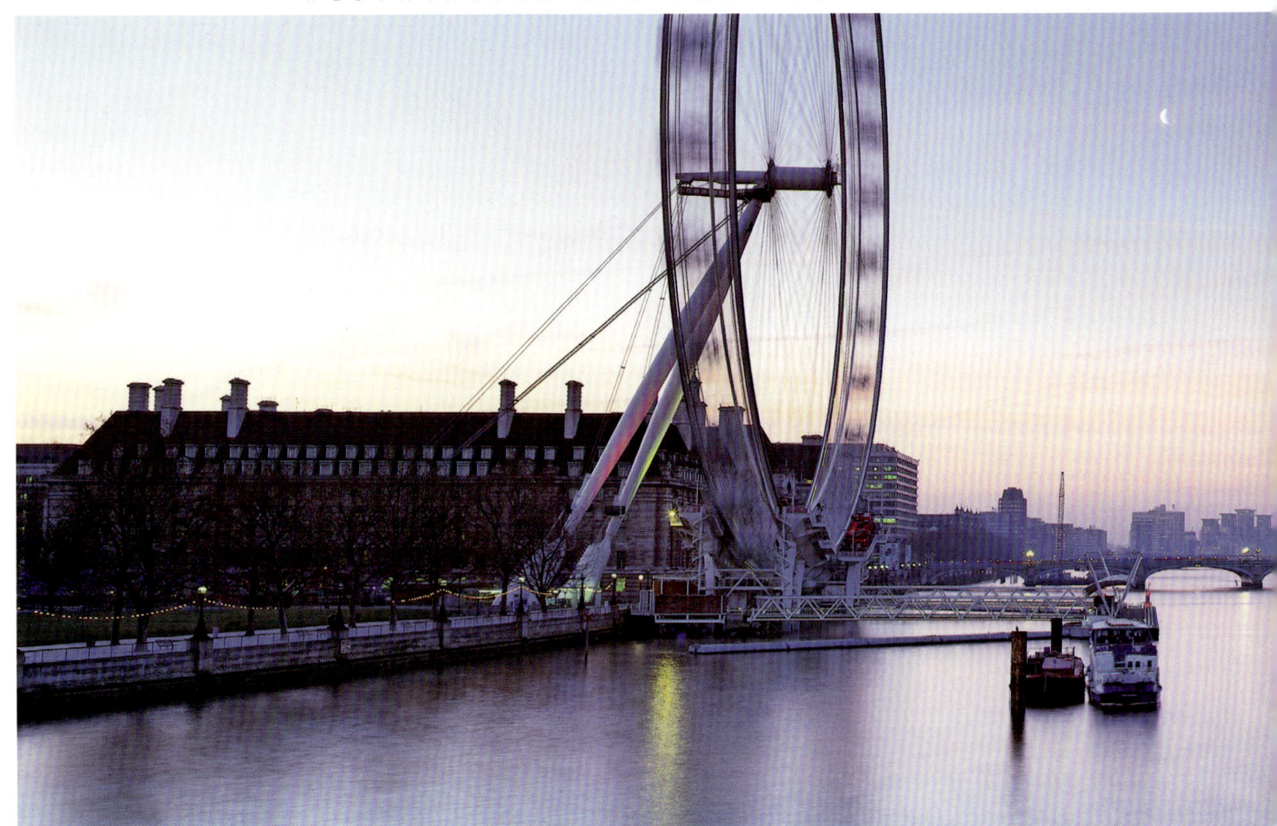

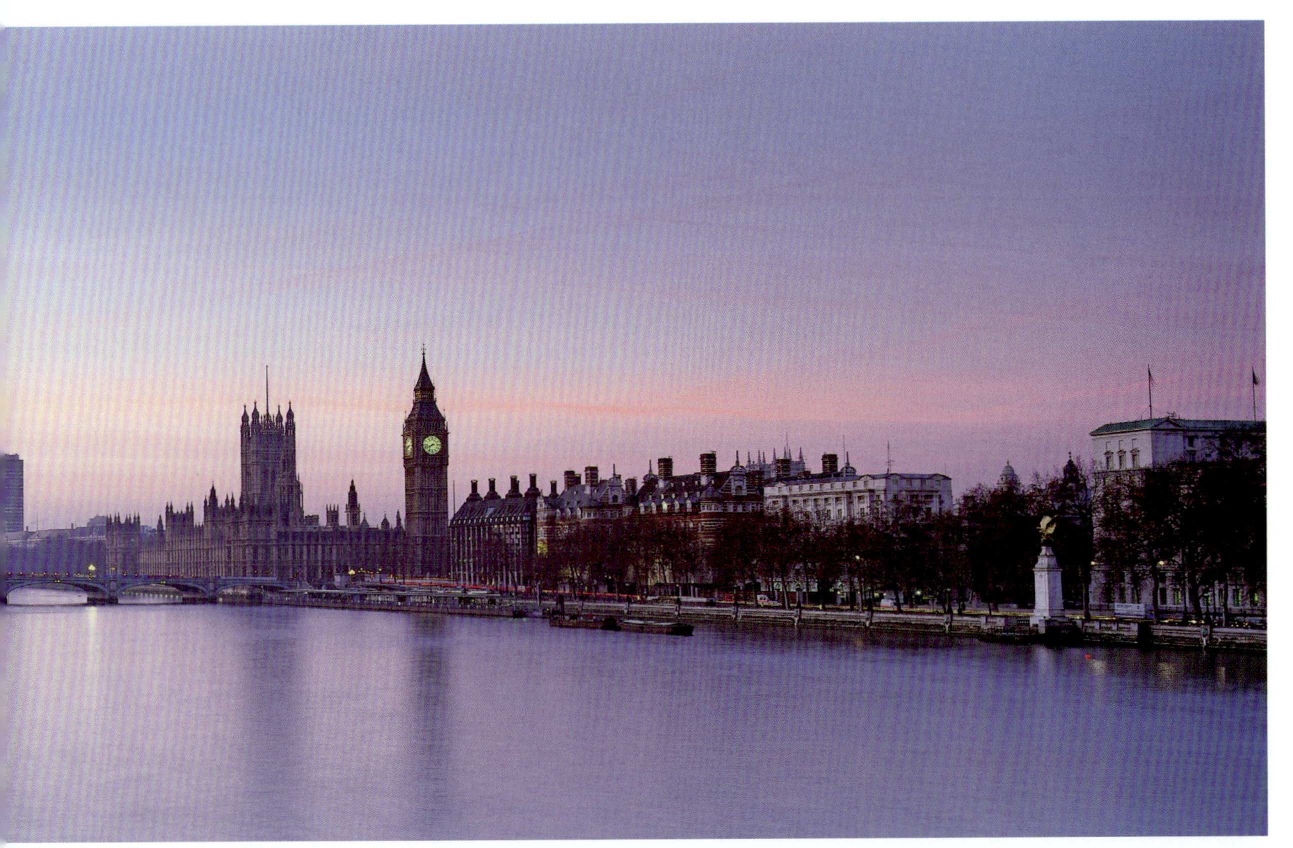

CRESCENT MOON AT DAWN, THAMES

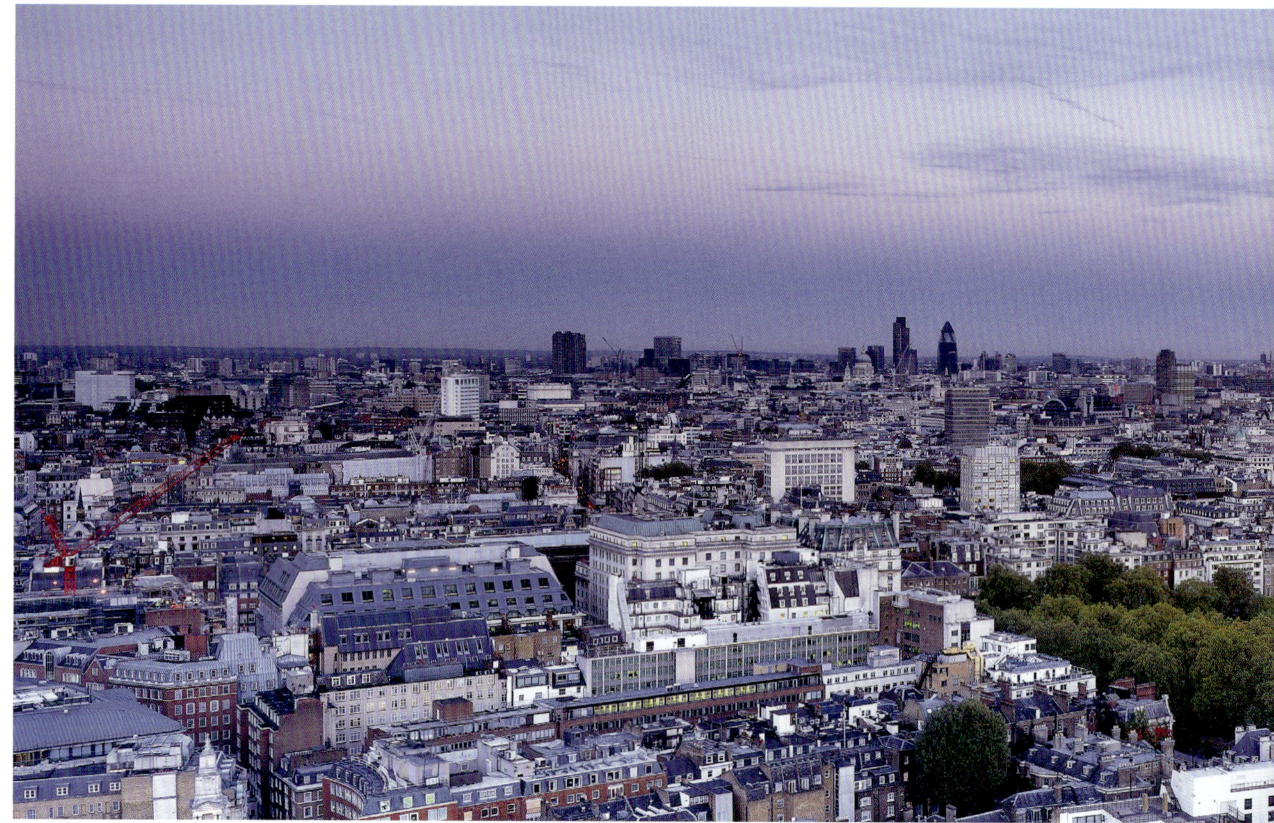

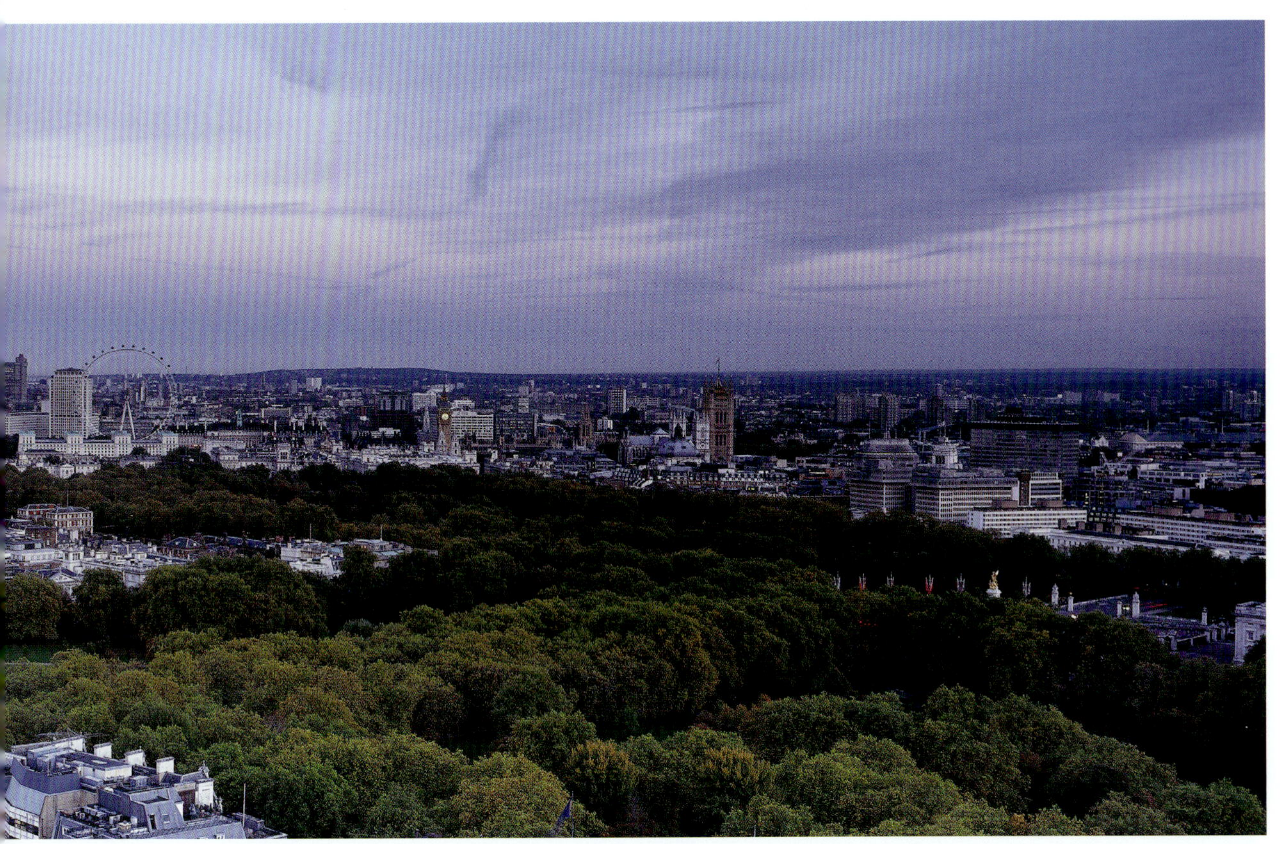

VIEW EAST, FROM PARK LANE HILTON

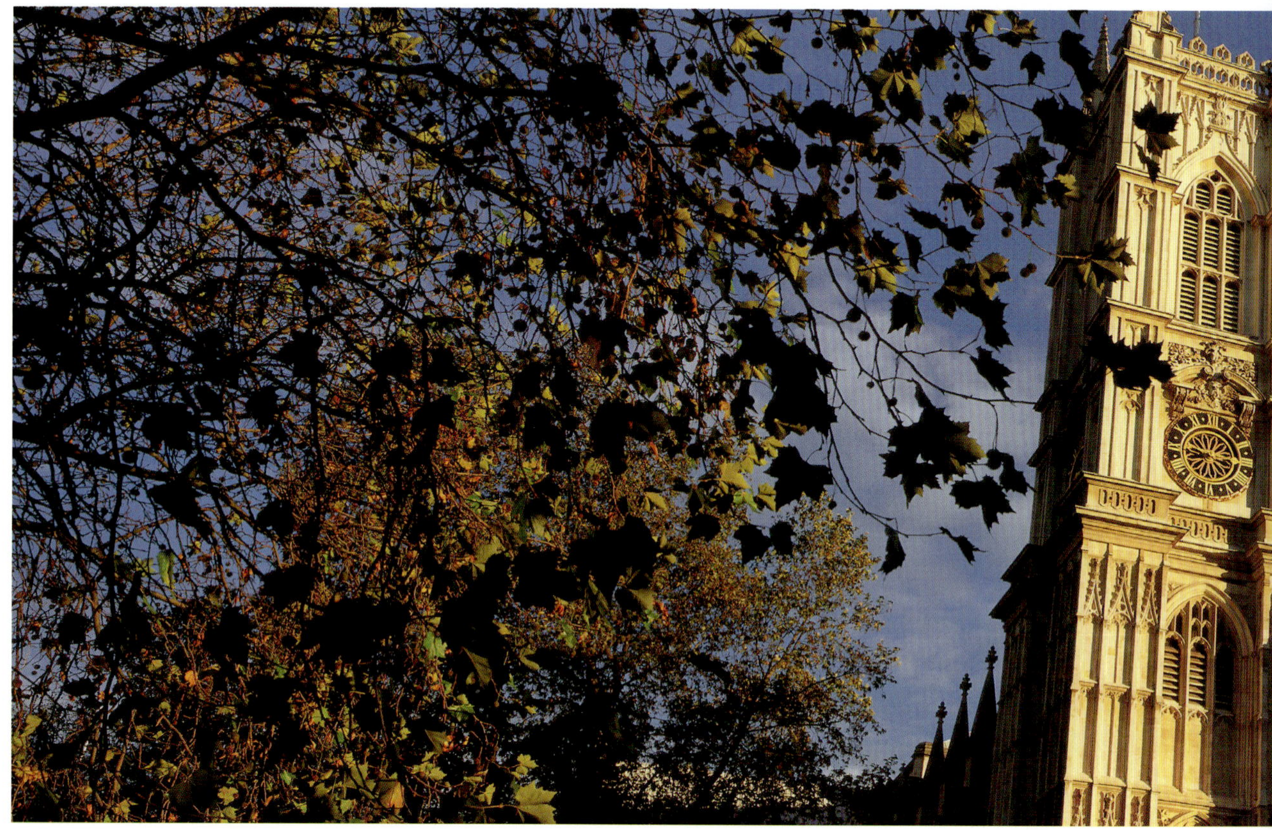

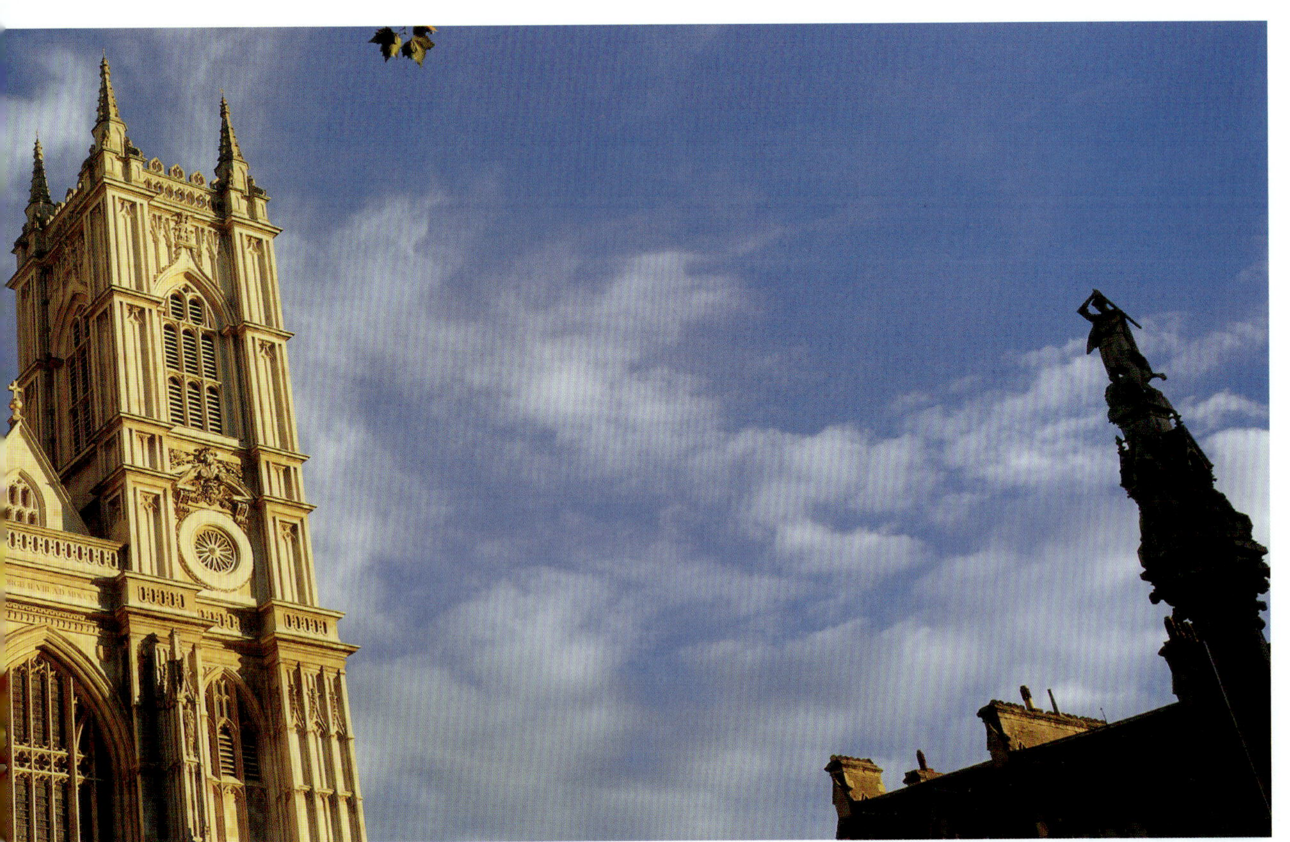

WESTMINSTER ABBEY, AUTUMN LIGHT

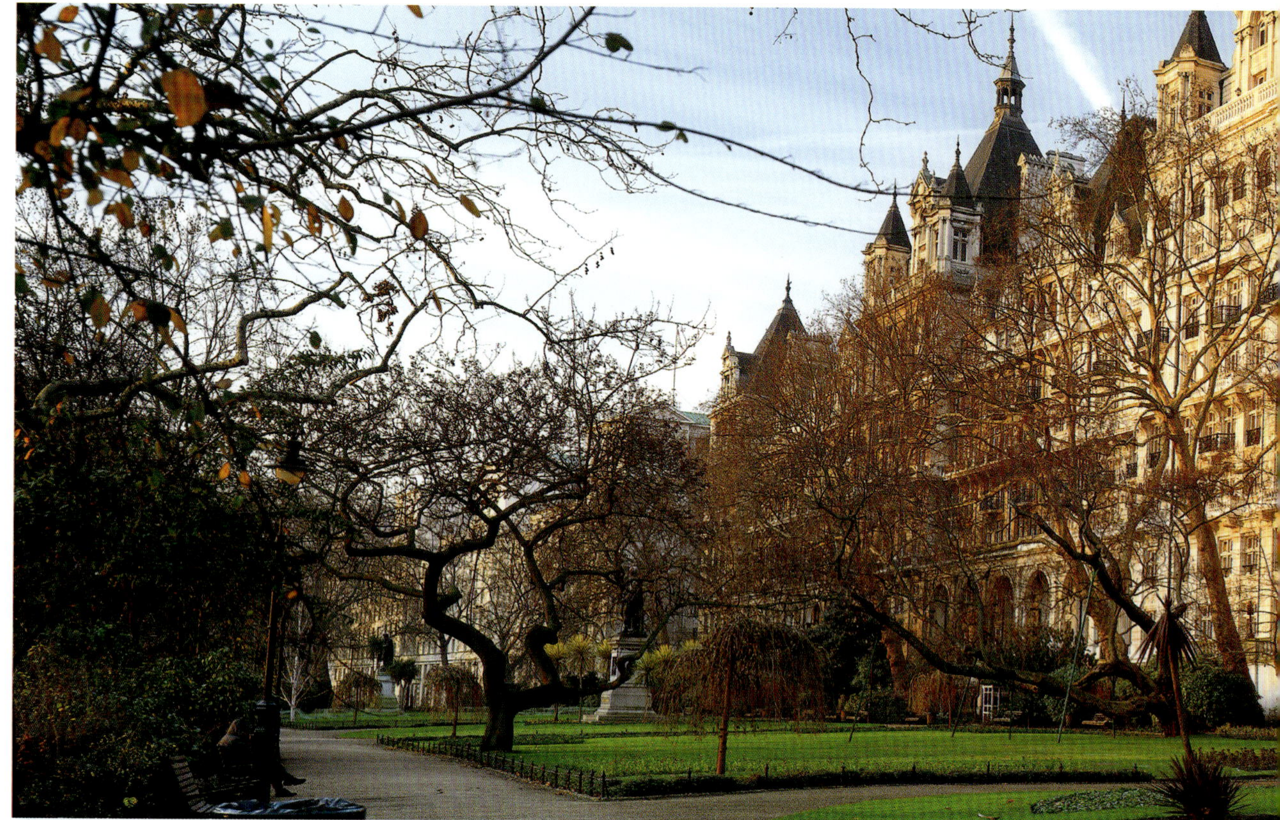

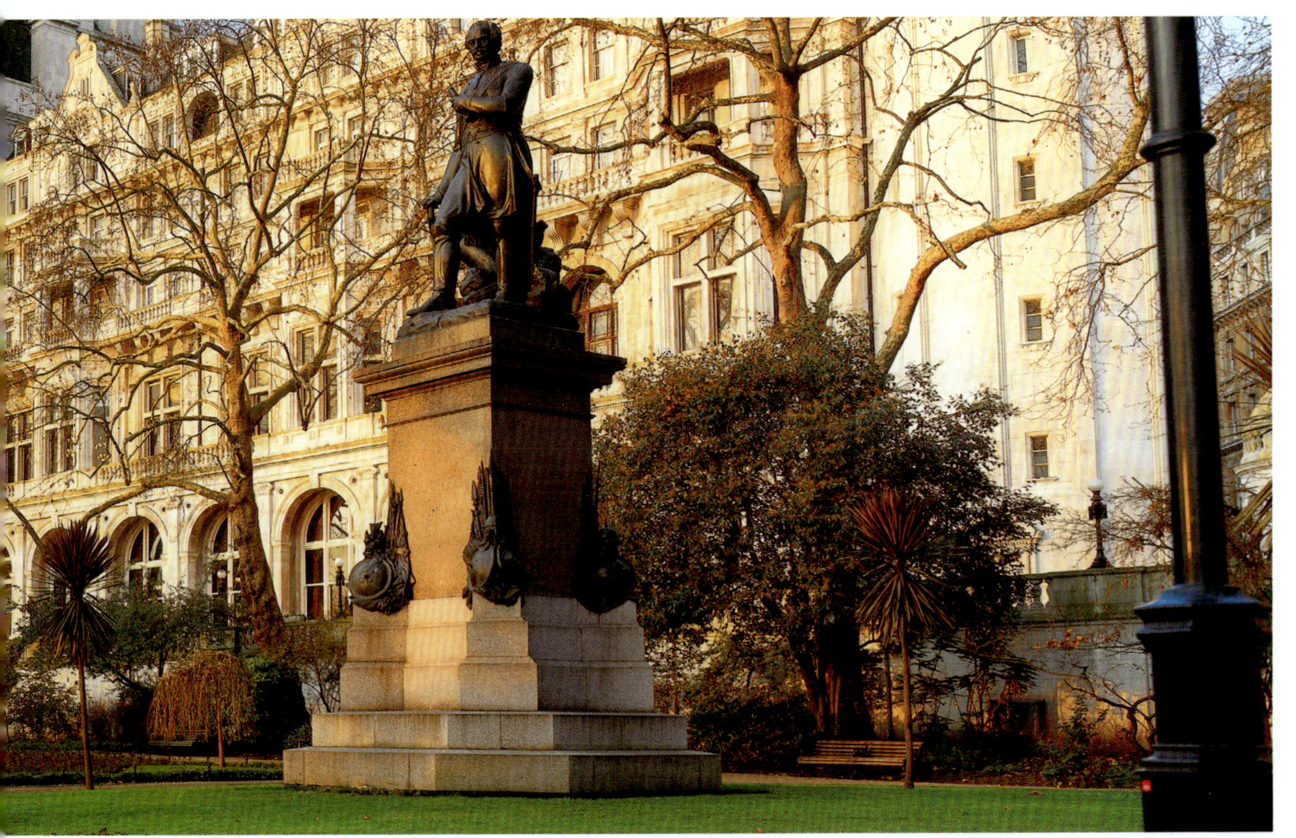

VICTORIA EMBANKMENT, DAWN

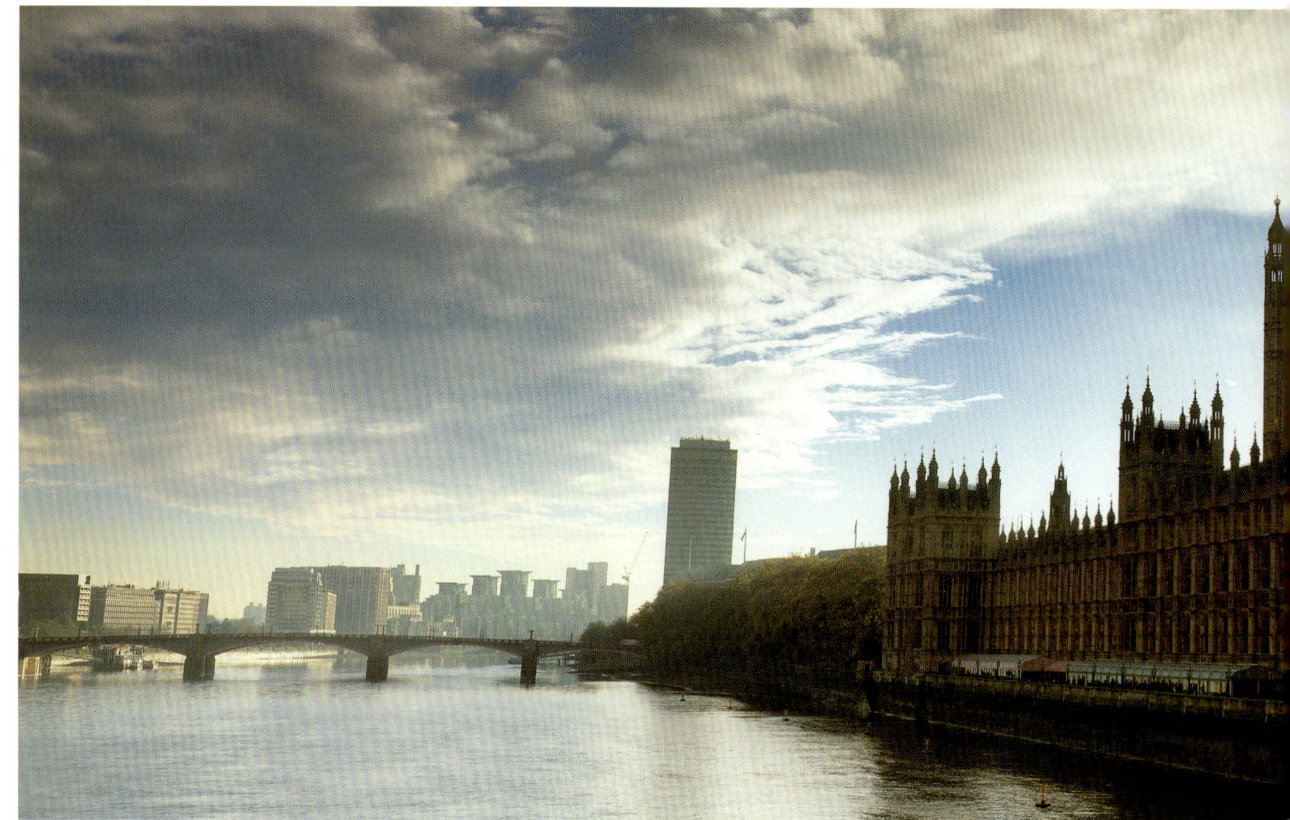

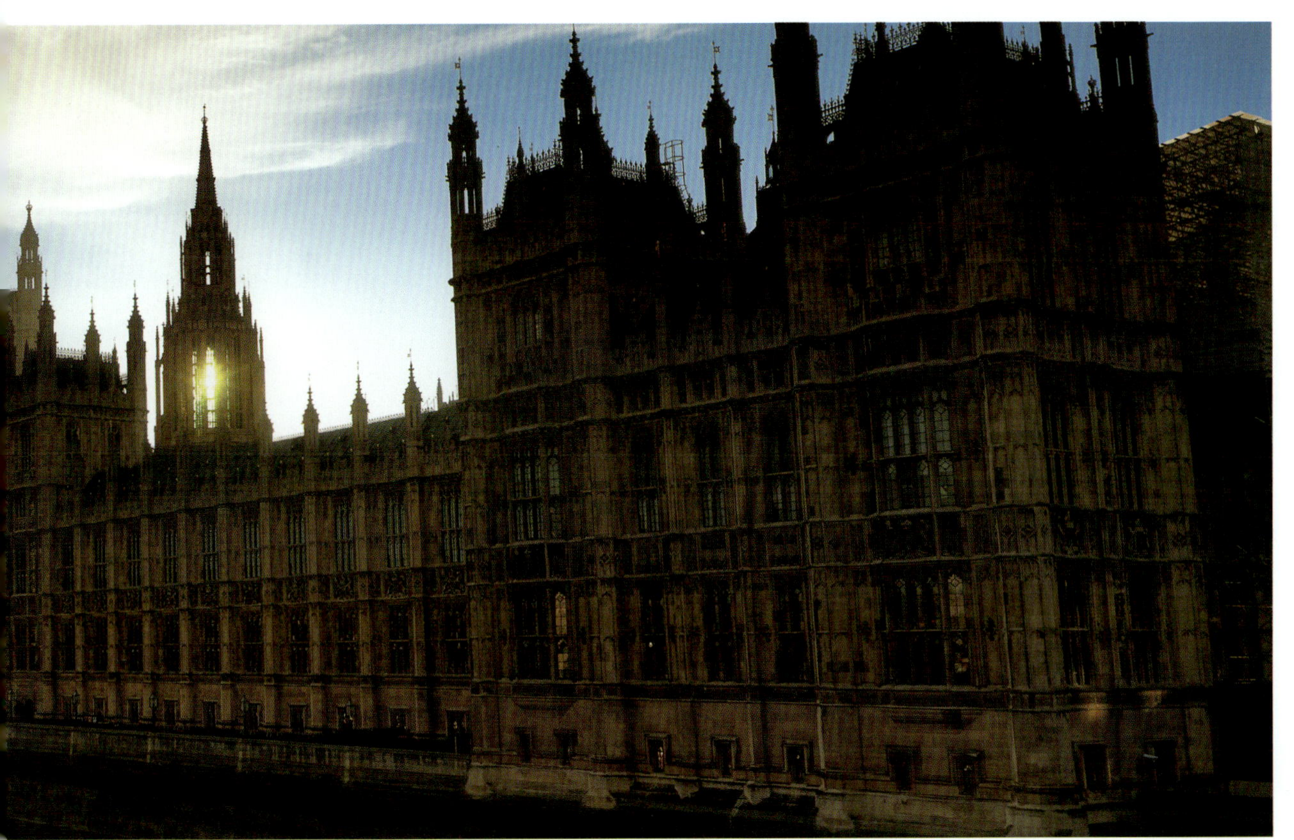

LIGHT IN THE TOWER, PALACE OF WESTMINSTER

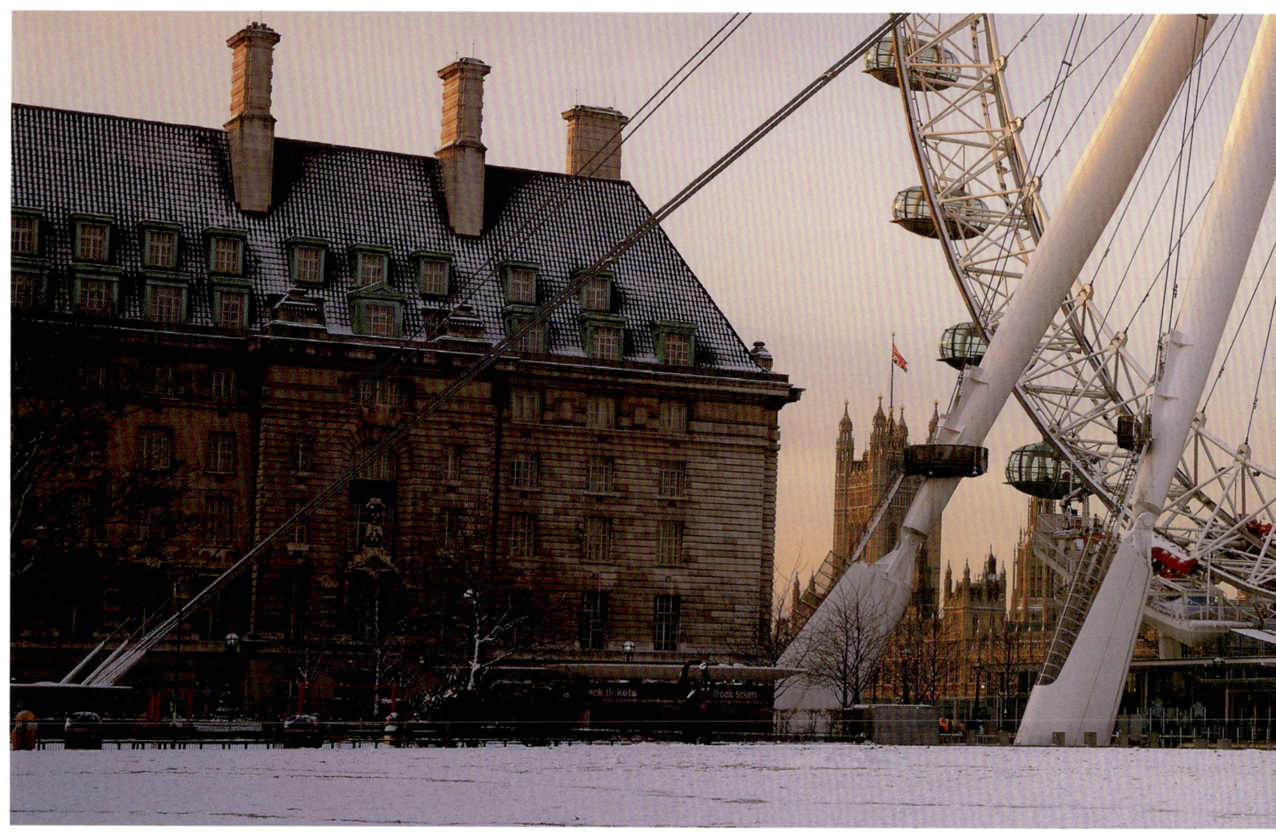

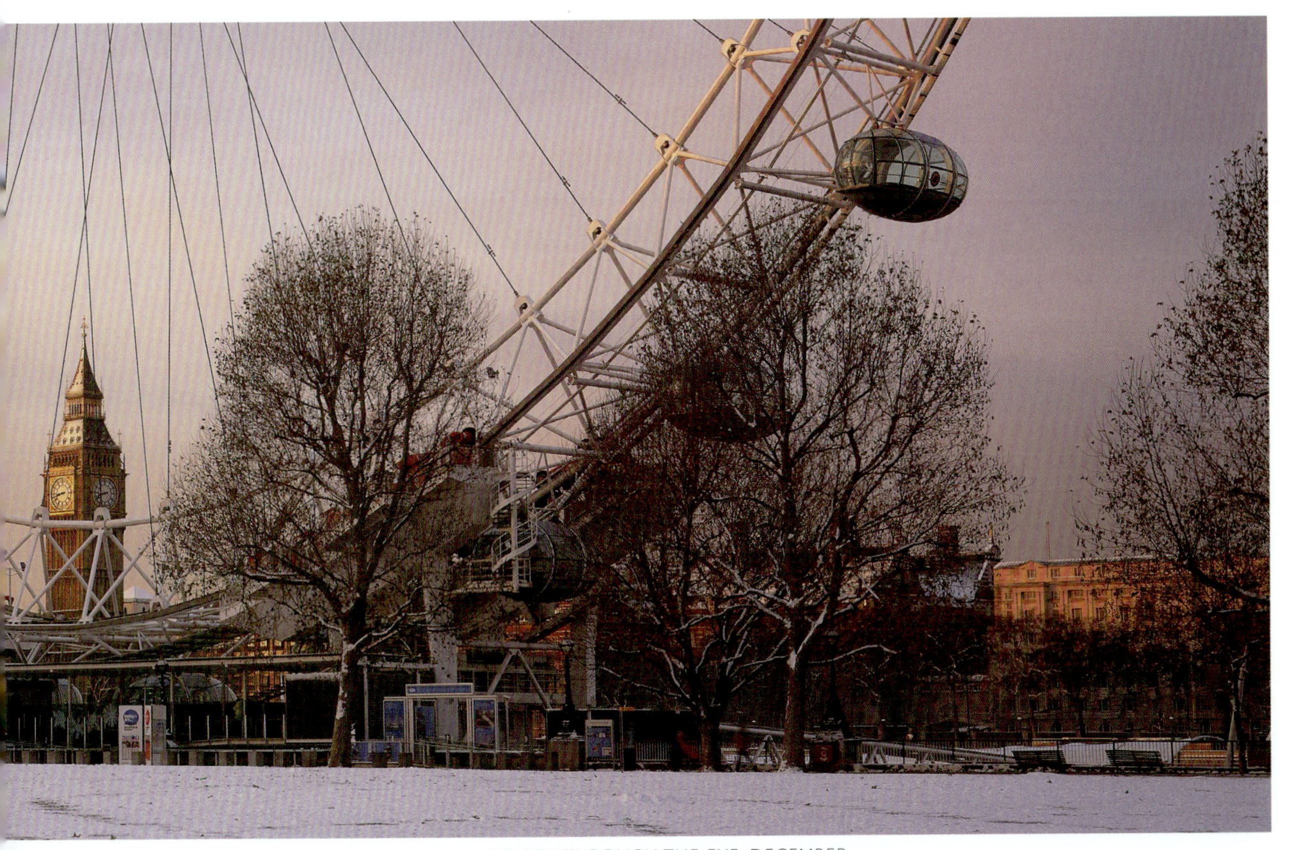

BIG BEN THROUGH THE EYE, DECEMBER

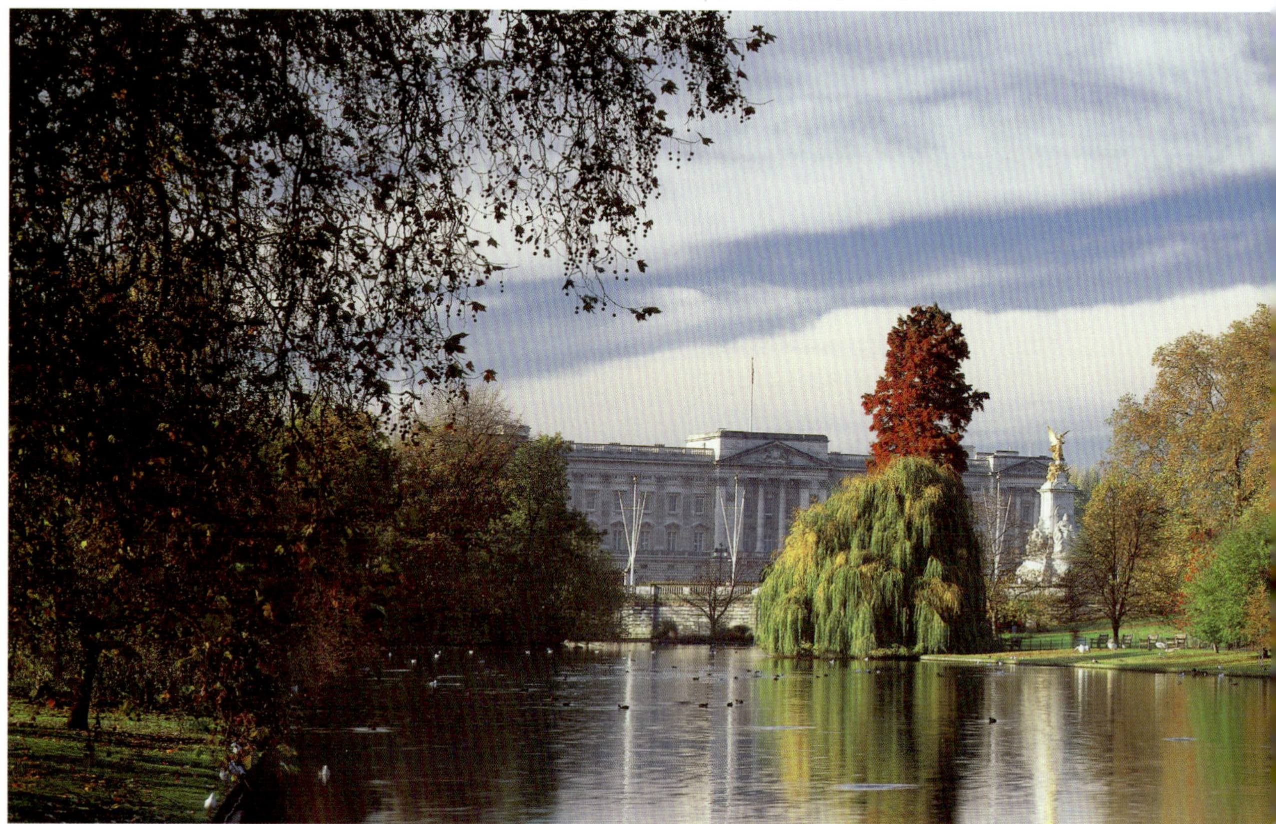

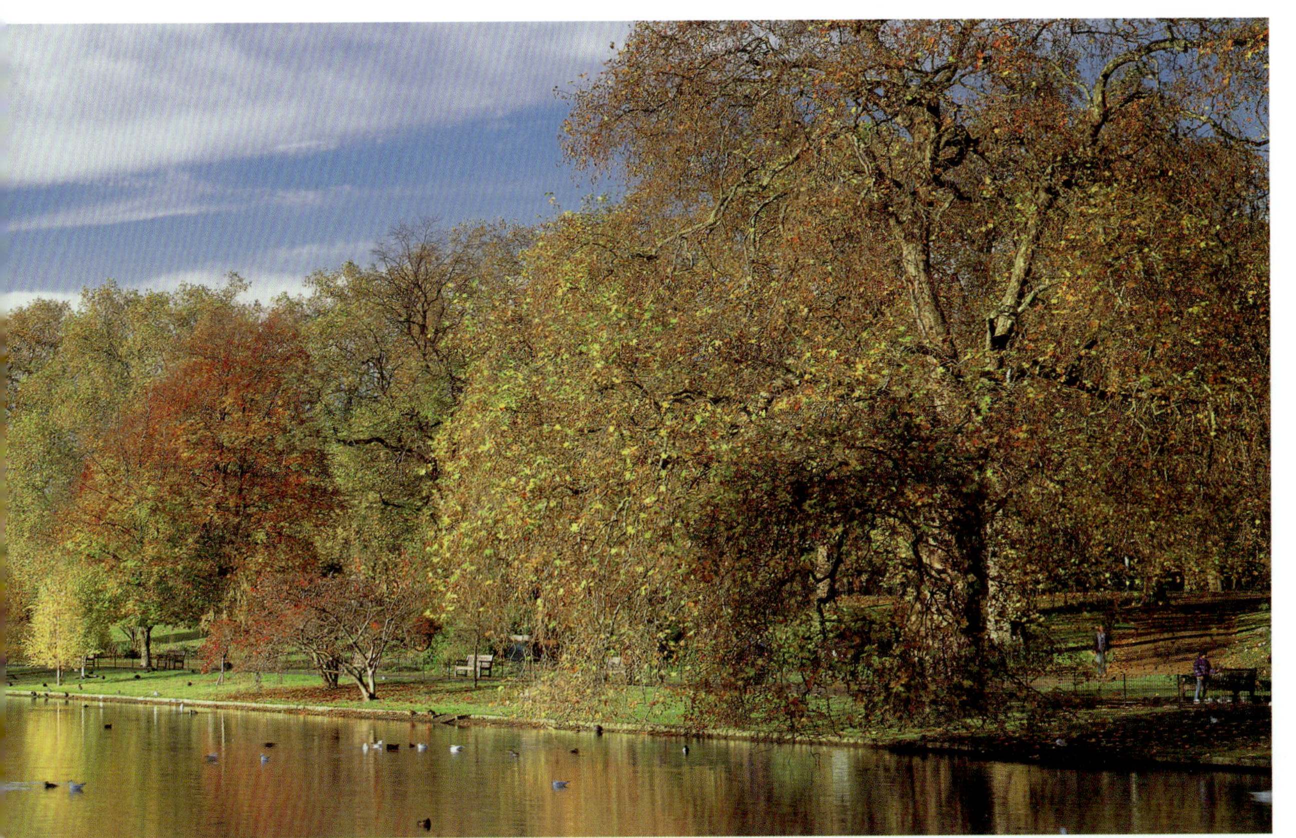

BUCKINGHAM PALACE IN AUTUMN, FROM ST JAMES'S PARK

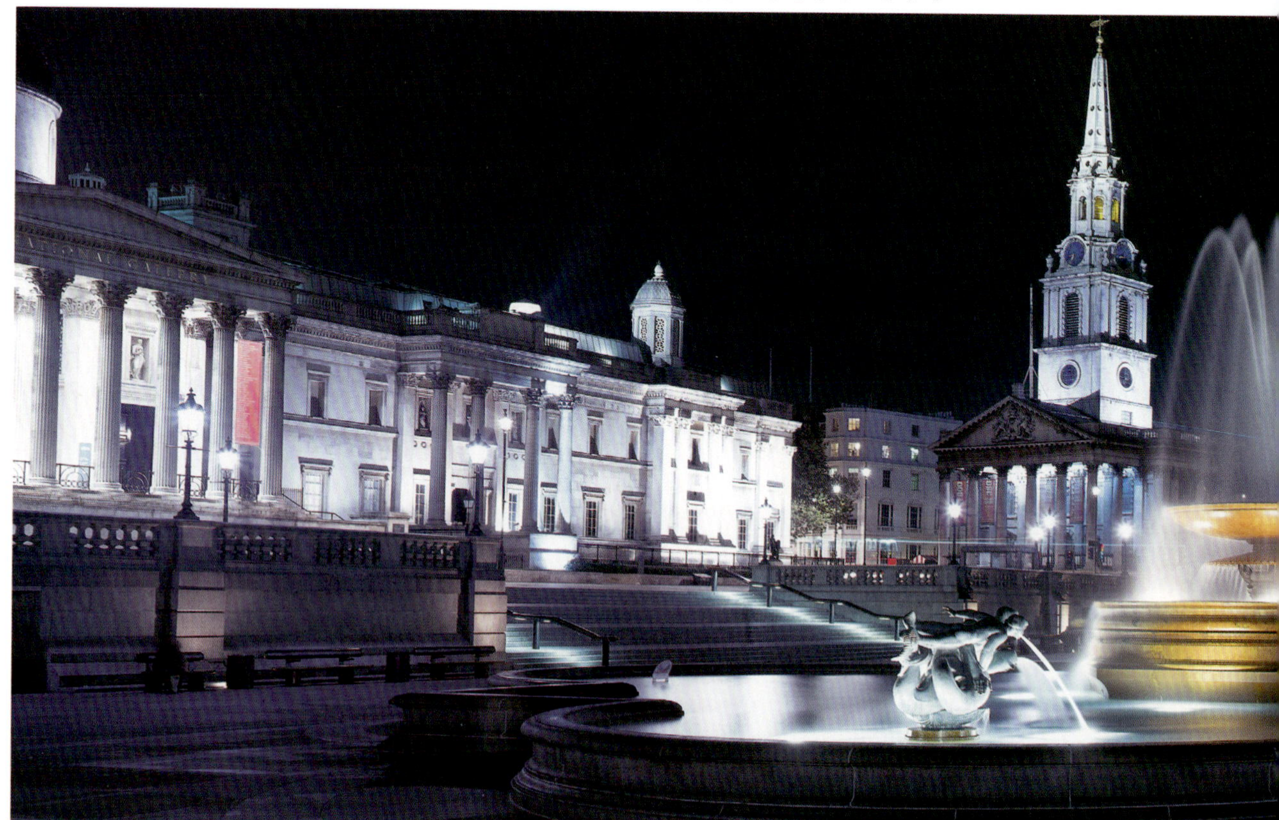

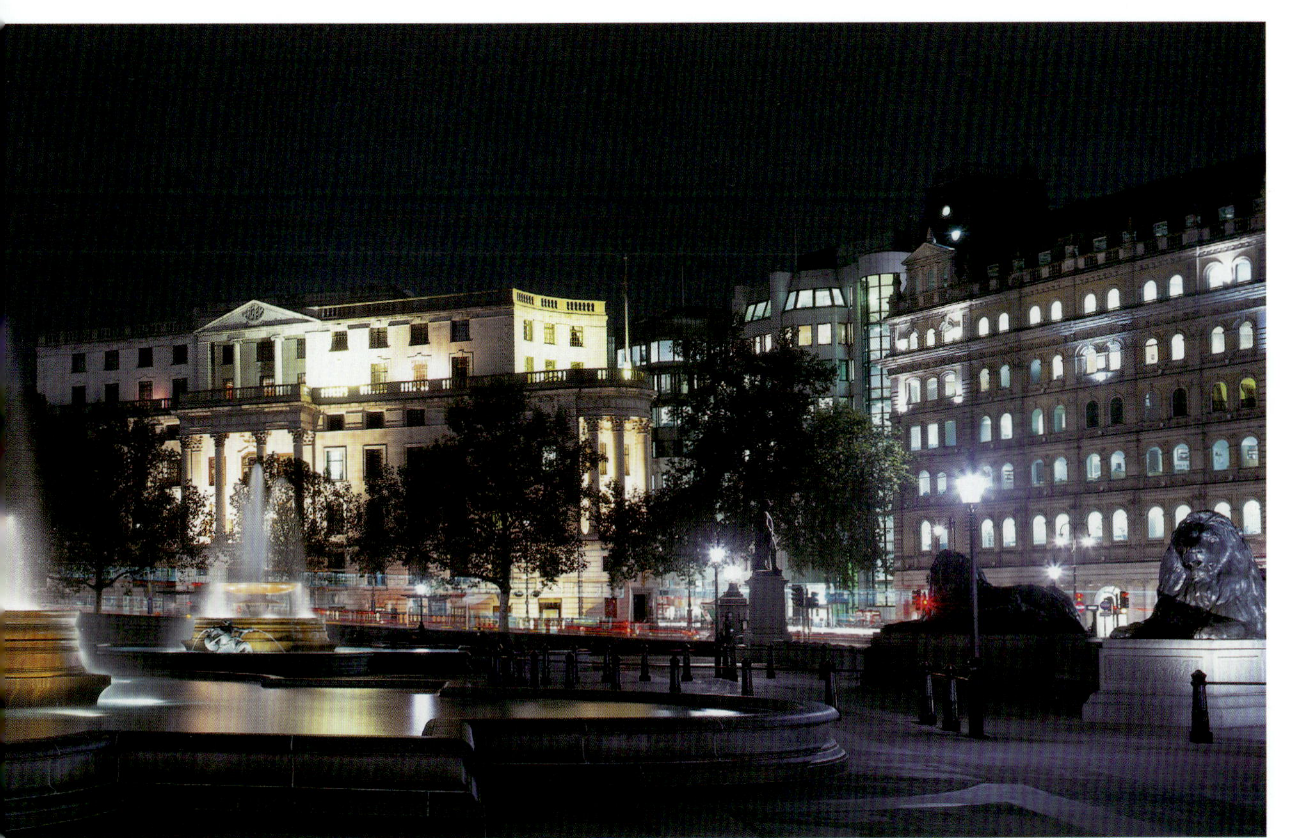

TRAFALGAR SQUARE BY NIGHT

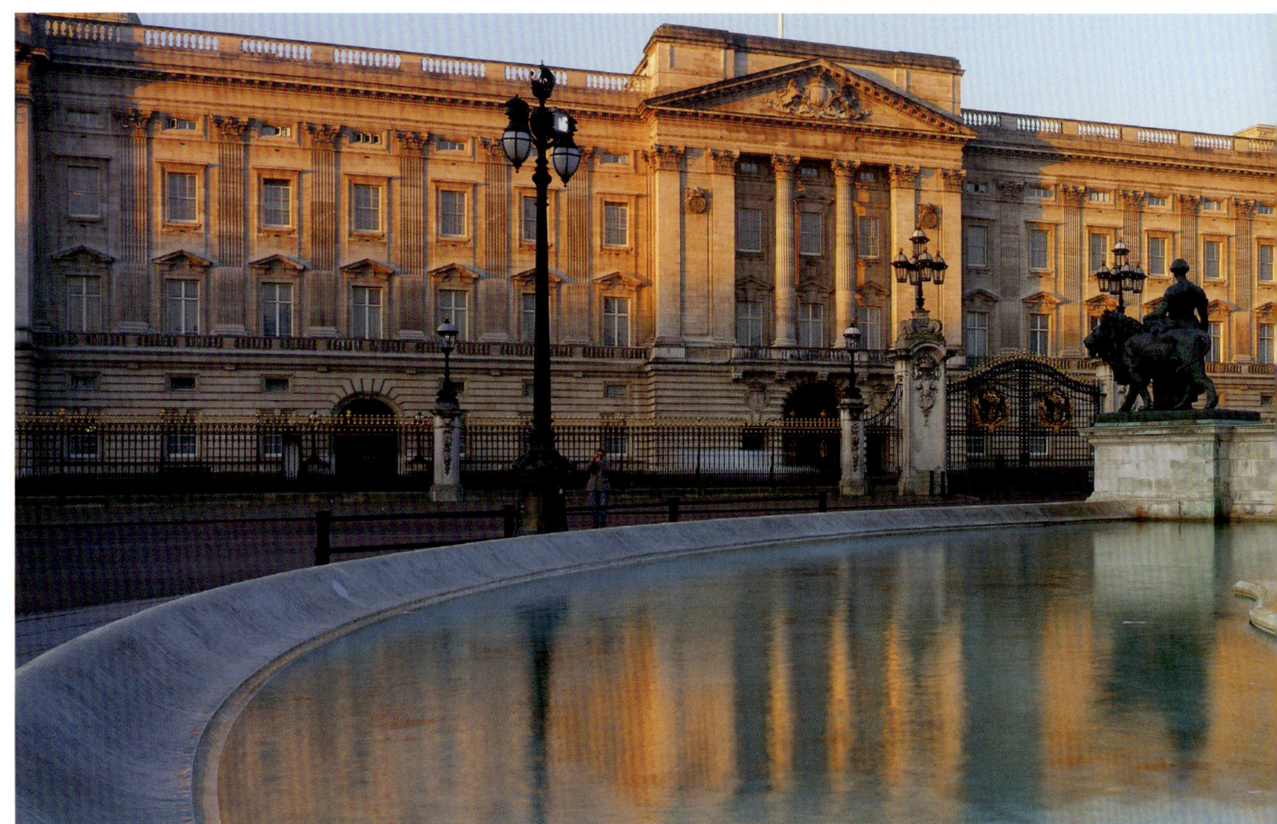

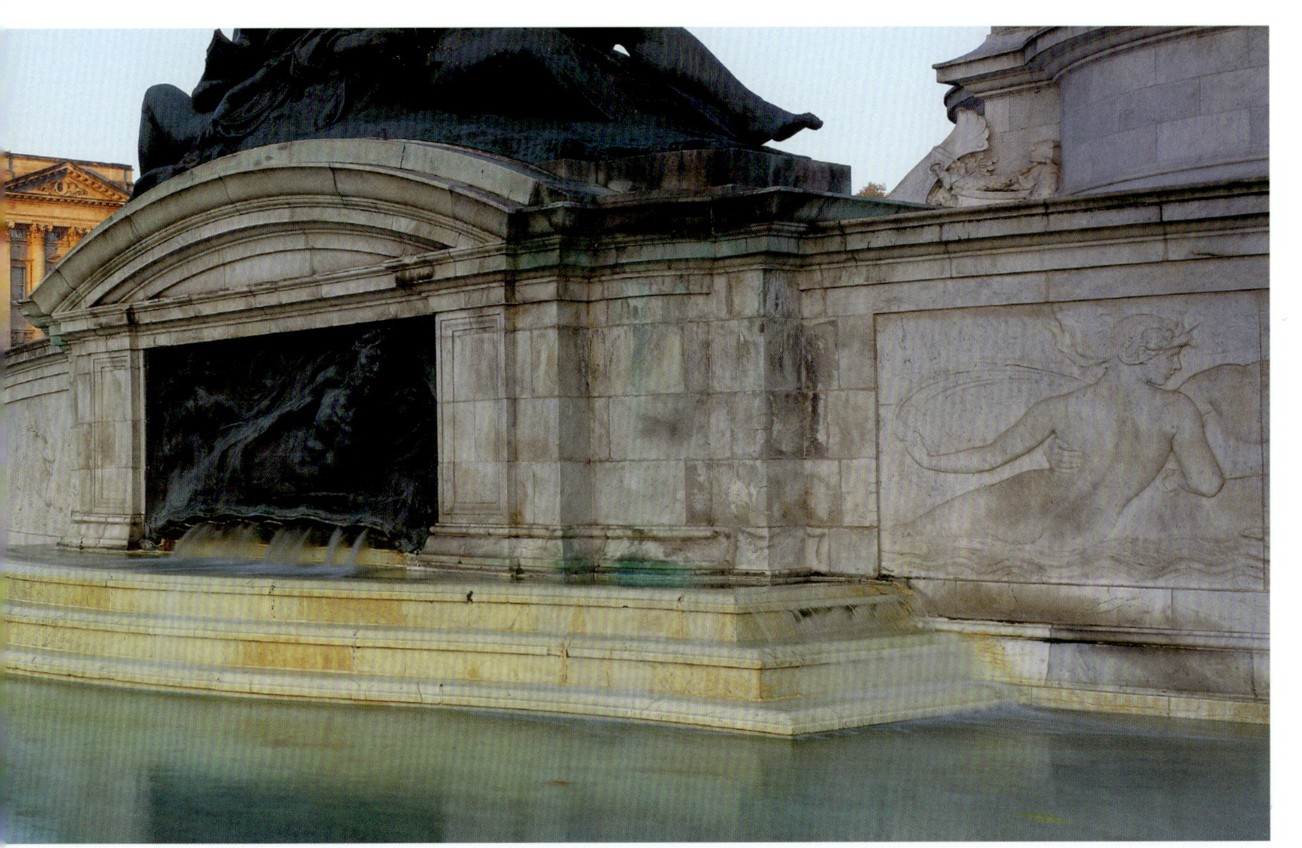

FOUNTAIN REFLECTIONS AT BUCKINGHAM PALACE

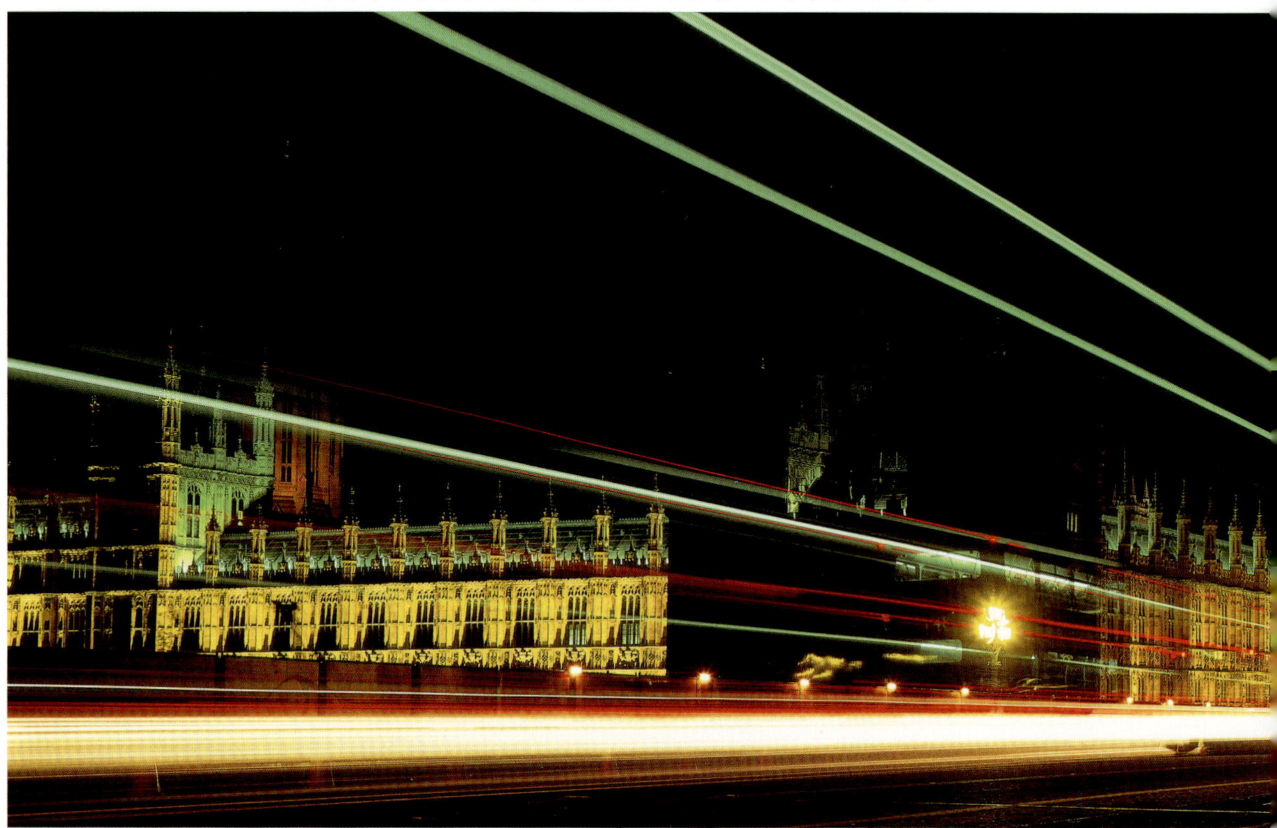

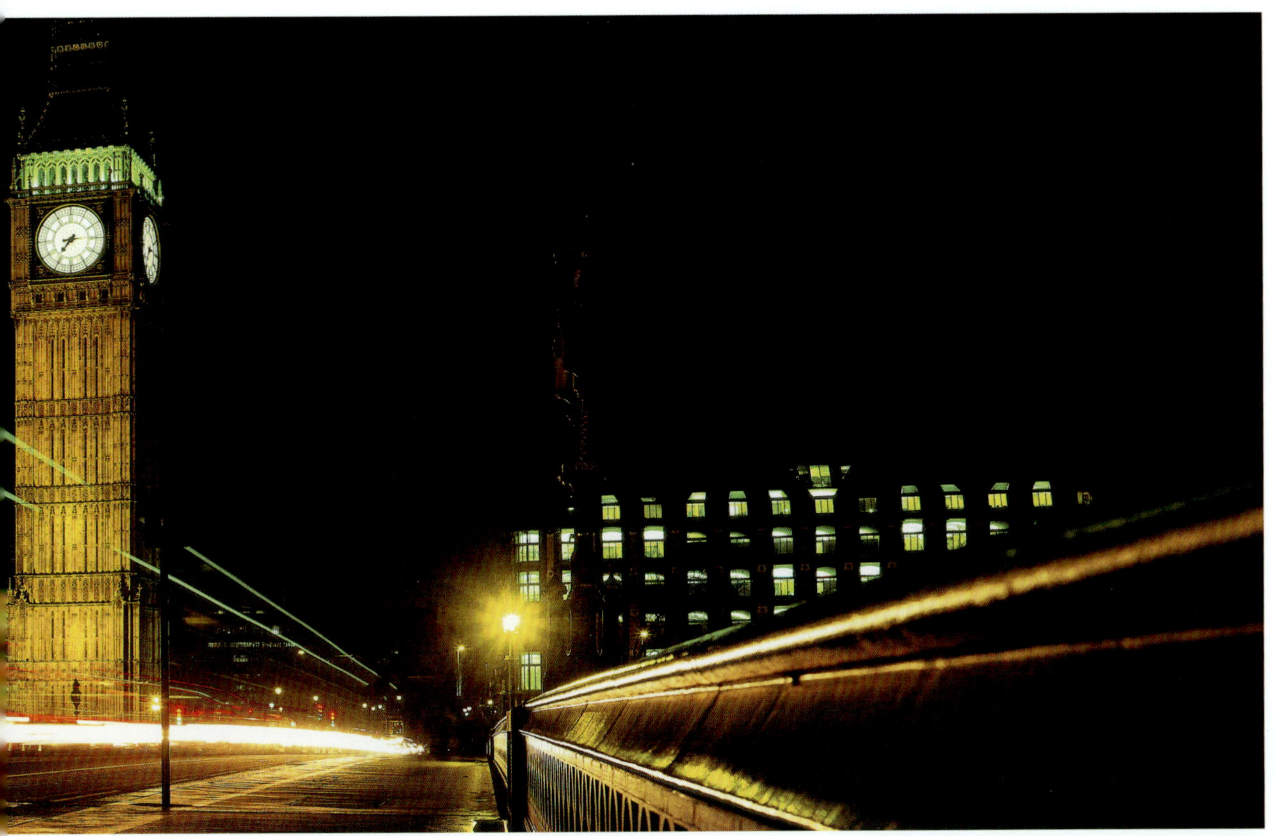

BIG BEN AND TRAFFIC TRAILS

THE CITY AND DOCKLANDS

Before it became Europe's most sprawling metropolis, London was the City and the docks – the latter providing the conduit for a vast global trade, the former turning the ensuing wealth into architectural grandeur. The City's ancient taverns and coffee houses also provided the setting for artistic endeavours, frequented by the likes of Samuel Pepys and William Shakespeare.

London Bridge was originally the only crossing over the Thames. The bridge went through various incarnations, one of which was later bought by a American, believing he was buying the famous Tower Bridge. As London expanded more bridges were added, but all were to the west of London Bridge, since the river to the east needed free flow of shipping as the hub of one of the world's busiest ports.

By the mid-1800s, the east end of London had become so densely populated that public pressure mounted for a bridge east of London Bridge. Over 50 designs were put forward to build a bridge that wouldn't disrupt river traffic, and eventually Horace Jones provided the solution in the shape of Tower Bridge, the superbly engineered drawbridge still in operation today.

While historic buildings remain throughout the City of London, many became surrounded by nondescript architecture as London grew careless of its beautiful heritage. Views of St Paul's Cathedral became a particular battleground, with increasing protests over buildings that might obstruct sightlines of this iconic landmark. The building of the Millennium Bridge was a breakthrough in the campaign for a more thoughtful attitude to London's appearance. This graceful structure was not only the first new Thames crossing since the completion of Tower Bridge in 1894, but also a victory for those keen to open up London to the admiring gaze. The bridge creates a breathtaking sightline connecting St Paul's with the equally striking Tate Modern art gallery.

The City skyline now shows the Swiss Re building – whose shape earned it the immediate nickname of 'The Gherkin'. Located at 30 St Mary's Axe (characterful old street names are a pleasure of any City walk), this 40-storey beauty is often credited to architect Sir Norman Foster but the original design was by Foster's then-associate Ken Shuttleworth – the architect also behind the Millennium Bridge and the giant arches of the new Wembley Stadium.

Two decades before 'The Gherkin', another iconic skyscraper emerged on the London skyline. Rather than appearing in the heart of the City, the Canary Wharf Tower rose above the derelict docks of the Isle of Dogs – a regenerative move that is typical of London's ongoing desire for reinvention. For years, it stood proudly alone as the major landmark on the east London skyline, surrounded by patches of water on which old boats and machinery were left as mementoes of past industrial glory.

A sudden spurt of building in the last decade has seen the Canary Wharf Tower joined by a series of companion skyscrapers. For an overview of the changes transforming Docklands and the east of London – even more so after London's successful bid for the 2012 Olympics – take a trip on the Docklands Light Railway (DLR), from the heart of the City to the eastern edge of the former docks.

Back in the City, some things are being left as they were. Leadenhall Market – named after a lead-roofed mansion that stood nearby in the fourteenth century – is built on the site of a Roman forum, and has been a food market since the Middle Ages. The present building is Victorian, built in 1881 by architect Horace Jones, who also found time to design two of London's other famous food markets, Billingsgate and Smithfield, as well as Tower Bridge. A visit to this trio of City markets would start with early morning fish (6-8am, not Monday) at Billingsgate, moving on to meat at Smithfield (perhaps pausing for one of the famously filling breakfasts available at the morning pubs in the area) and ending with lunch at Leadenhall. A real taste of London life, in every sense.

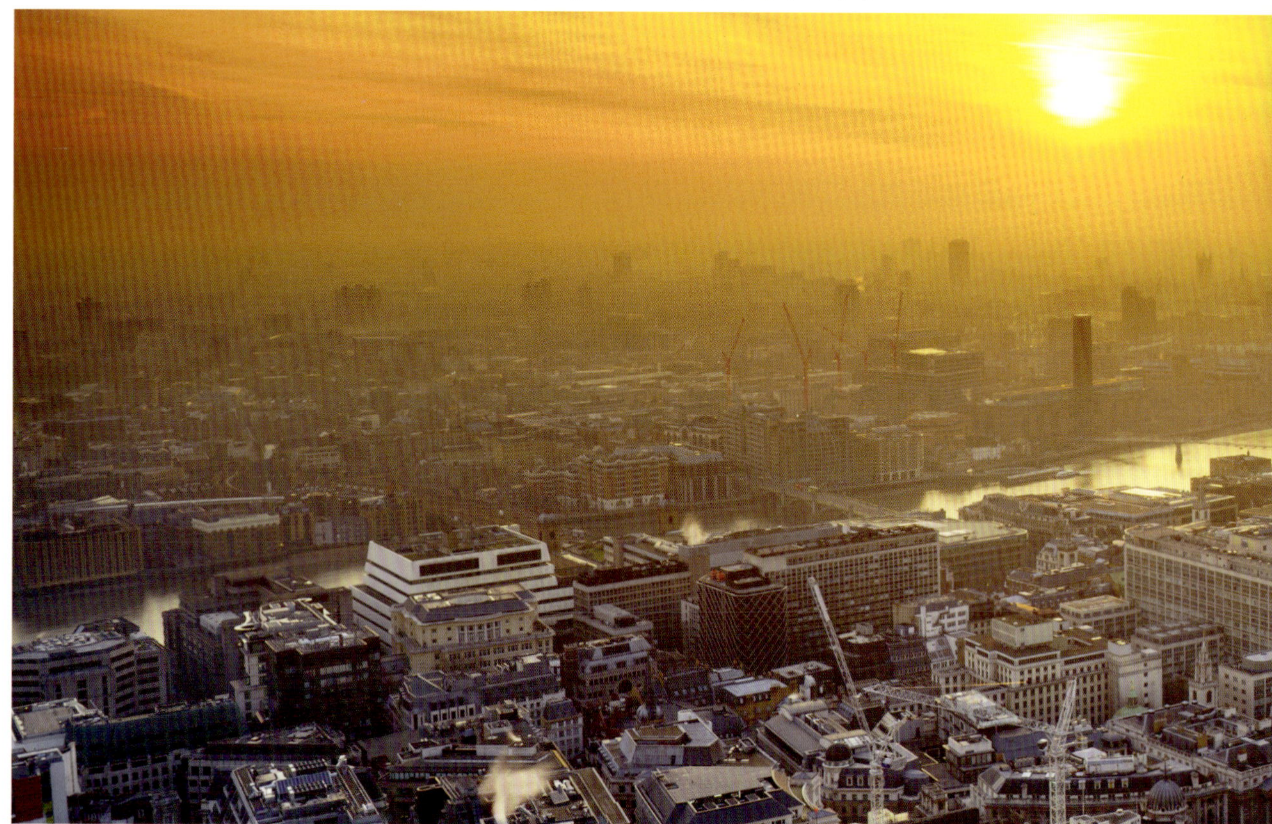

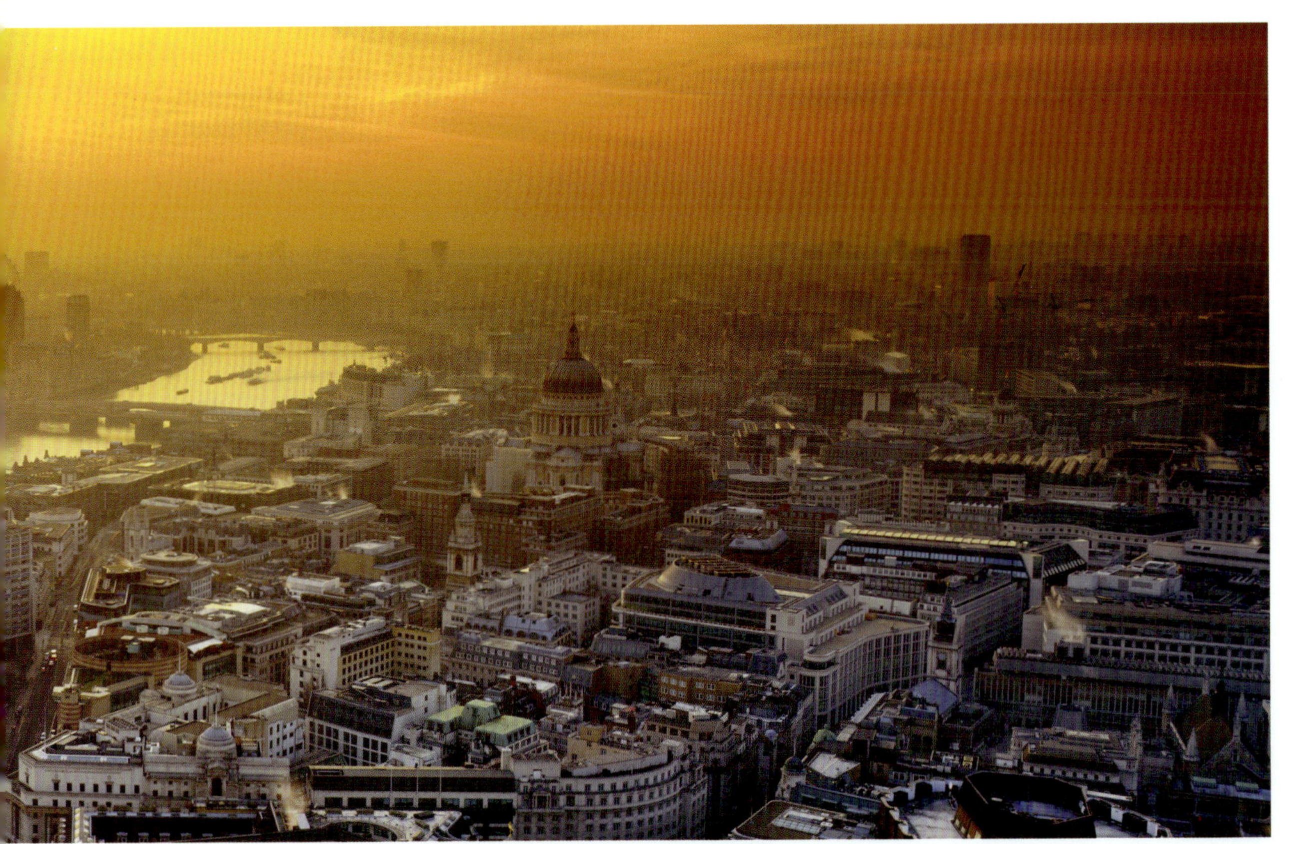

DYING SUN FROM TOWER 42

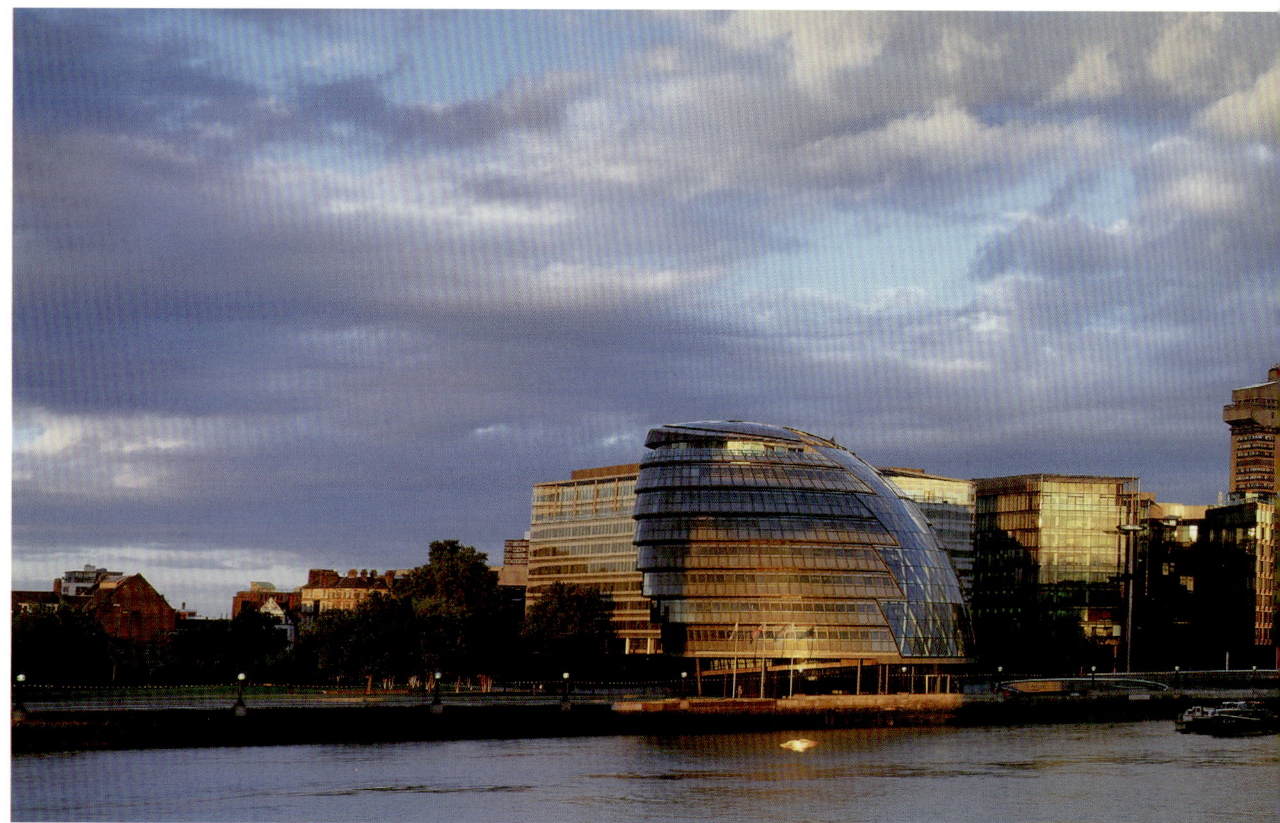

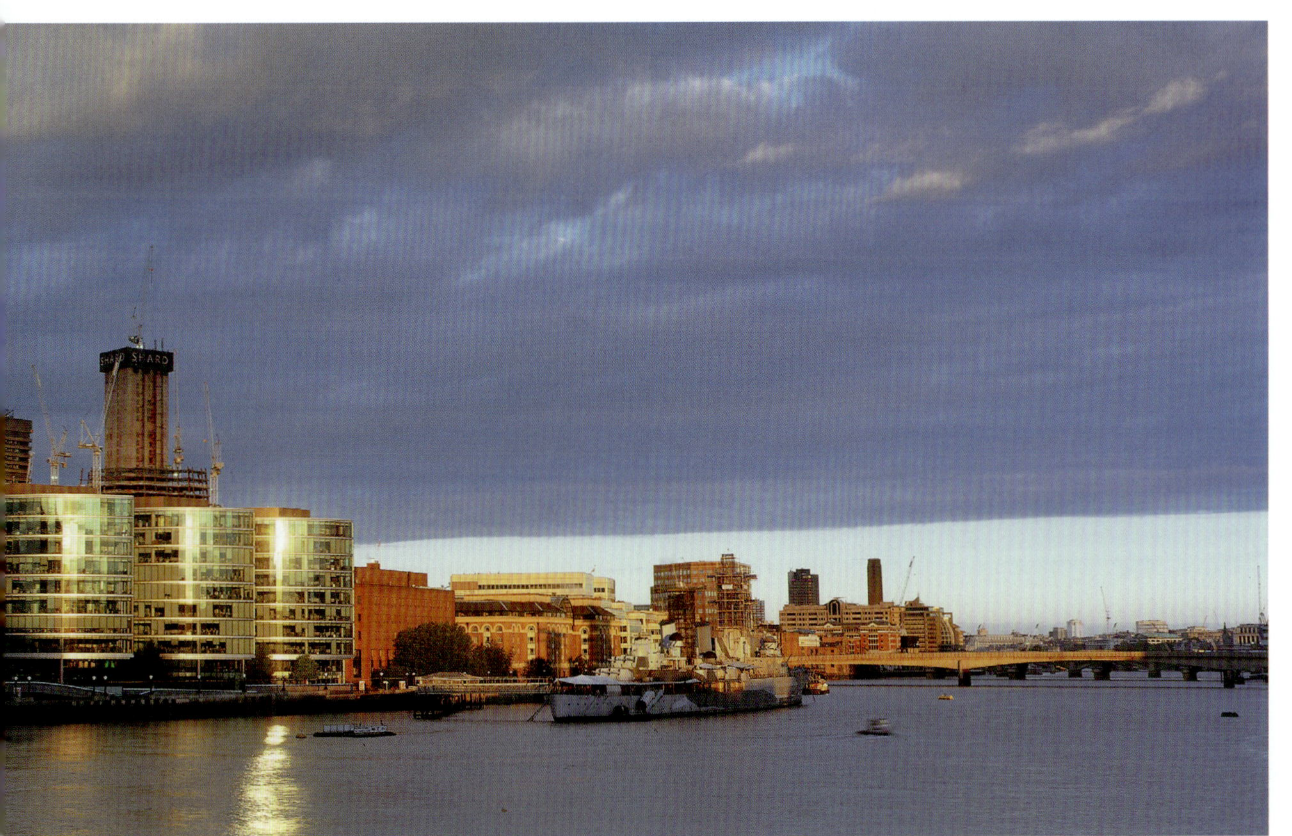

CITY HALL AND THE BEGINNINGS OF THE SHARD, FROM TOWER BRIDGE

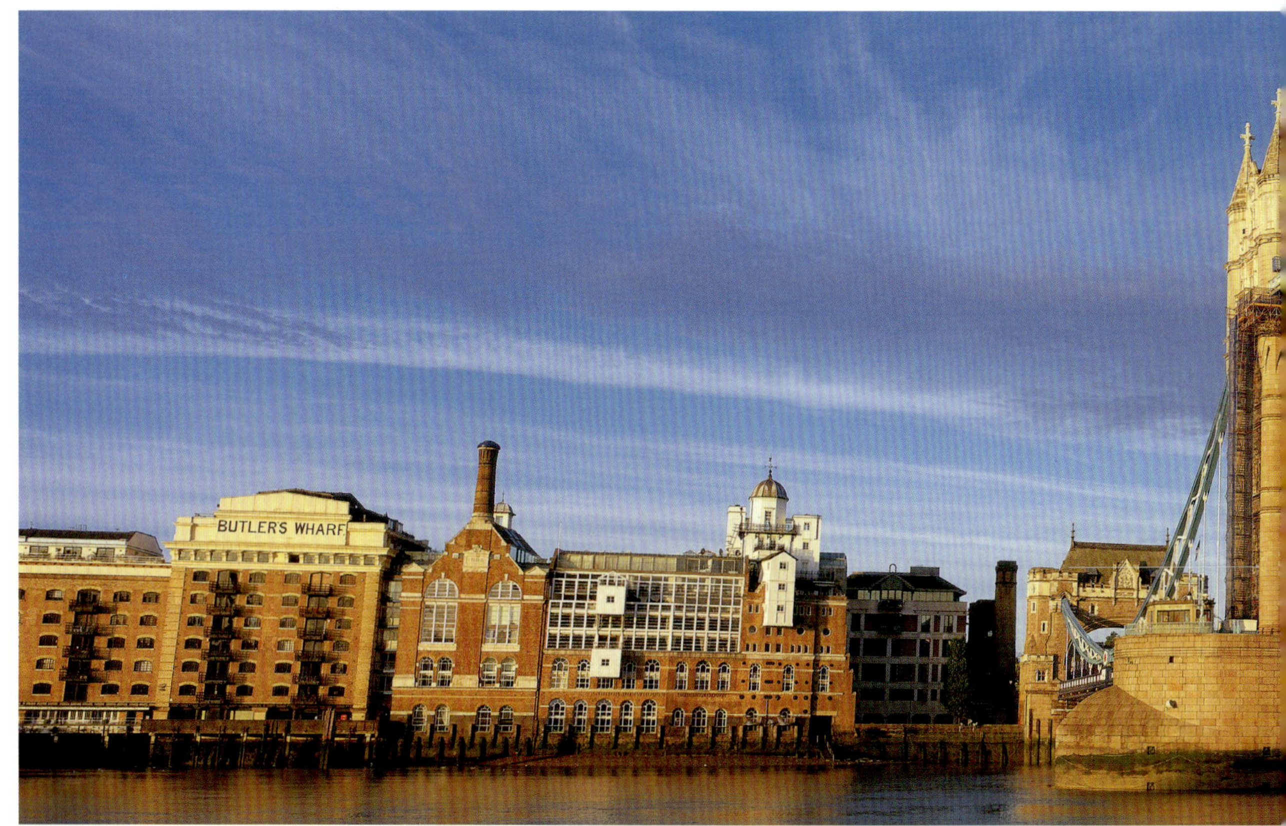
BUTLER'S WHARF

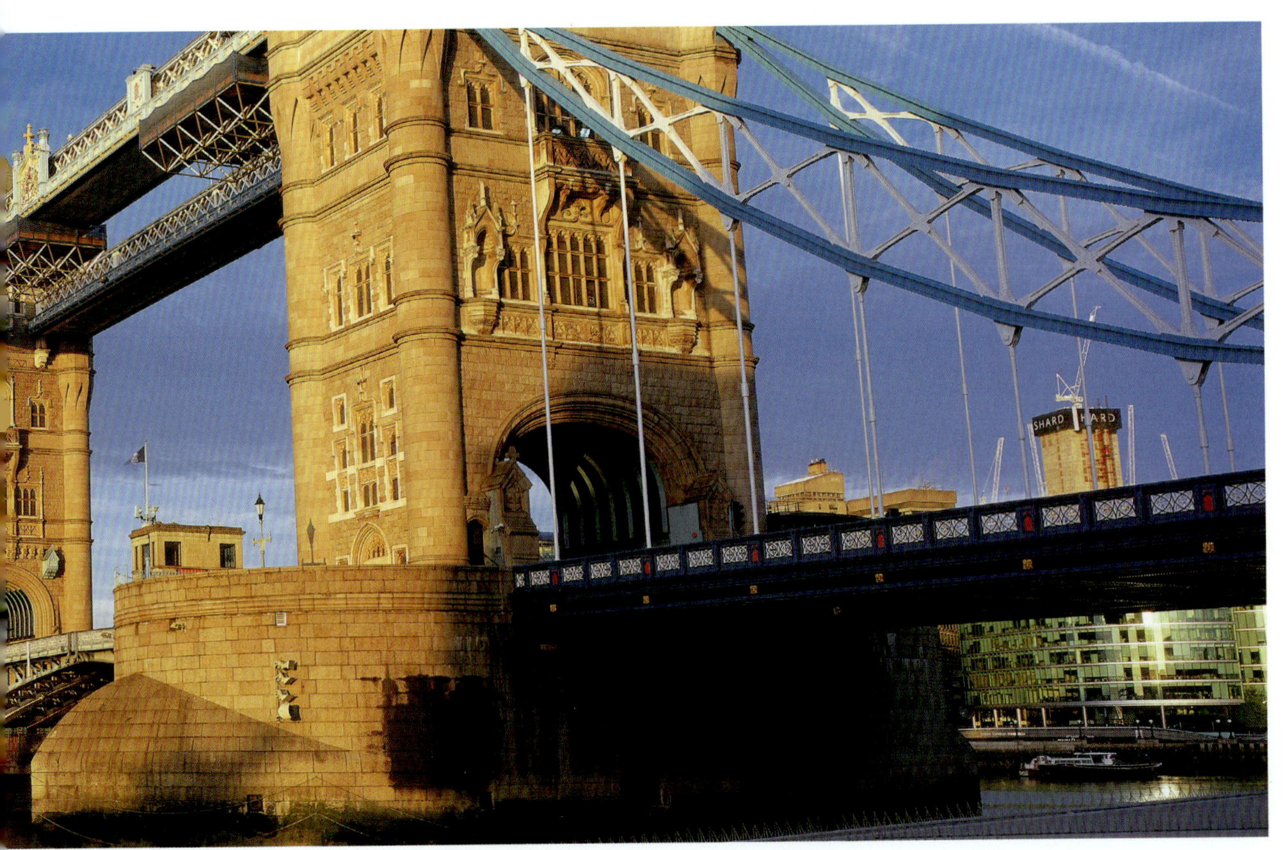

MORNING LIGHT ON TOWER BRIDGE

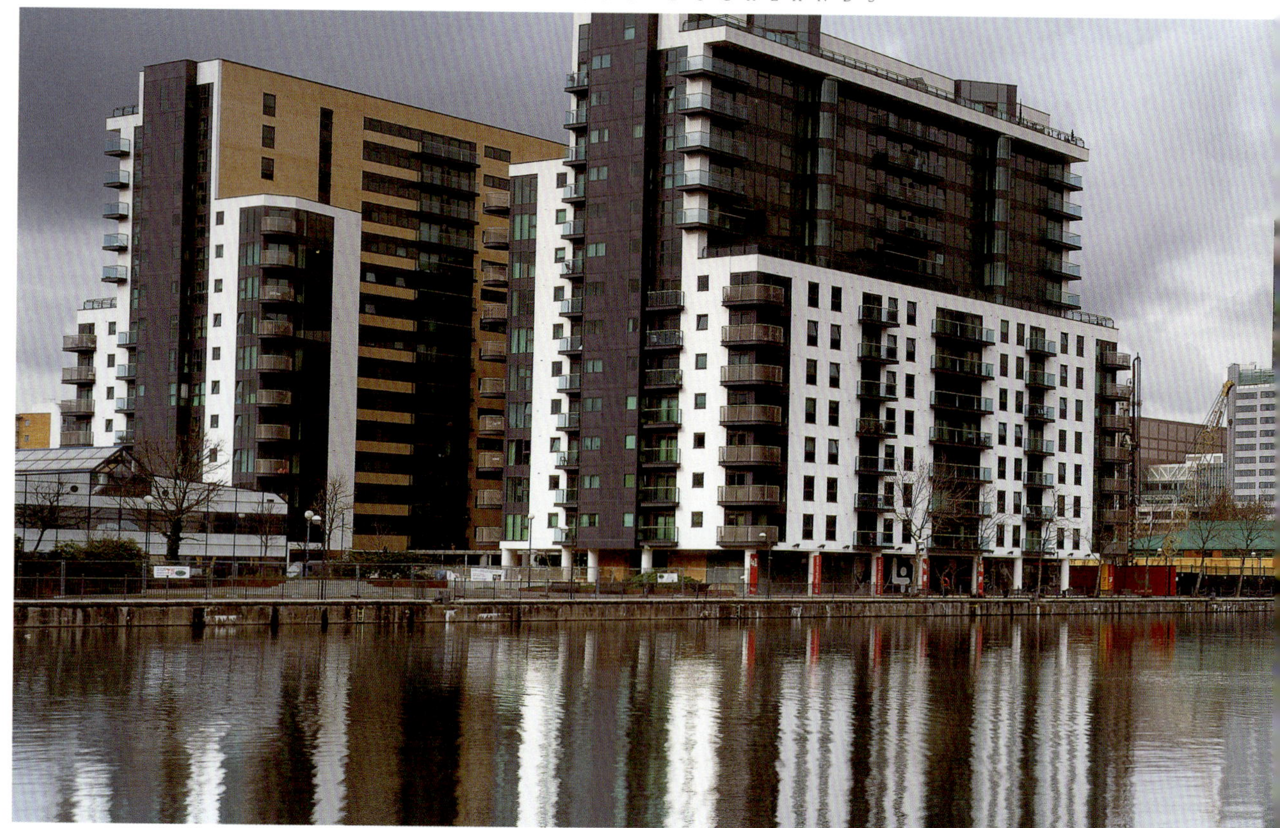

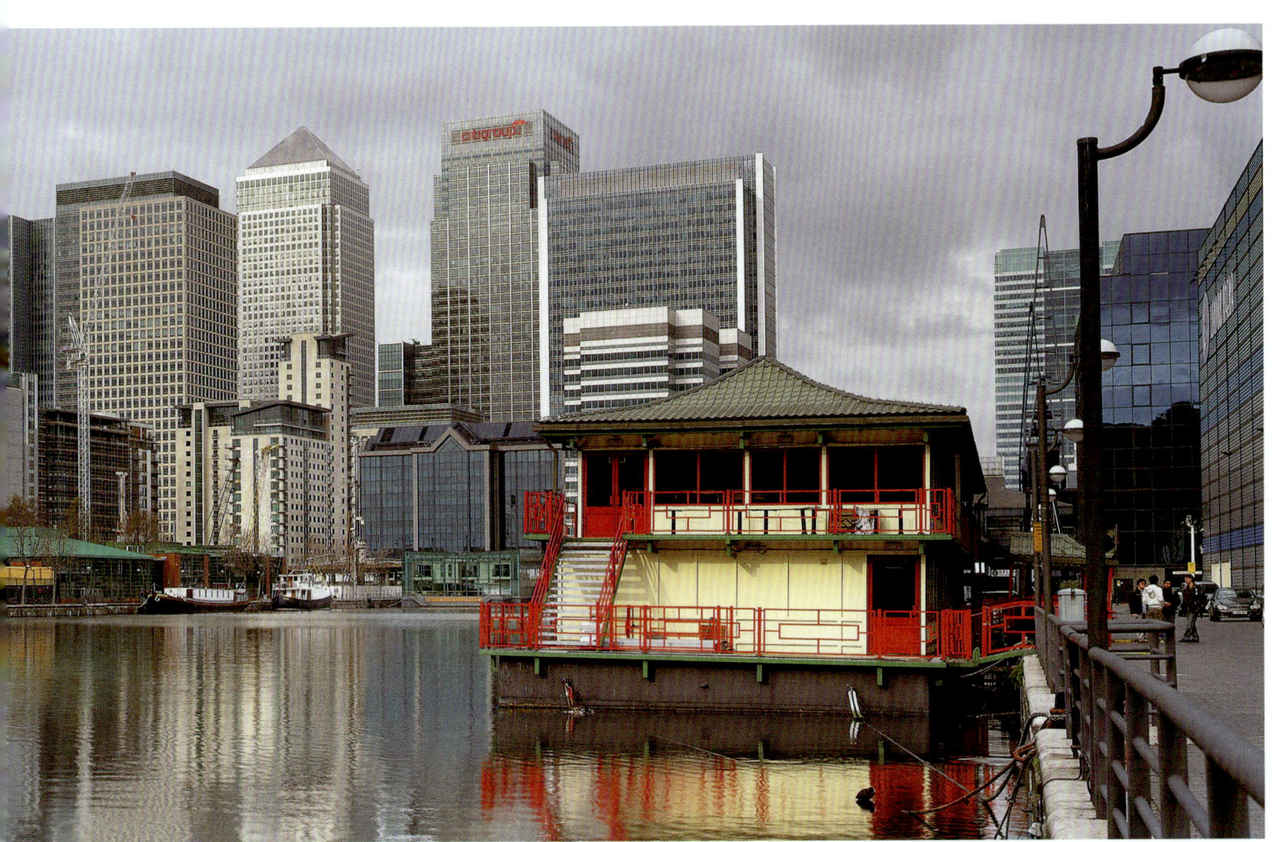

CHINESE BARGE, CANARY WHARF

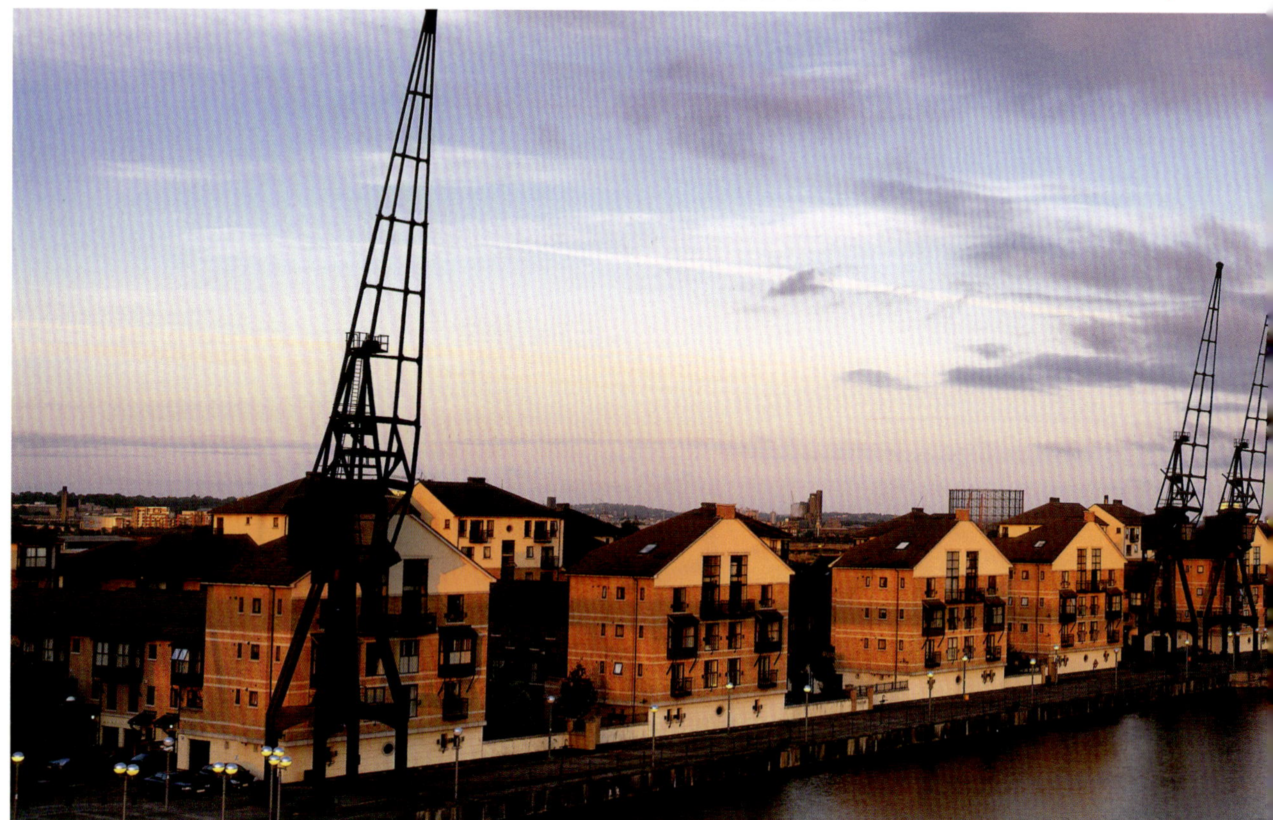

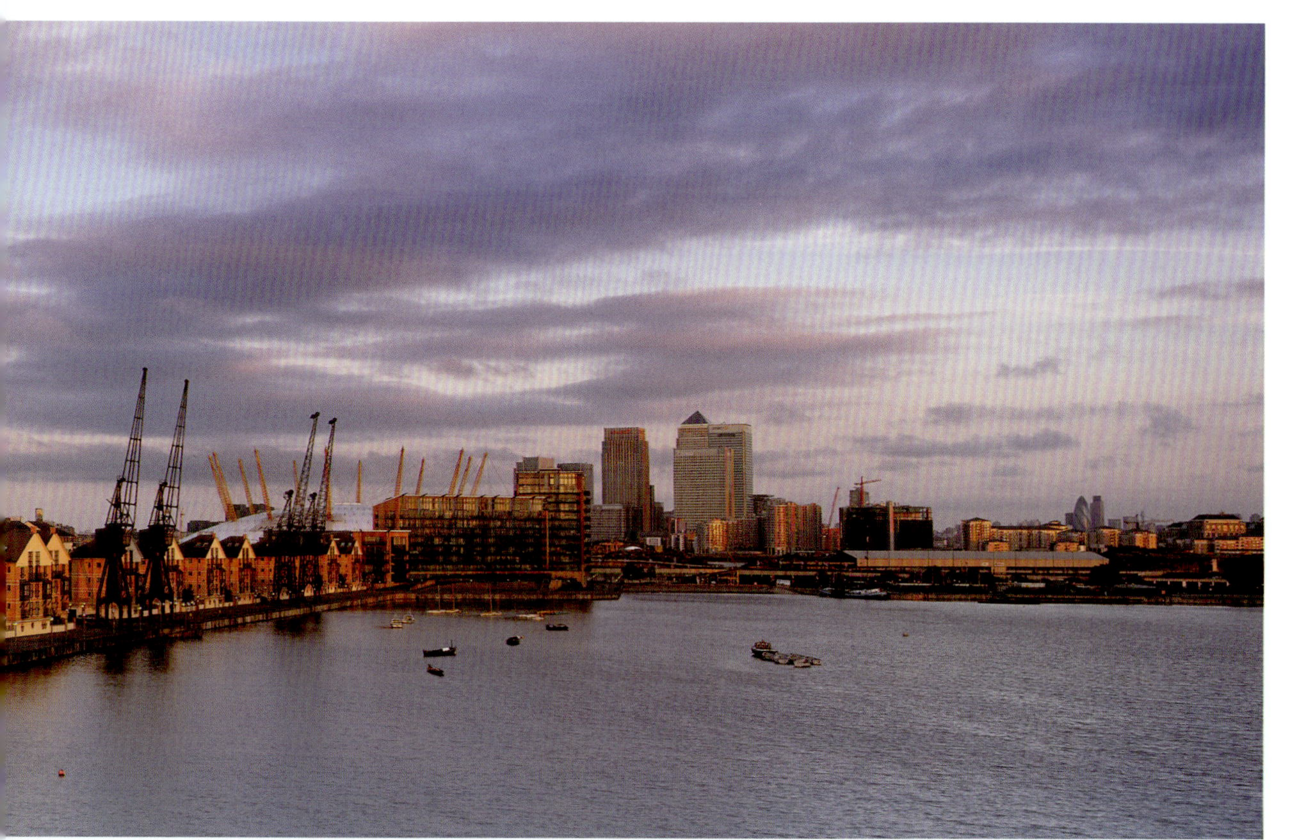

ROYAL VICTORIA DOCK AT DAWN

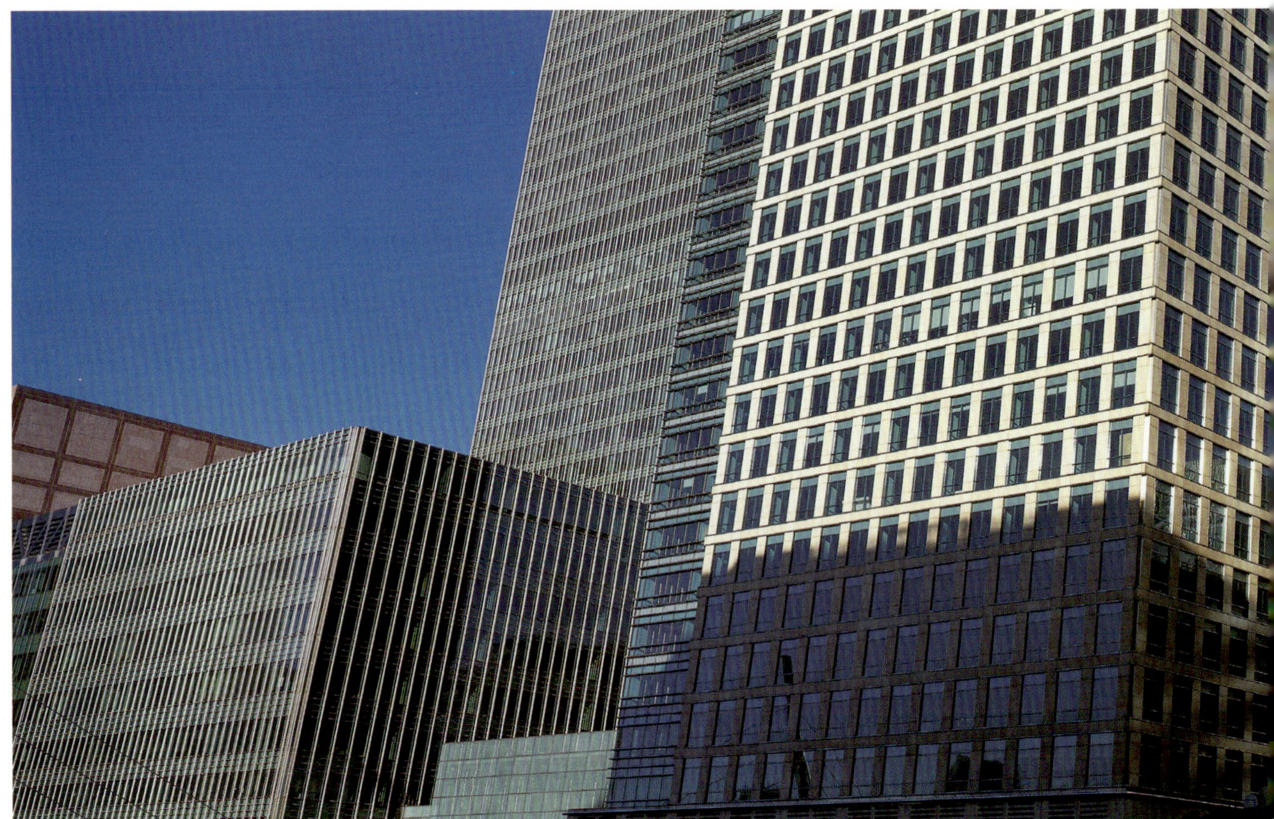

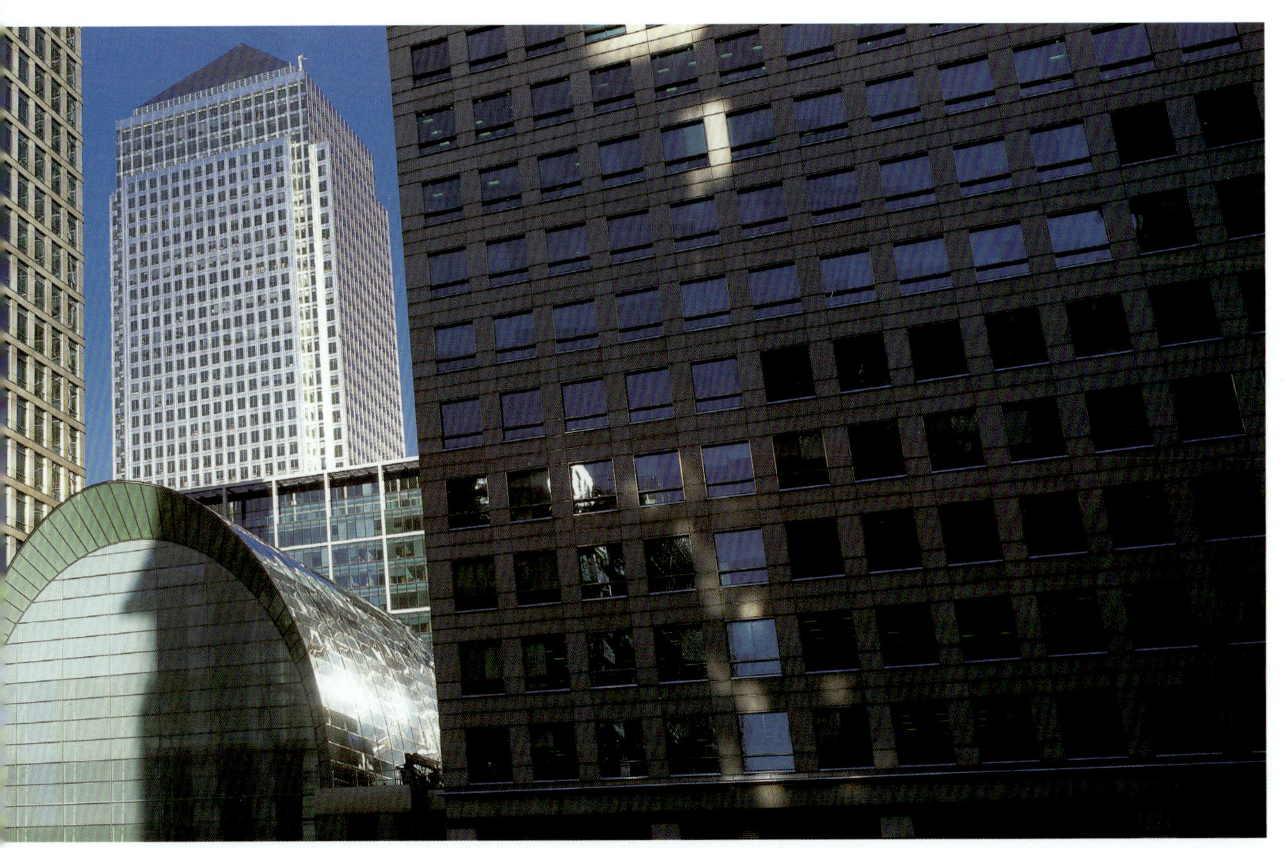

CANARY WHARF TOWERS AT HERON QUAYS

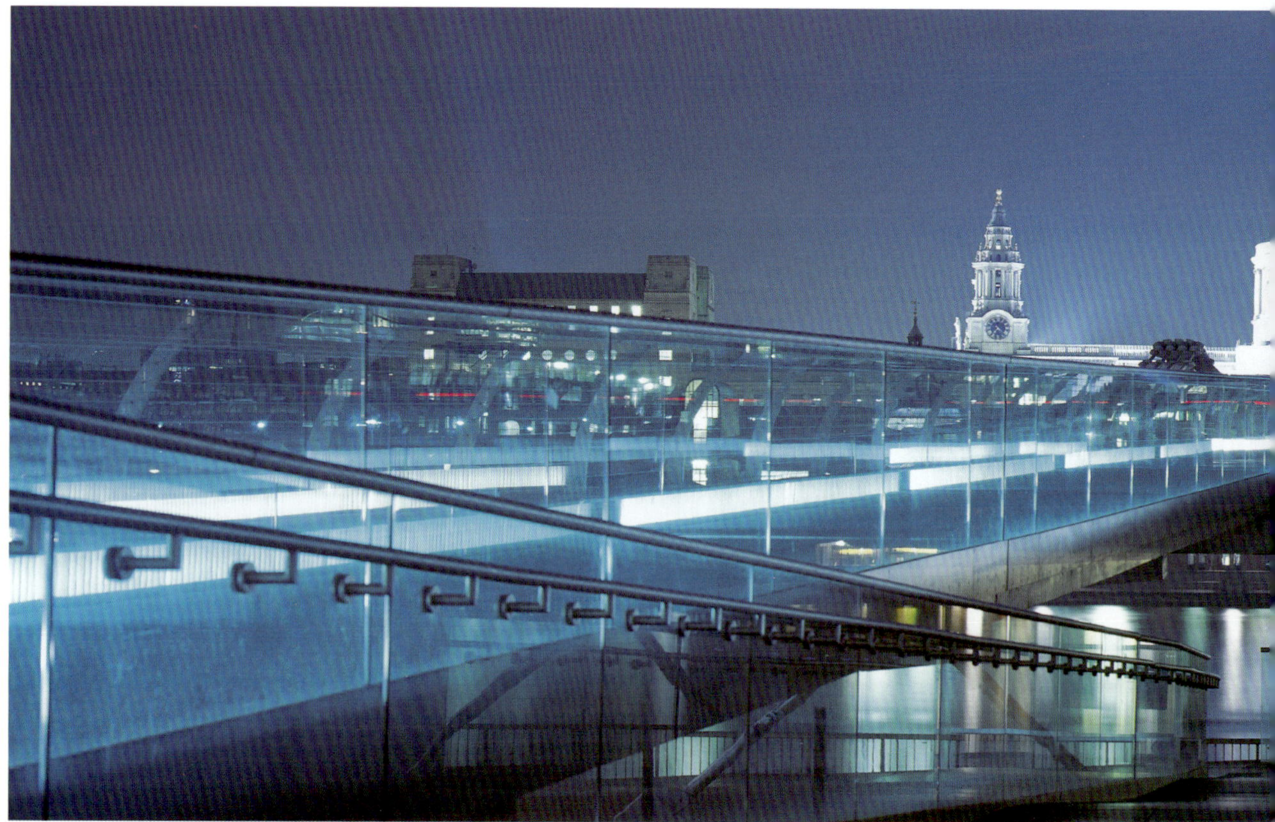

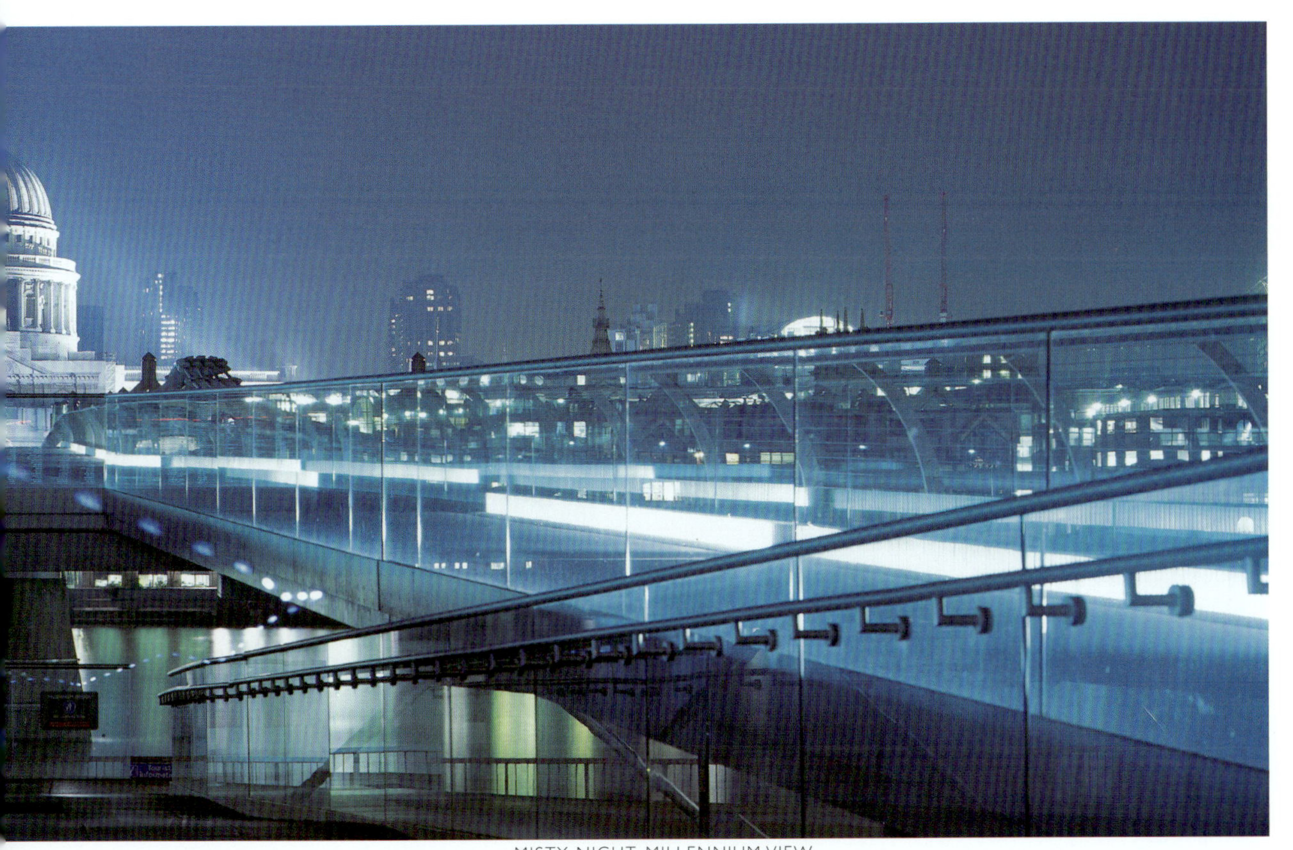

MISTY NIGHT, MILLENNIUM VIEW

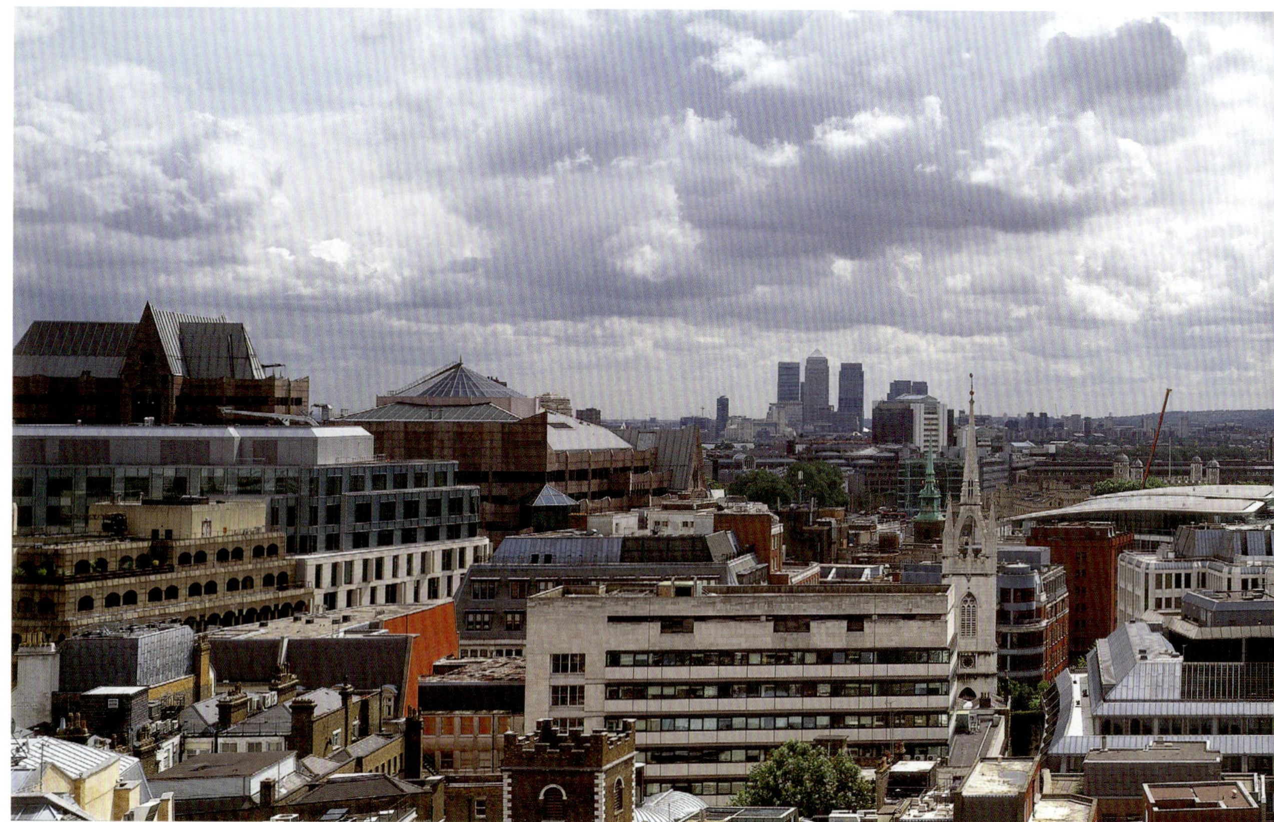

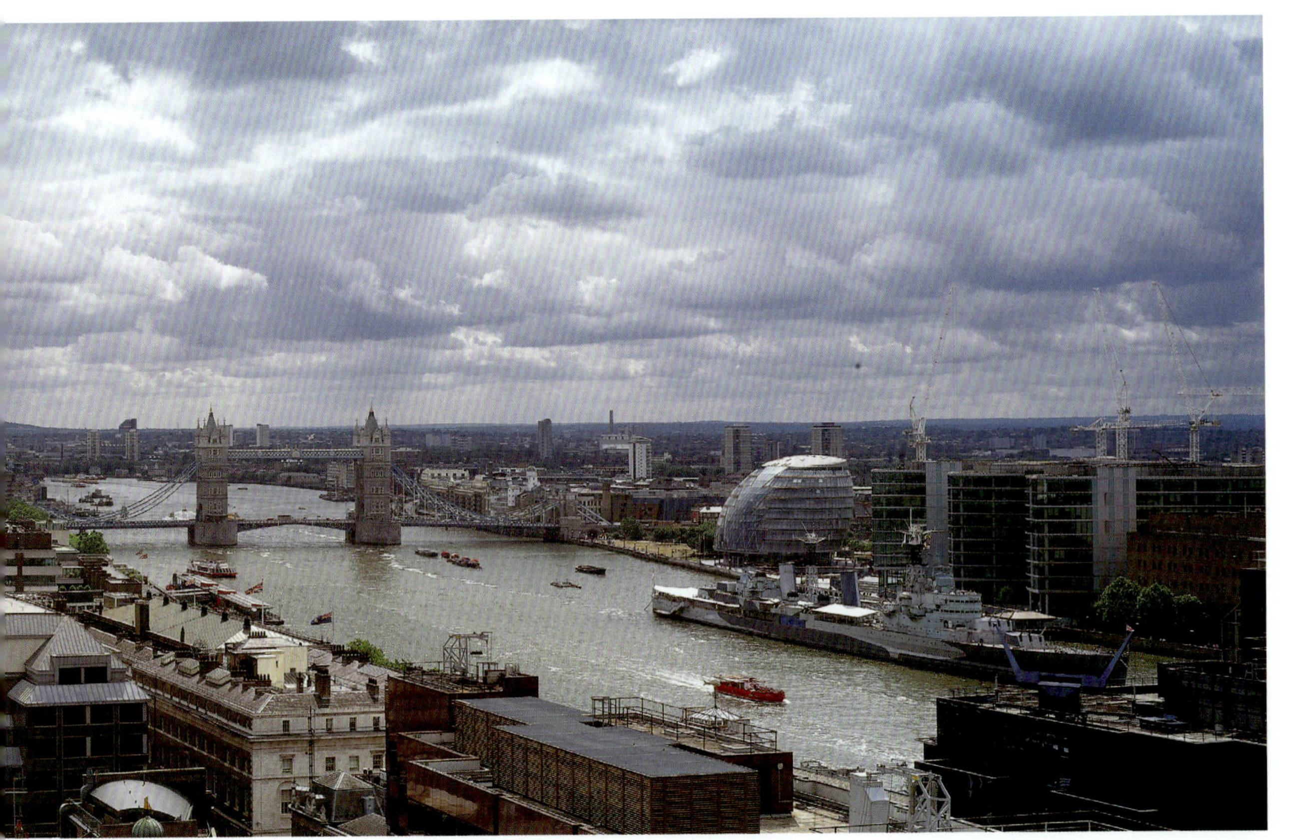

VIEW EAST FROM THE MONUMENT

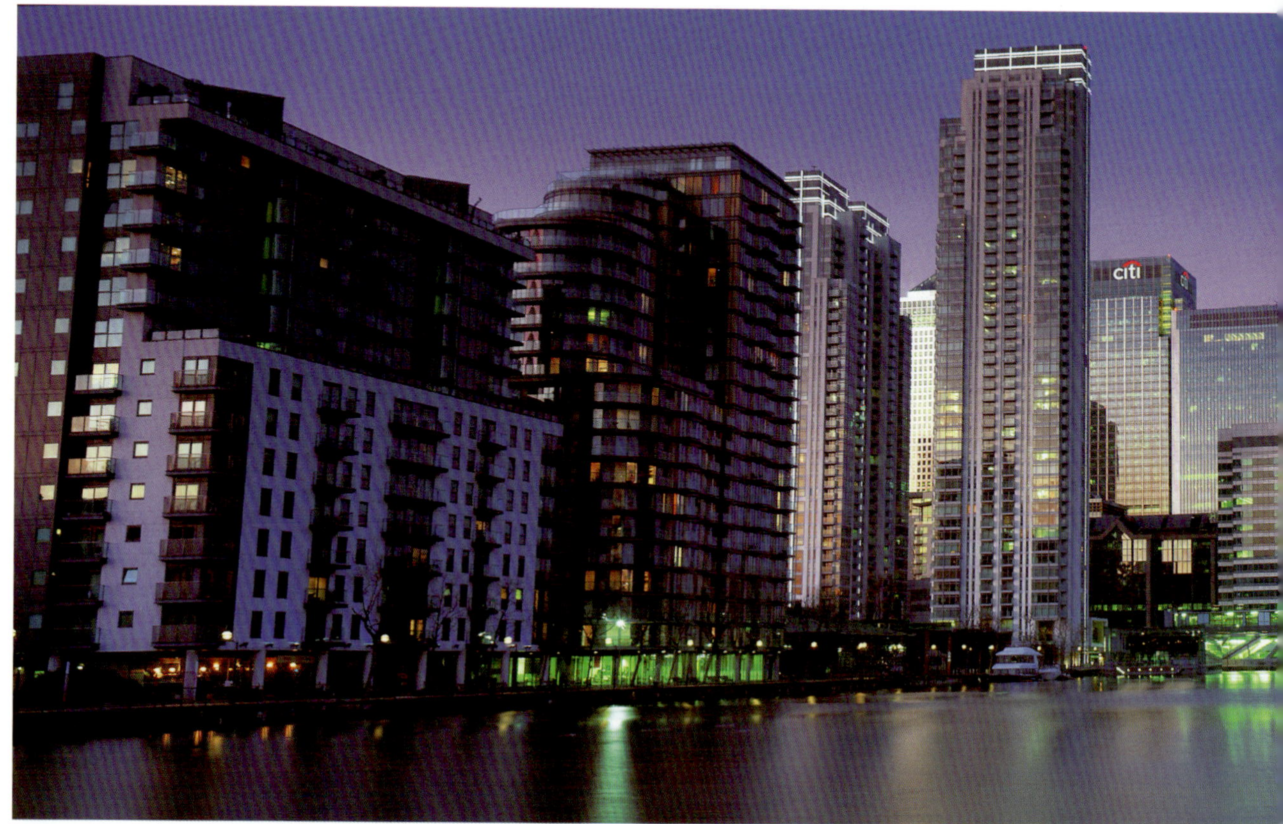
citi

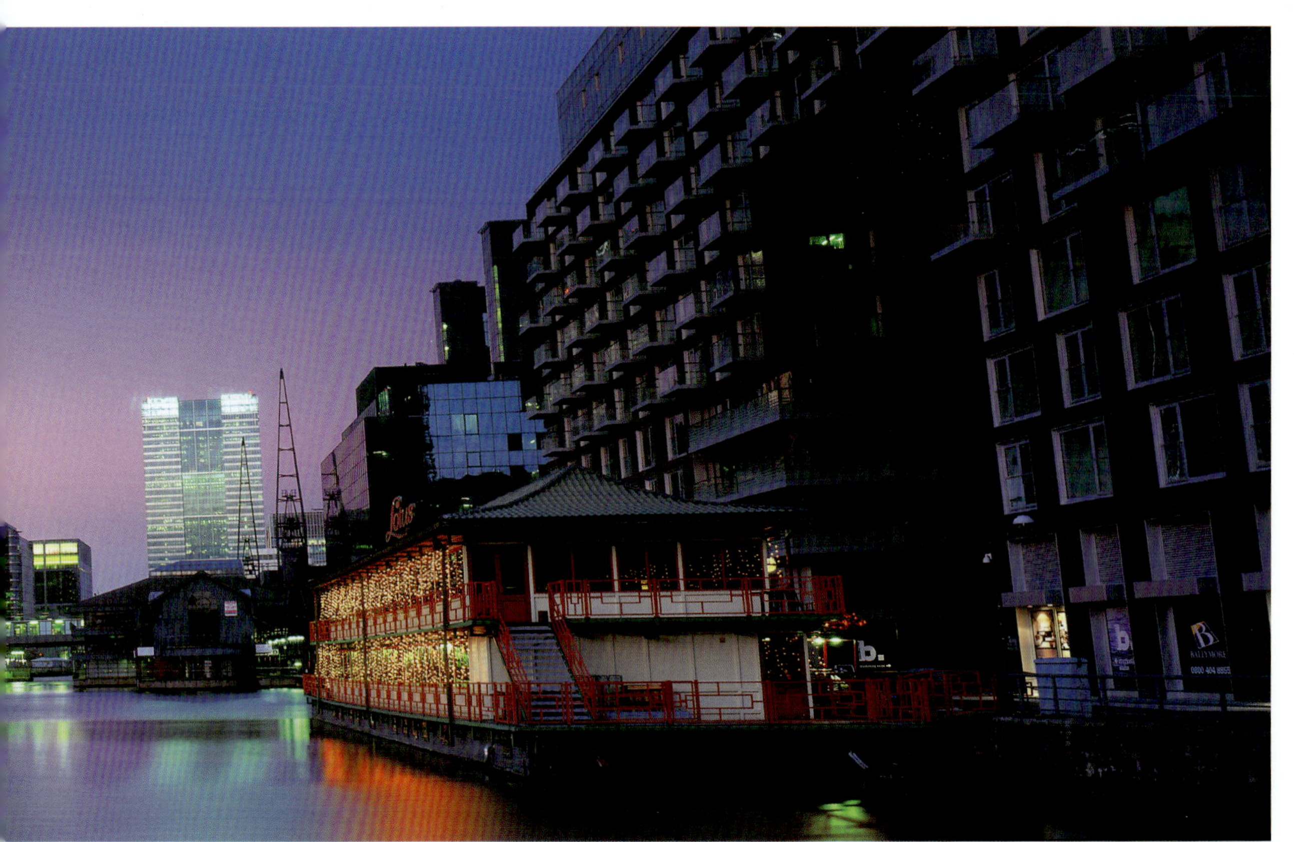

CHINESE BARGE REVISITED, CANARY WHARF

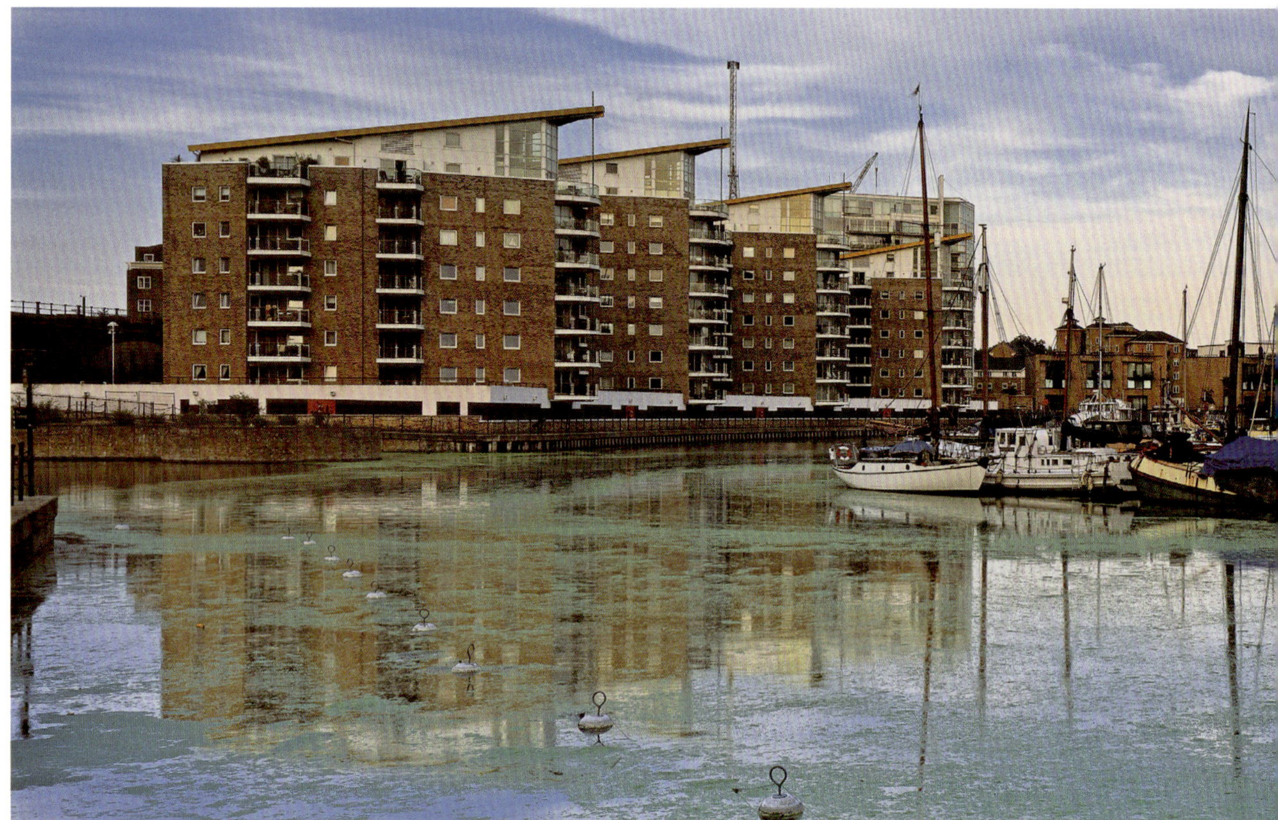

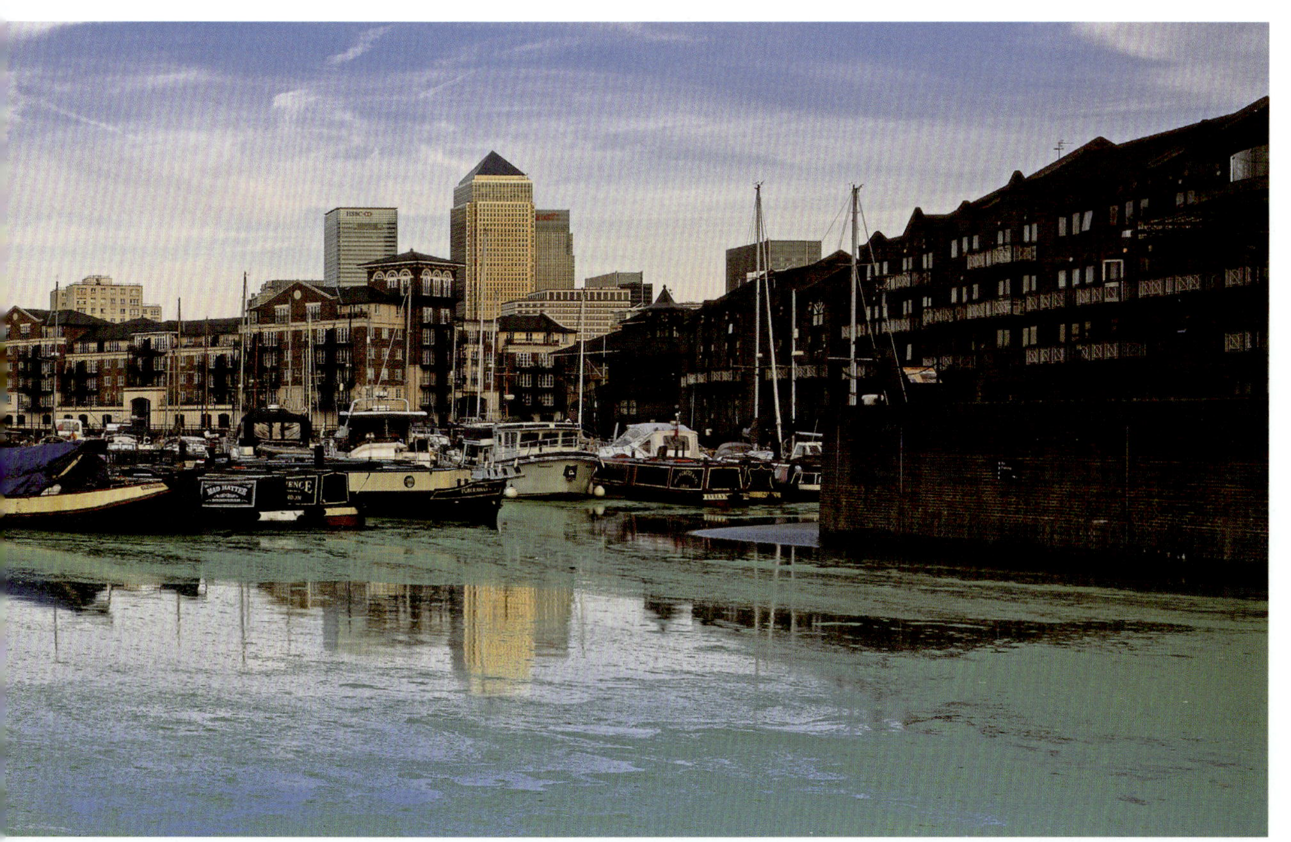

EVENING, LIMEHOUSE BASIN

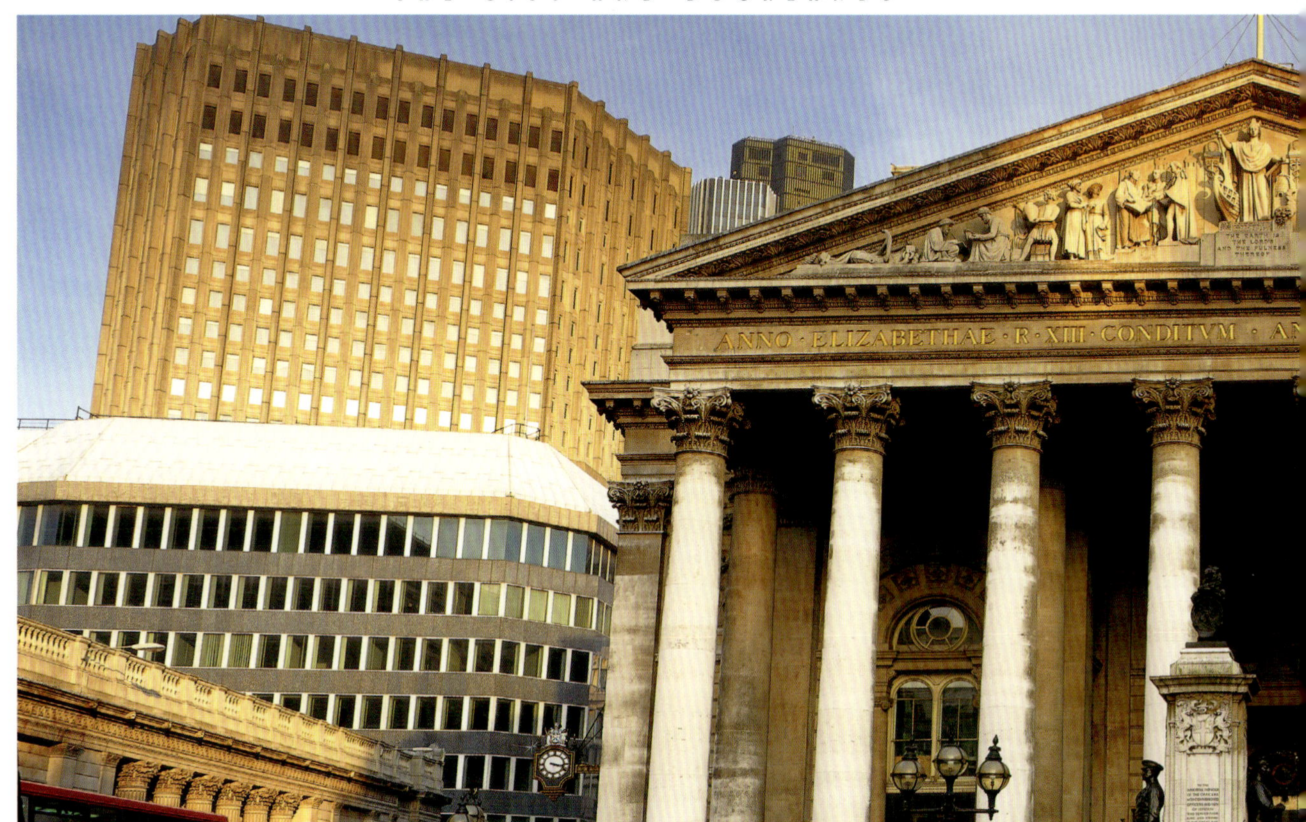
ANNO · ELIZABETHAE · R · XIII · CONDITVM ·

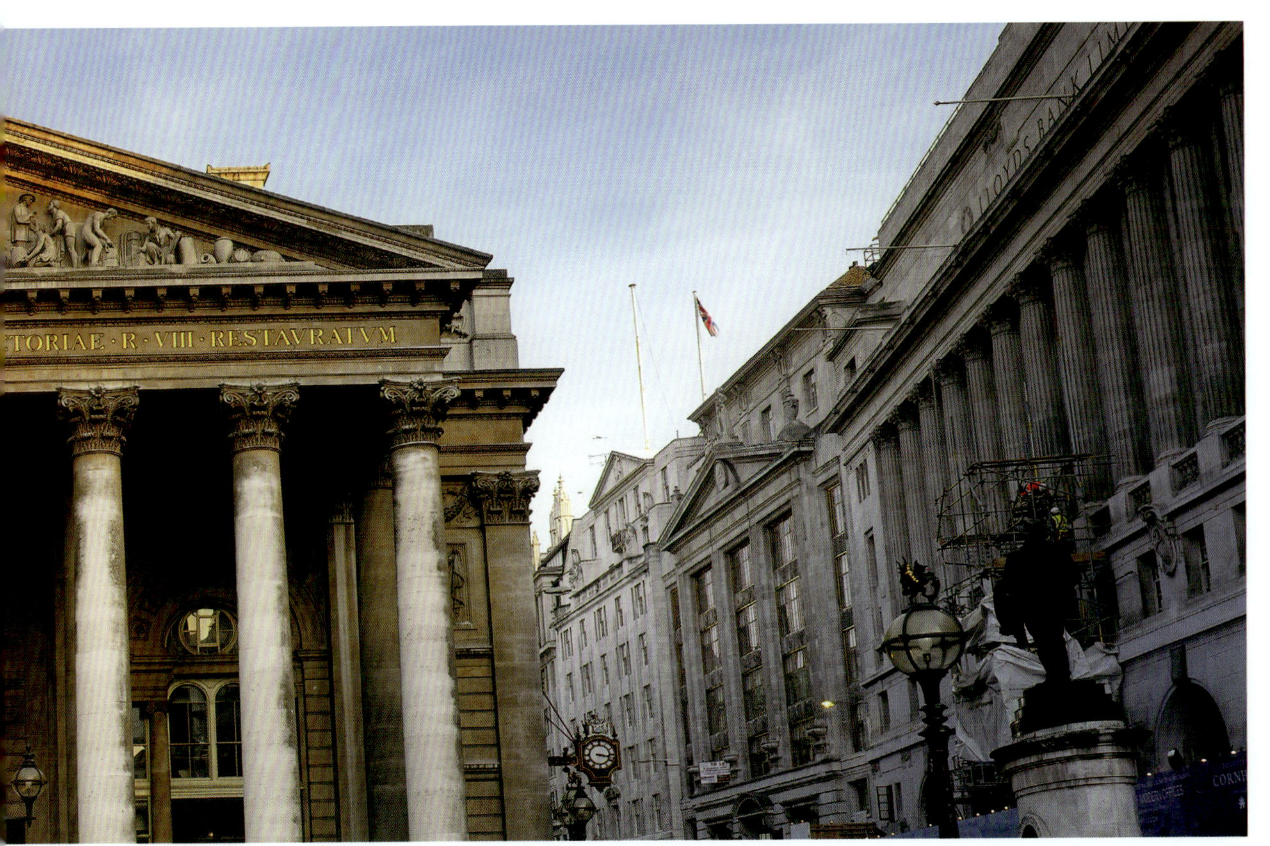

ROYAL EXCHANGE, THE CITY

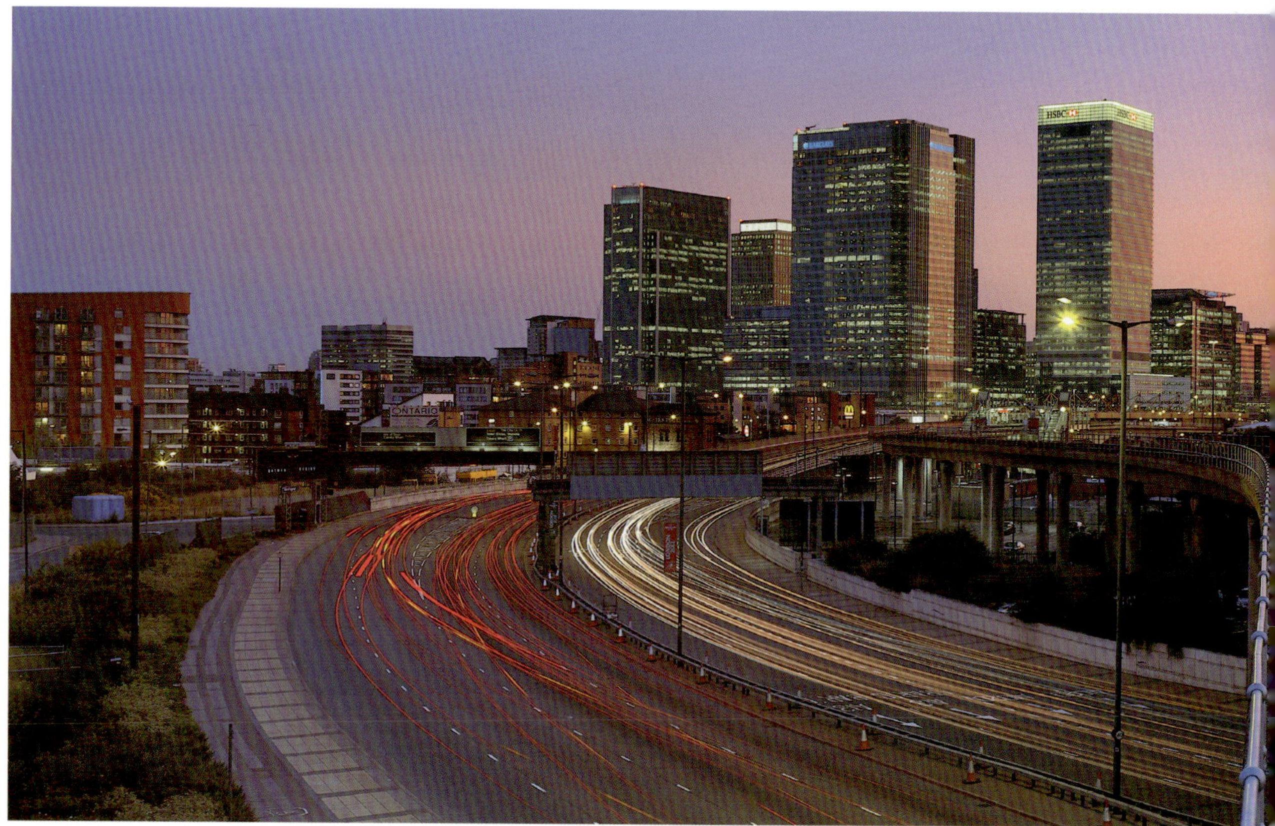
HSBC
HSBC
ONTARIO

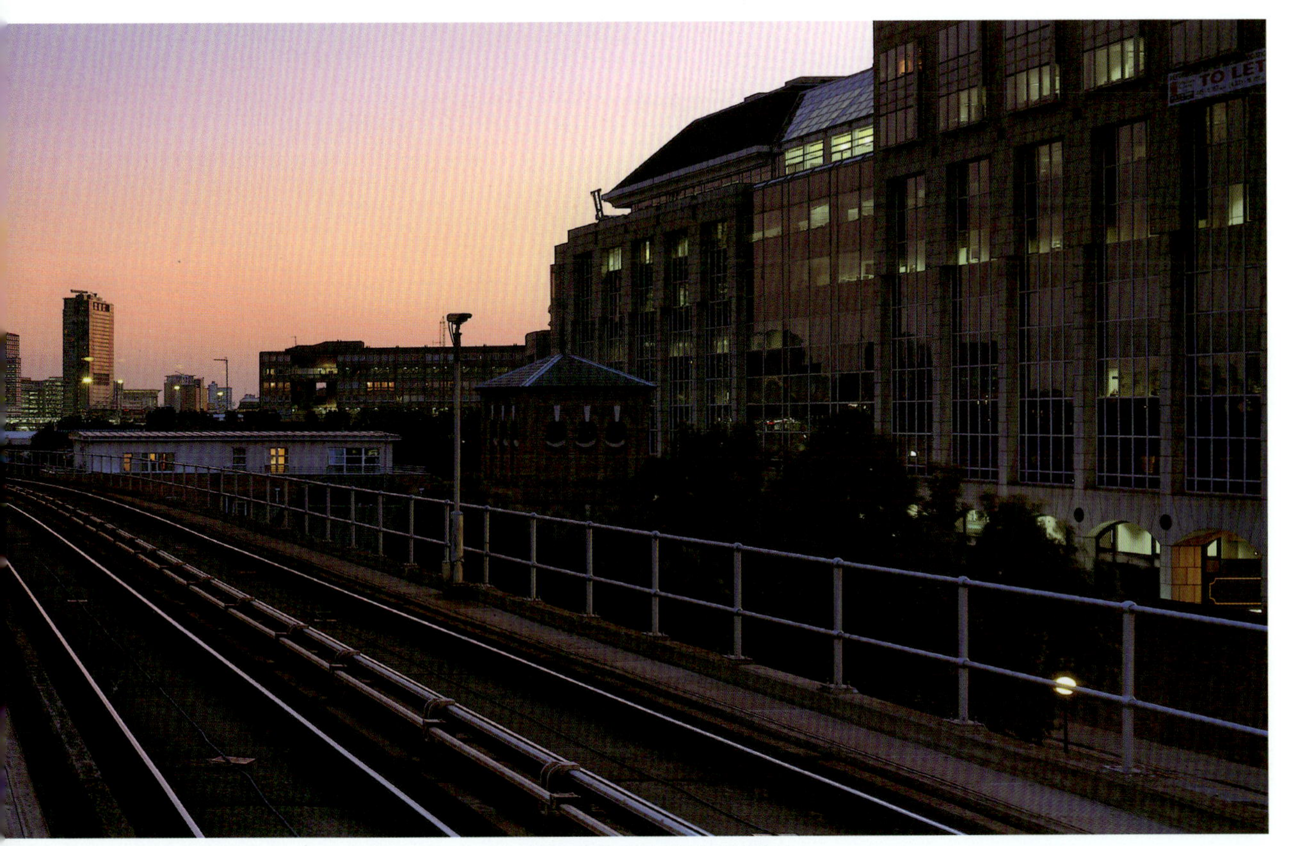

NEW CITY FROM EAST INDIA

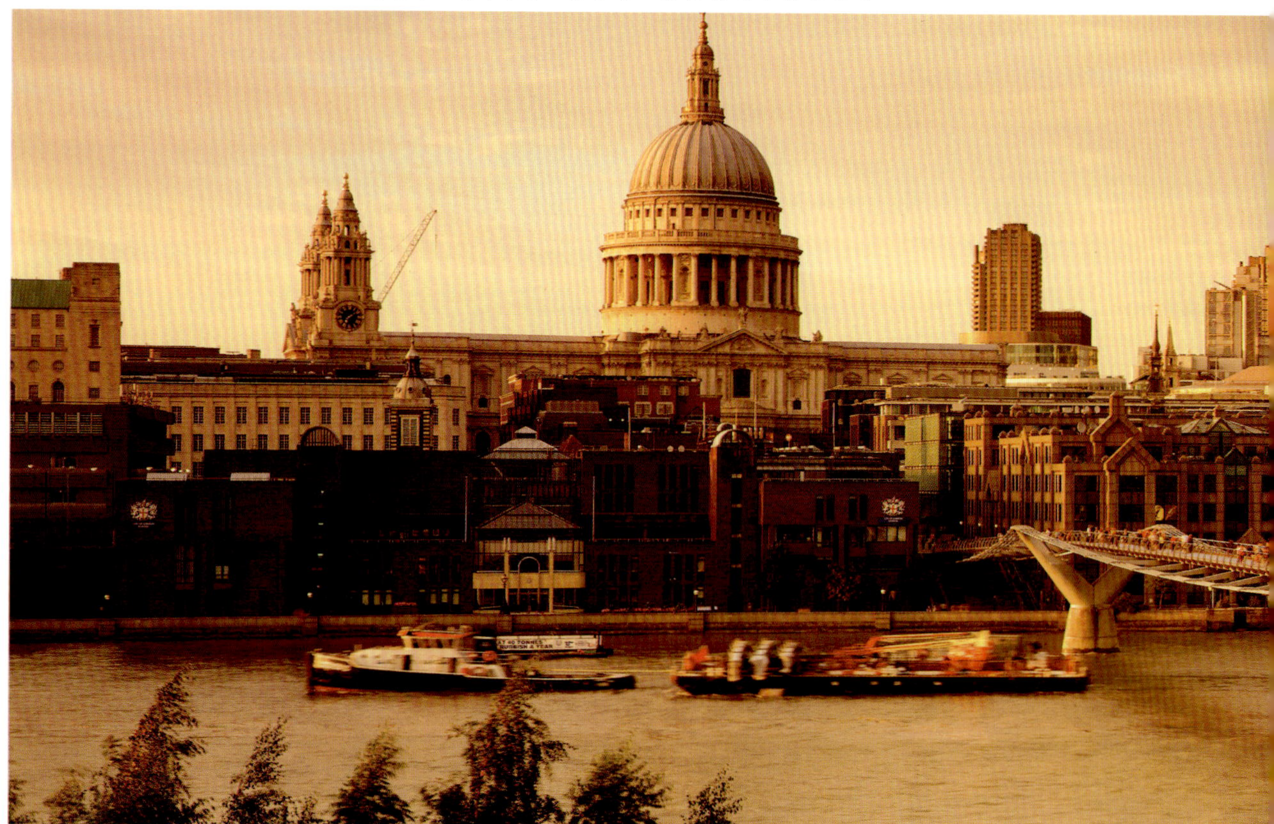

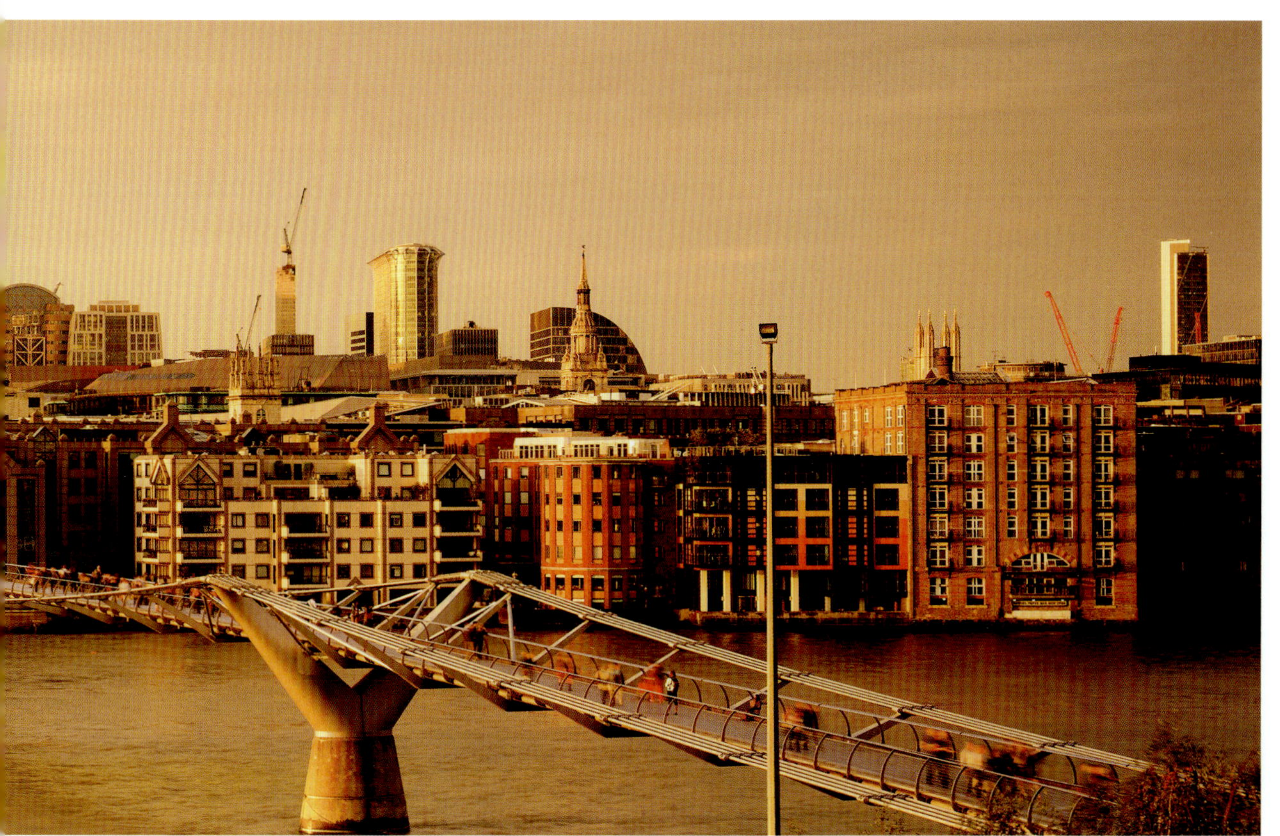

EVENING LIGHT ON ST PAUL'S, RIVER THAMES

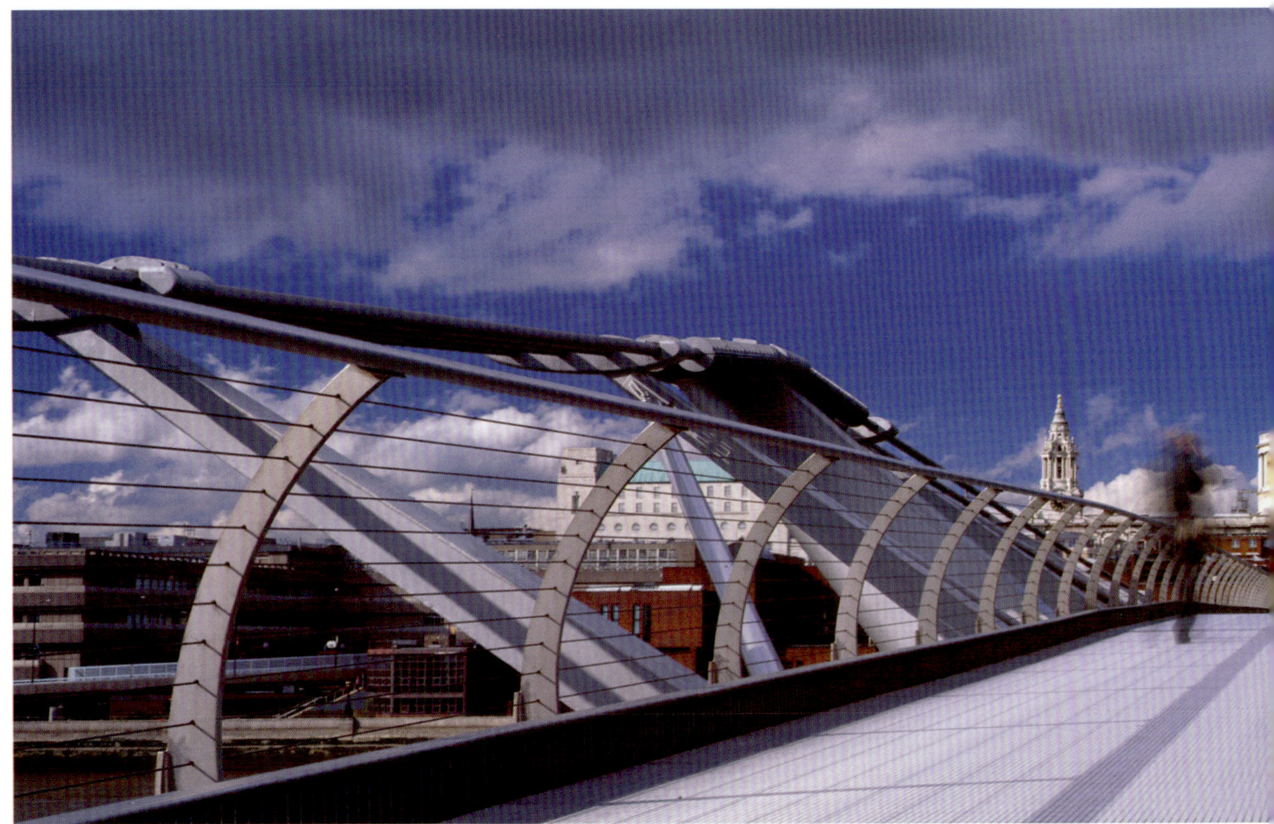

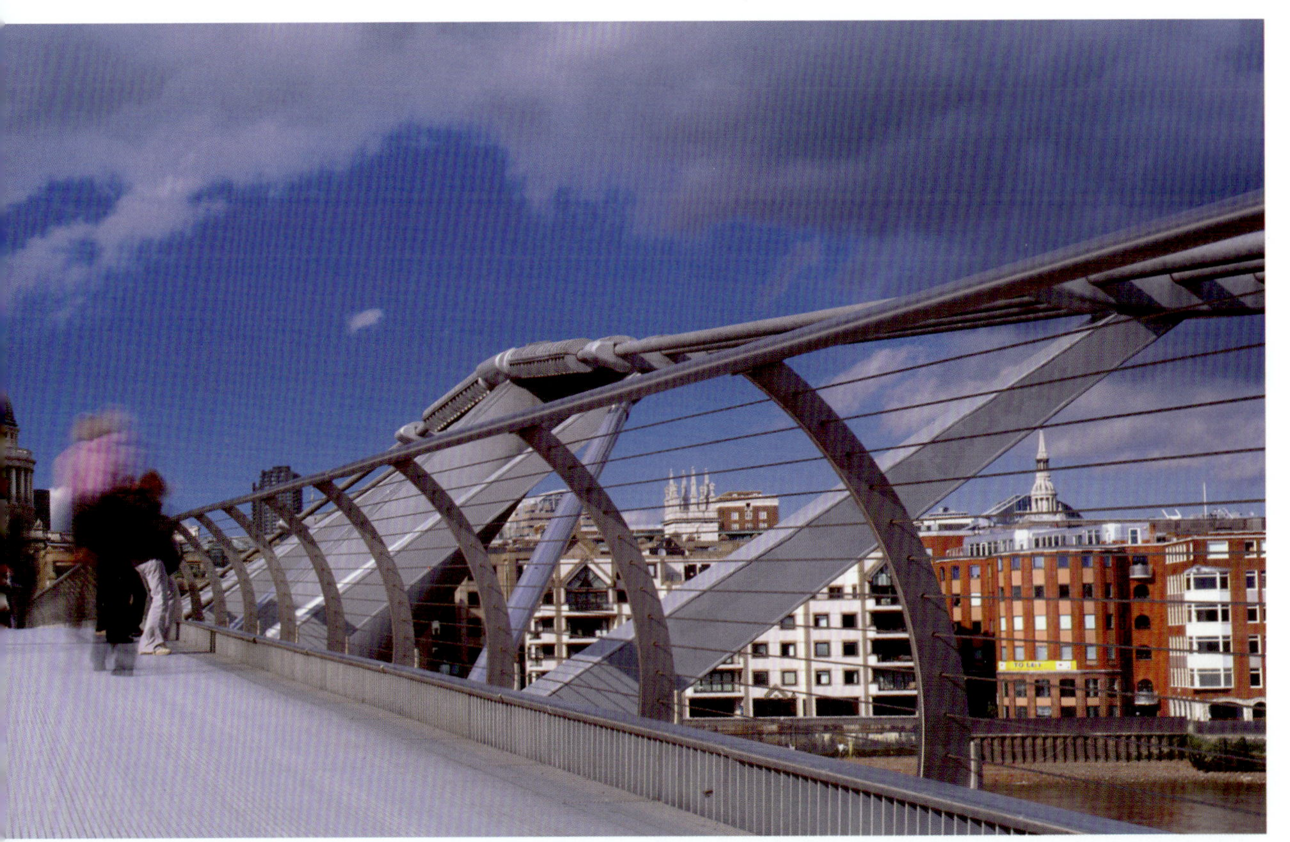

ST PAUL'S FROM MILLENNIUM BRIDGE

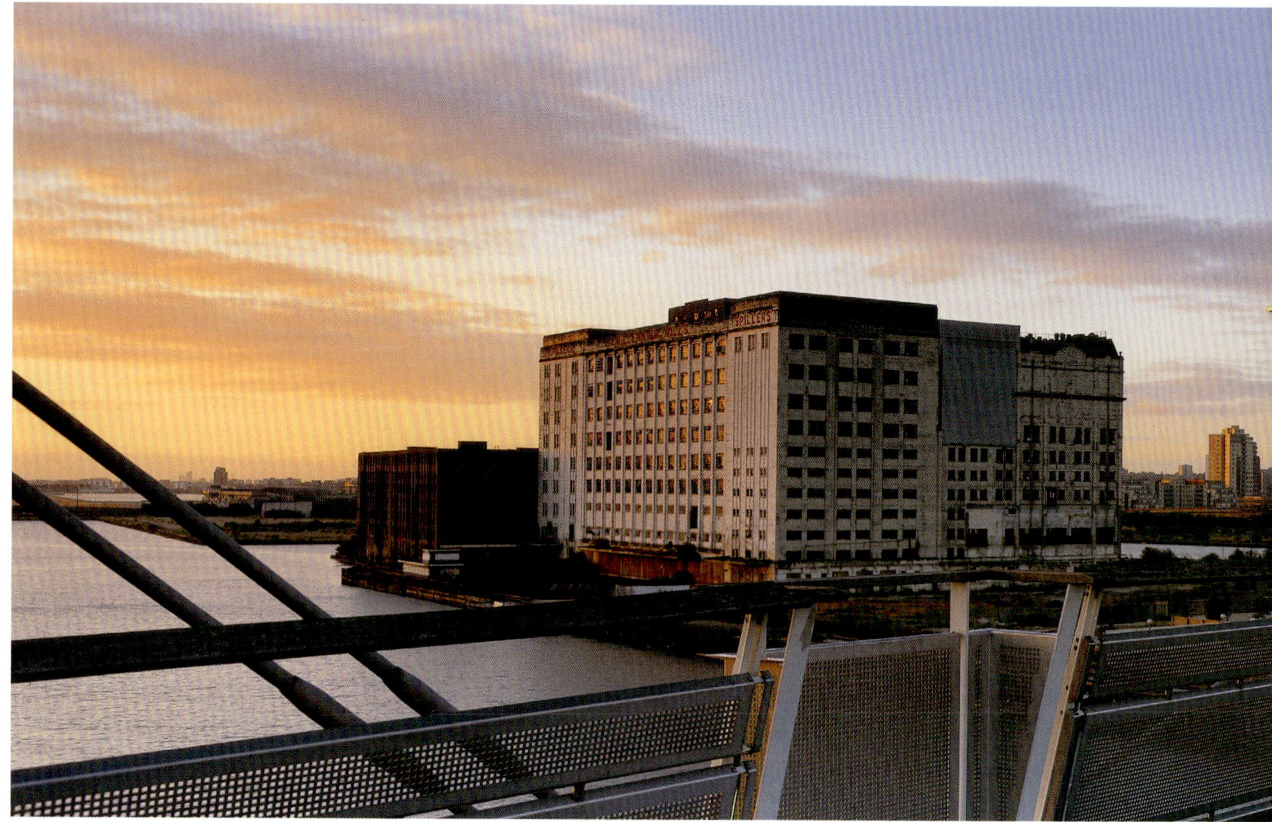
SPILLERS

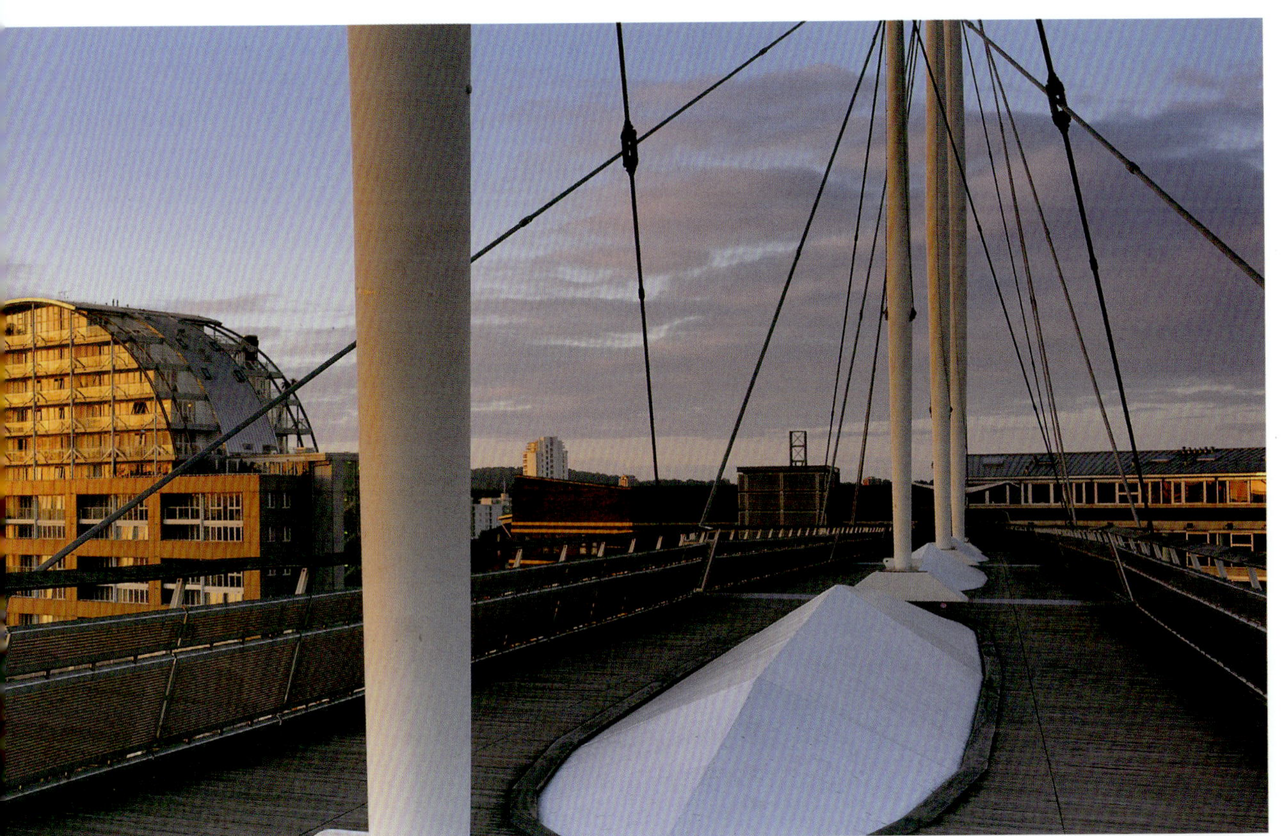

MILLENNIUM MILL, ROYAL VICTORIA DOCK

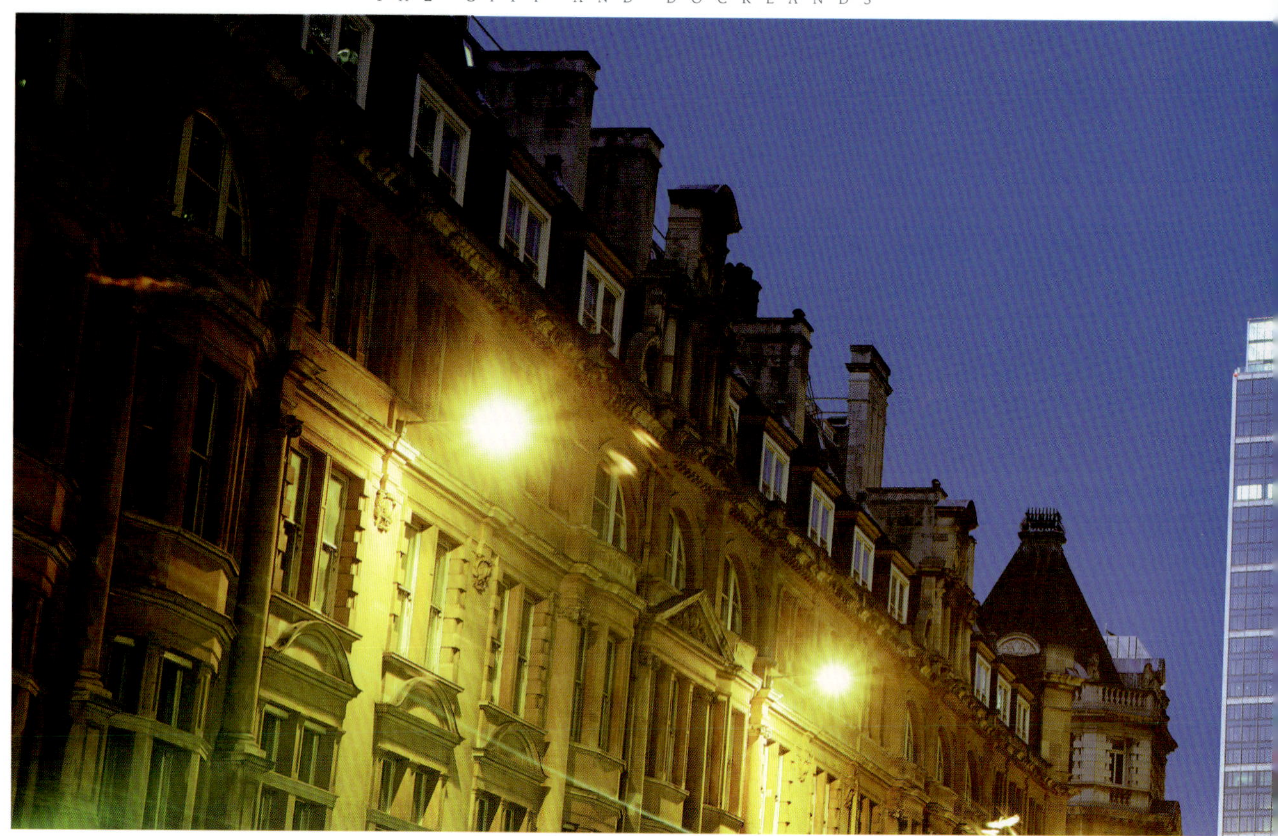

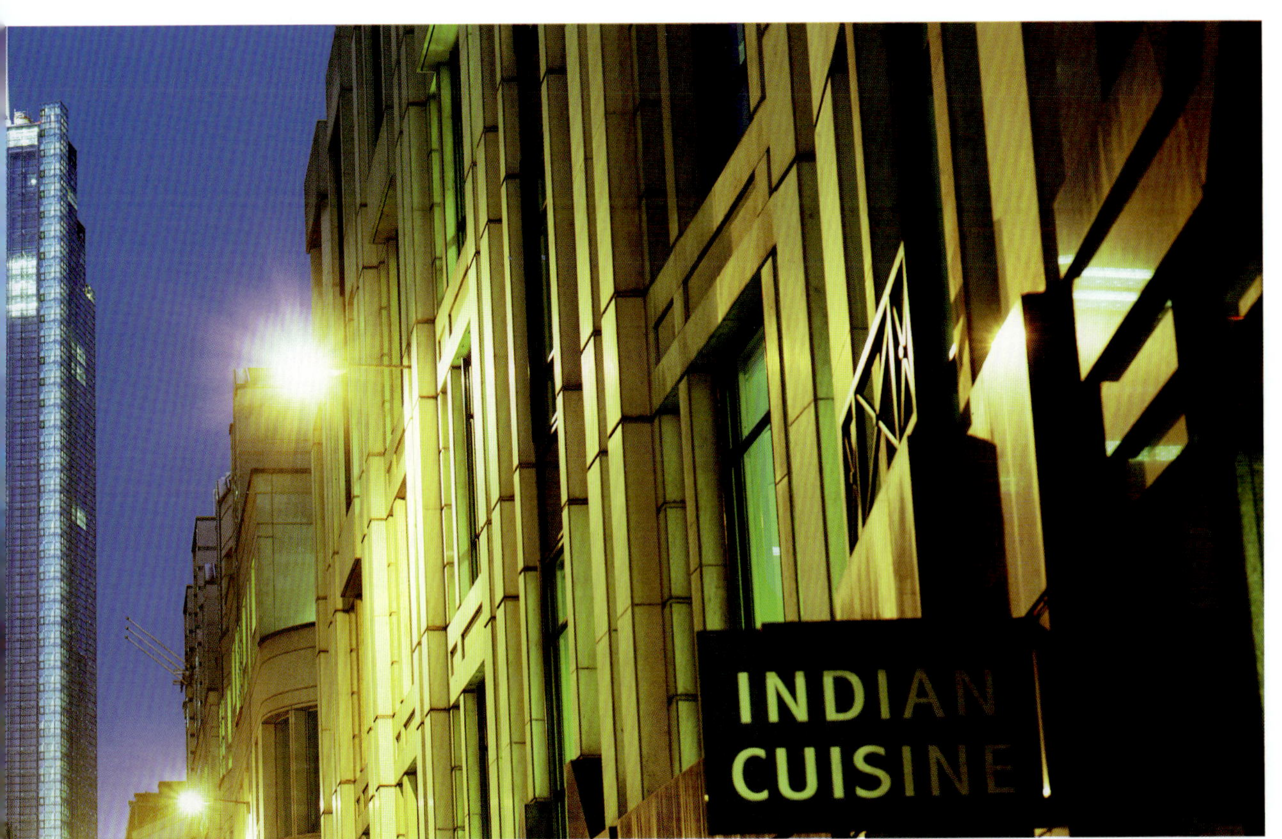

HERON TOWER FROM LONDON WALL

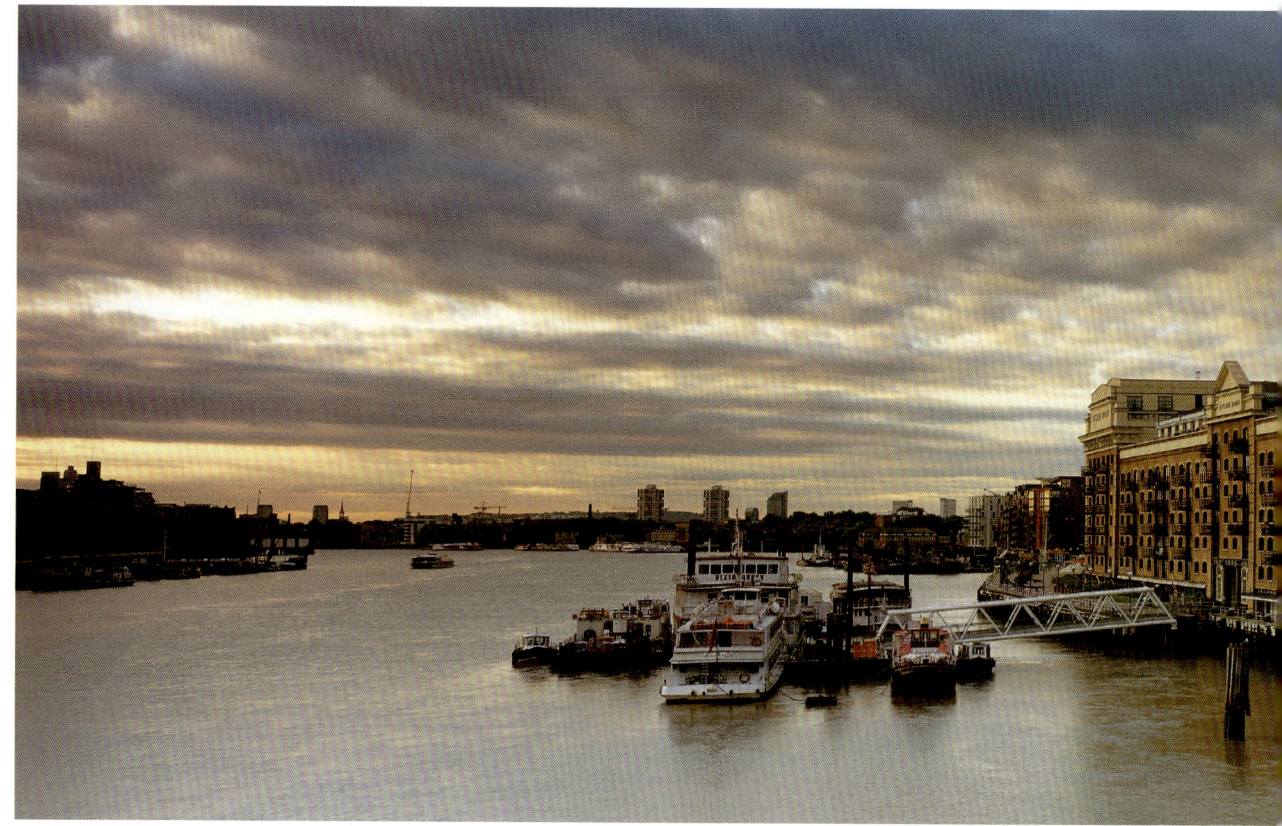

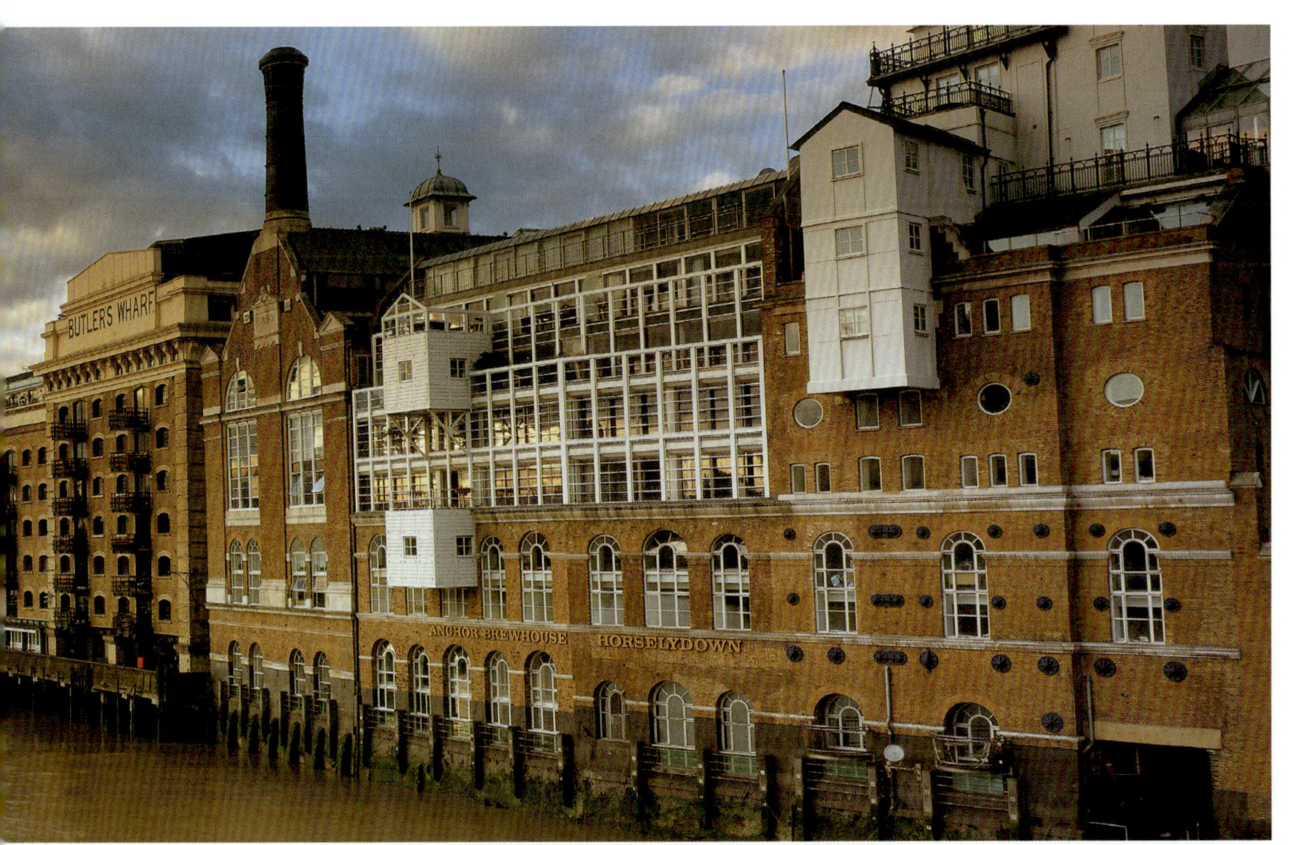

BUTLER'S WHARF AT DAWN, FROM TOWER BRIDGE

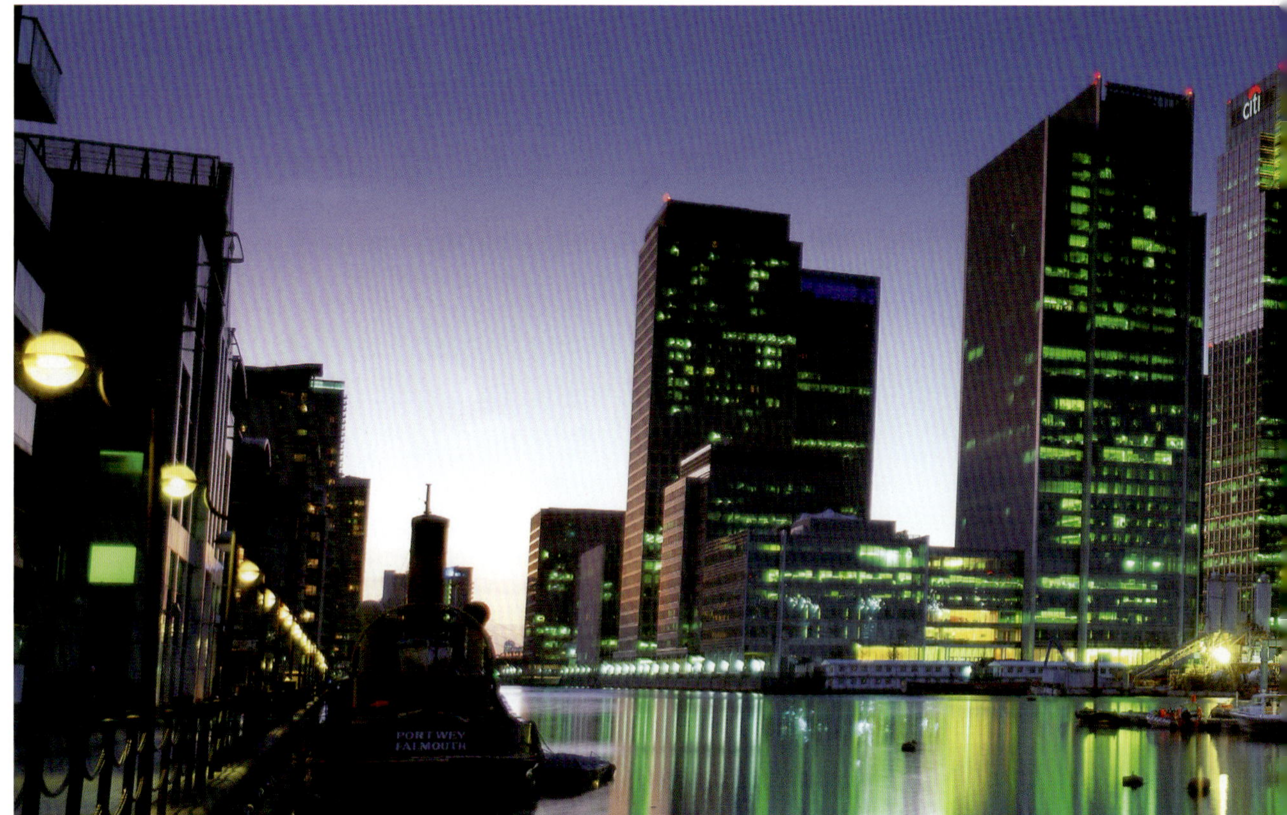
citi
PORTWEY
FALMOUTH

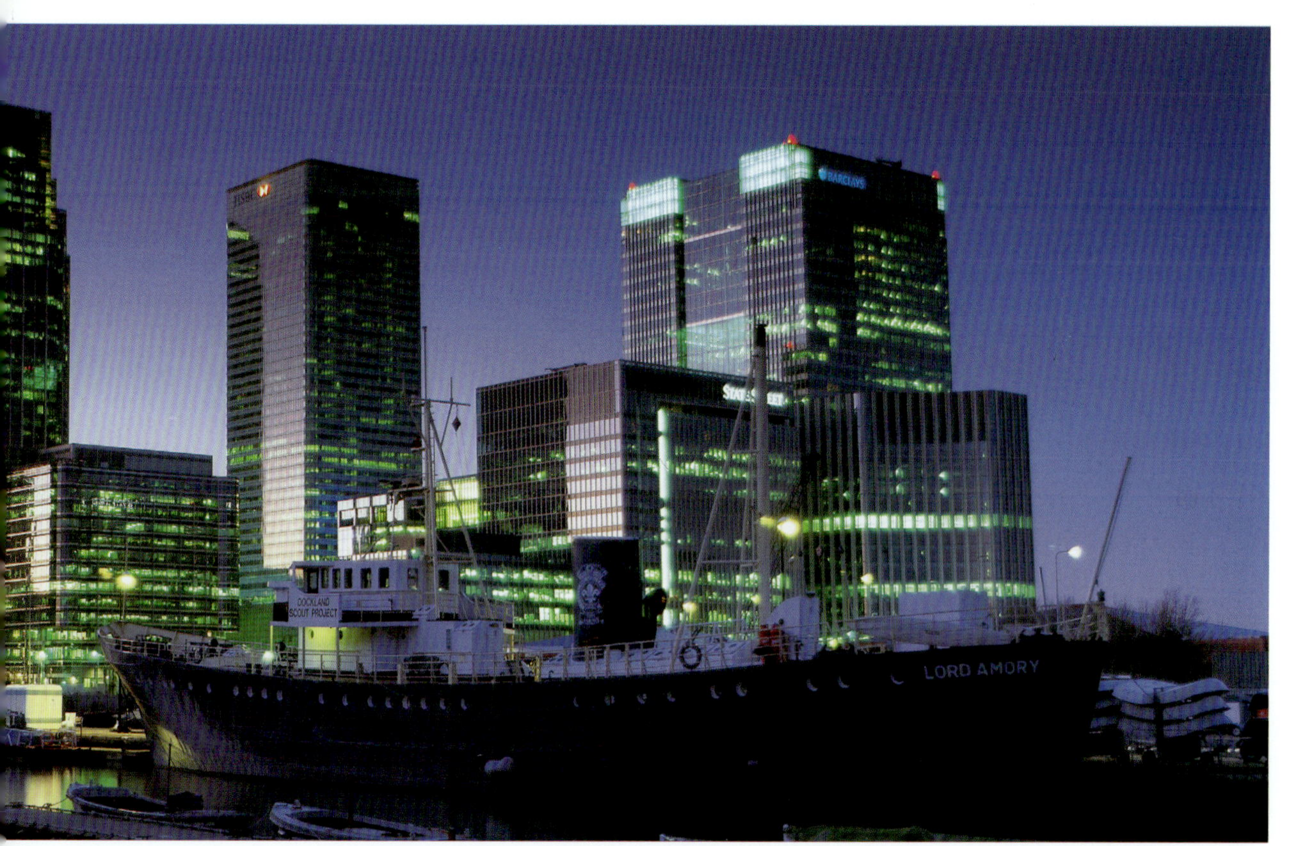

CANARY WHARF FROM WEST INDIA DOCKS

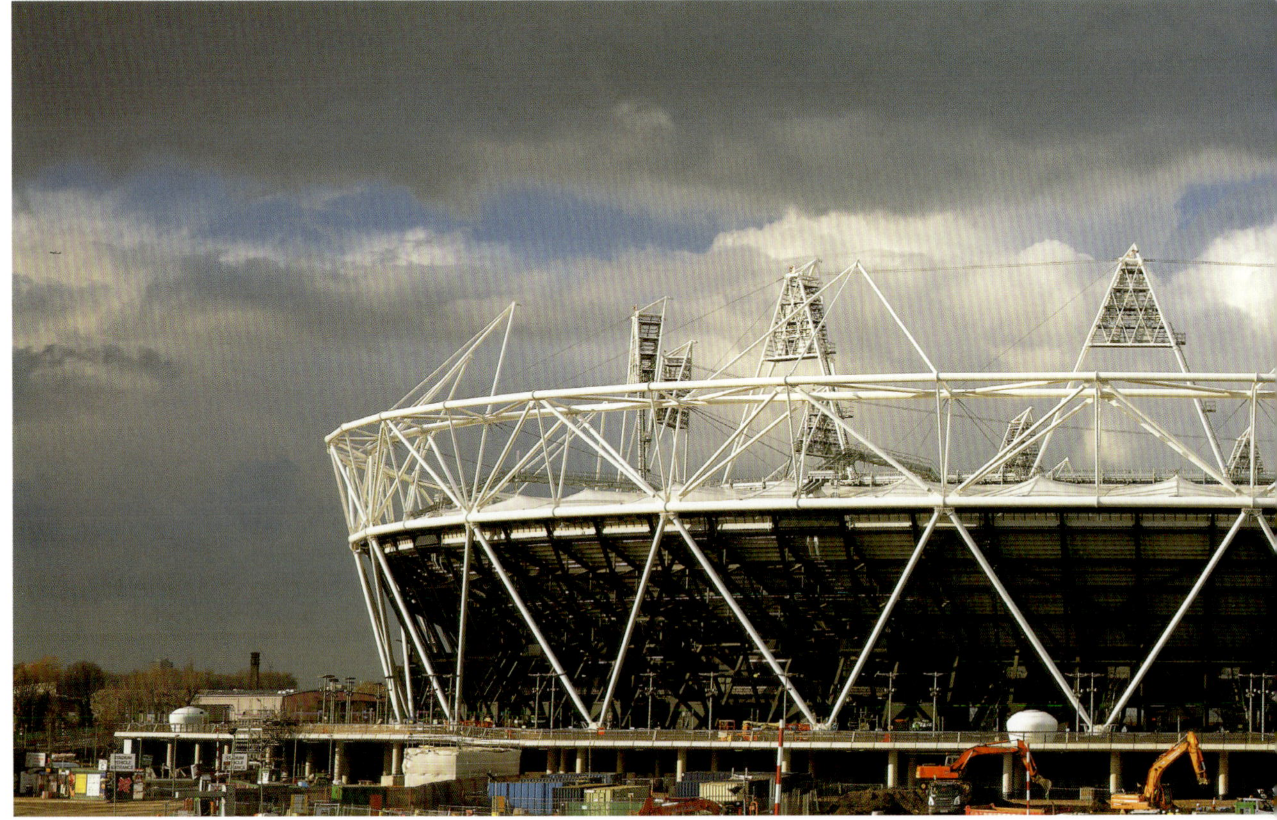

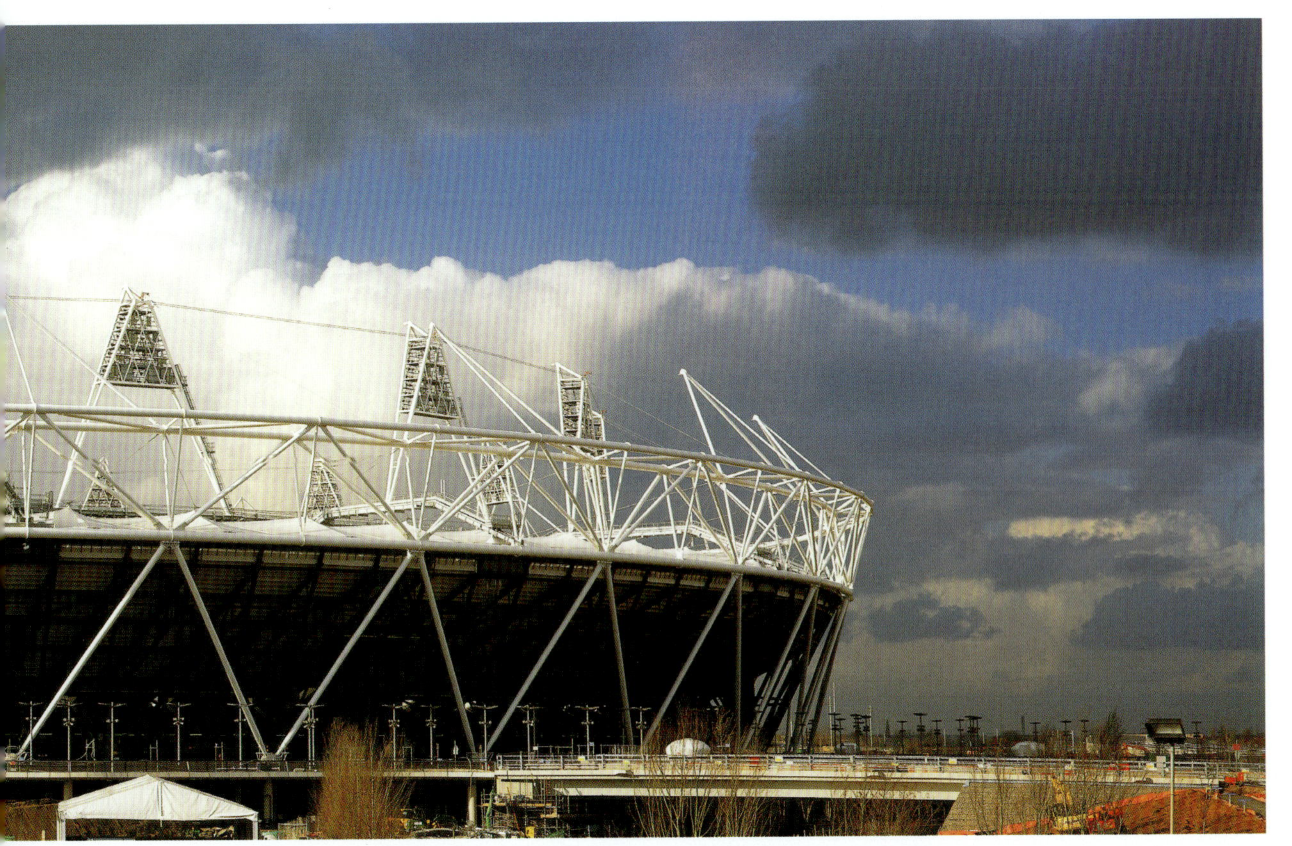

STORM CLOUDS BEYOND THE OLYMPIC STADIUM, STRATFORD

BLOOMSBURY AND TO THE NORTH

To any well-read Londoner, the mention of Bloomsbury immediately conjures up the names of the Bloomsbury Set who took up residence in this neighbourhood just north of the West End in the years before the First World War. Today Bloomsbury remains a centre of learning – from the vast British Museum to the London colleges clustered around Russell Square. A little farther out, the lanes of Hampstead, the streets around Regent's Park and the pretty waterways of Little Venice are home to many of London's creative A-list.

As befits an area where thoughtful wandering is in order, this slice of north London has its share of green spaces, of which the 800-acre (325-hectare) Hampstead Heath is the most beautiful. First recorded in 1312, this former area of rough moorland supplied firewood to London for centuries, as well as water. The Heath is still famous for its 25 ponds, some of which provide London's most characterful places to swim.

Hampstead Heath's most famous building is Kenwood House, built in the early 1600s. For over half a century, classical concerts have been held by the lake in its formal gardens, attracting thousands of people each summer. Beside the Heath, Parliament Hill was dubbed Traitors Hill when it became a meeting place for troops loyal to Parliament during the English Civil War. Now it is a mecca for kite flyers, as well as offering one of the finest views of London.

Also built on an elevated position is Alexandra Palace. Despite its name, it has nothing to do with royalty. Sited on the highest point of Muswell Hill in 1873, it was intended to be a 'People's Palace', a place of entertainment to rival the Crystal Palace (see Hyde Park To Hampton Court). Nicknamed 'Ally Pally', it also became the location of the world's first public TV service in 1936 when the BBC began broadcasting from here.

While Alexandra Palace's star has faded, the 487-acre (200-hectare) Regent's Park remains a magnet for Londoners in search of entertainment – a popular place to play various sports, as well as home to both London Zoo and the city's Open Air Theatre with its summer stagings of Shakespeare. Three sides of the park are lined with elegant white terraces of houses designed by John Nash. The park also contains several villas, of which the most prominent is the Marquis of Hertford's Villa, now the American Ambassador's residence.

Running through the northern end of the park, Regent's Canal was once a major trade route connecting the Grand Union Canal from the north of England with the former London Docks. You can still walk along the canal from Little Venice in the north to the Limehouse Basin in the east, pausing perhaps at the London Canal Museum in King's Cross or at Camden Lock market.

Two other icons of London feature in this chapter, both legacies of the Swinging Sixties. The BT Tower – known as the Post Office Tower when it opened in 1964 to the north of Oxford Street in the West End – was the place to see a panorama of London long before the London Eye rose on the south bank of the Thames. The tower, alas, closed to the public in 1980.

Another London icon which enjoyed its finest hour in the 1960s was Wembley Stadium. Originally known as the Empire Stadium, Brazilian superstar Pele called it the 'church of football'. Built for the British Empire Exhibition of 1924, its famous 'Twin Towers' hosted England's international matches, five European Cup finals, and each season's final of the FA Cup. Now, a twenty-first century Wembley has finally been completed. Designed by Ken Shuttleworth – the architect behind the Millennium Bridge and the Swiss Re building – the new stadium replaces the former building's twin towers with a soaring arch. As London looks to a bright future, the new Wembley will play its role as a venue for matches in the 2012 Olympic Games.

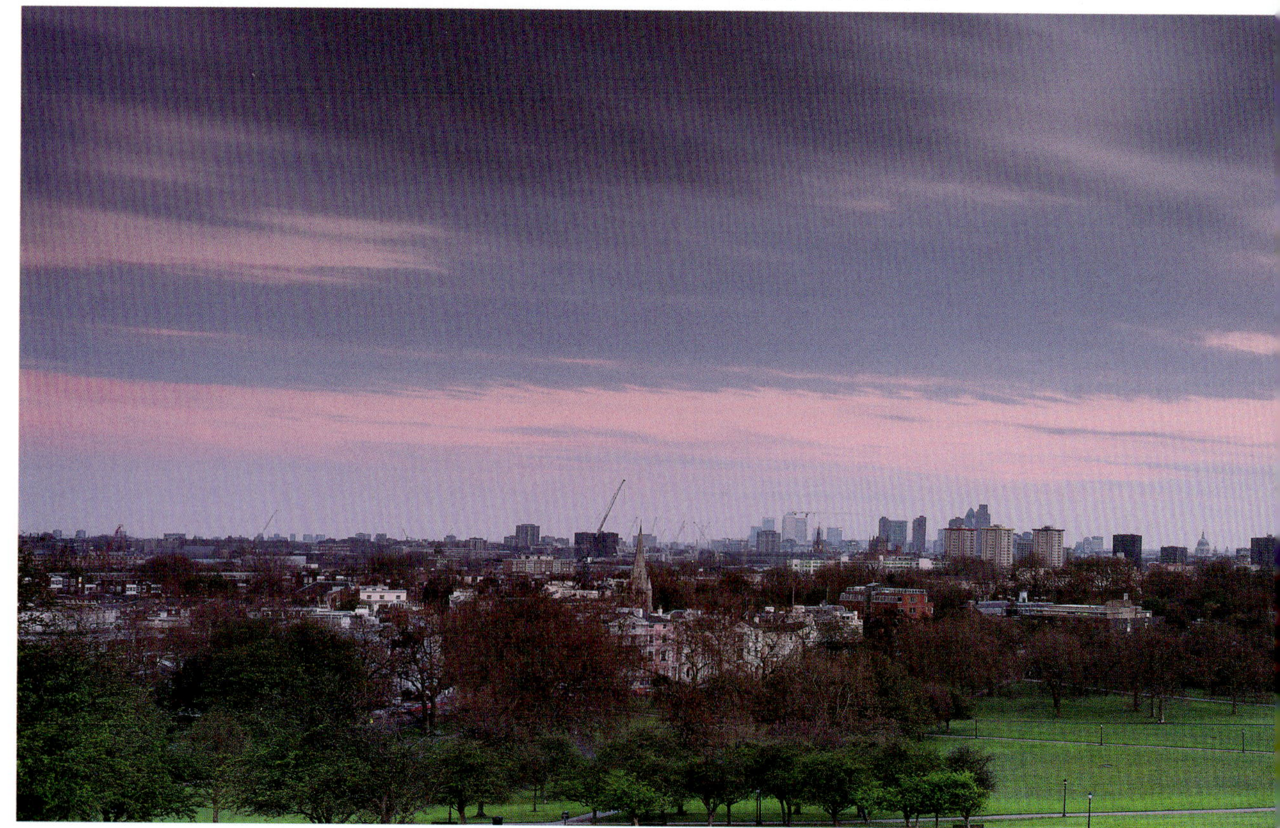

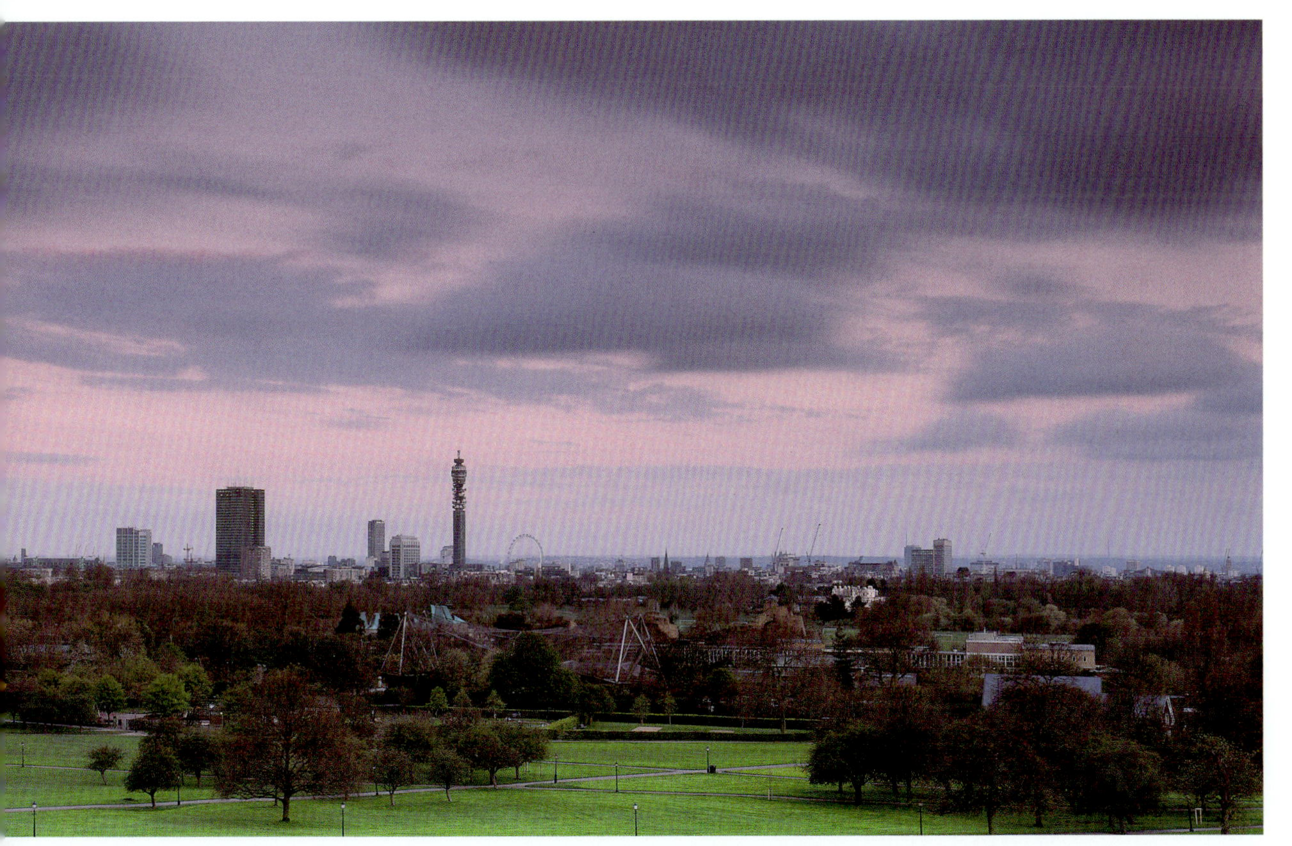

EVENING SKIES FROM PRIMROSE HILL

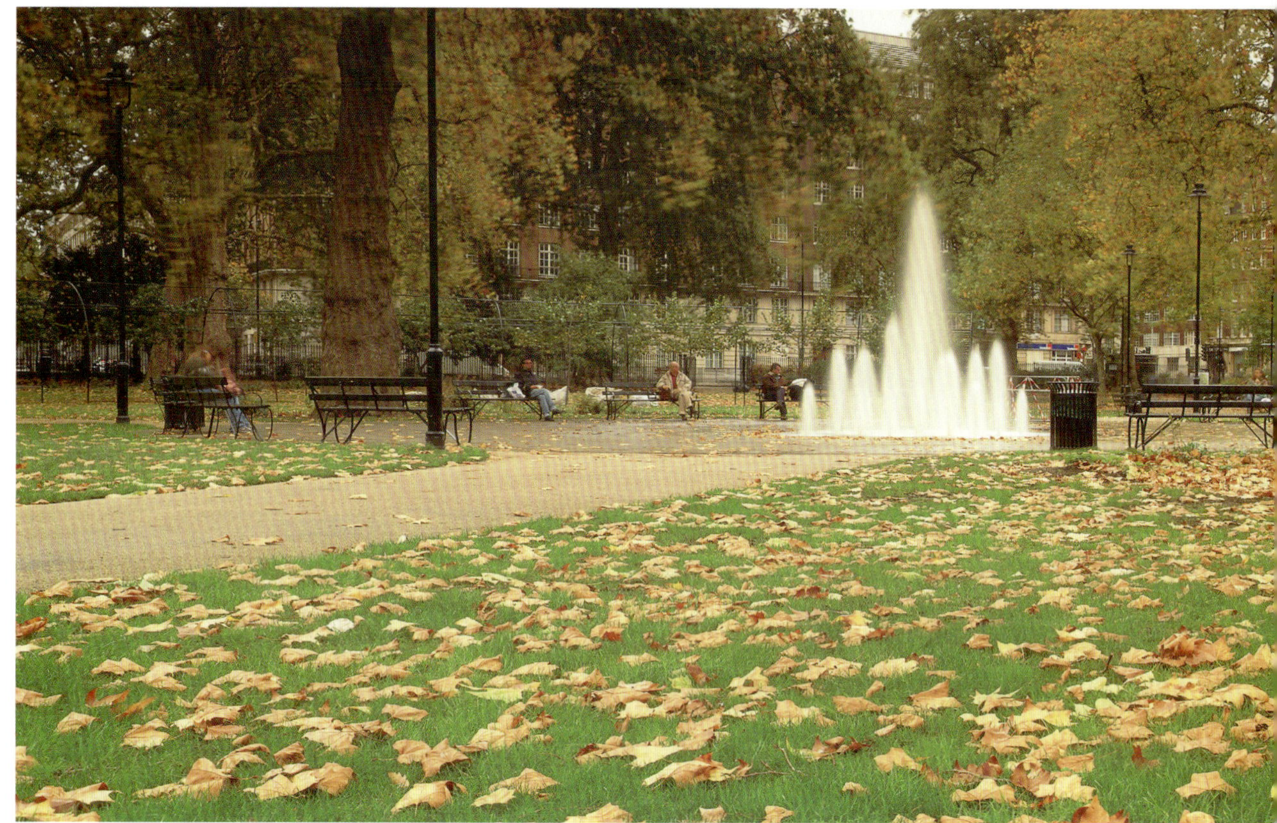

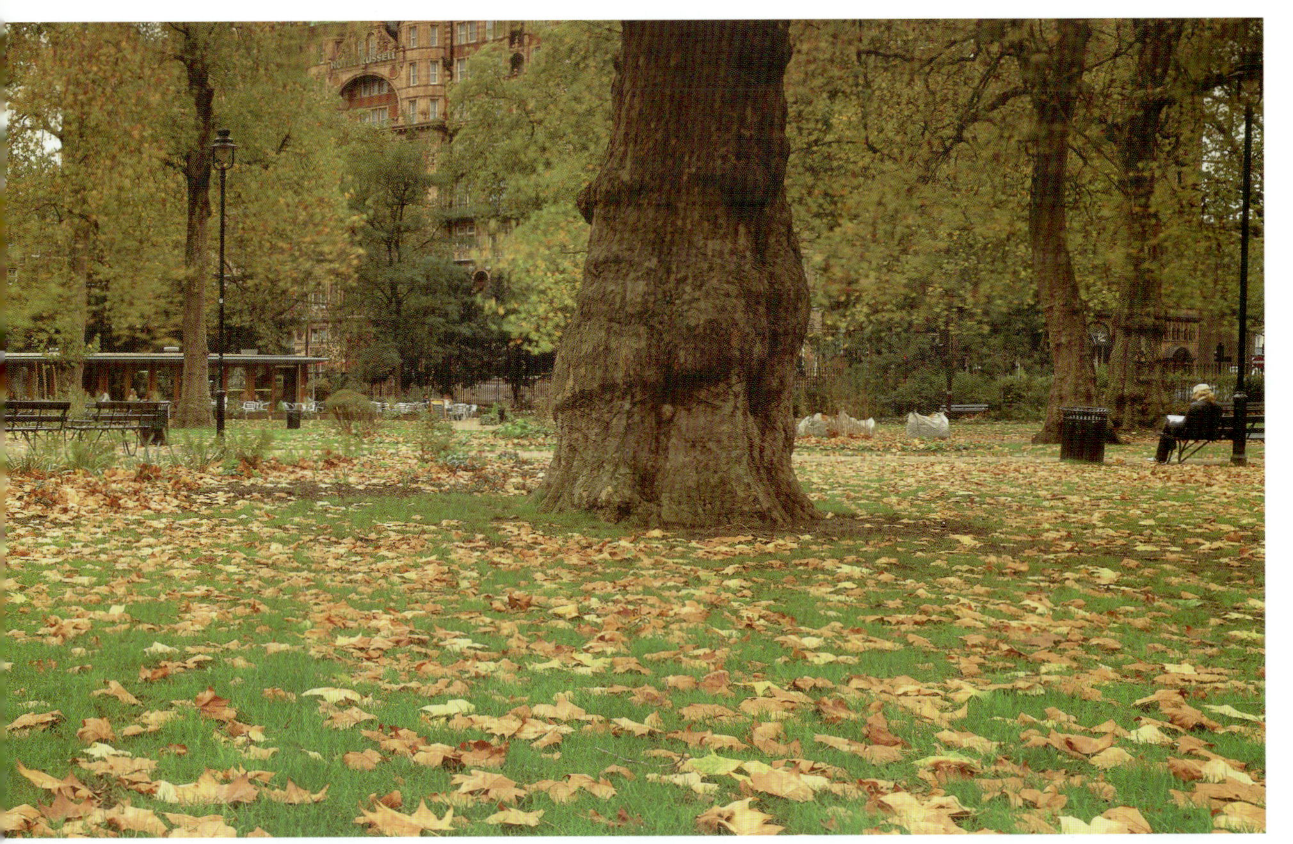

LEAVES, RUSSELL SQUARE

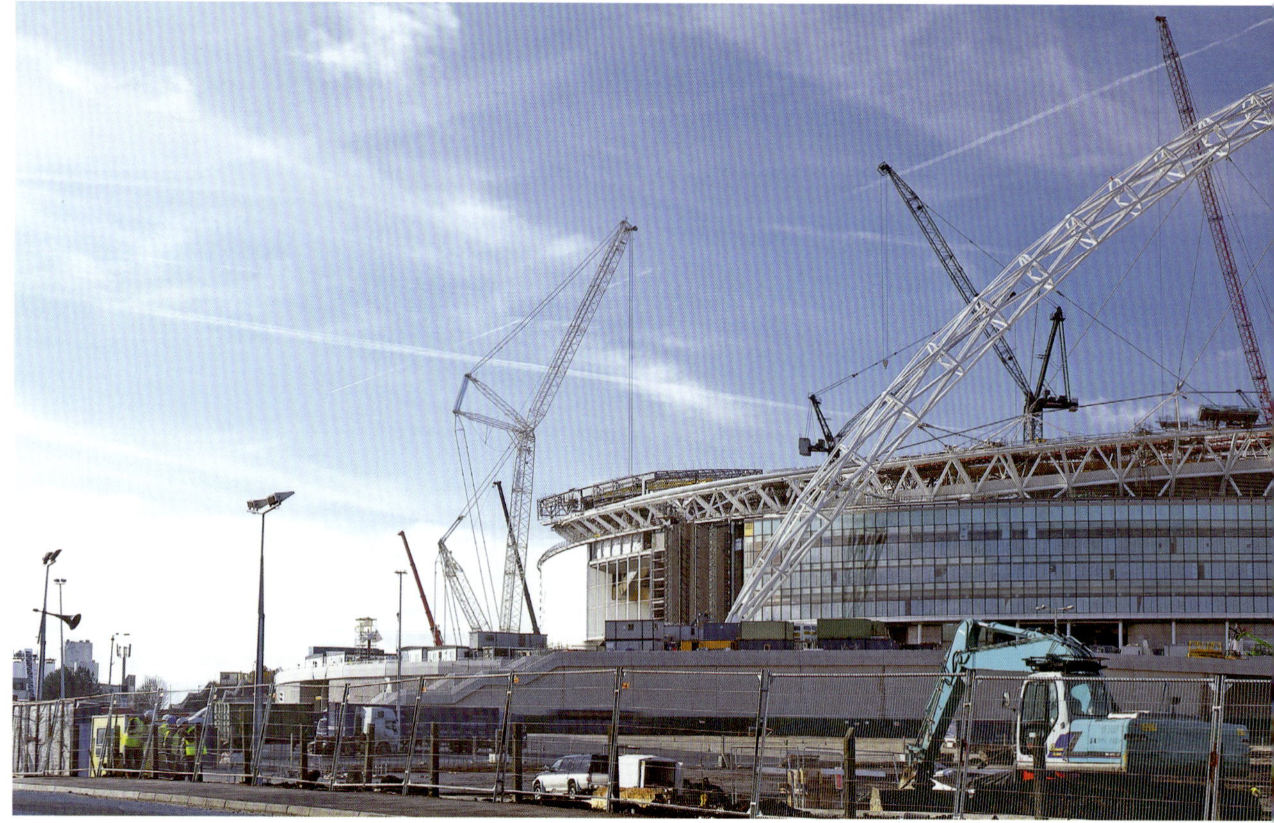

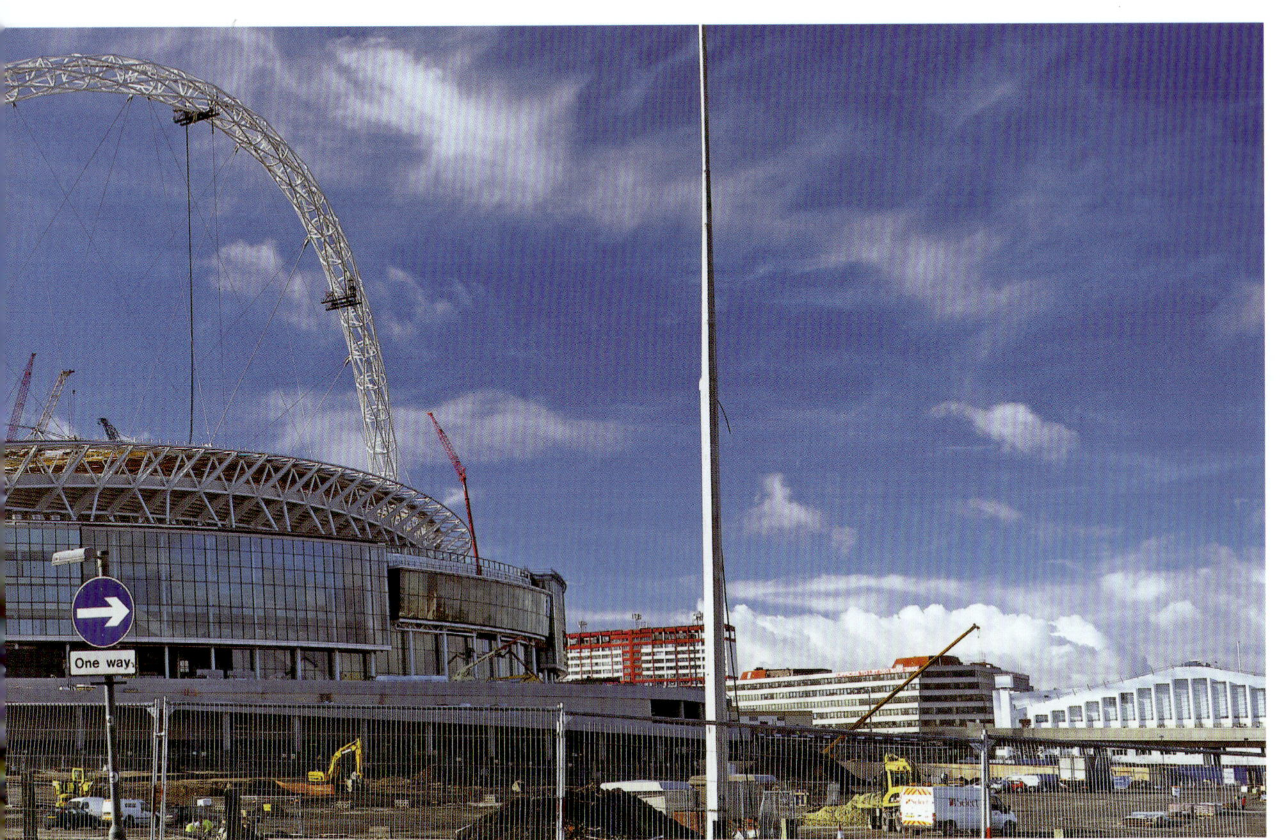

CRANES, NEW WEMBLEY STADIUM

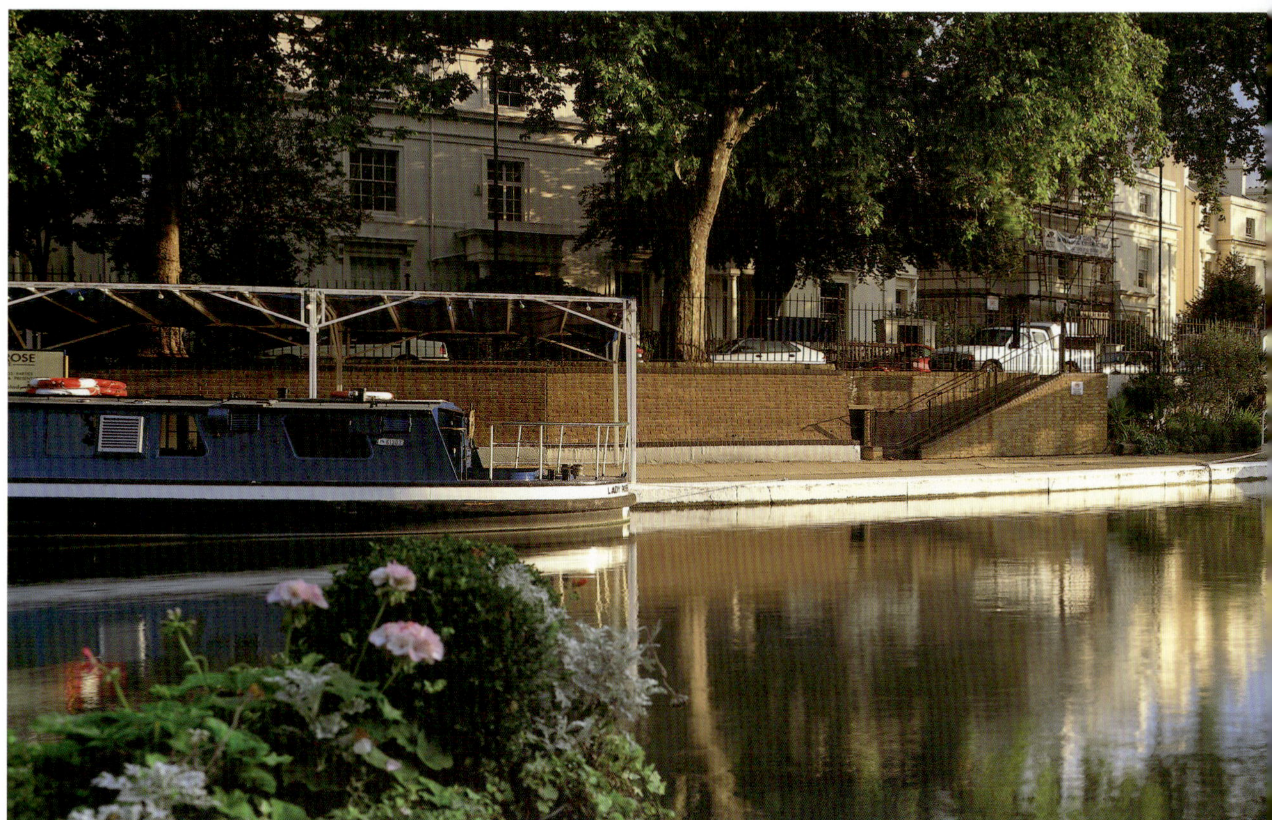
ROSE

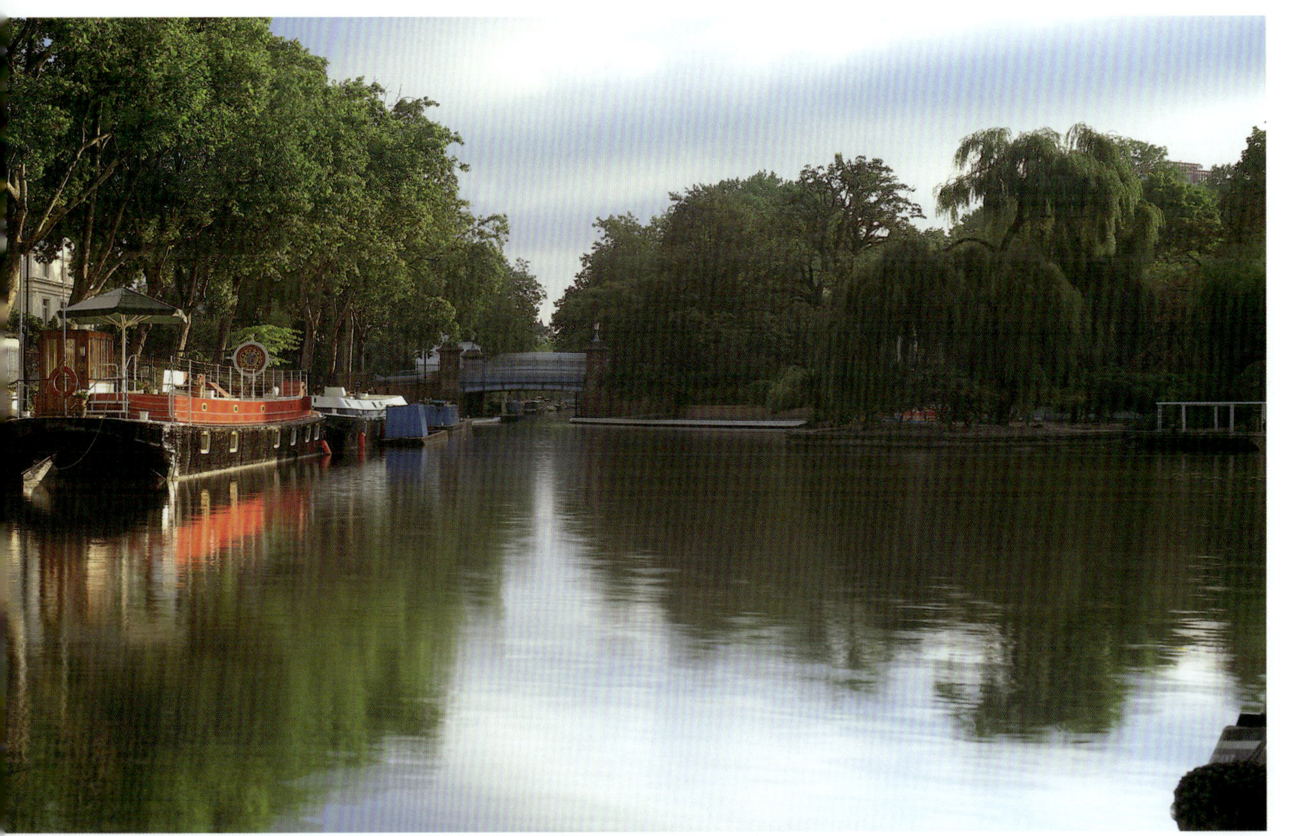

DAWN COLOURS, LITTLE VENICE

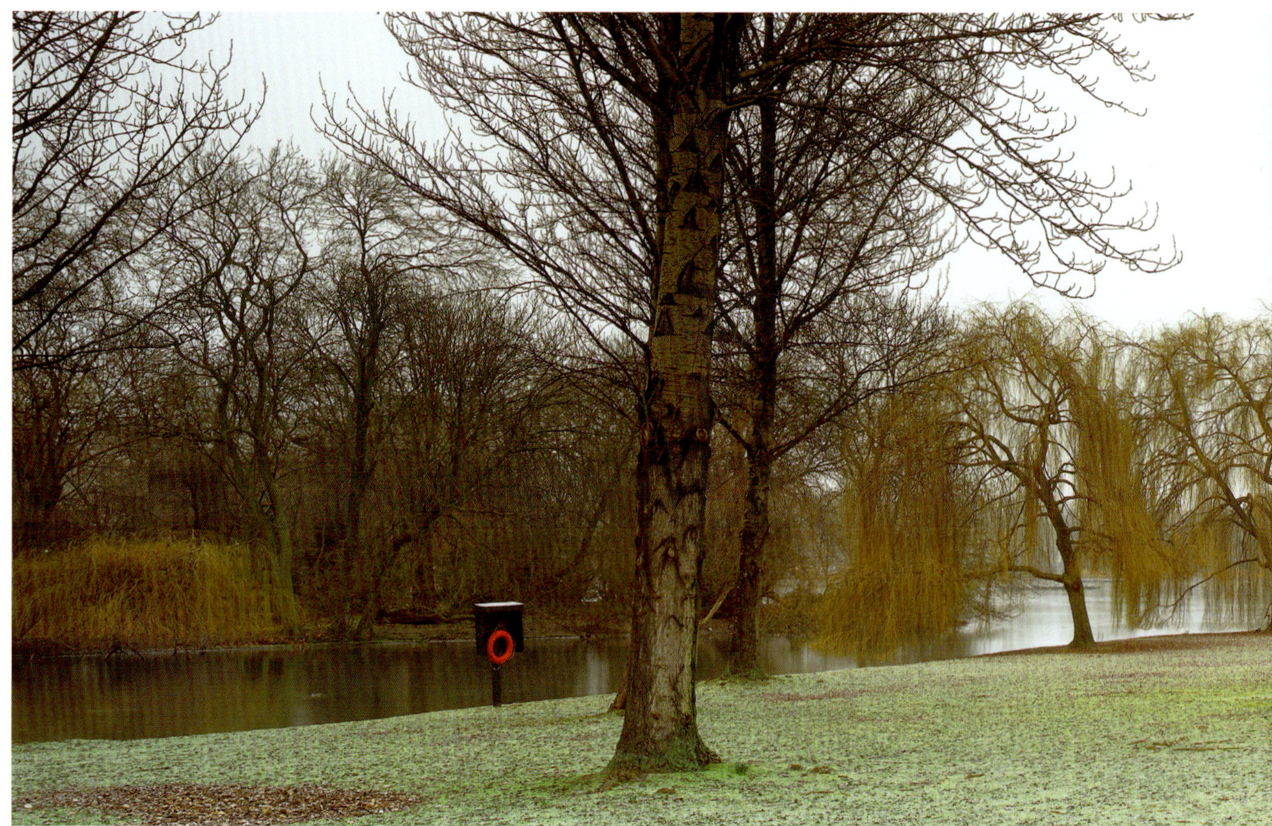

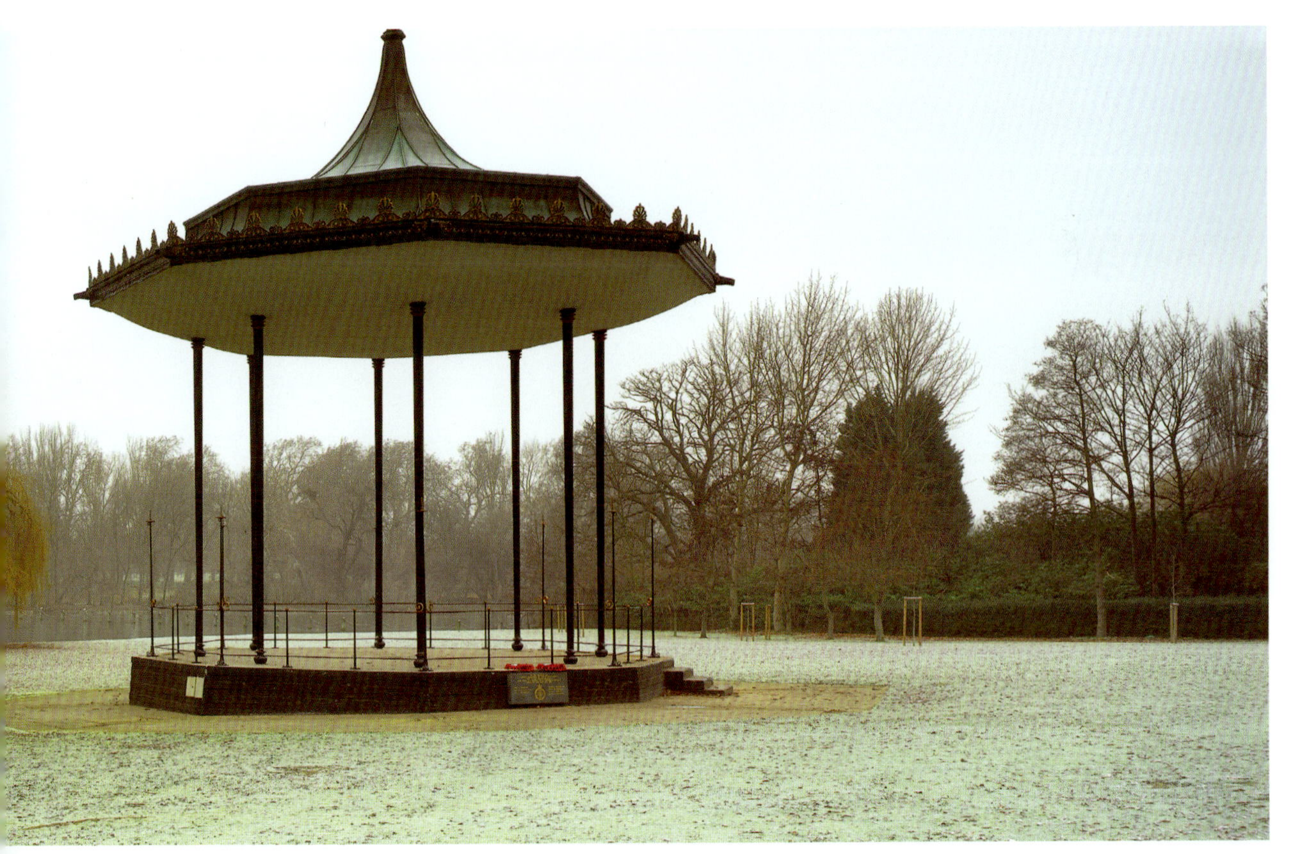

BANDSTAND IN WINTER, REGENT'S PARK

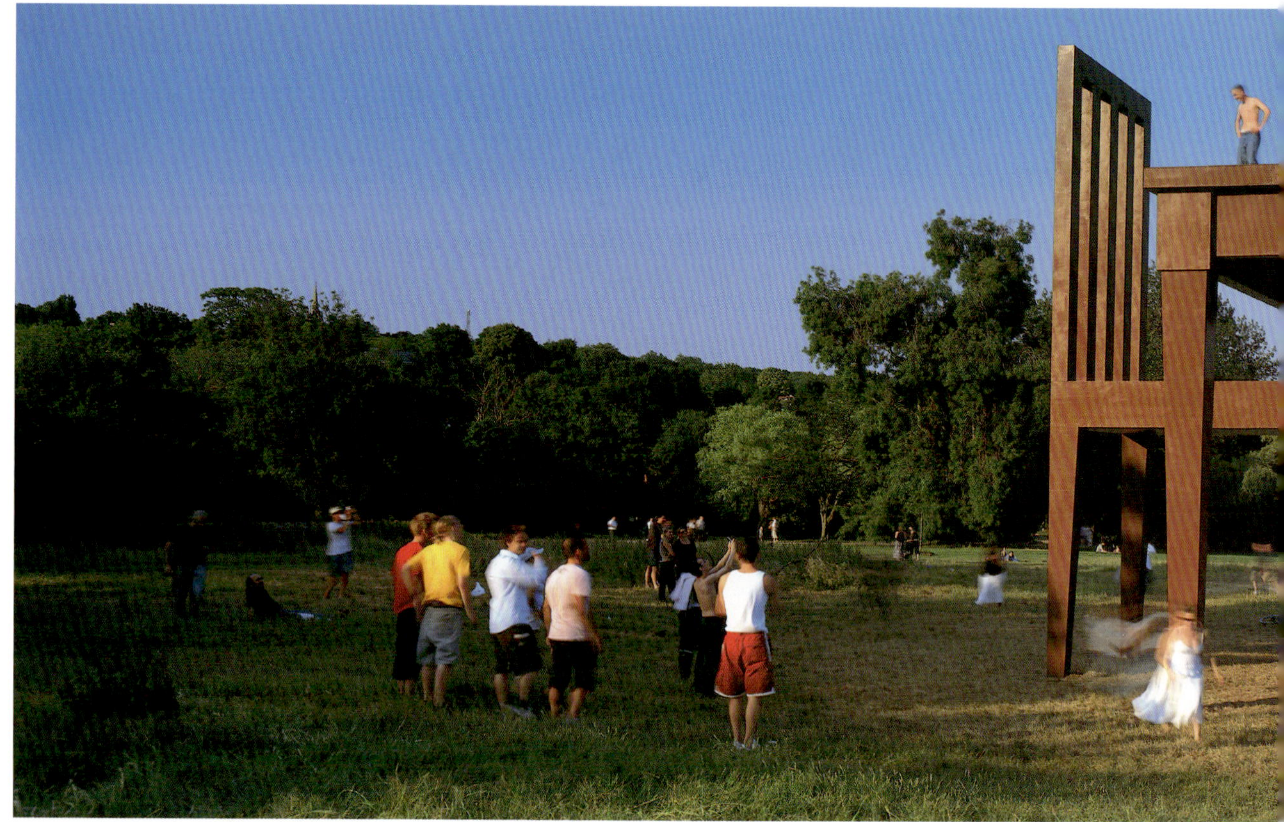

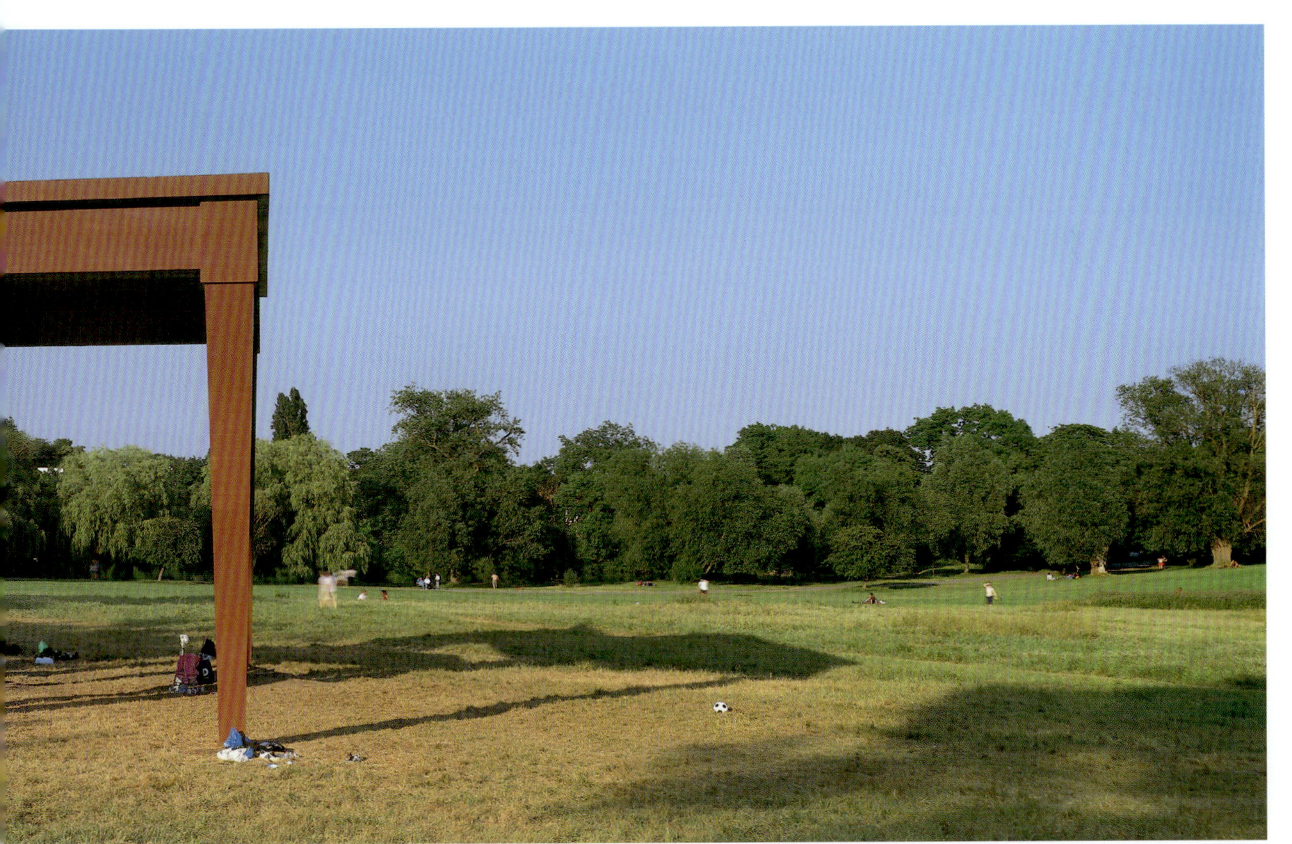

GARY CLIMBS THE WRITER, PARLIAMENT HILL

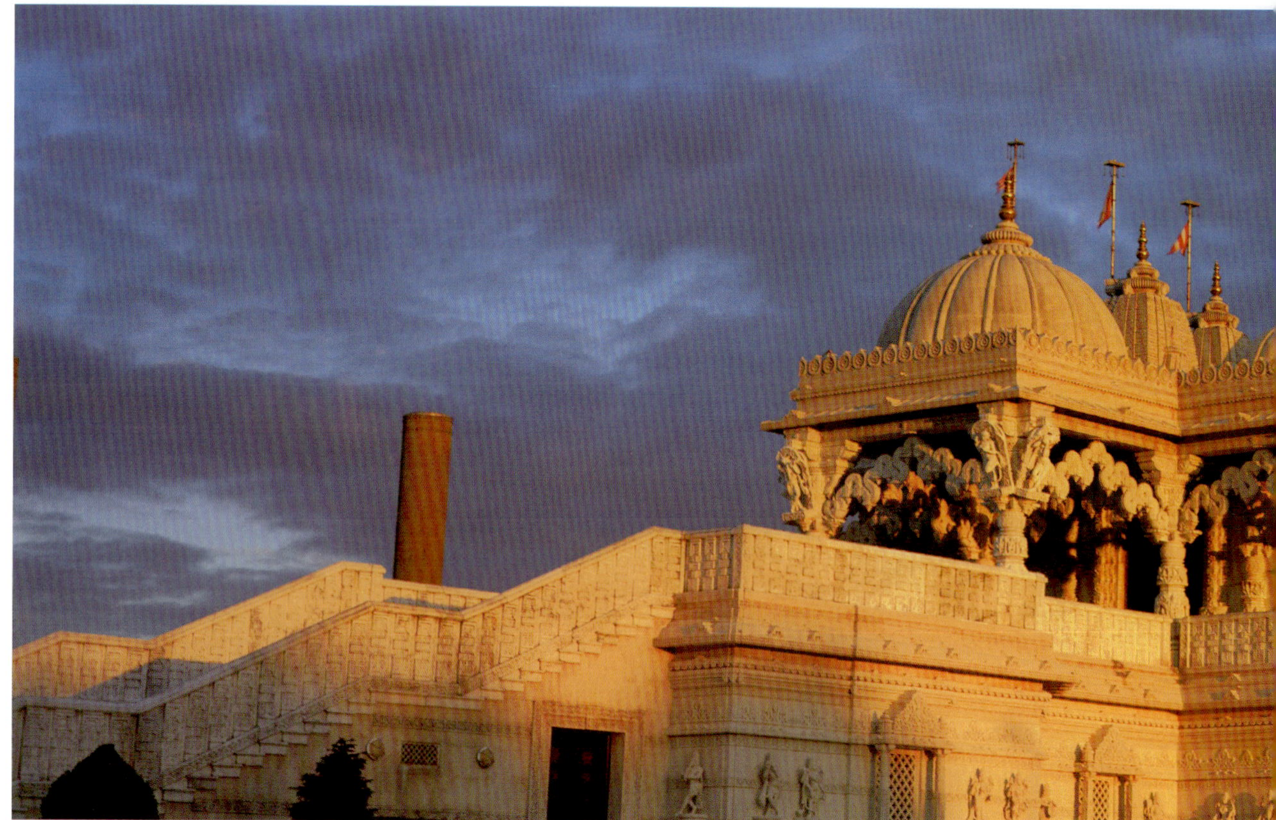

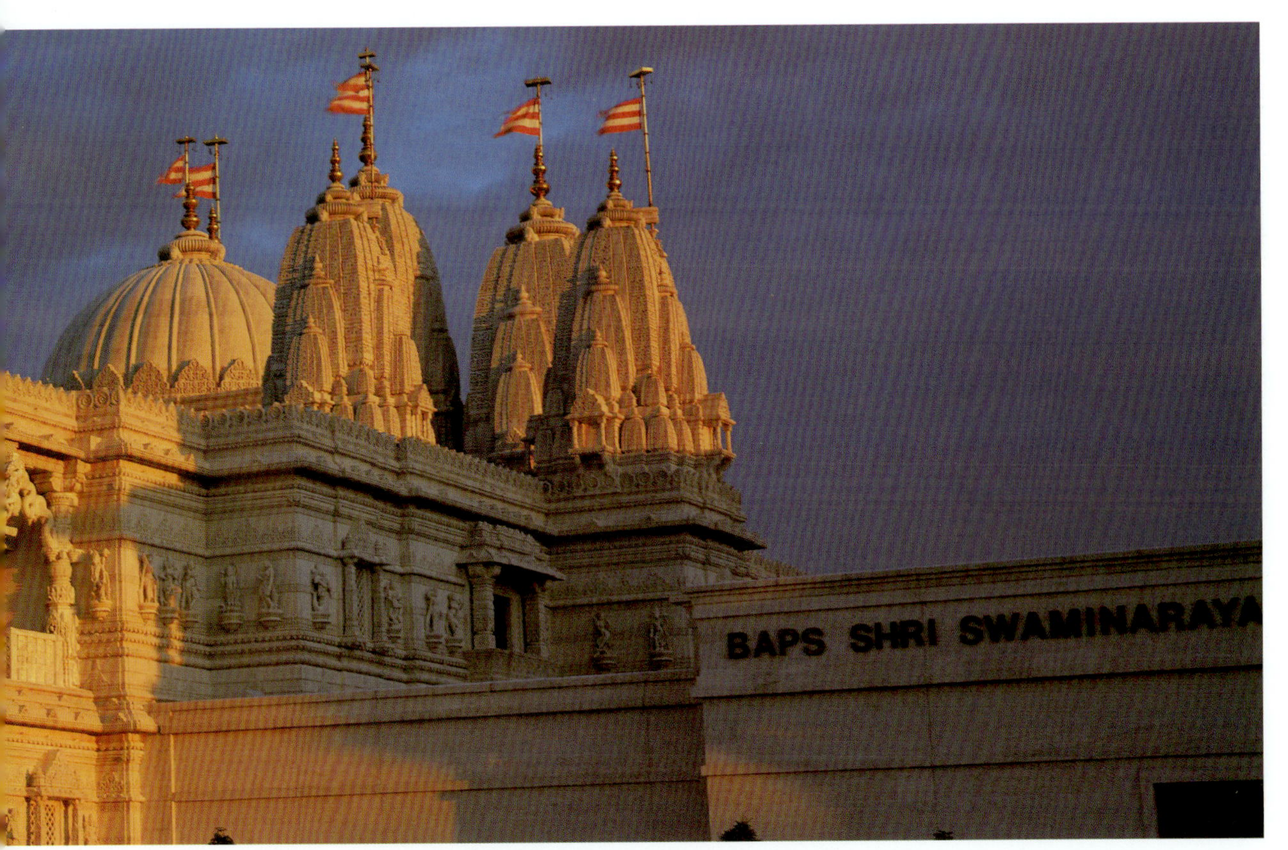

NEASDEN HINDU TEMPLE, EVENING LIGHT

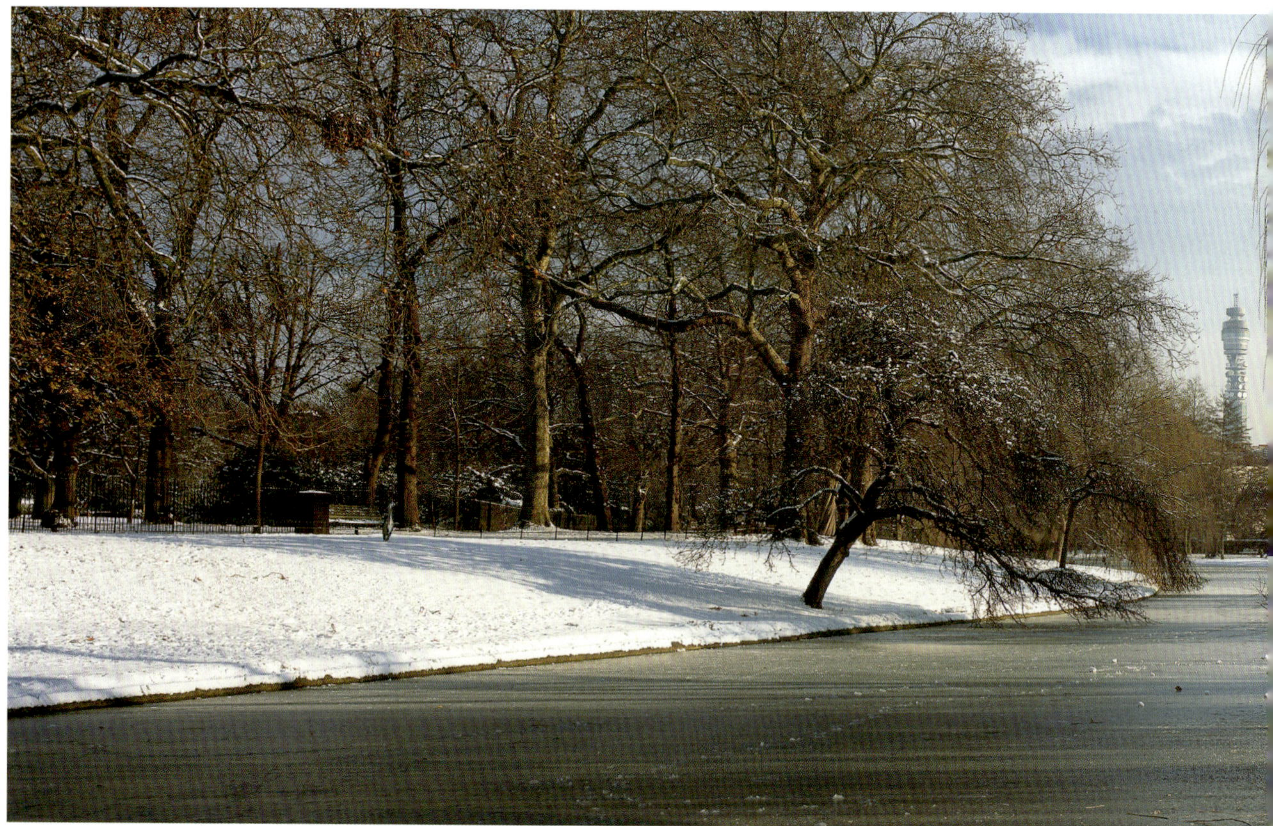

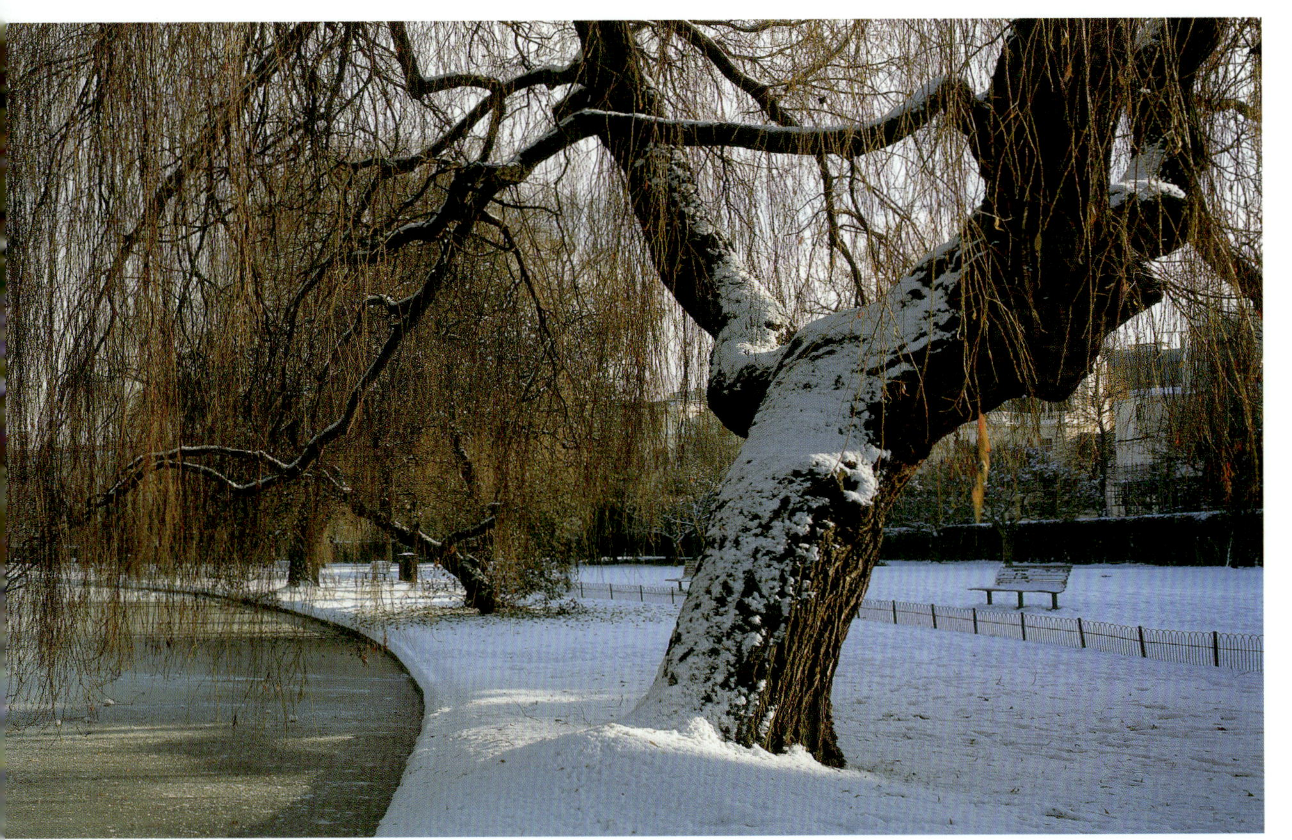

THICK SNOW IN REGENT'S PARK

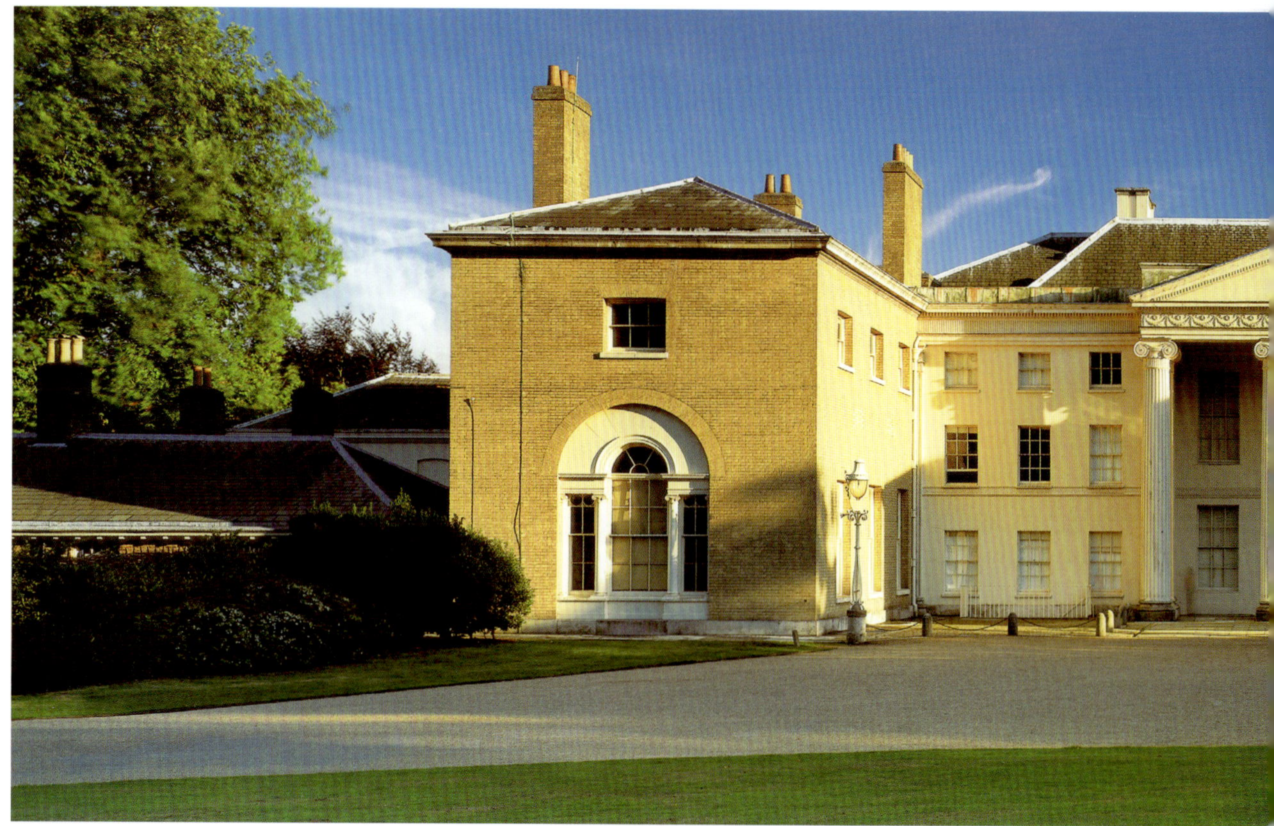

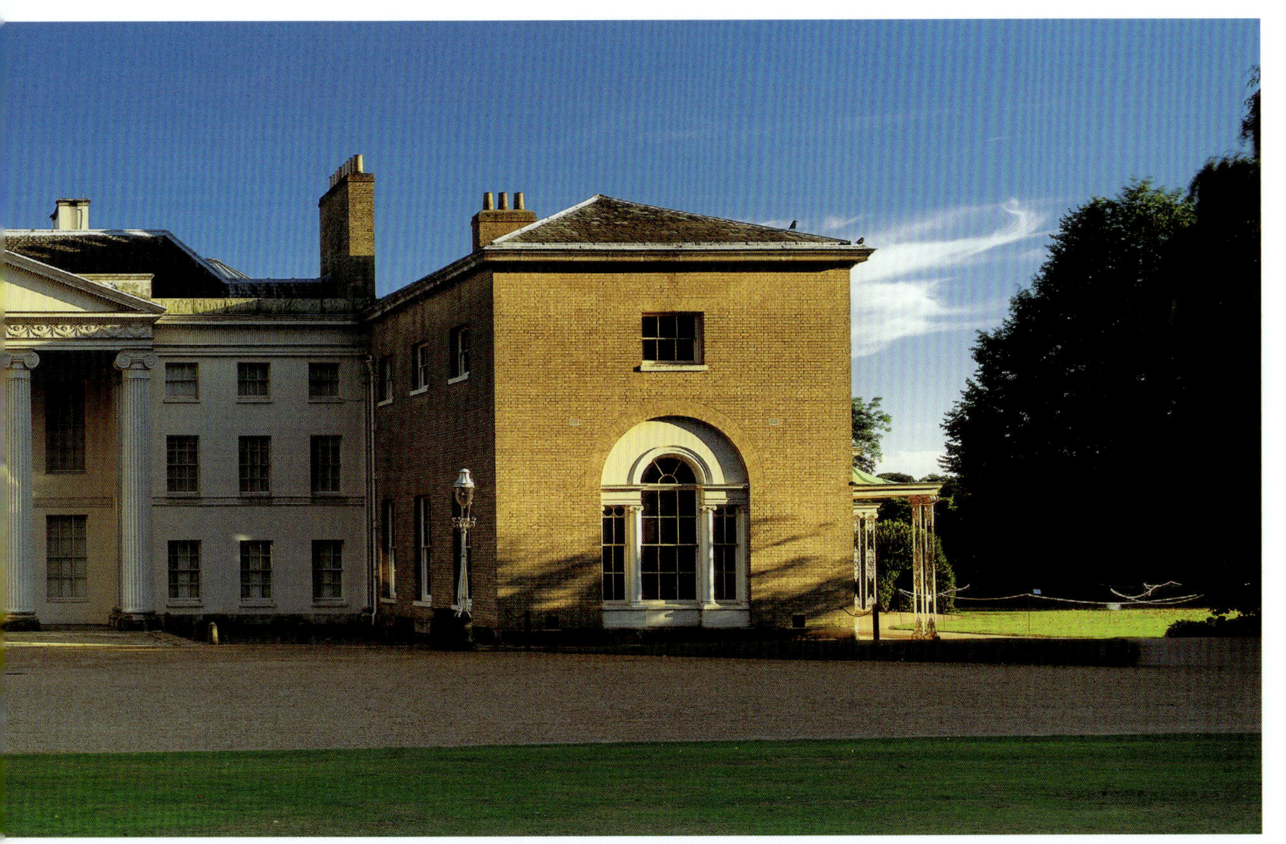

KENWOOD HOUSE, HAMPSTEAD HEATH

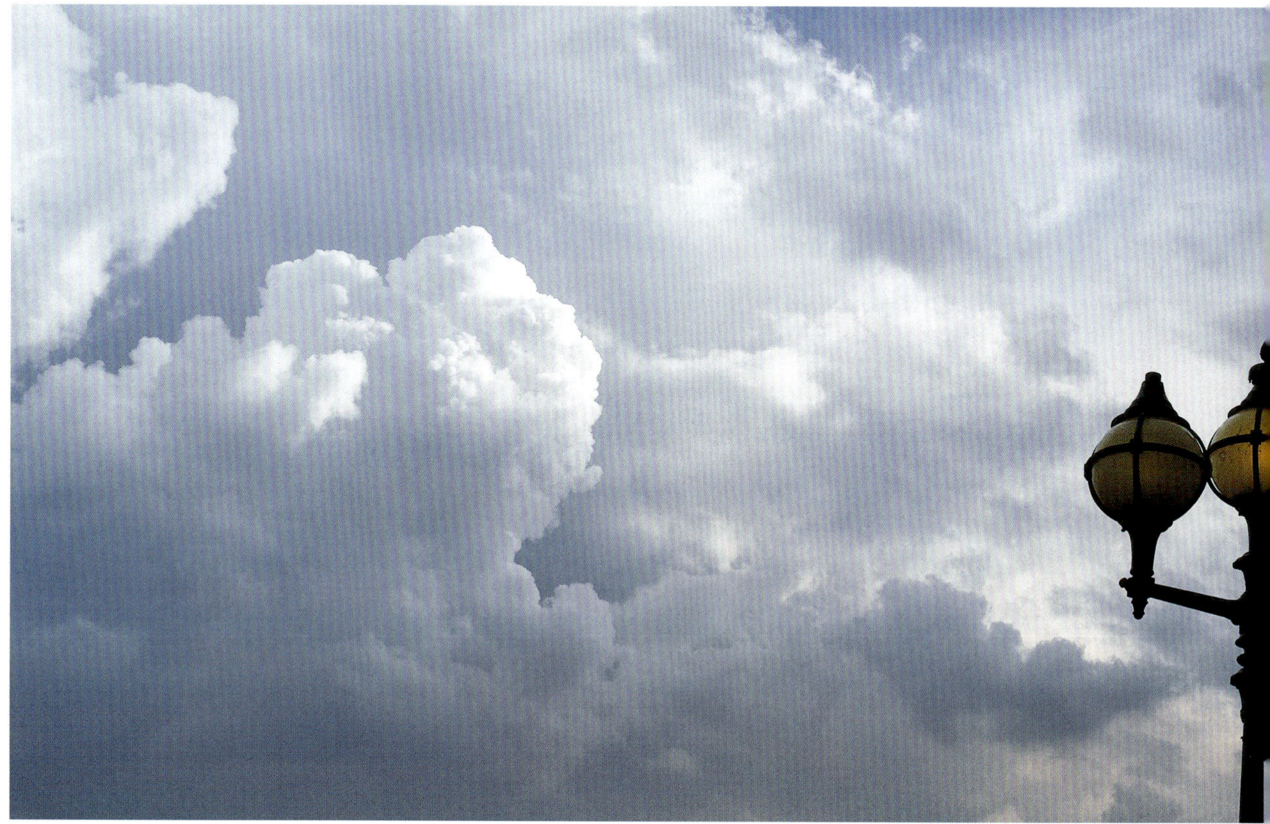

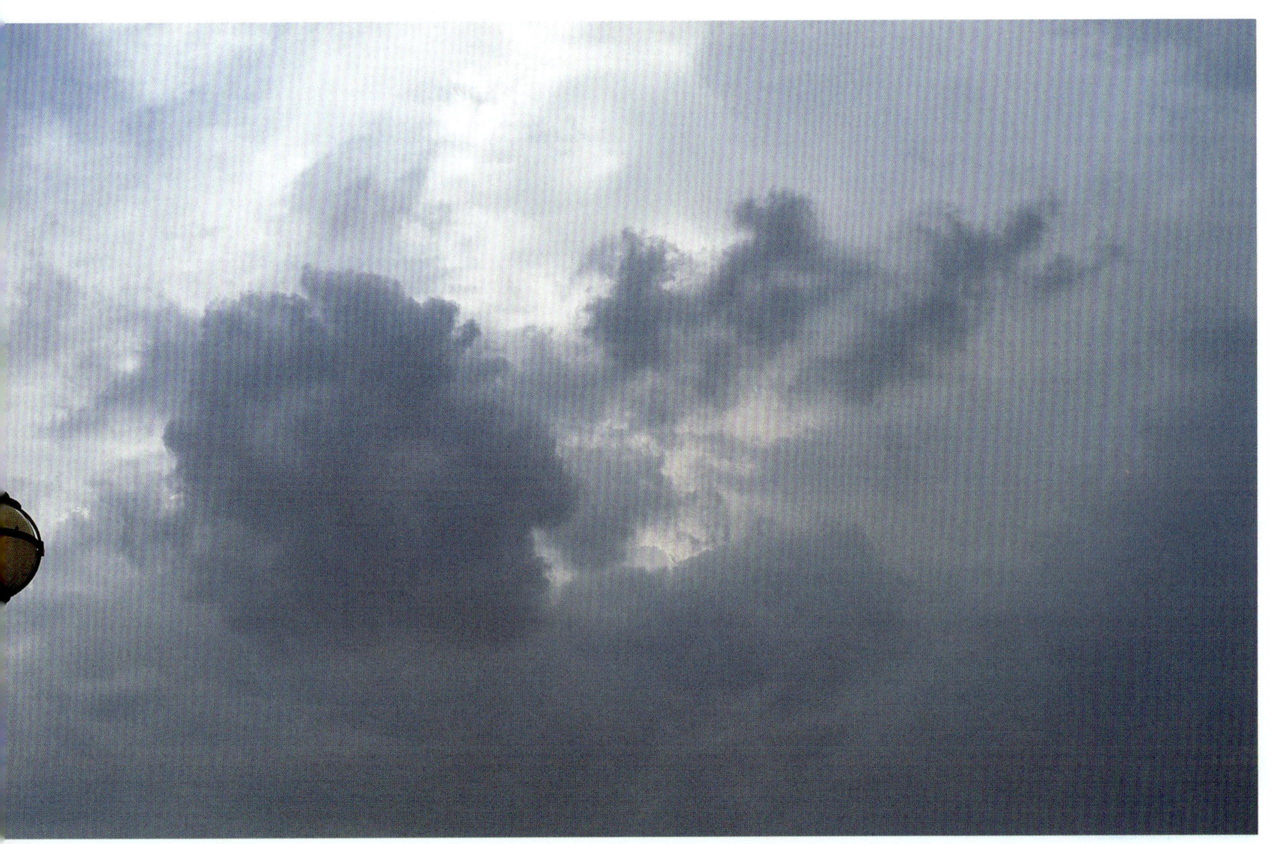

LAMPS, ALEXANDRA PALACE

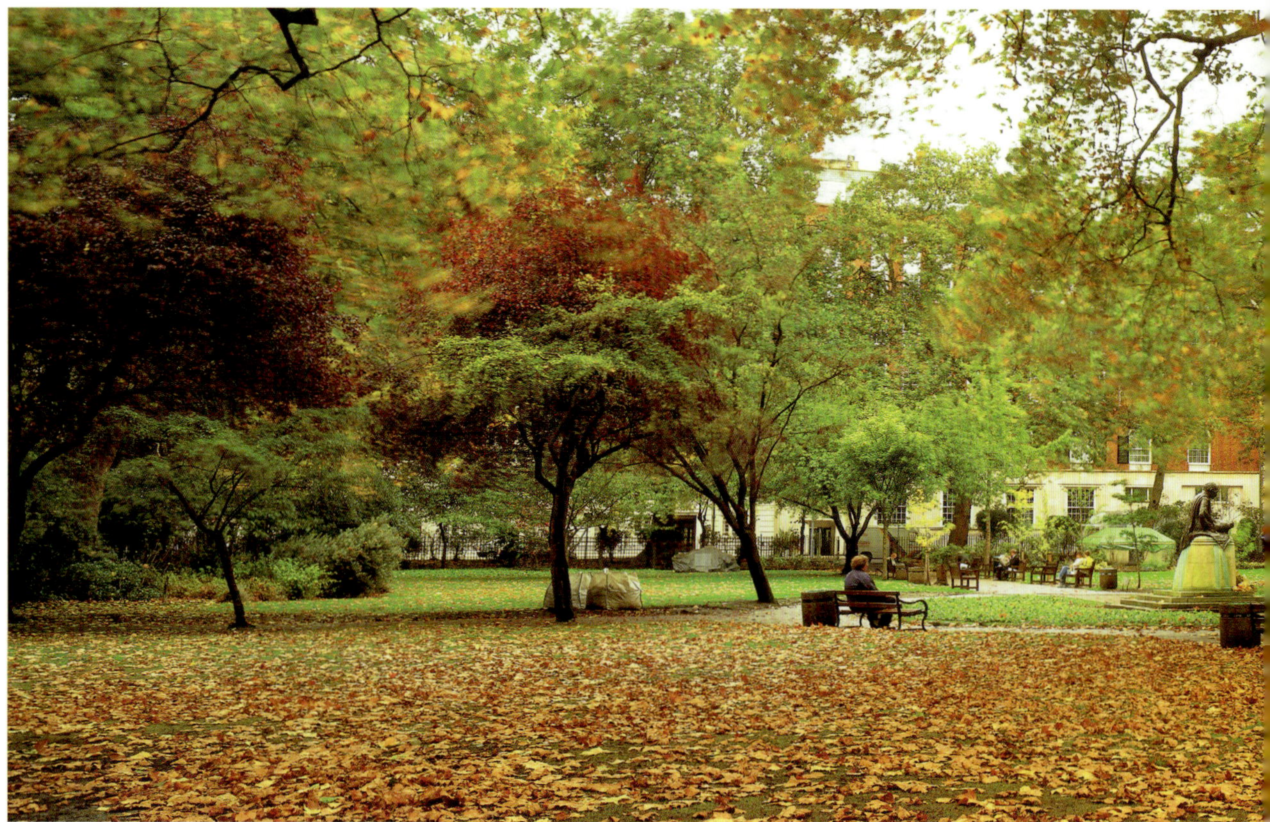

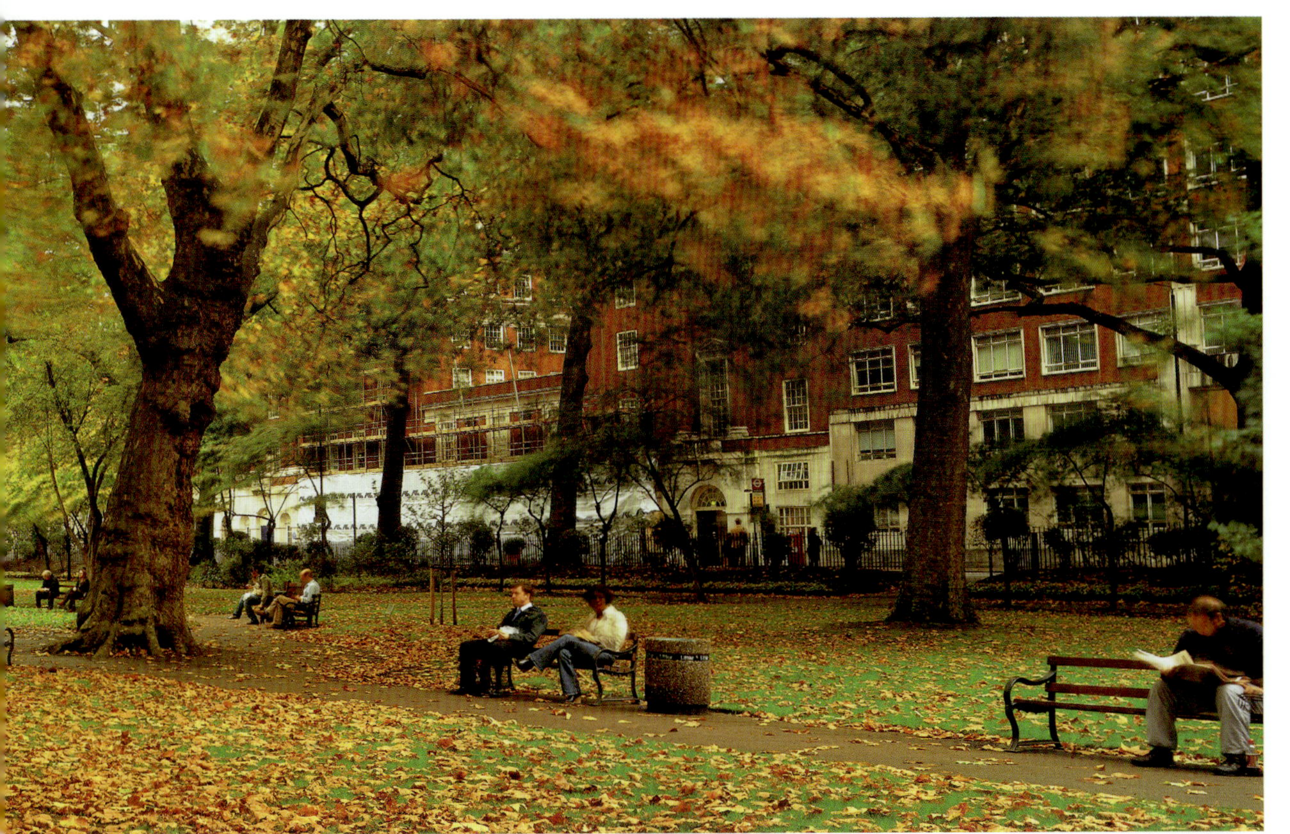

AUTUMN, TAVISTOCK SQUARE

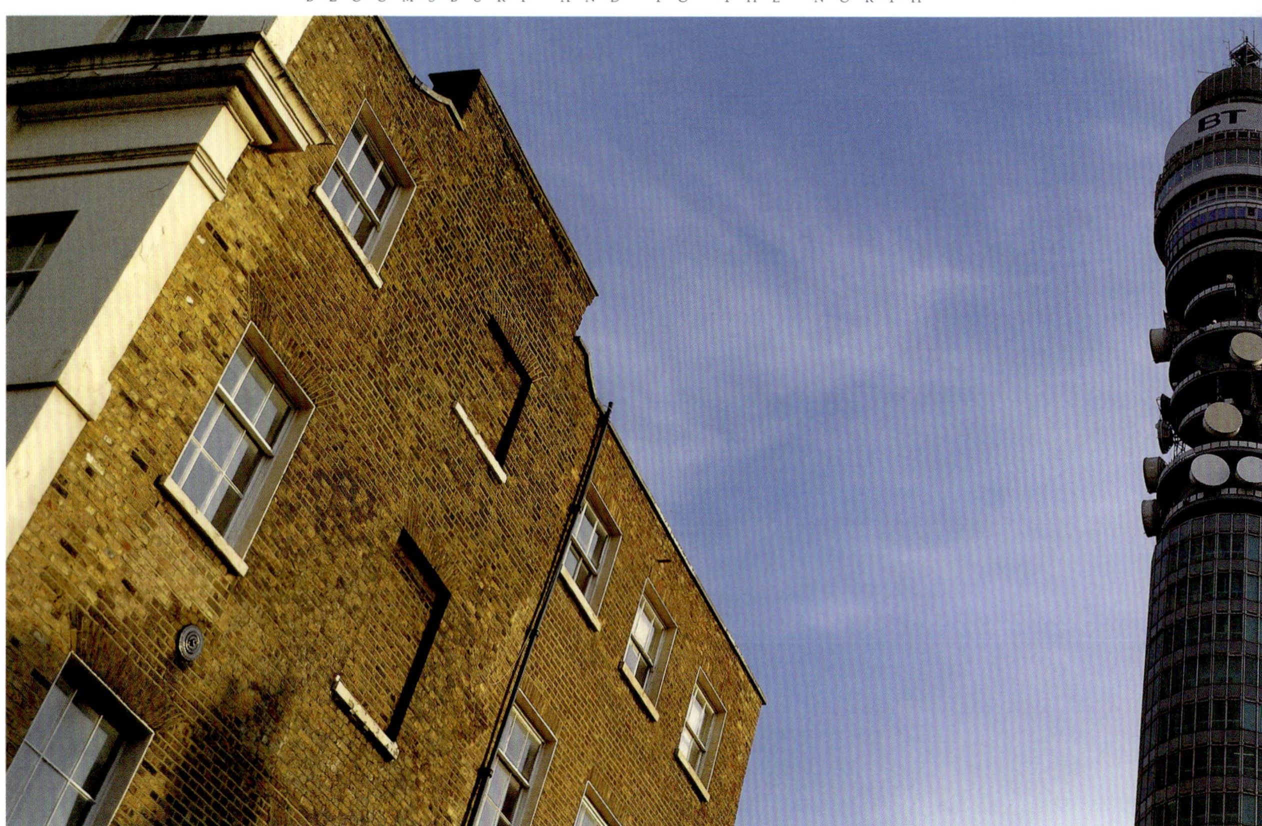
BT

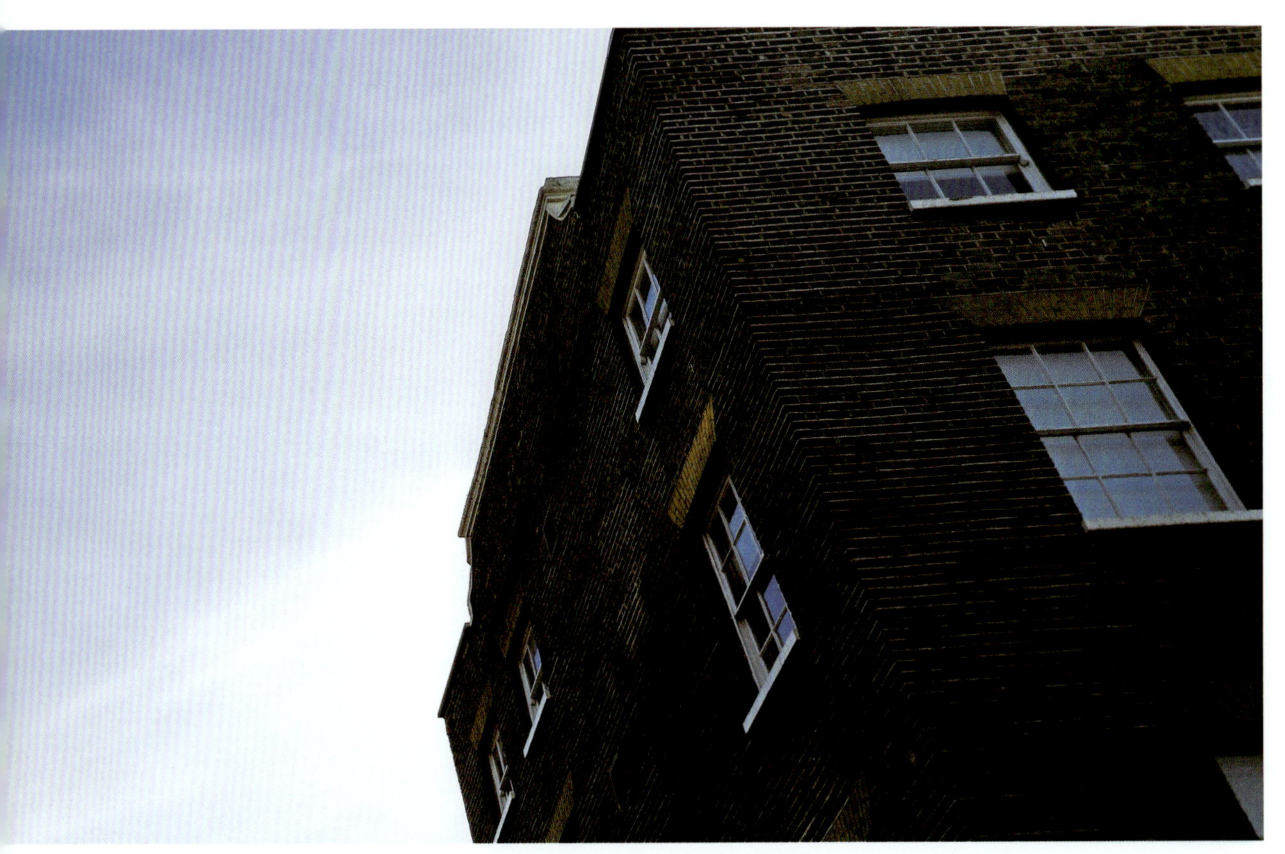

BT TOWER FROM CAPPER STREET

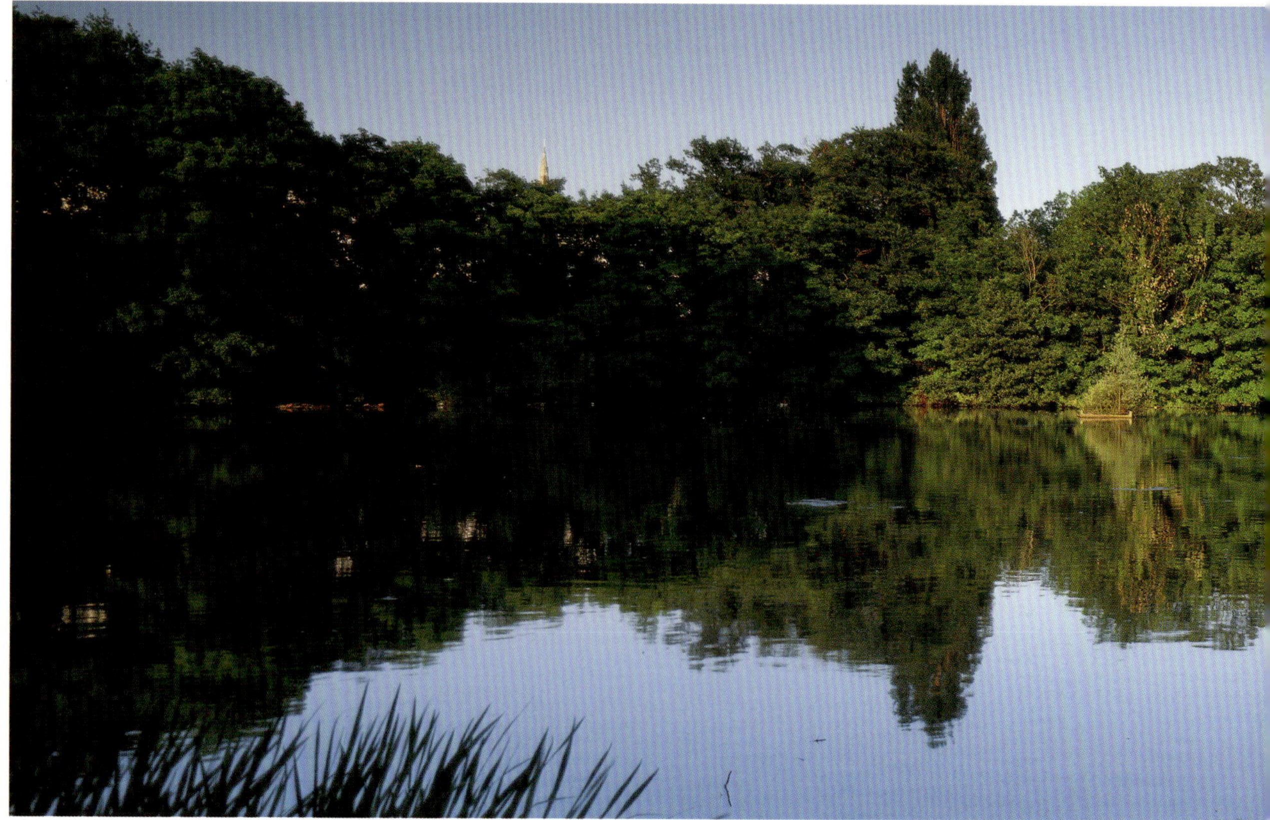

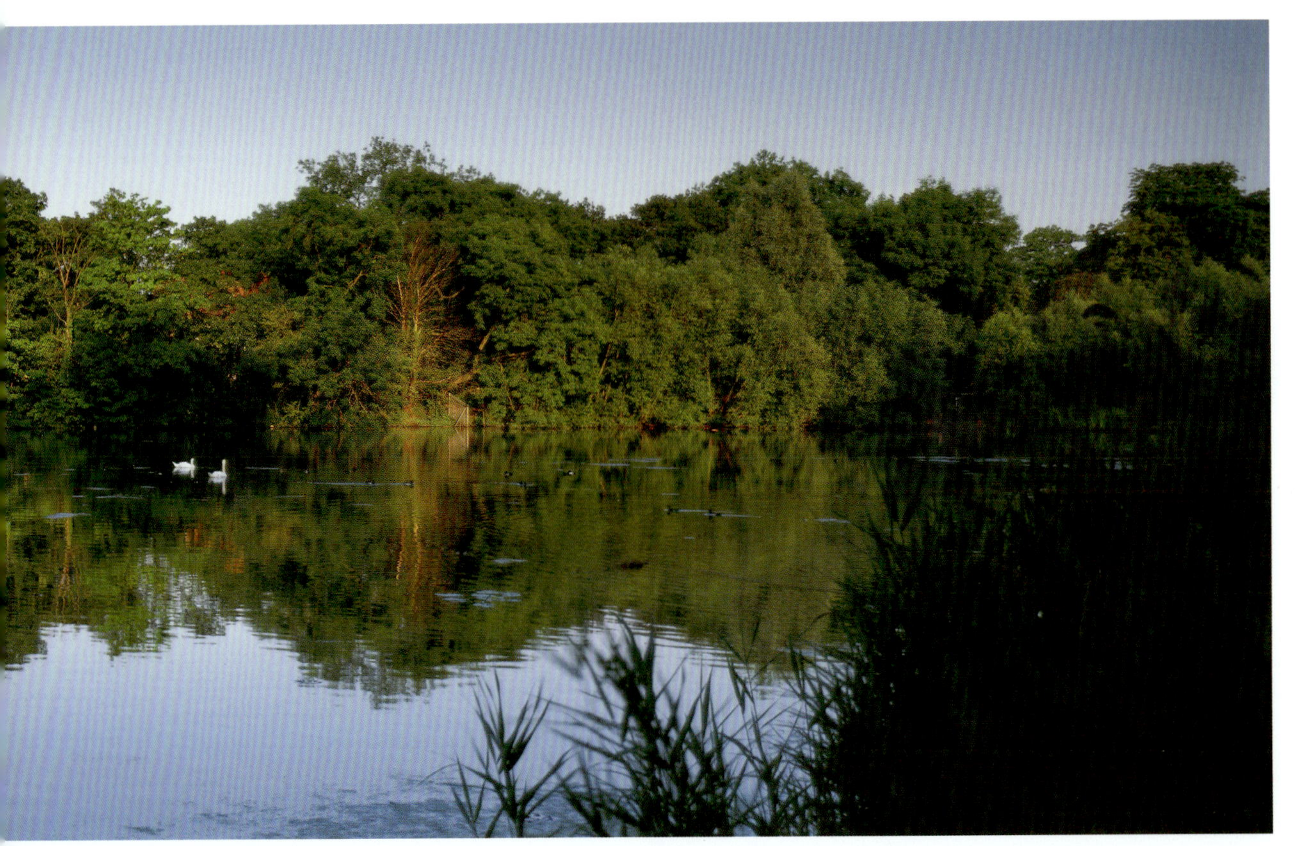

SWANS, HAMPSTEAD HEATH

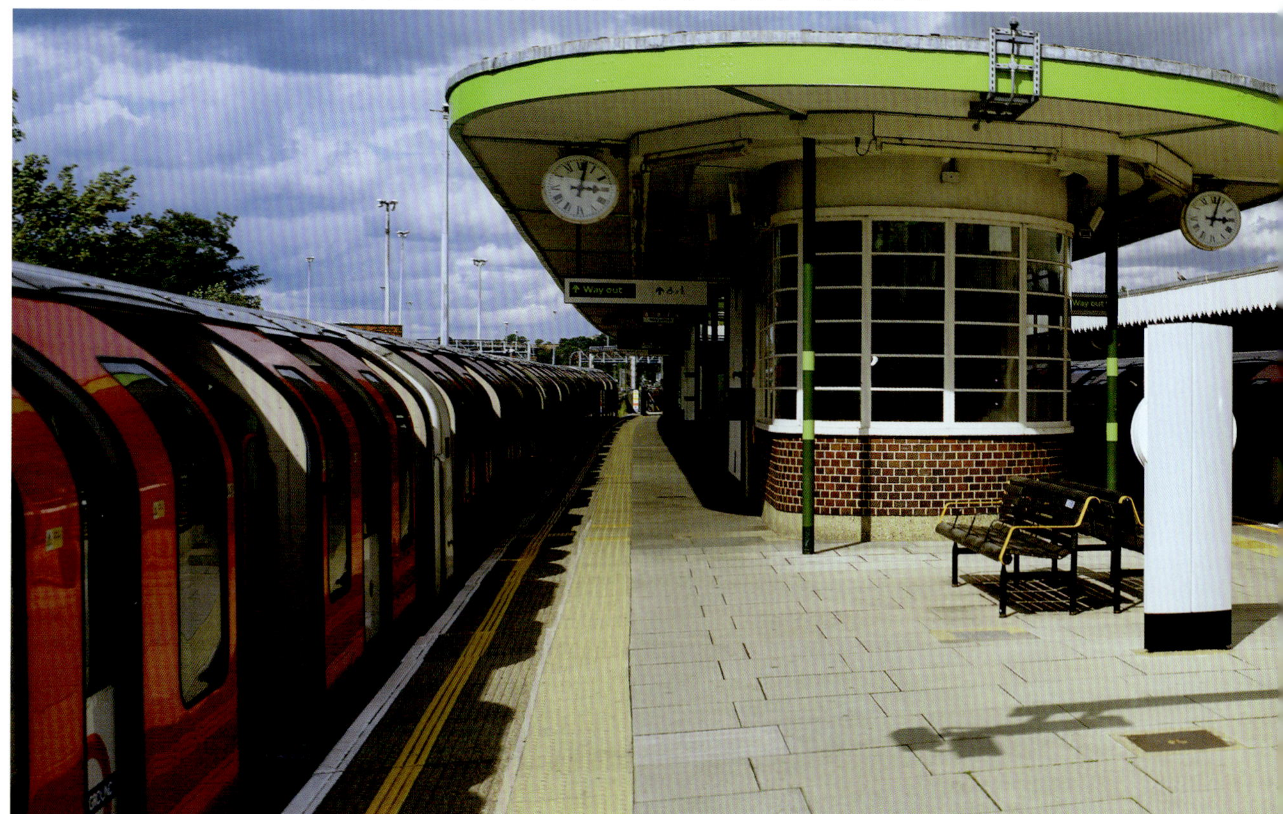
Way out

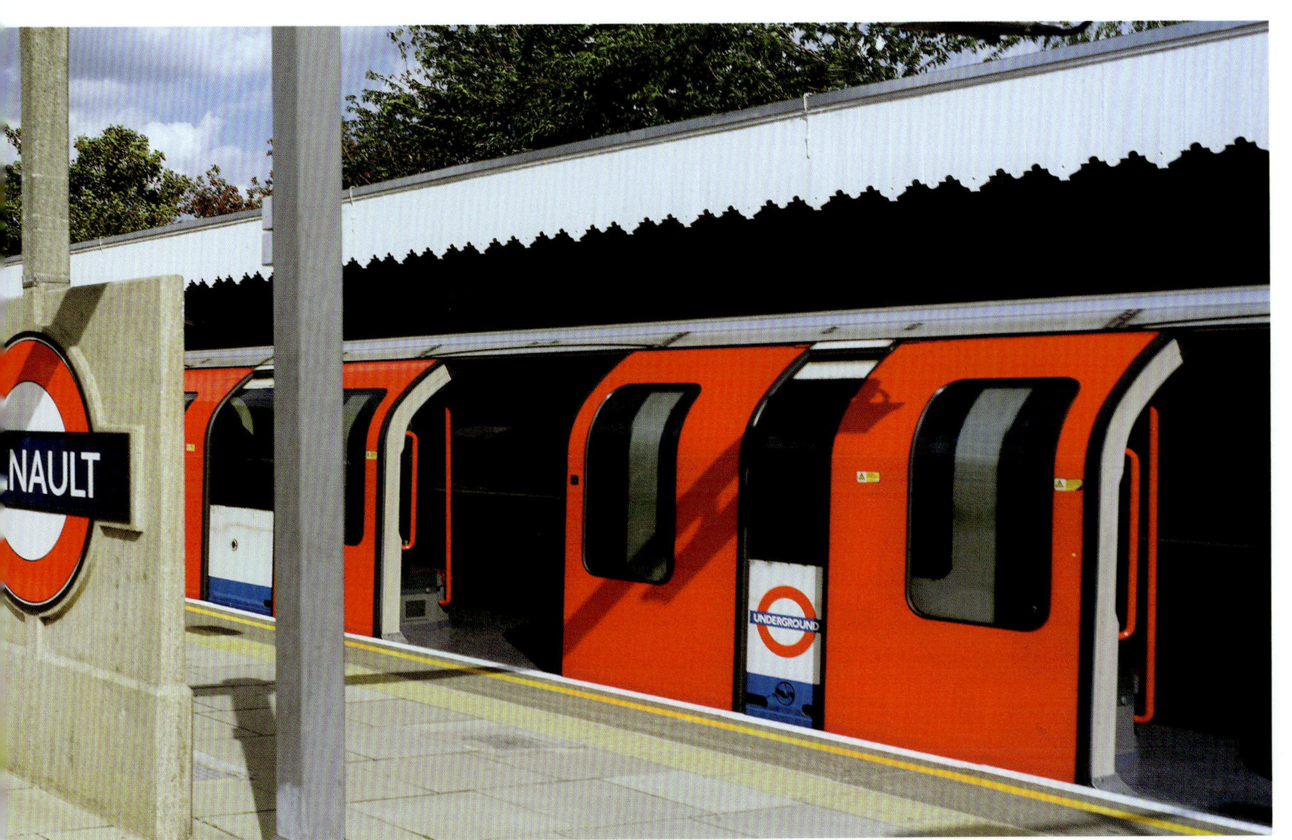

ART DECO WAITING ROOM AT HAINAULT, CENTRAL LINE

HYDE PARK TO HAMPTON COURT

The Thames may flow east towards its appointment with the North Sea but London's money has traditionally flowed the other way. For centuries, financial and trading fortunes made in the City of London or its dockland quays took on luxurious form in the west – from the present day wealthy trendsetters of Notting Hill to the historic palaces at Richmond, Kensington and Hampton Court.

West London is bookmarked by two of the city's great parks. Hyde Park, with its famous lake The Serpentine (created in the 1730s by Queen Caroline, wife of George II), marks the edge of the West End shopping district, while Richmond Park marks the western edge of London itself.

Covering 350 acres (140 hectares), Hyde Park was owned by the monks of Westminster Abbey until 1536 when it was acquired by Henry VIII as a private hunting ground. Charles I opened the park to the public in 1637, and two decades later it became a sanctuary for thousands fleeing the Great Plague that struck the City of London in 1665. The park remains a sanctuary today from the traffic thundering past the imposing Marble Arch, moved to the park's north-east corner from Buckingham Palace in 1851. Hyde Park also possesses its own Royal palace: Kensington Palace, best known today as the home of the late Princess Diana.

During the Great Exhibition of 1851 the famous iron-and-glass Crystal Palace was built along the route now bearing the evocative name Rotten Row, before being moved to south London, where it burned down in 1936. More recently, rock concerts have brought vast crowds to the park, from the legendary 1969 free concert by the Rolling Stones to the Live 8 show of 2005.

Mementoes of Queen Victoria's consort Prince Albert imprint the landscape as you move west. The Albert Memorial was unveiled by Victoria in 1876 following Albert's death from typhoid aged just 42. A few hundred yards away, the soaring dome of the Albert Hall encloses a unique circular auditorium which is one of London's major music spaces. The hall's annual 'Proms' classical concerts are as much part of London's summer social calendar as Wimbledon or the Chelsea Flower Show.

Head south, past Harrods and a cluster of London's great museums – the Victoria & Albert, Natural History Museum and Science Museum – and you come to the Albert Bridge. Opened in 1873, the bridge was almost demolished after the Second World War because of structural problems. Though strengthened, it still bears wartime signs telling soldiers from nearby Chelsea Barracks to break step when marching over it in case vibrations caused a collapse!

West along the riverbank you pass the houses of London's super-rich – from luxury houseboats to Marble Hill House, the Palladian villa built in the 1720s for Henrietta Howard, mistress of George II, where she entertained not only her royal lover but also great writers of the day such as Jonathan Swift.

The western edge of London comes at Richmond Park, a designated nature reserve whose ancient woods and grassland have changed little since its foundation in the 13th century. Today Richmond offers a feel of the countryside while still having a view of St Paul's Cathedral, 12 miles (19 kilometres) to the east.

Nearby is London's most famous Victorian greenhouse, the Palm House in Kew Gardens. The Gardens were created as a pleasure garden for Prince Frederick in 1731, becoming the Royal Botanic Gardens in 1759. Some of the earliest of its 50,000 botanical specimens were brought back by Captain Cook from his famous Pacific voyages. Built in the 1840s, the Palm House is one of London's most recognisable structures. Built using techniques developed from ship-building, the building has been compared to the upturned hull of a graceful ocean liner. Kew can be reached by river – a cruise from Westminster Pier takes just over an hour.

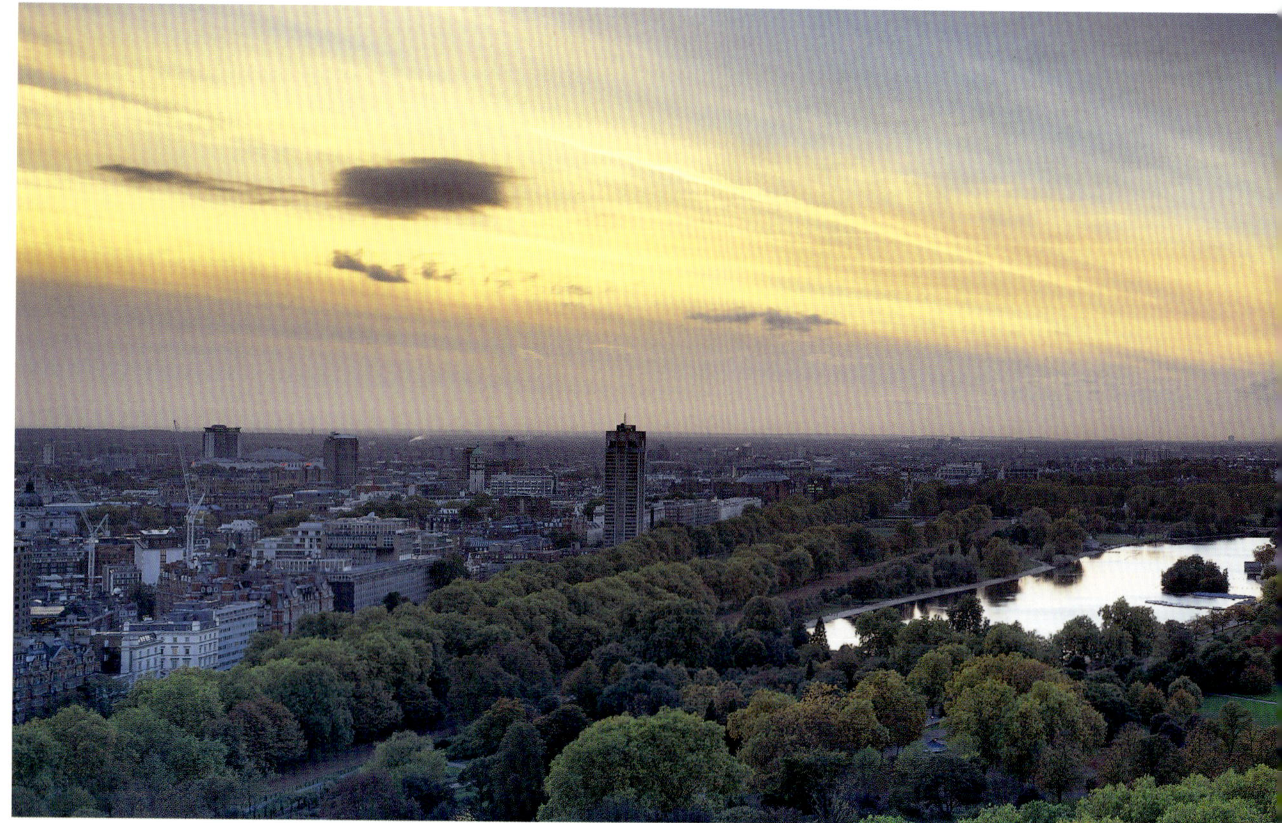

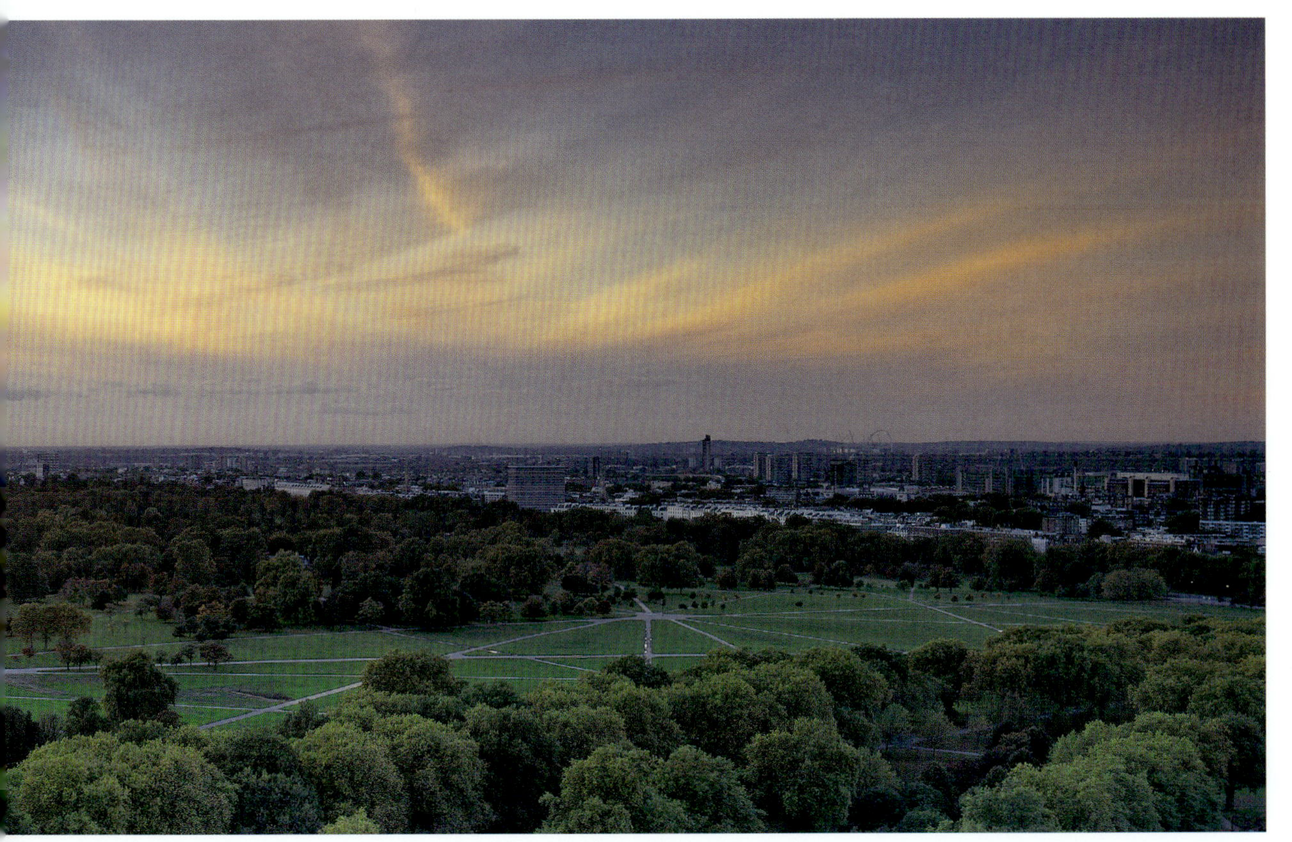

VIEW WEST, PARK LANE HILTON

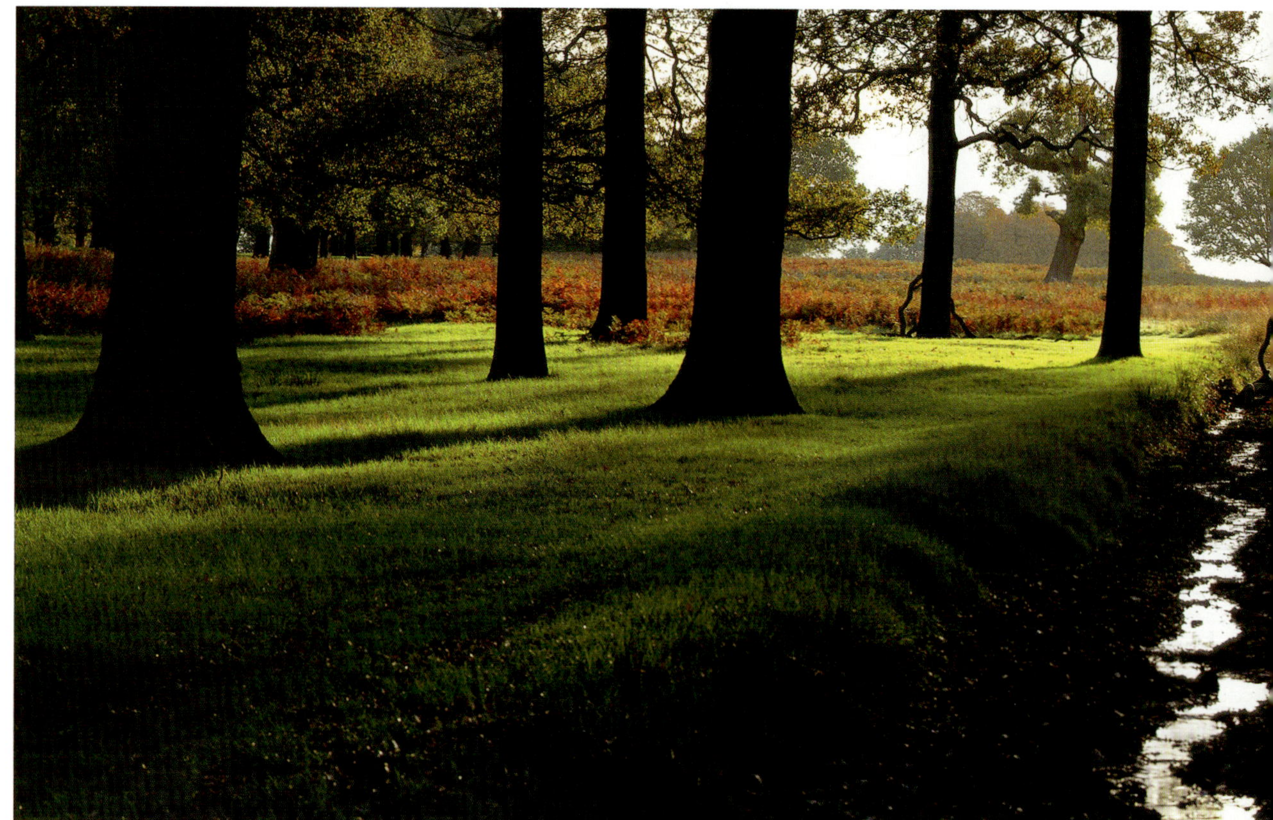

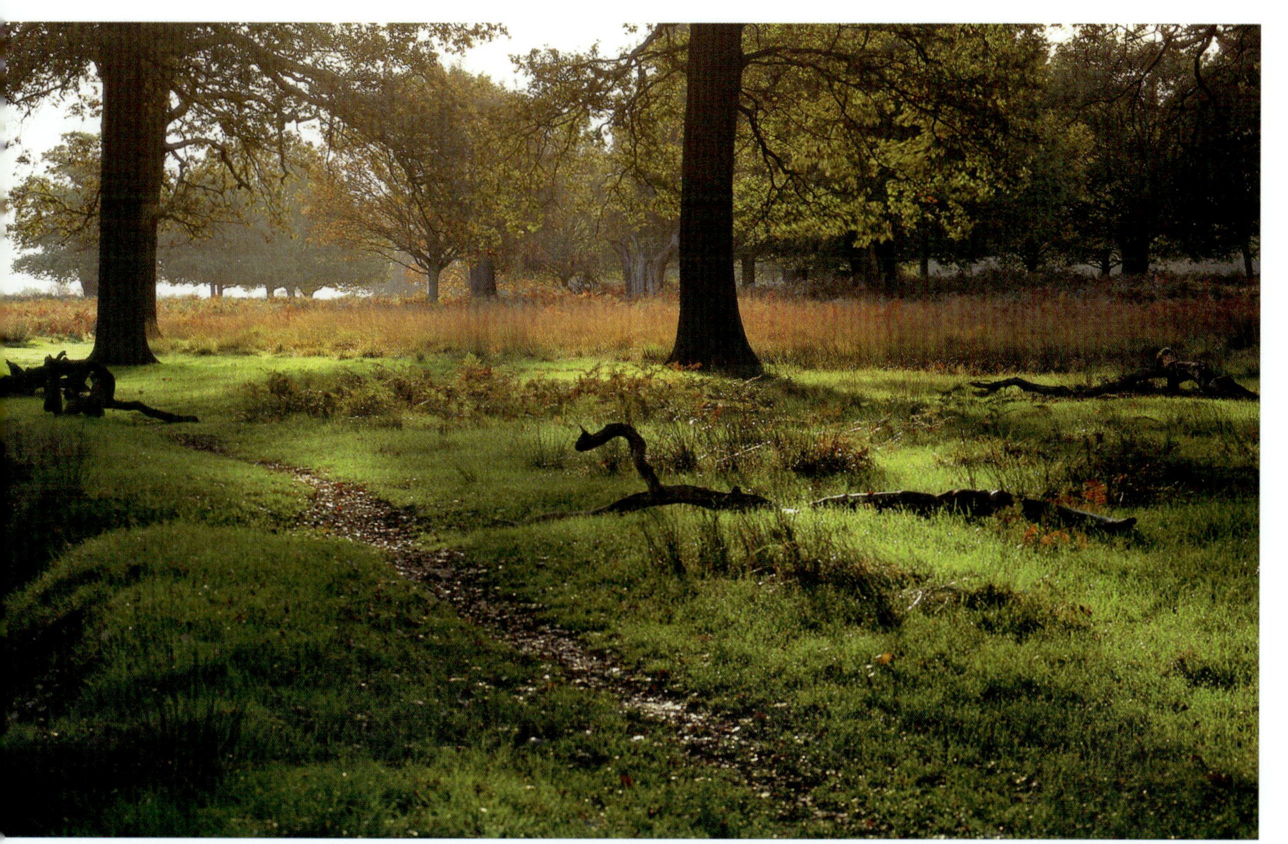

STREAM, RICHMOND PARK

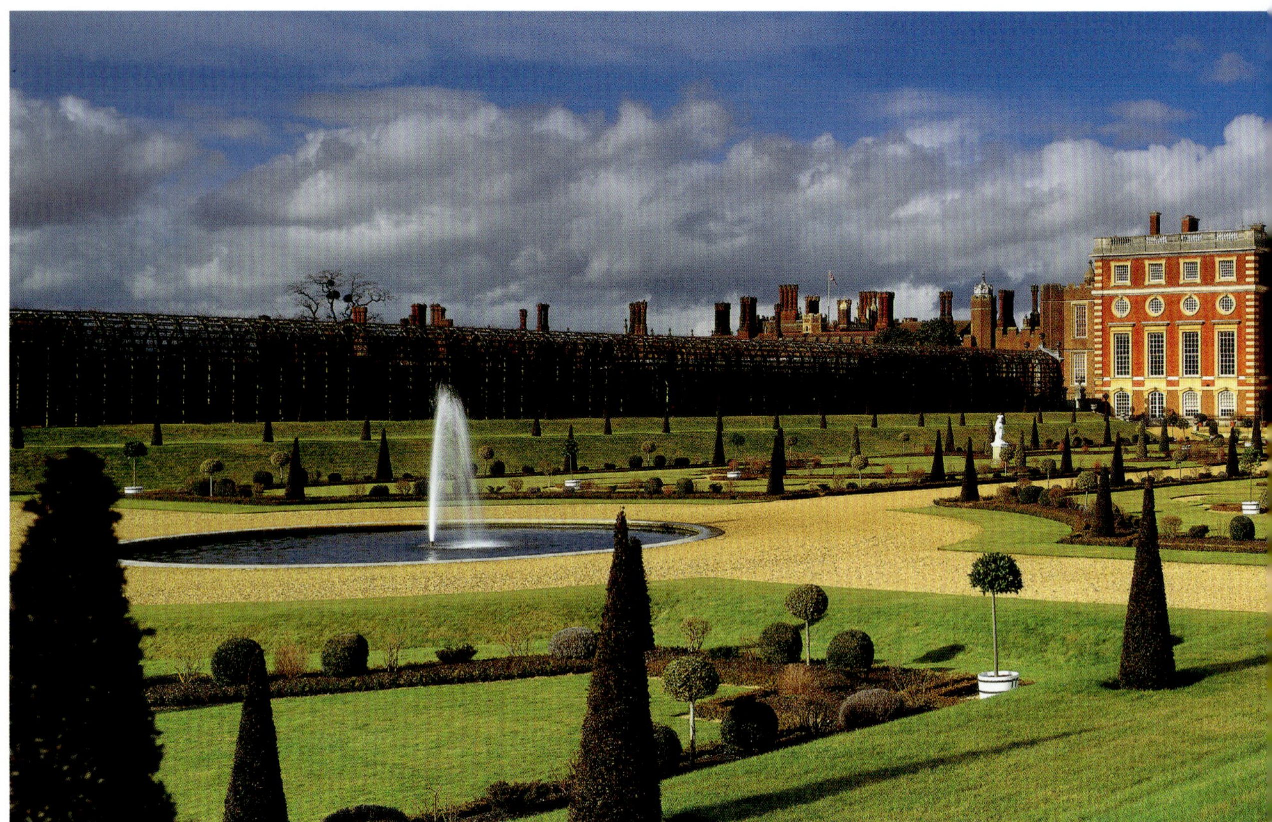

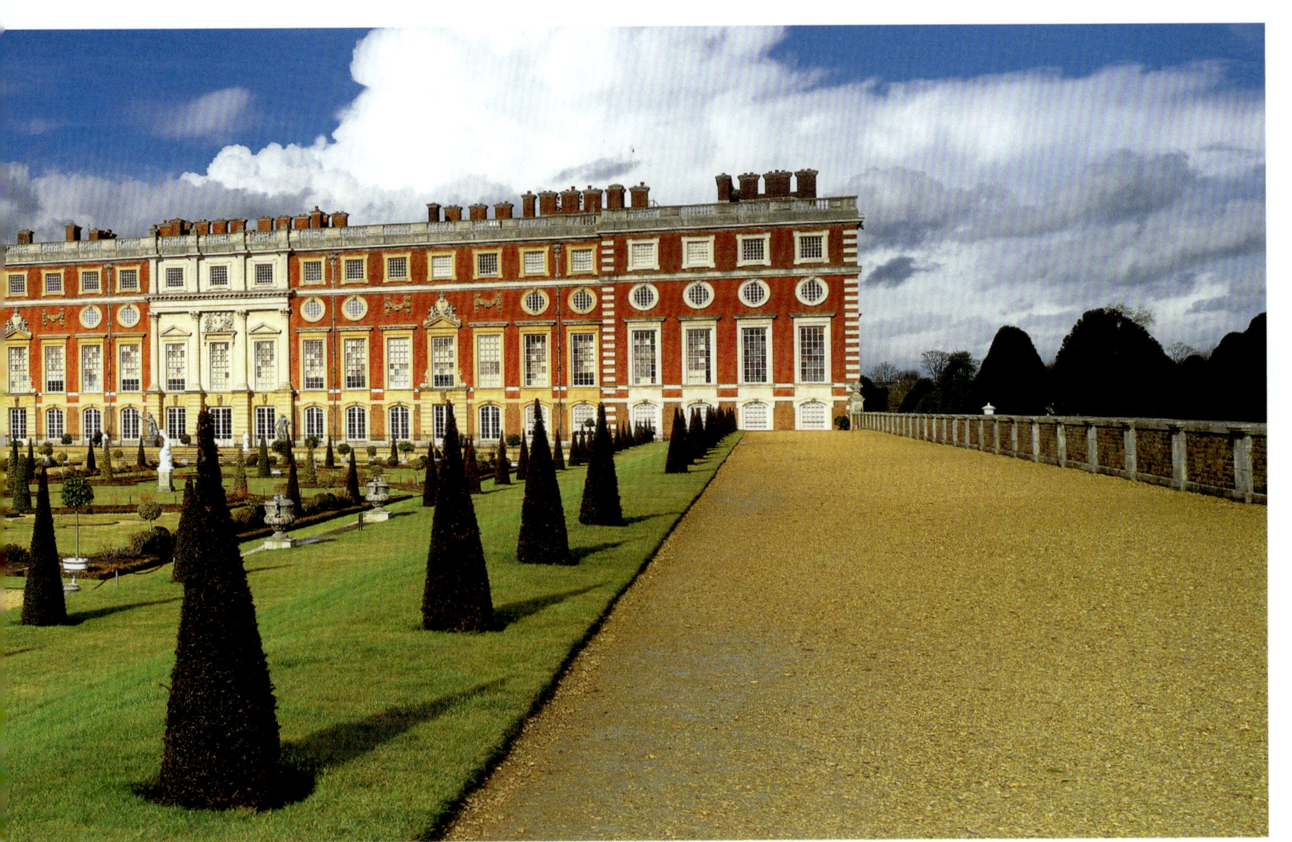

FLUFFY CLOUD, HAMPTON COURT PALACE

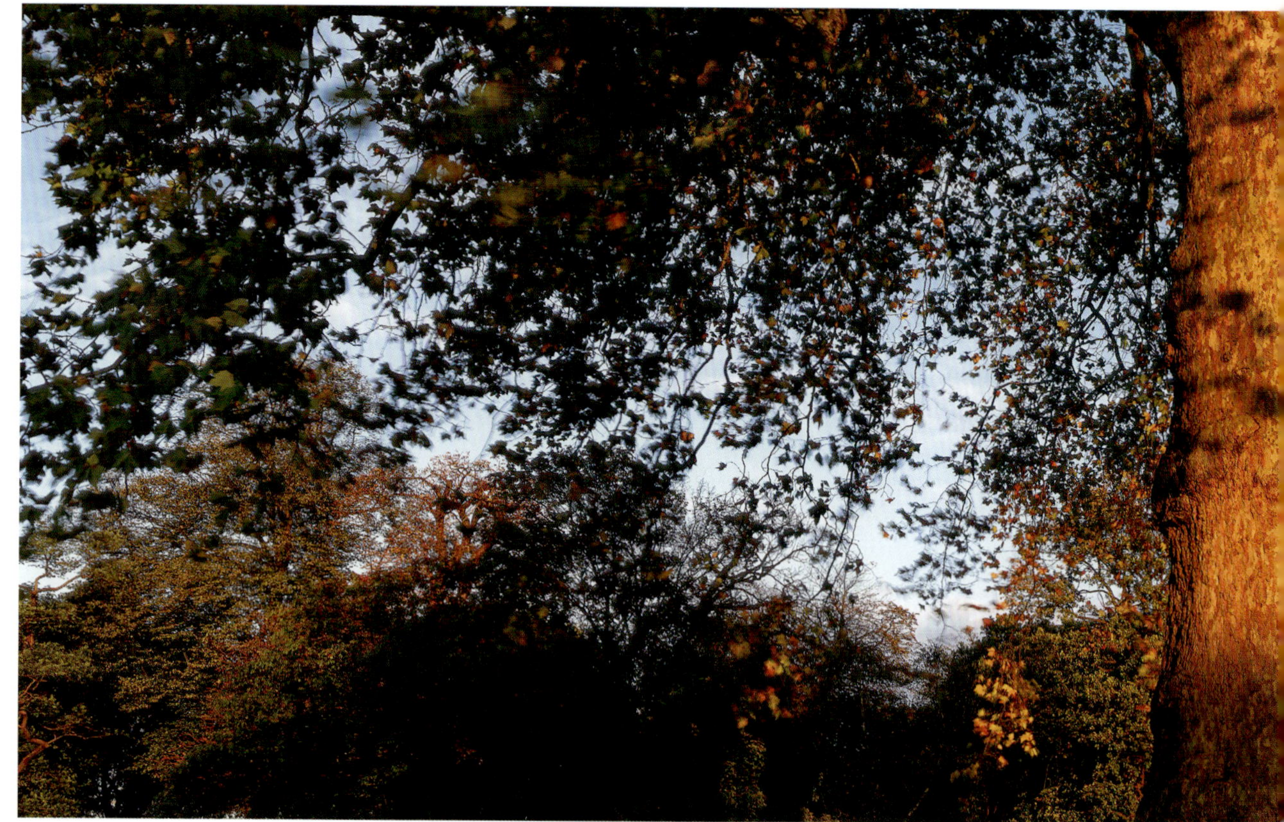

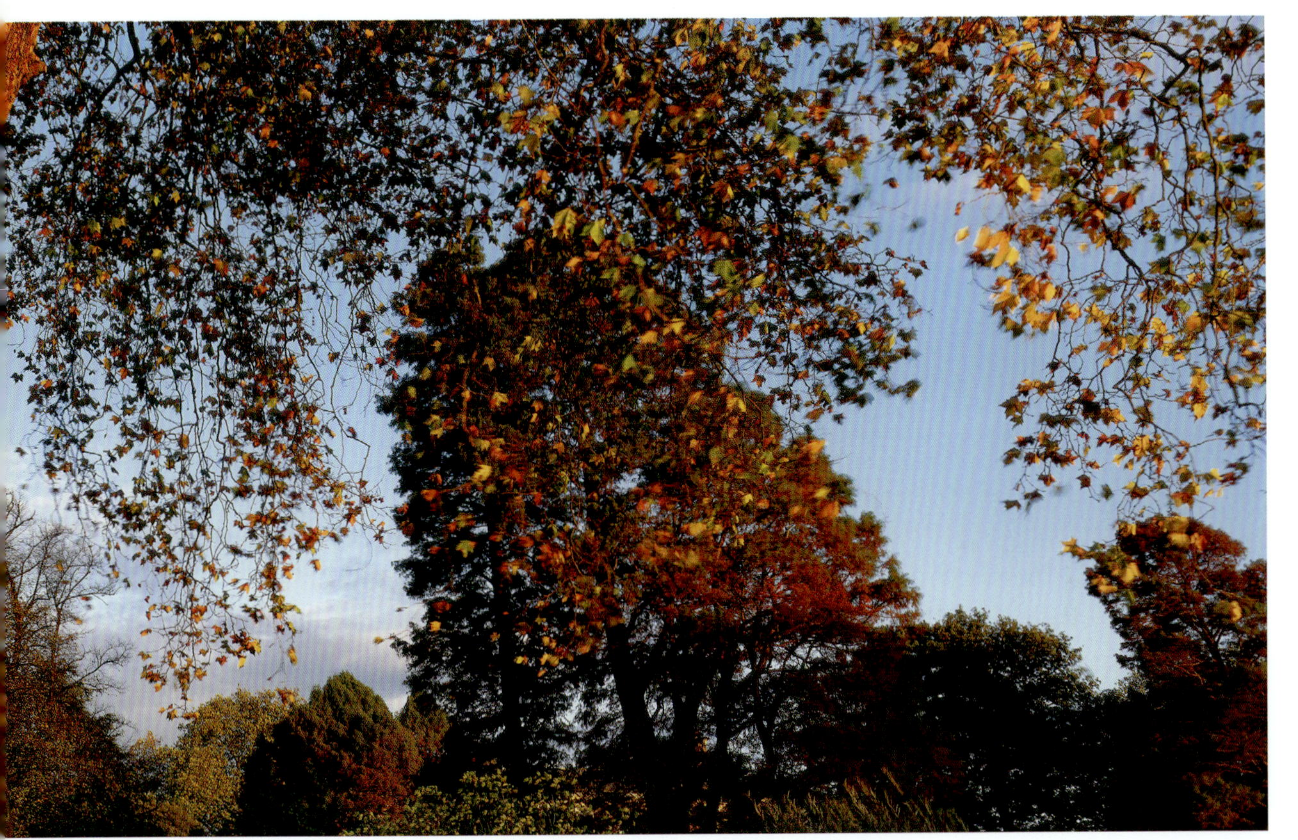

LEAF SHOWER, KEW

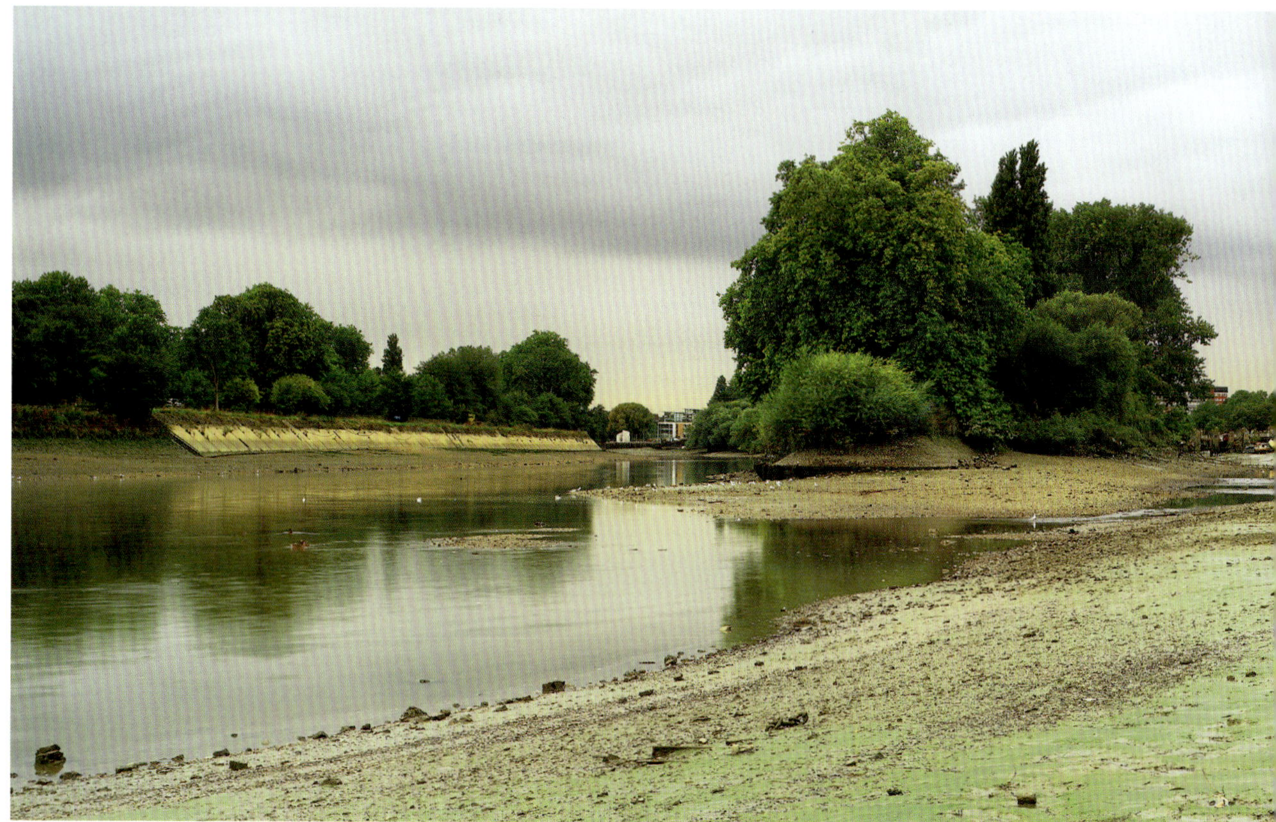

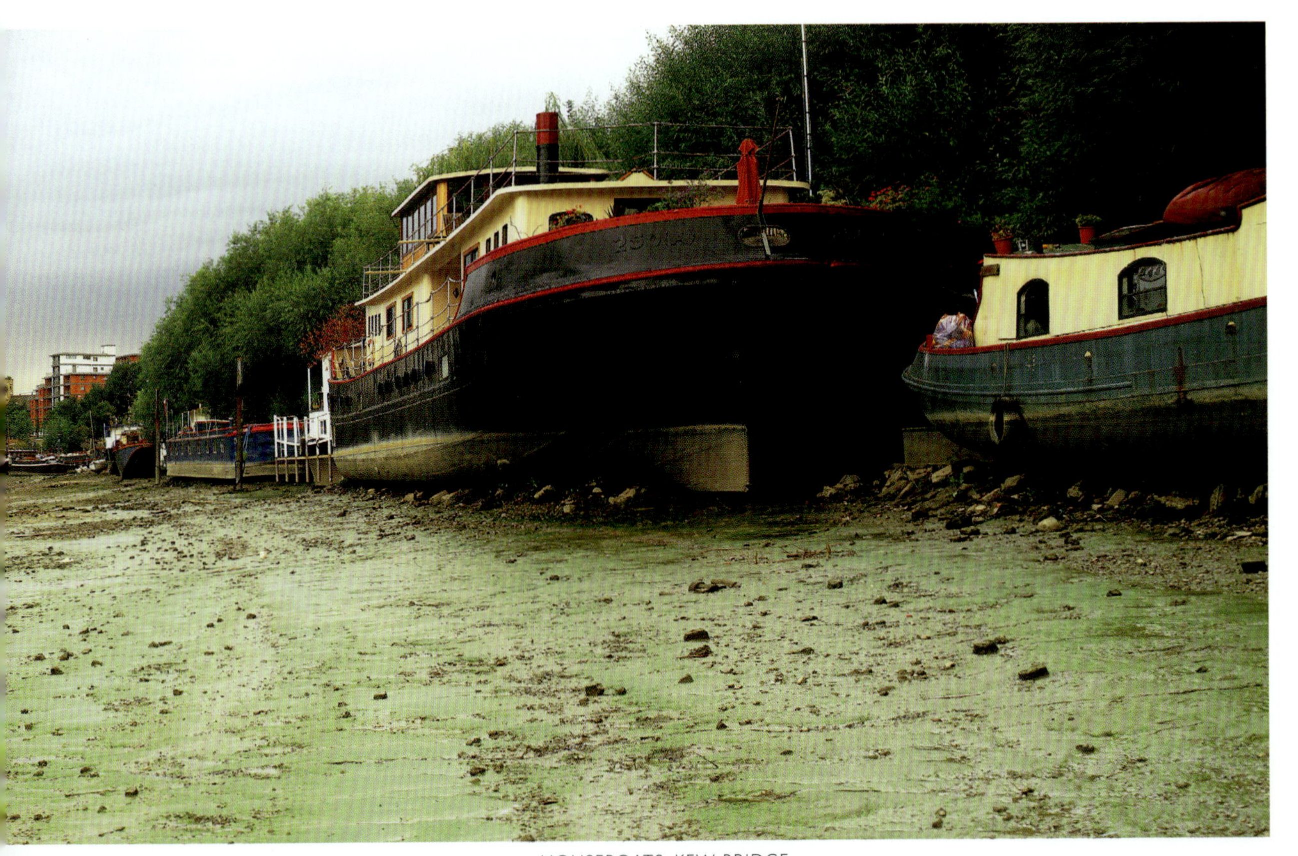

HOUSEBOATS, KEW BRIDGE

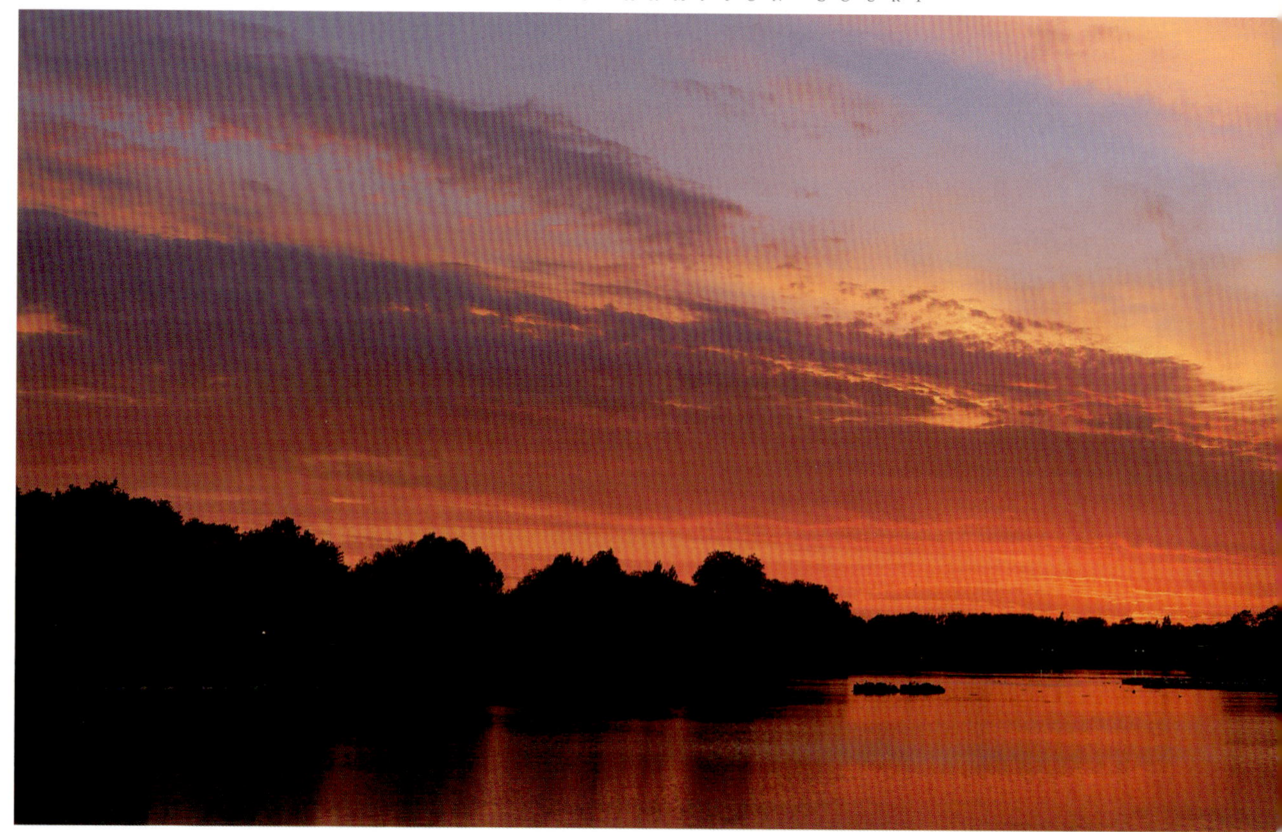

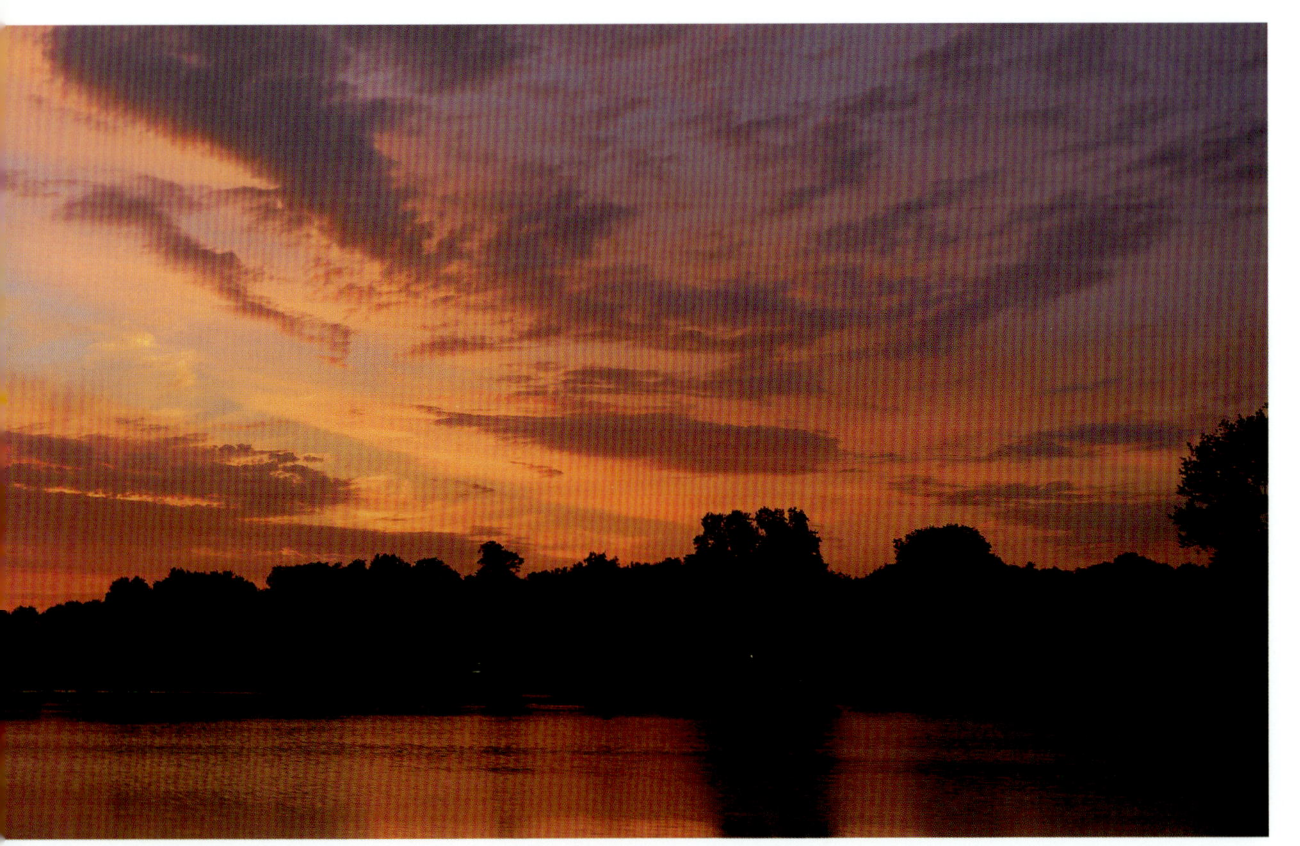

SERPENTINE SUNSET, HYDE PARK

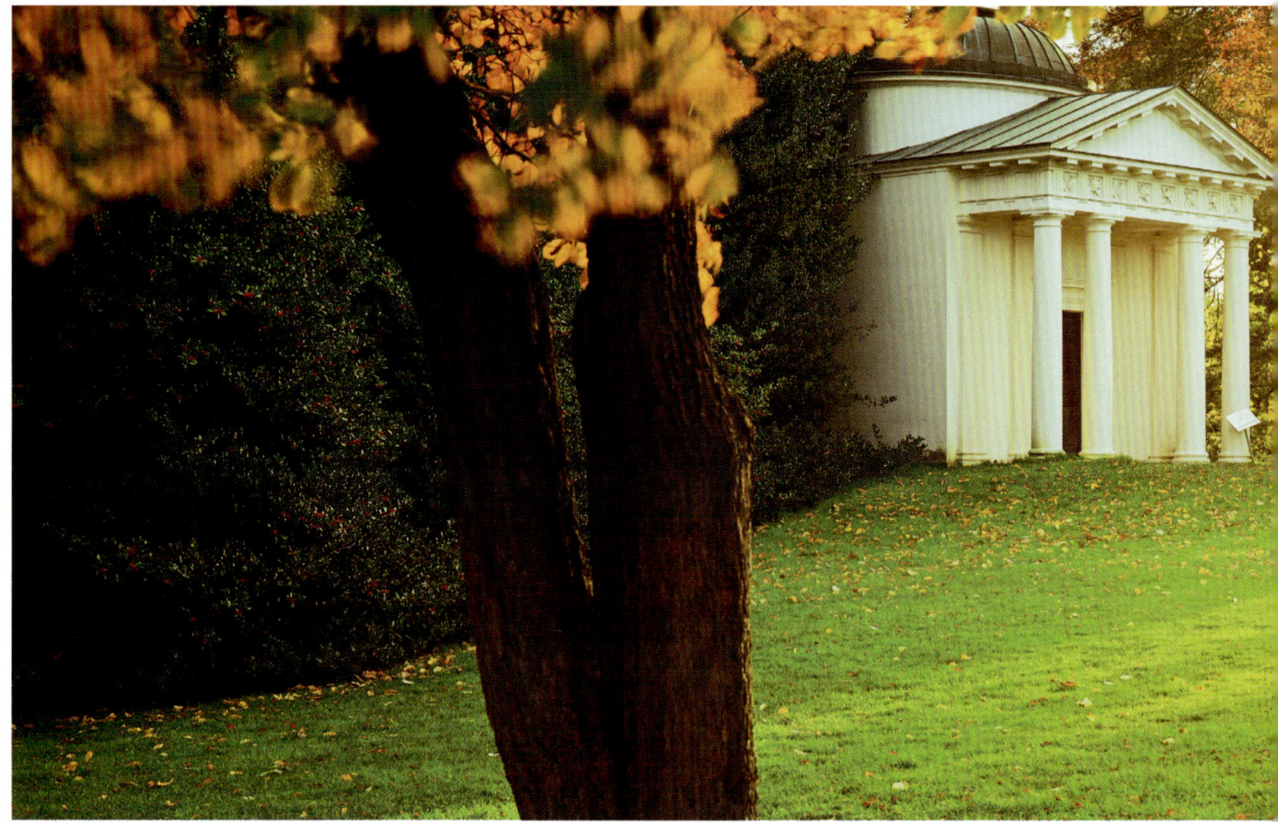

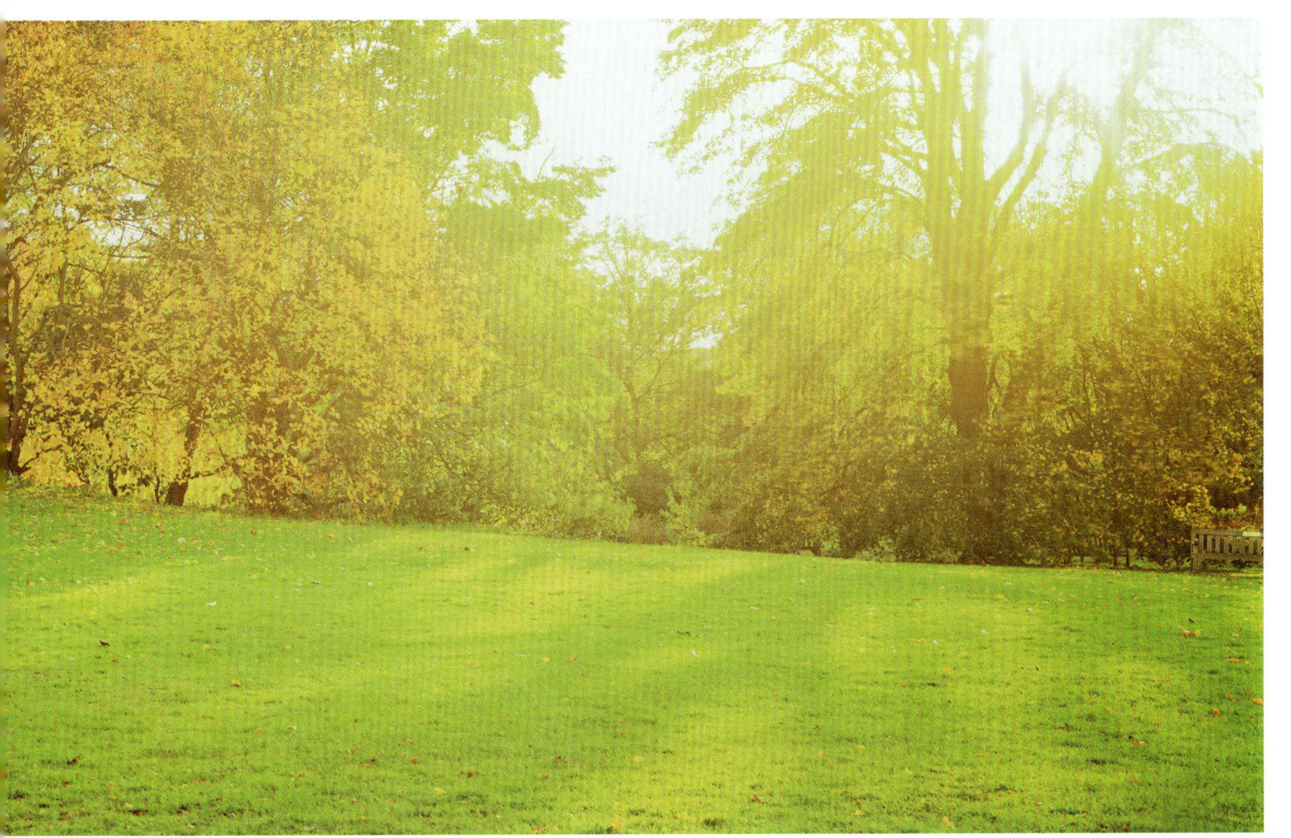

TEMPLE, KEW GARDENS

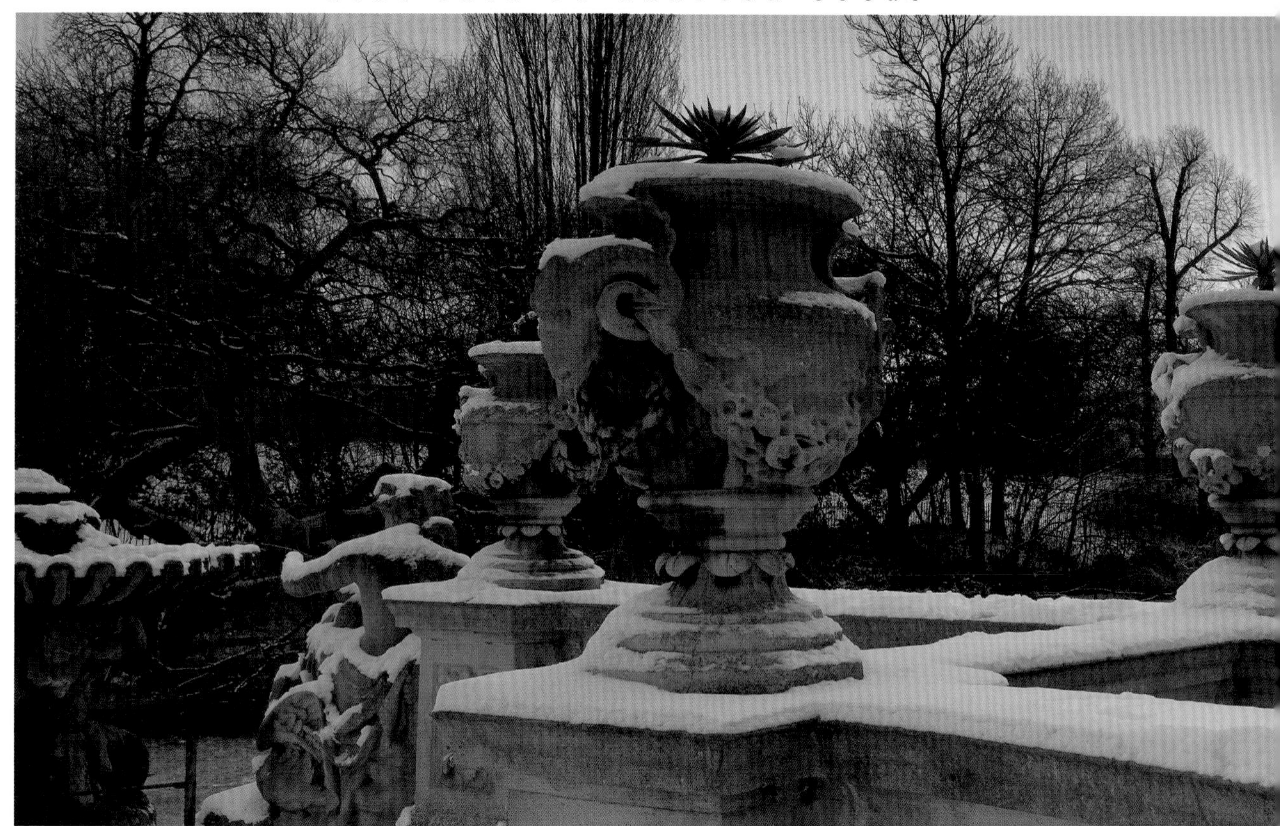

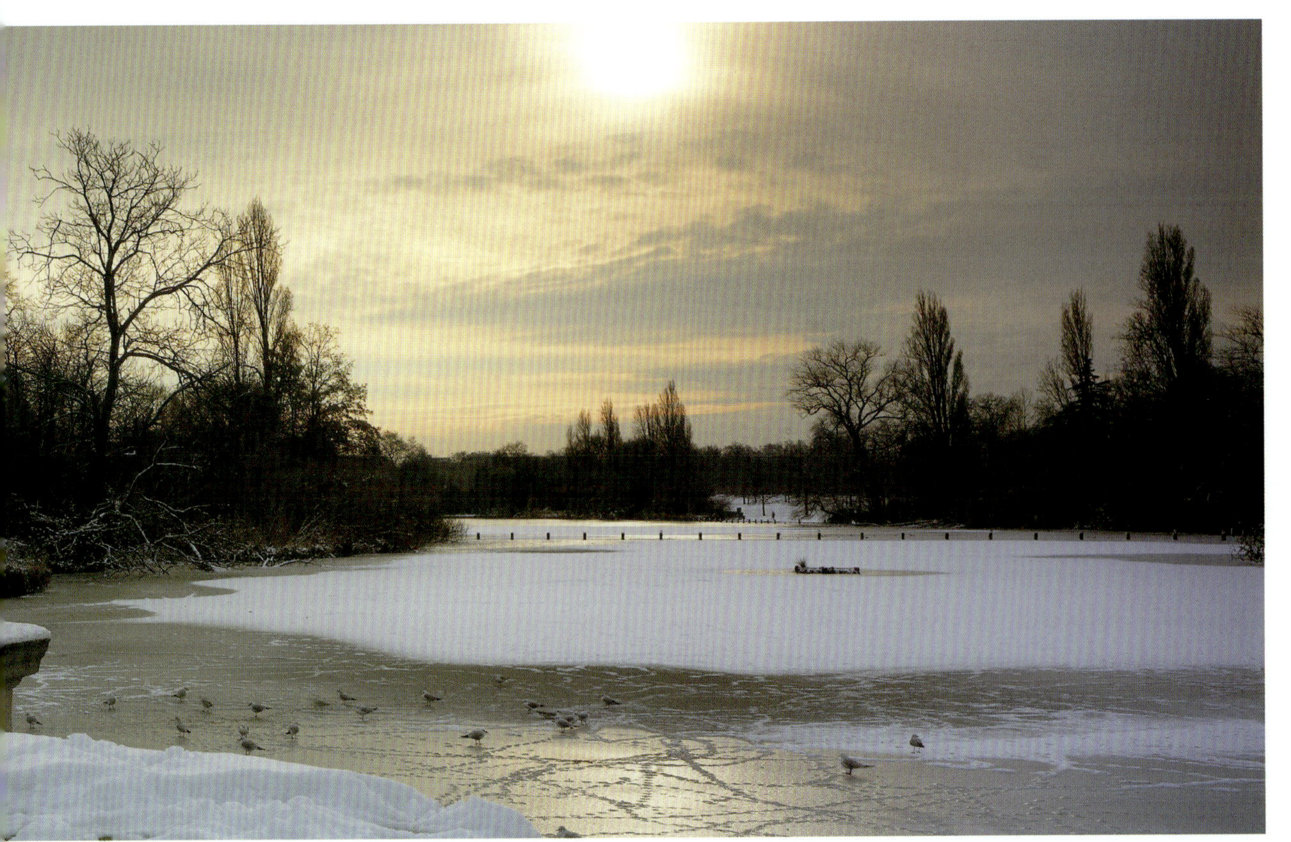

ITALIAN GARDENS, SERPENTINE, HYDE PARK

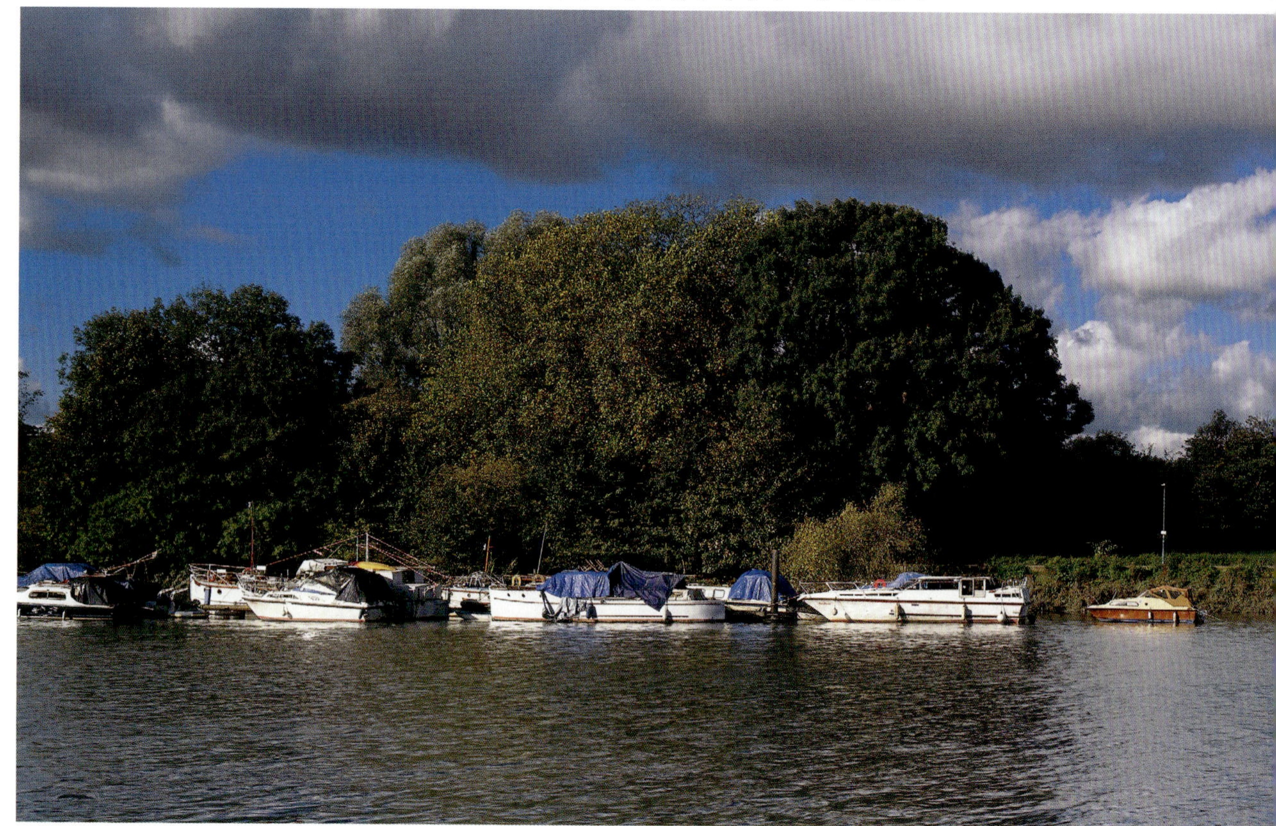

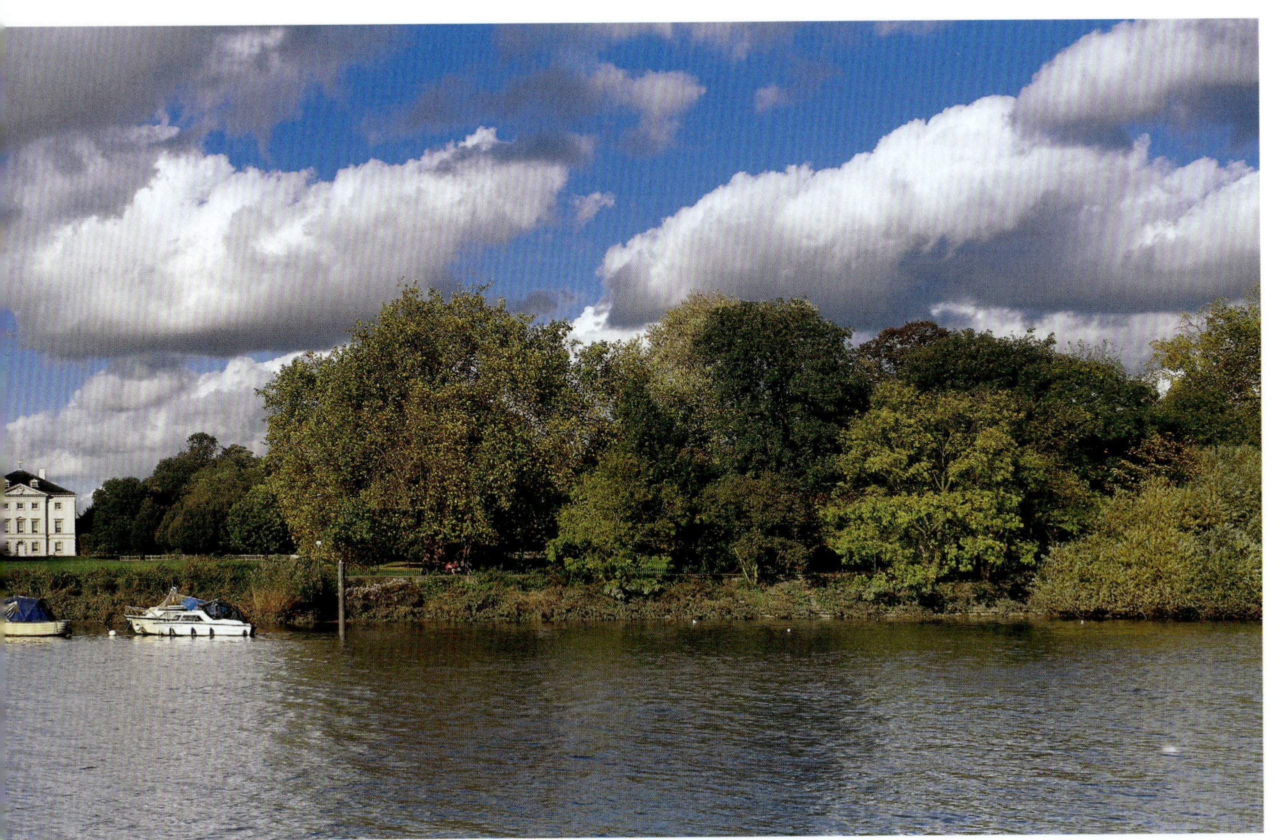

MARBLE HILL HOUSE, RIVER THAMES

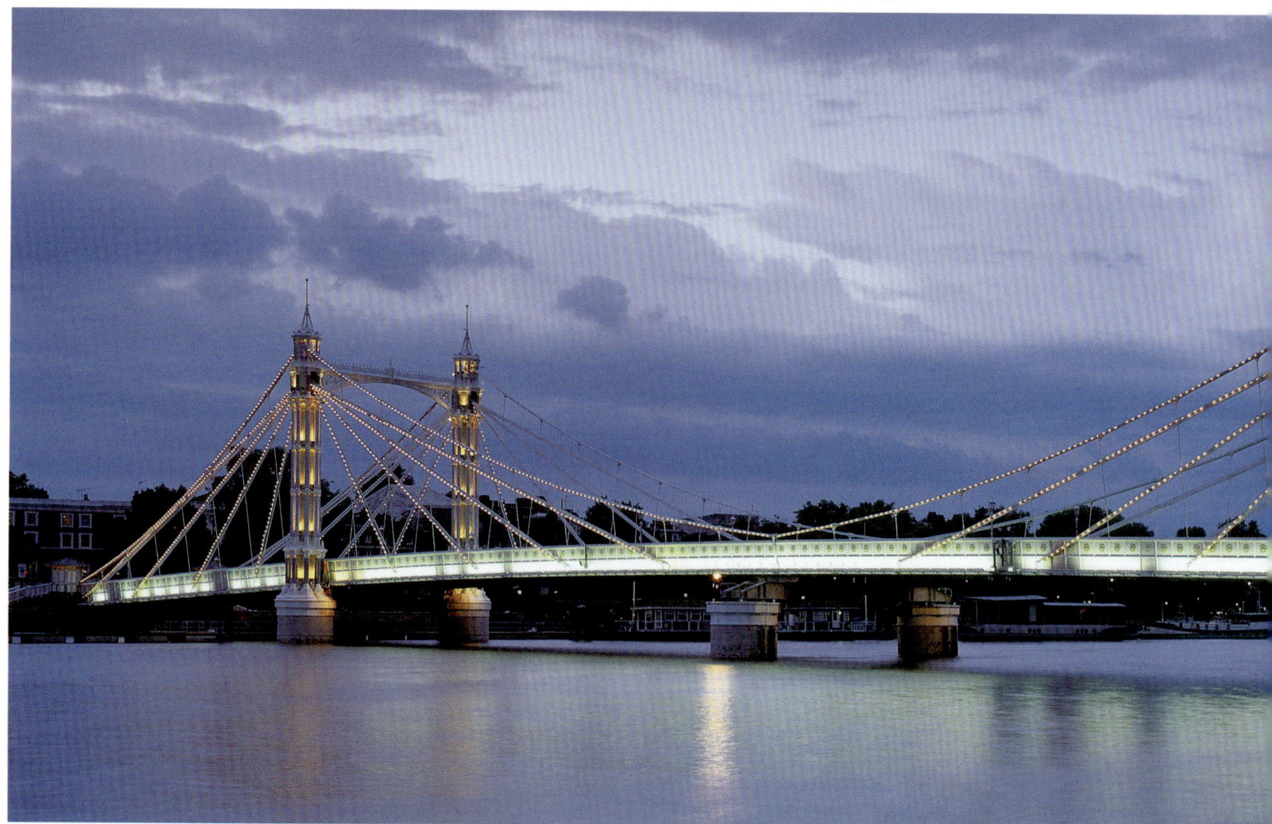

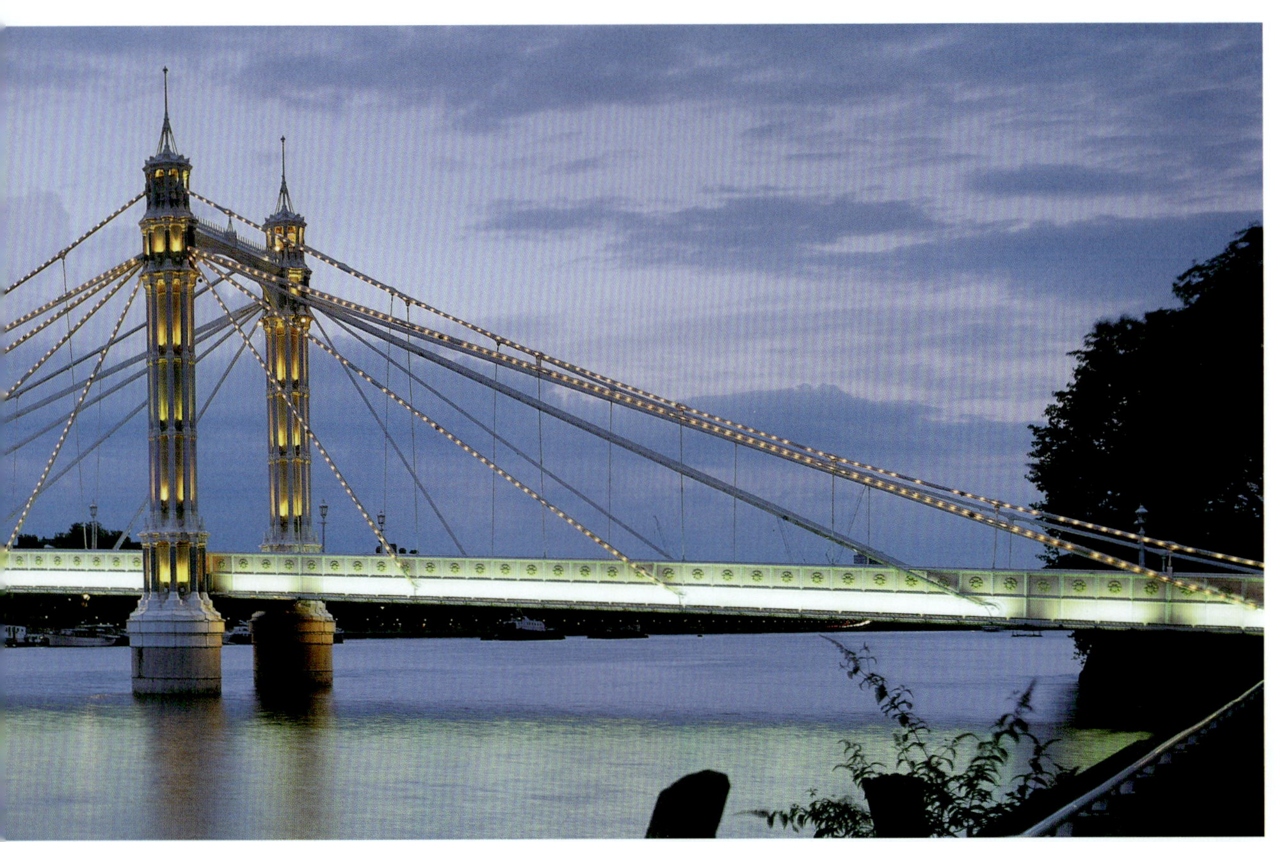

BLUE DUSK, ALBERT BRIDGE

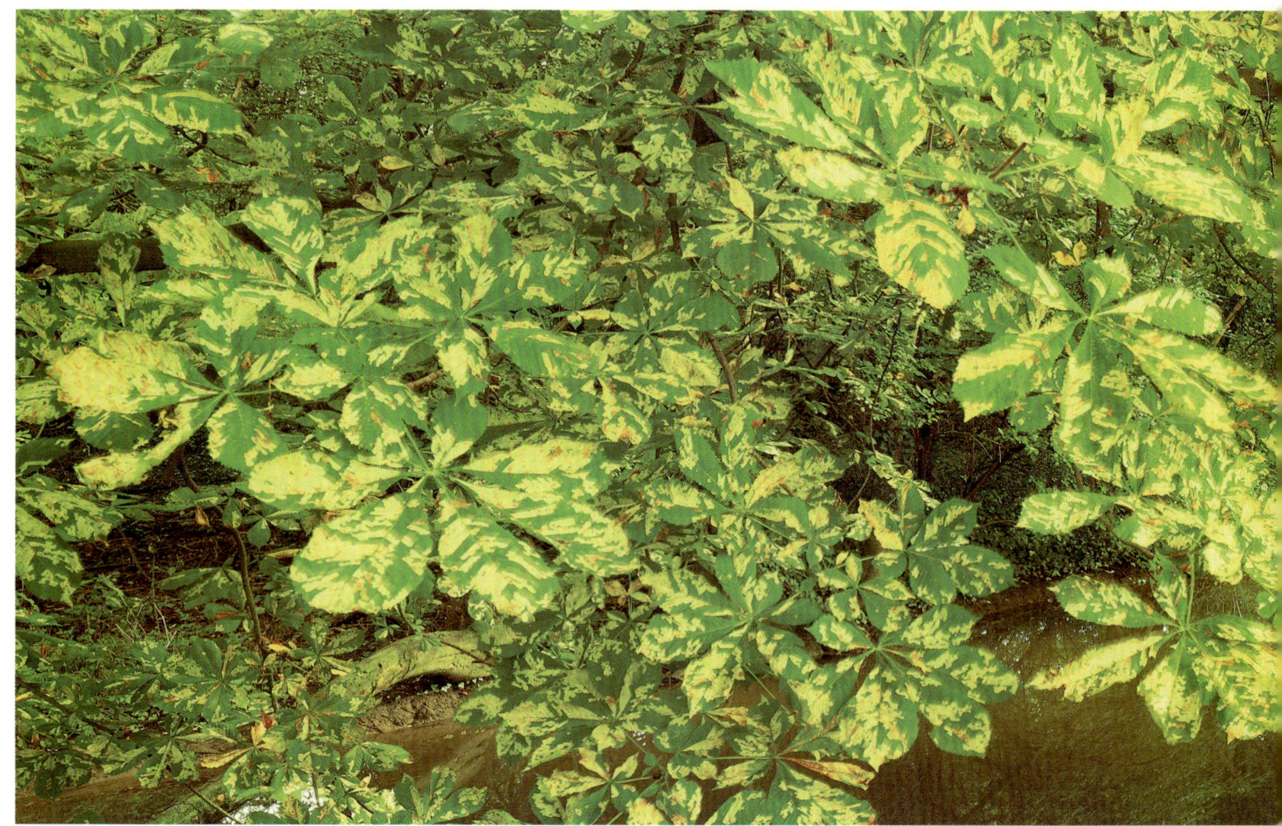

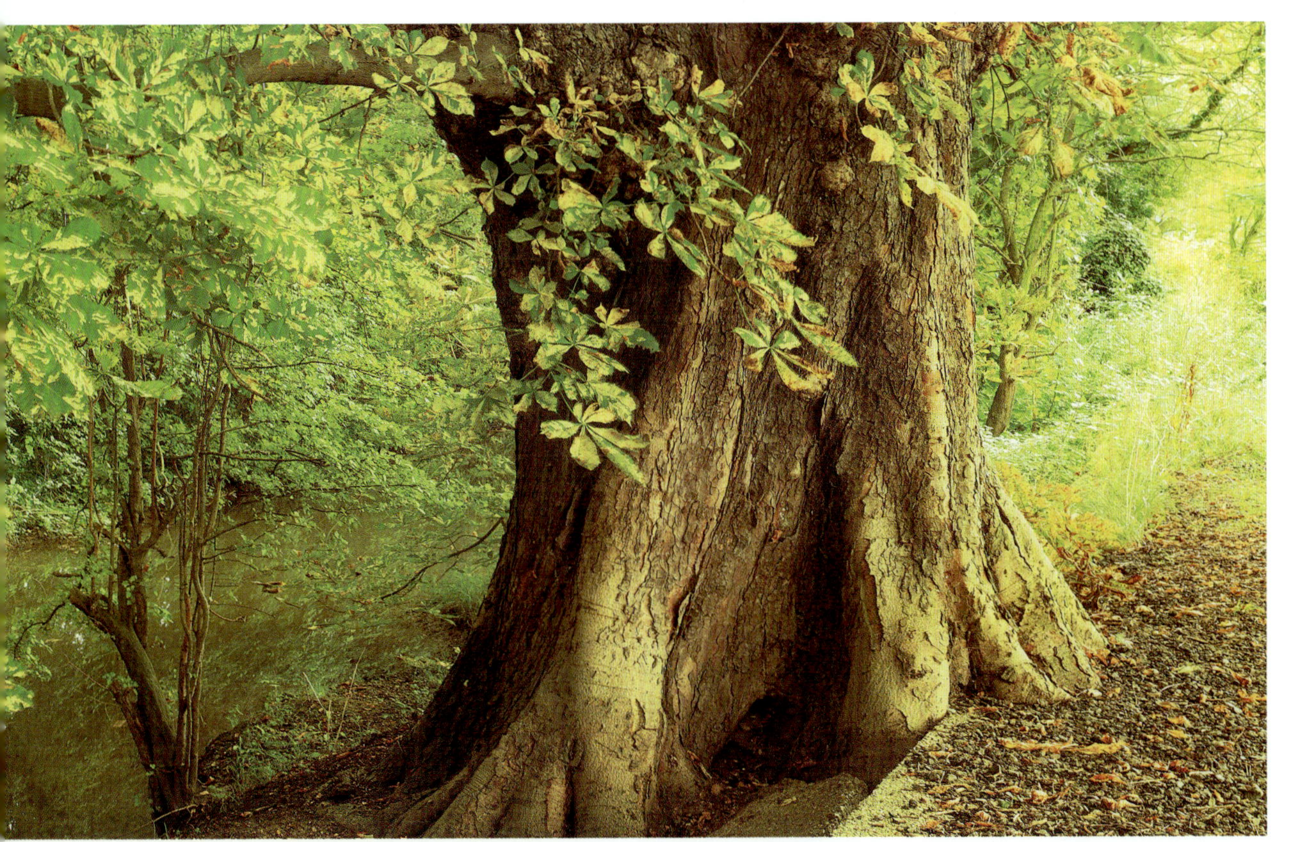

HORSECHESTNUT, THAMES PATH

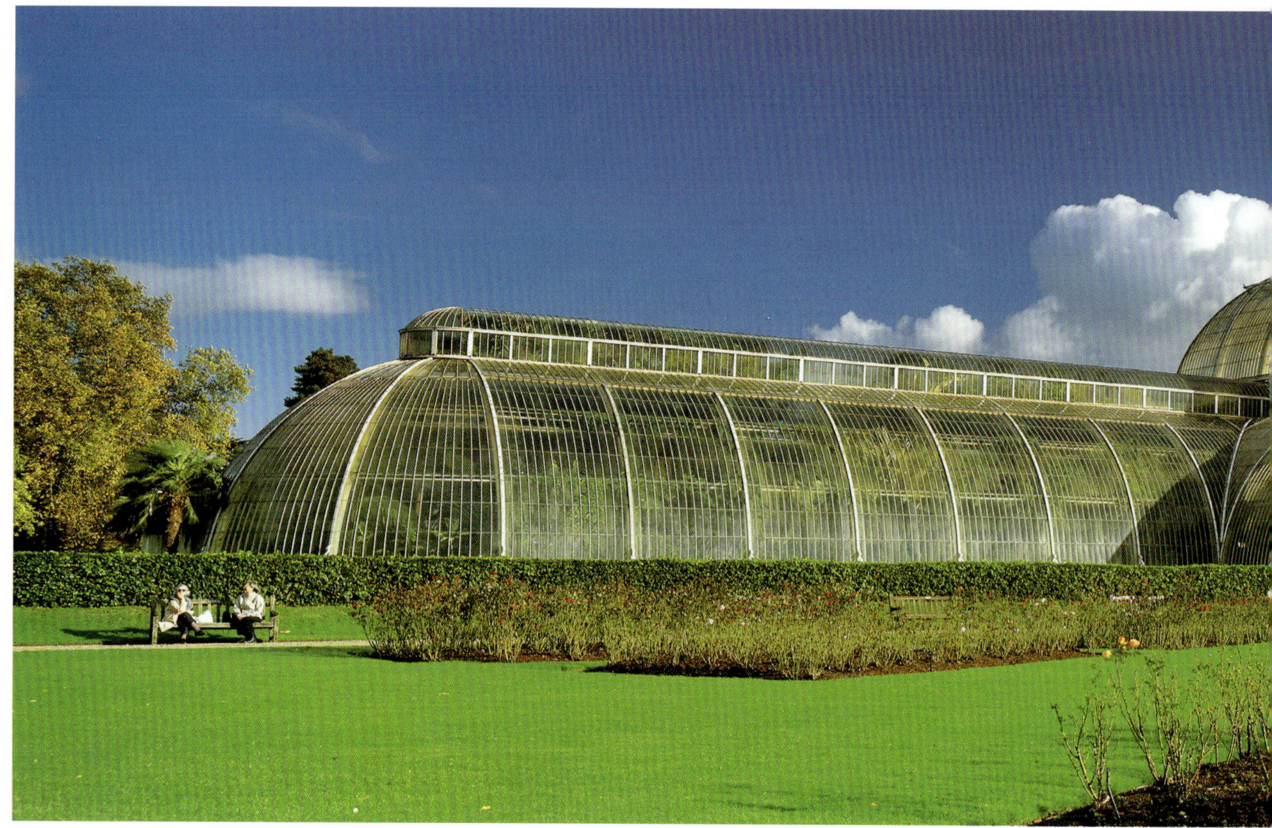

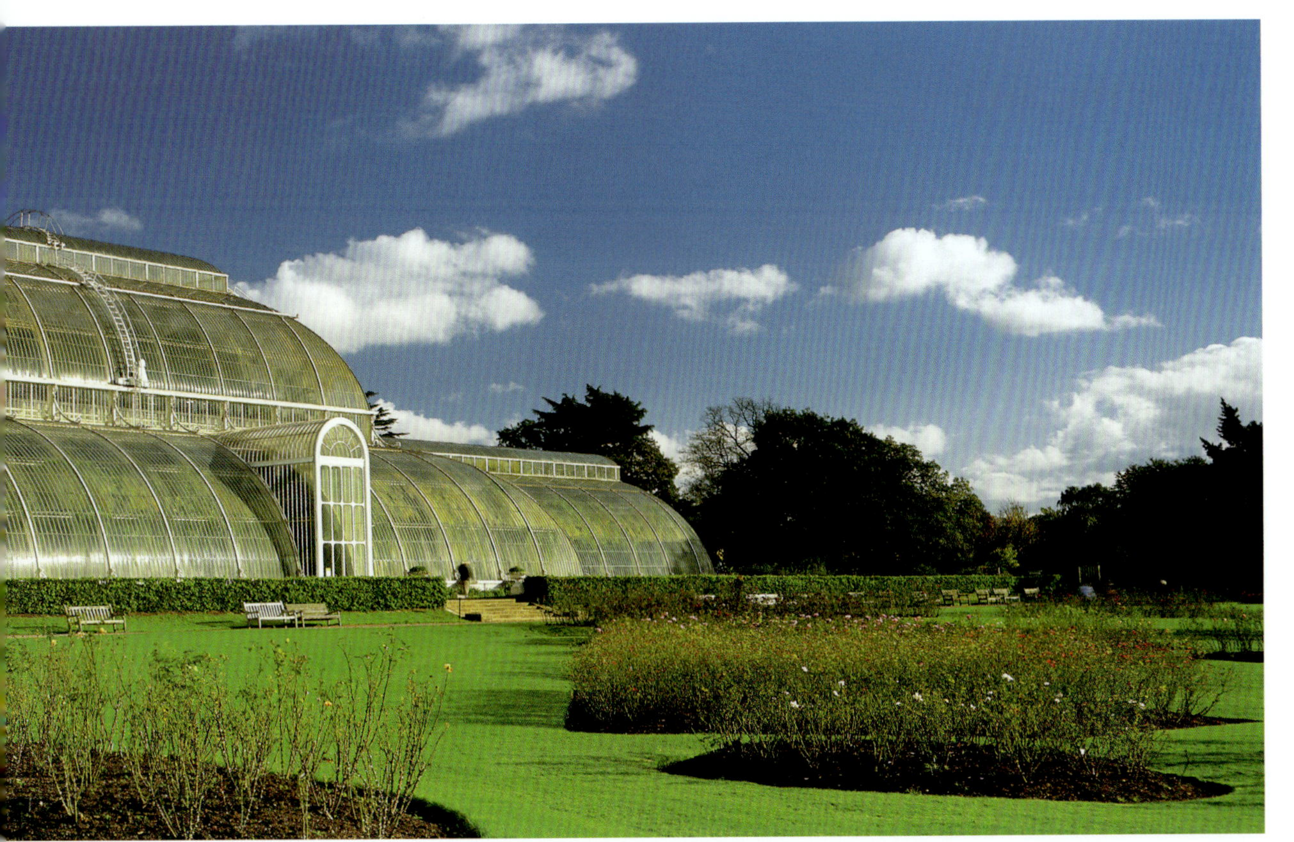

FLUFFY CLOUDS, PALM HOUSE, KEW GARDENS

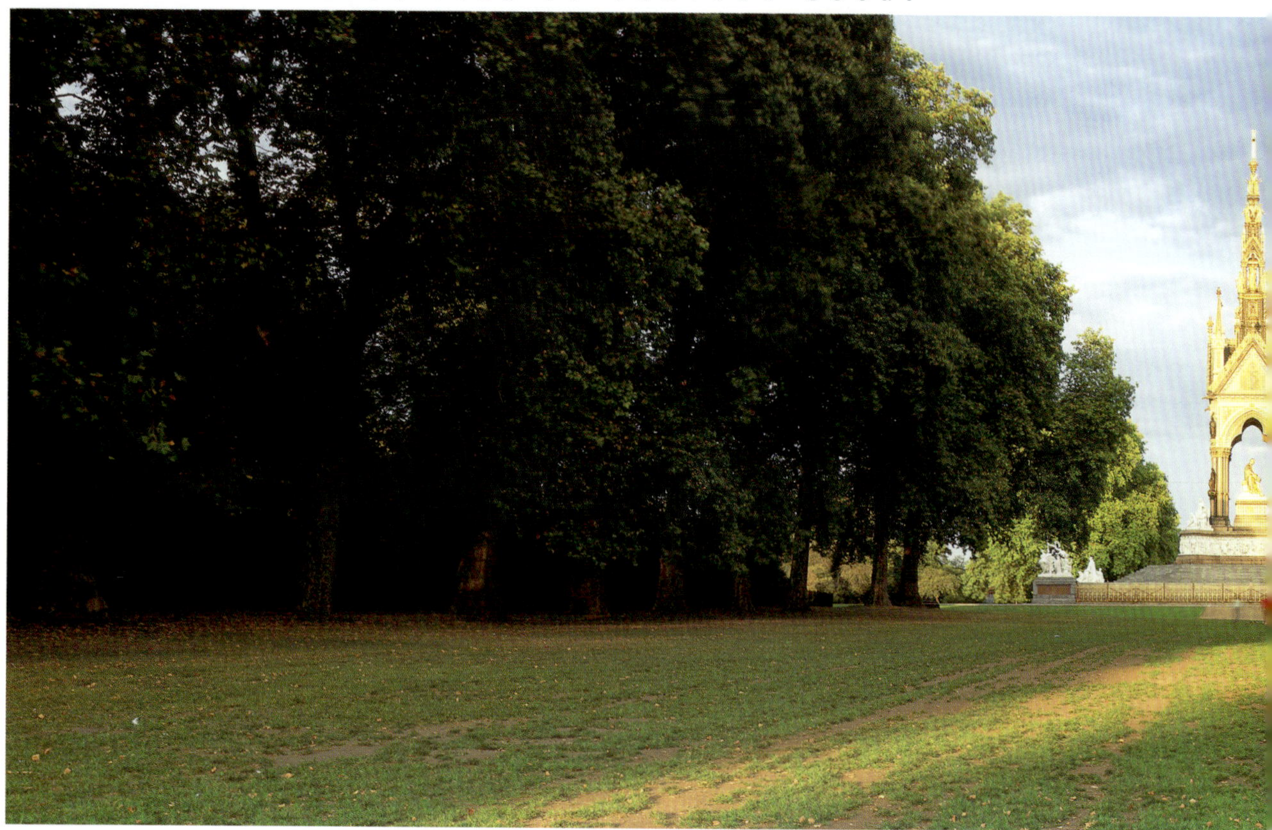

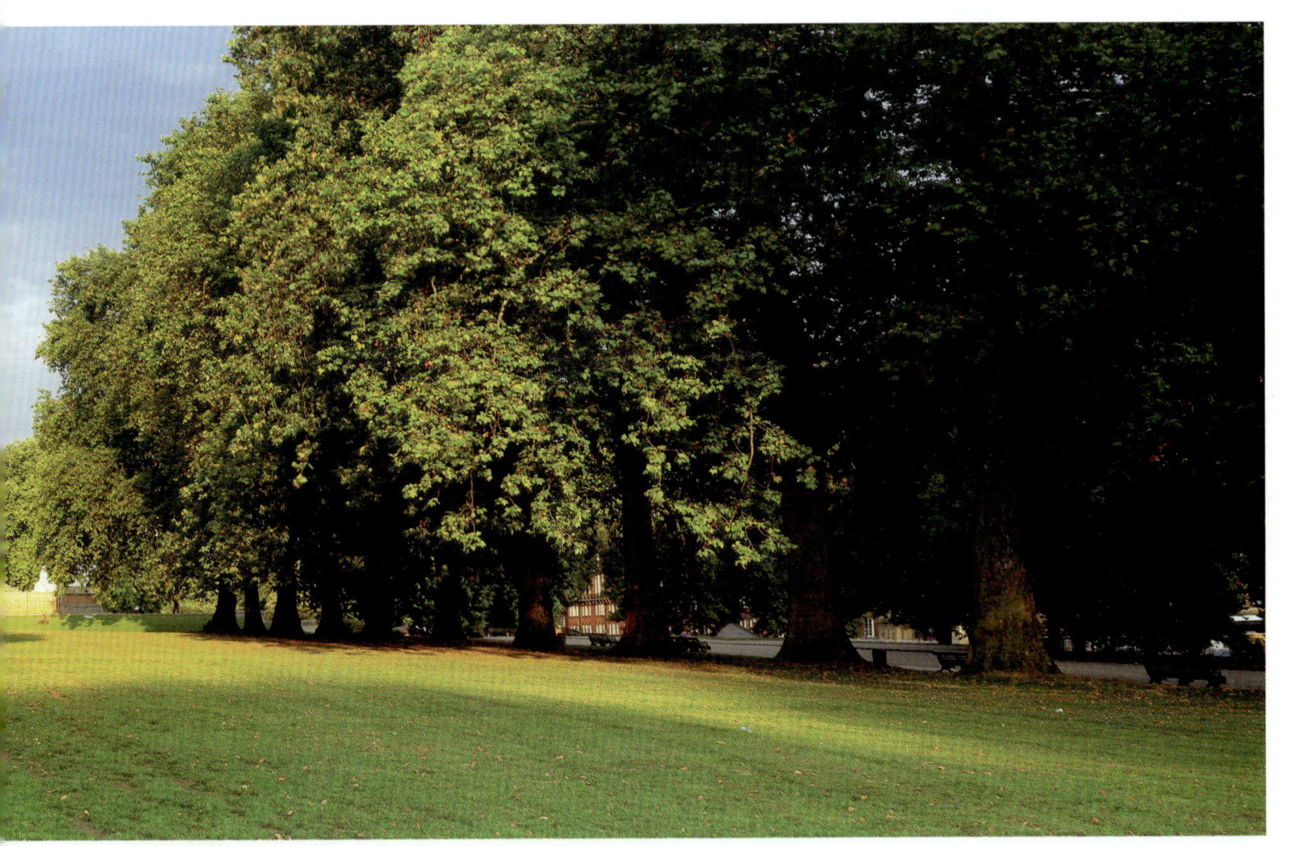

ALBERT MEMORIAL, HYDE PARK

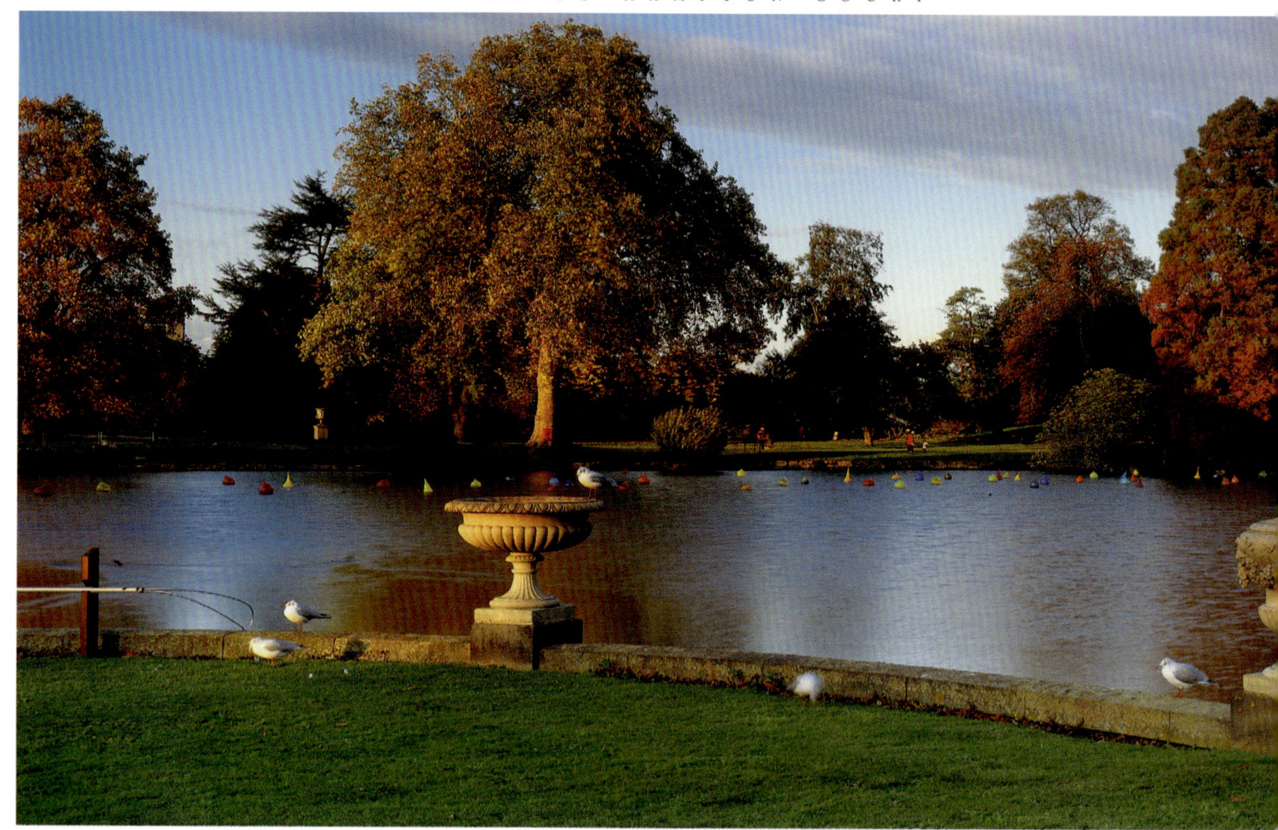

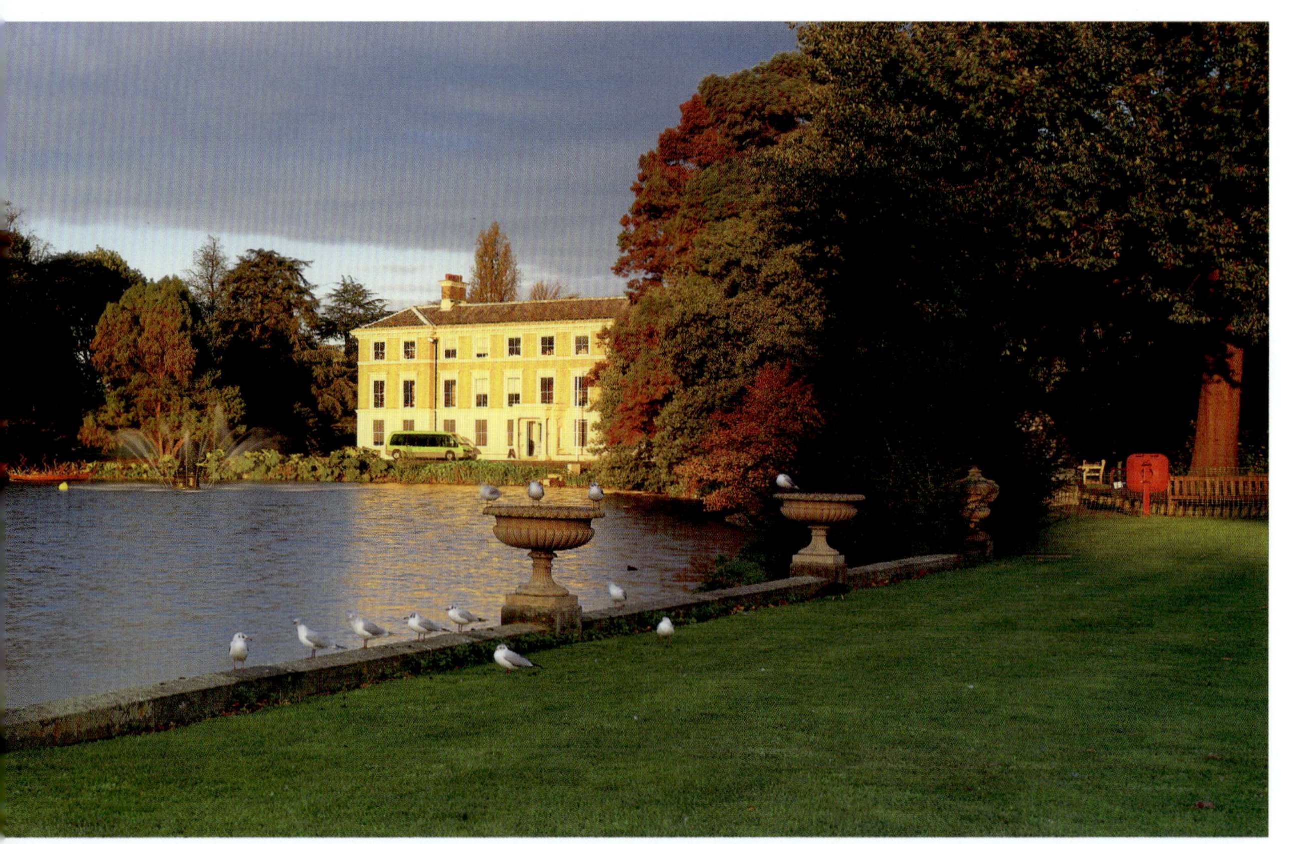

LAKE AT KEW GARDENS

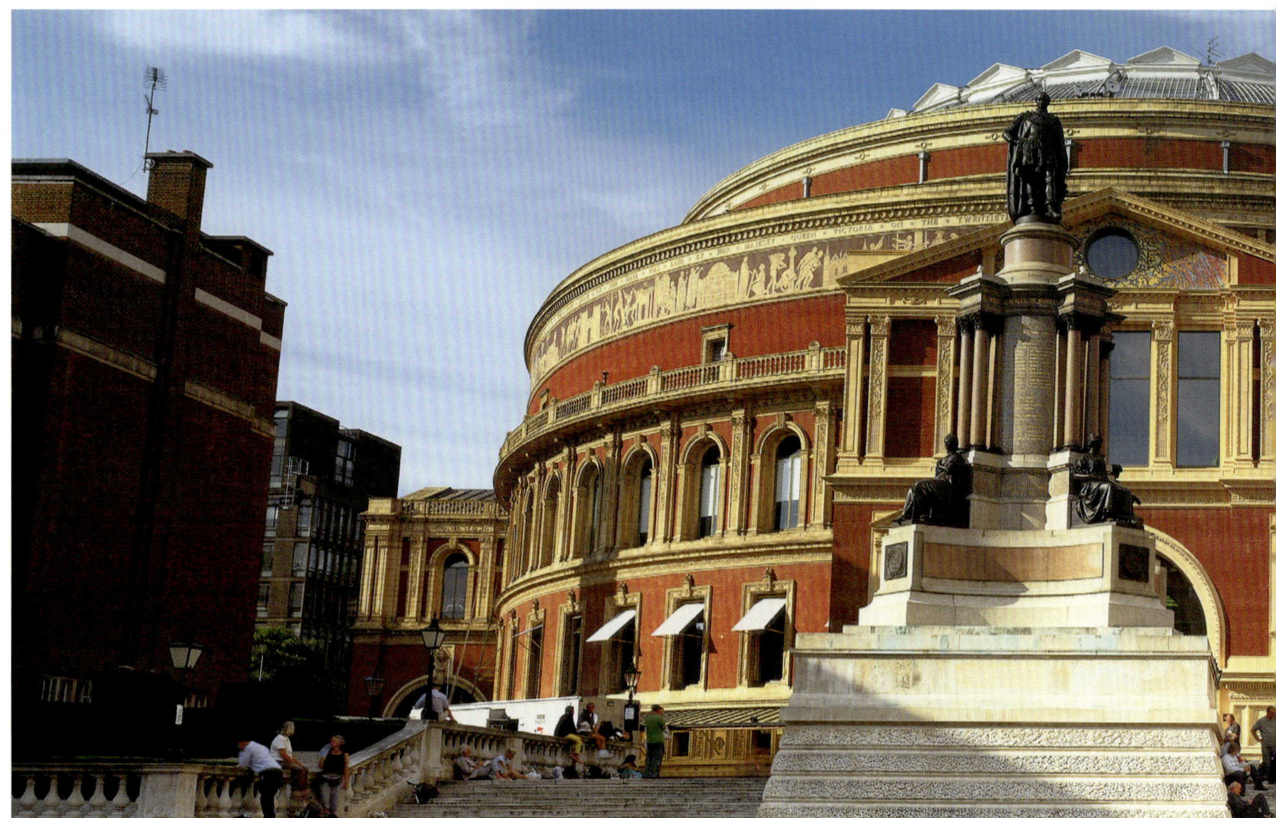
HALL • WAS • LAID • BY • HER • MAJESTY • QUEEN • VICTORIA • ON • THE

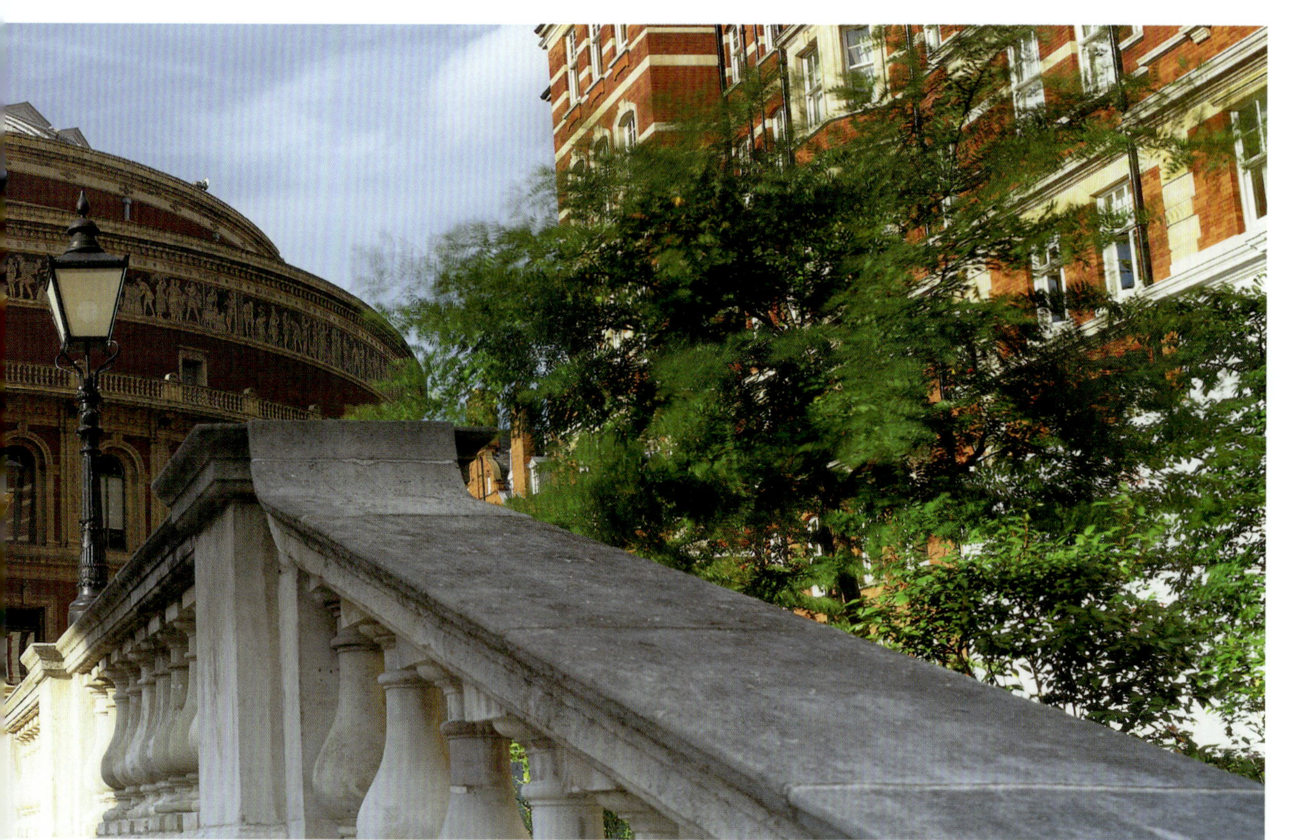

ROYAL ALBERT HALL, AFTERNOON SUN

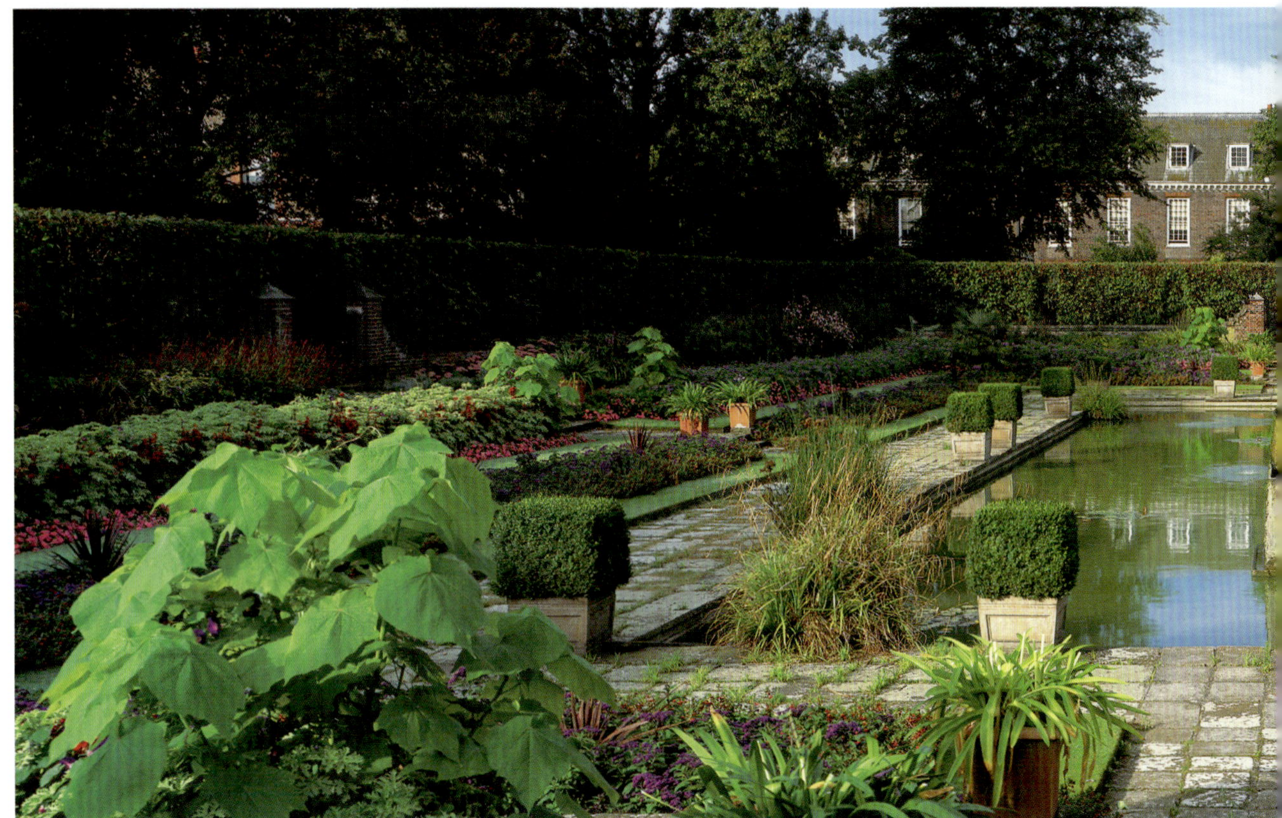

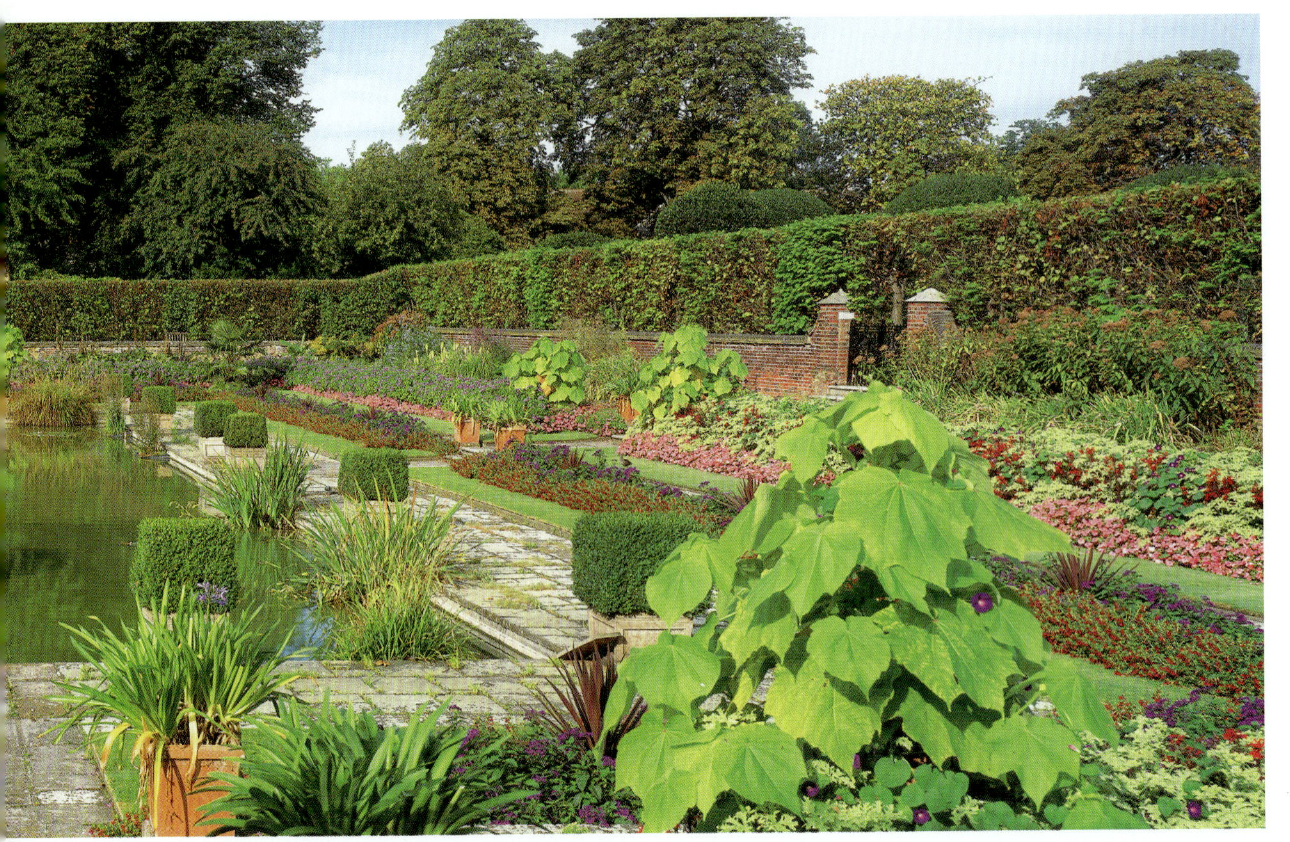

GARDENS, KENSINGTON PALACE

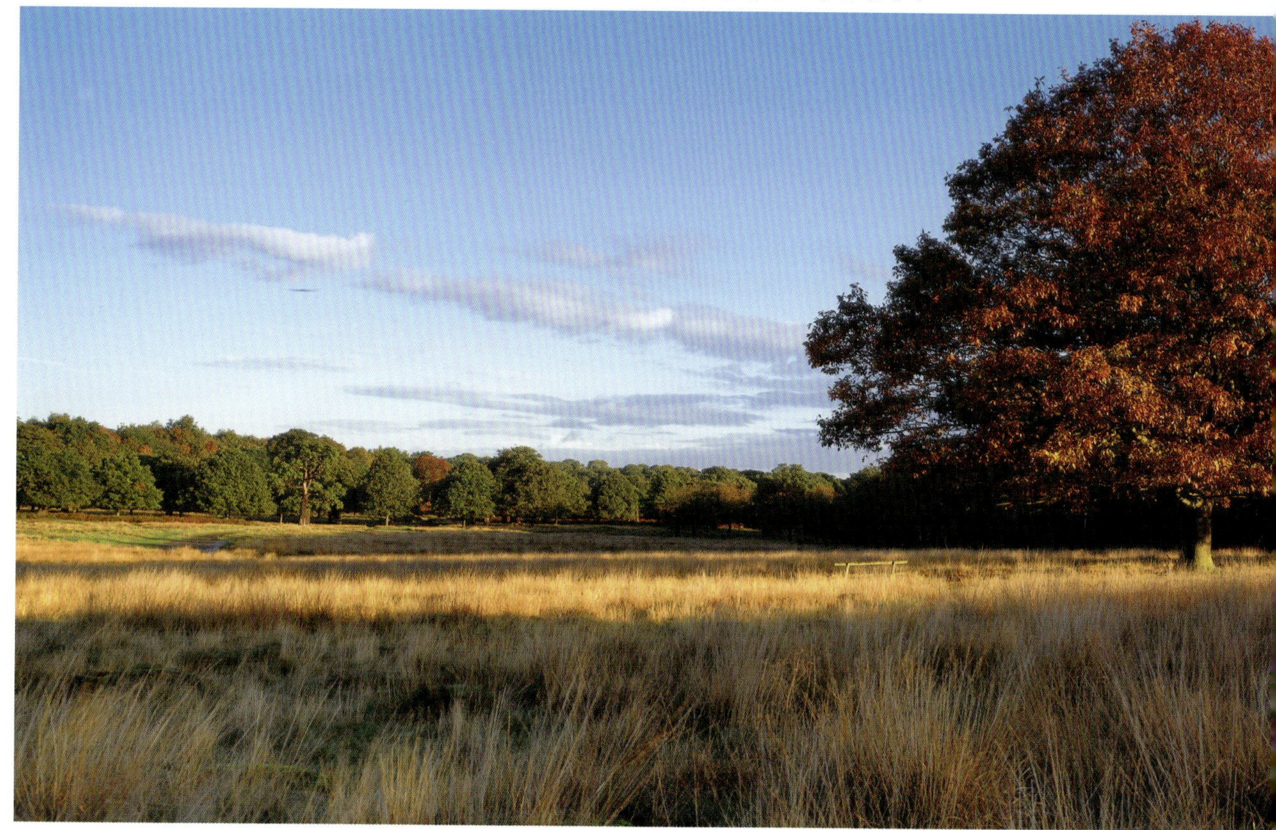

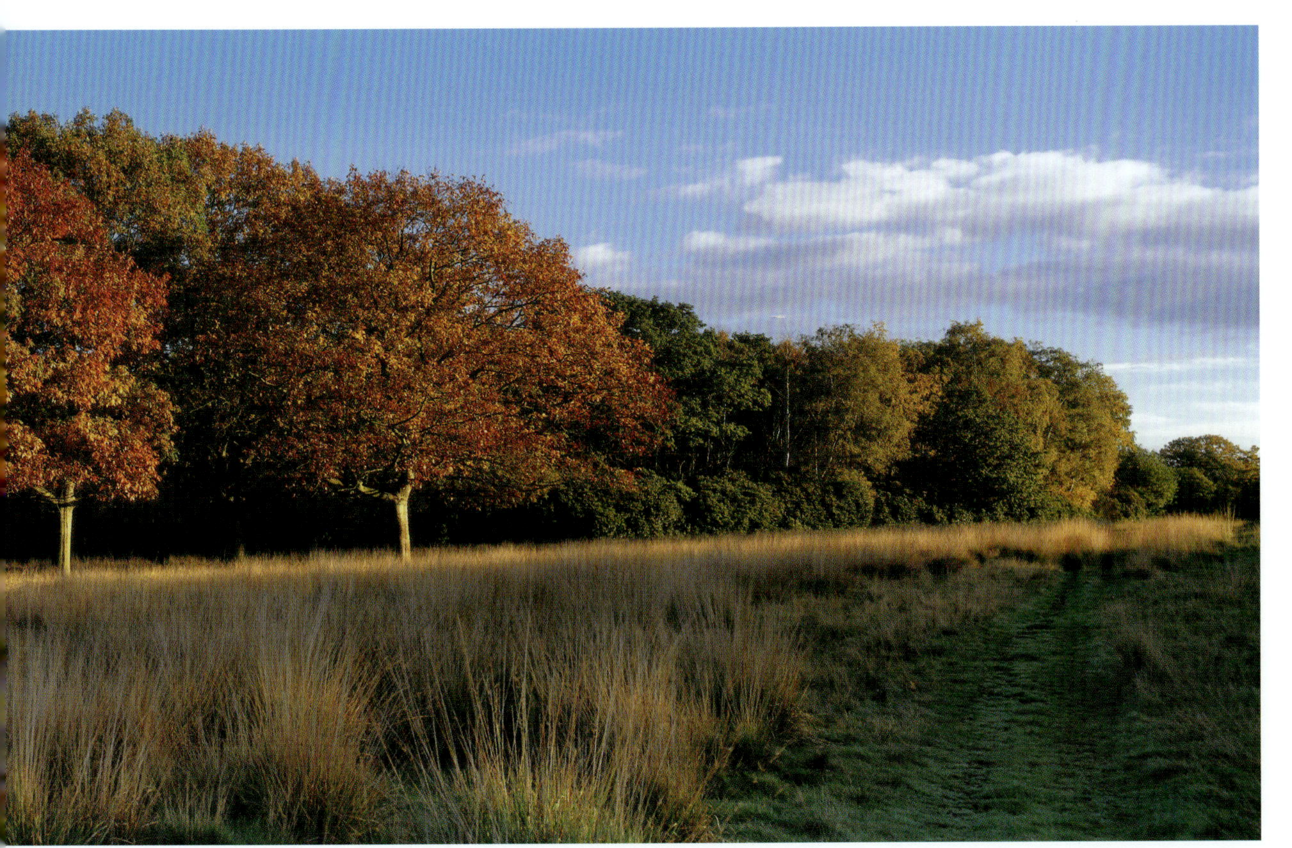

AUTUMN TREES, RICHMOND PARK

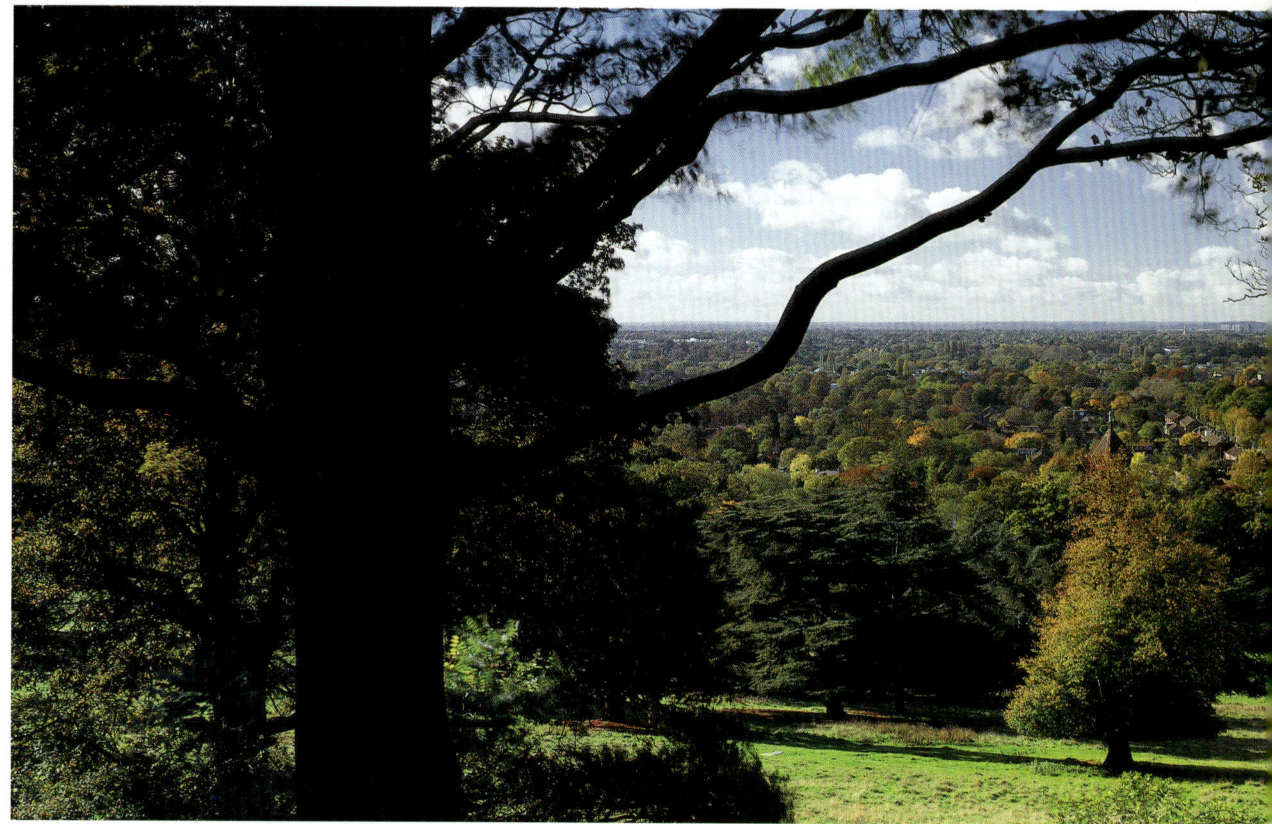

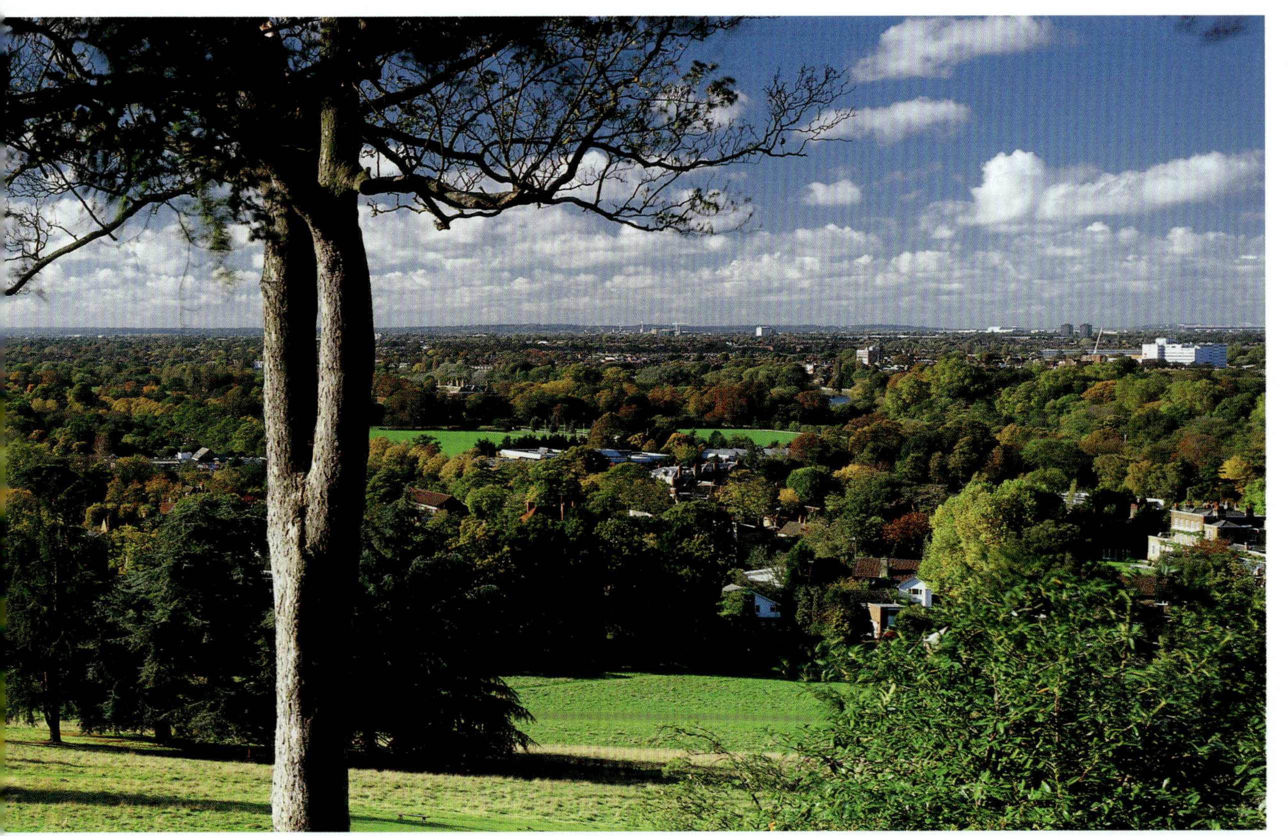

VIEW FROM HENRY VIII'S MOUND, RICHMOND PARK

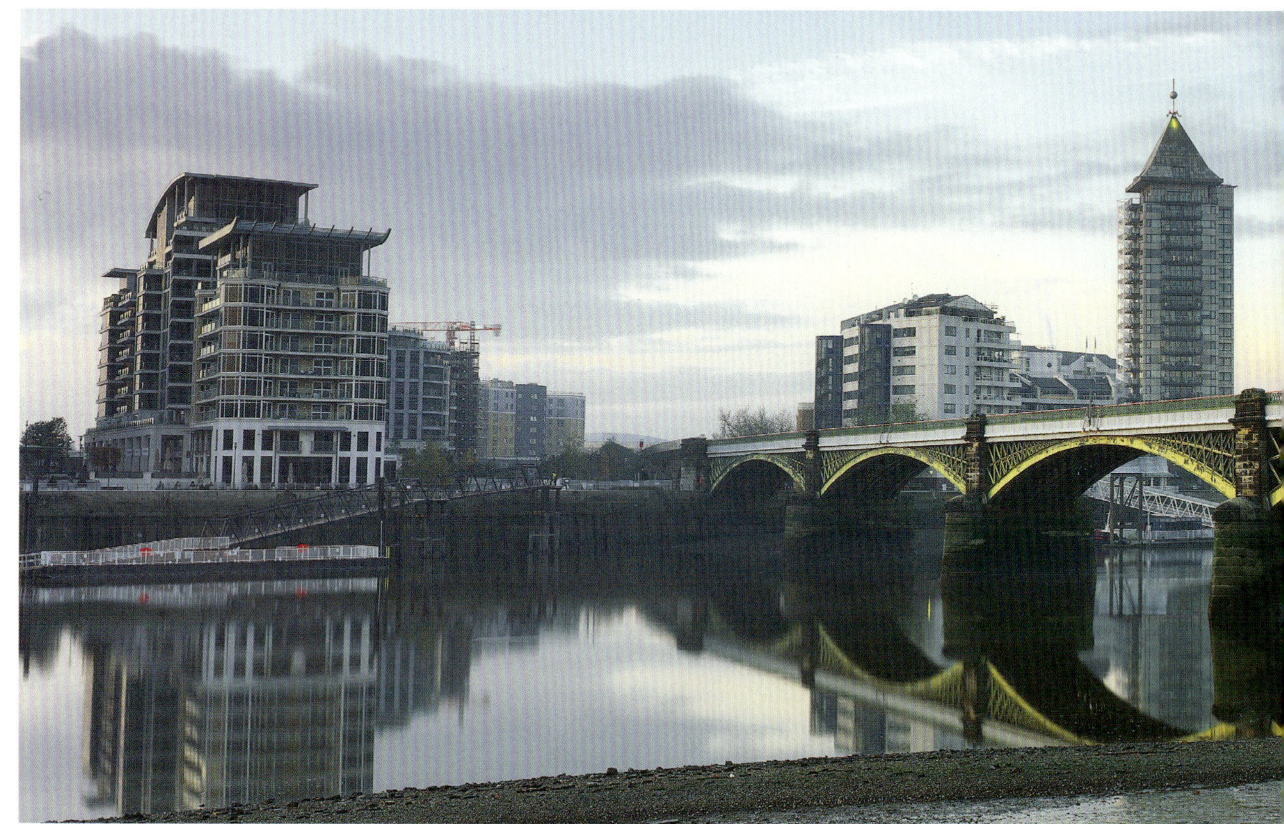

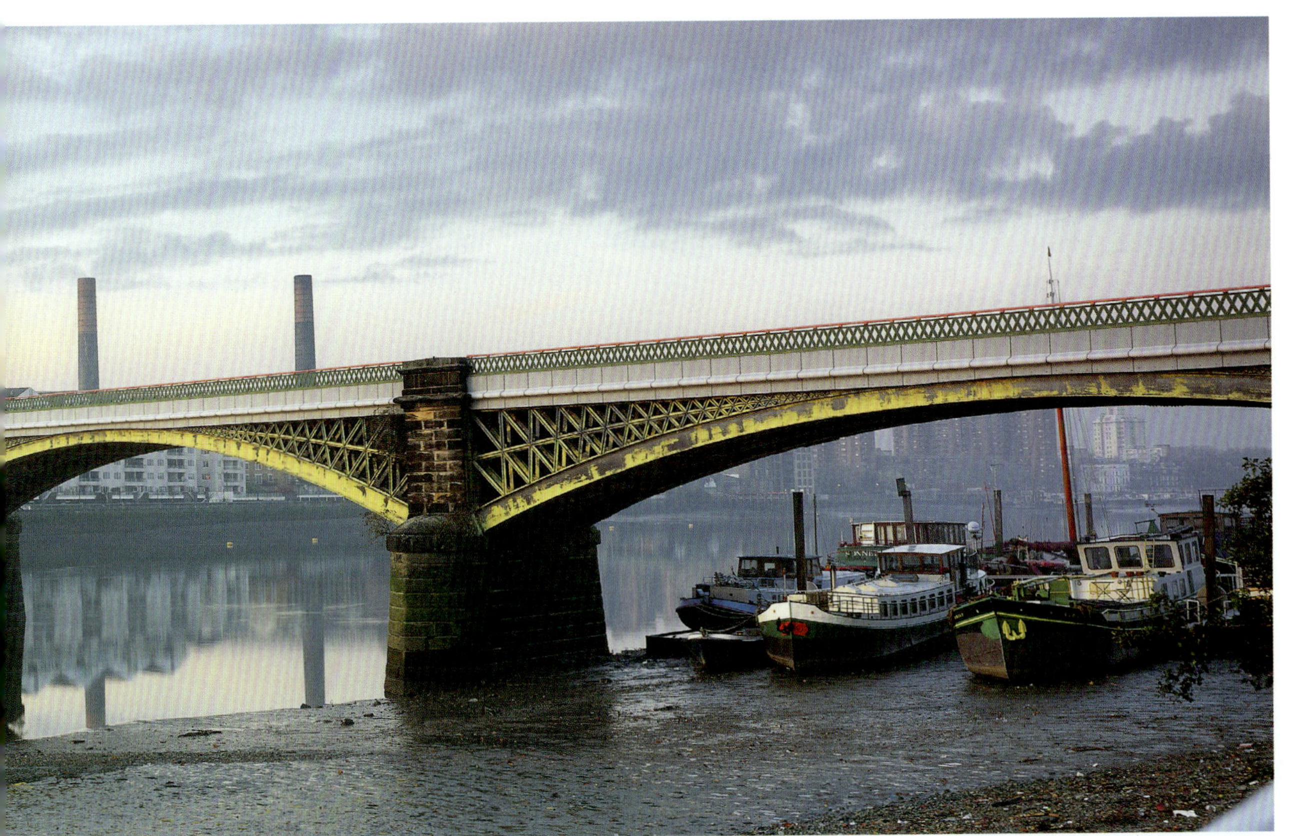

BELVEDERE TOWER, CHELSEA HARBOUR

THE SOUTH BANK

Since London's foundation in Roman times, the Thames has loomed large in the city's daily life – a major thoroughfare as well as the conduit for the maritime trade that brought London prosperity.

The river frontage on the south side puts the north bank to shame. From just east of Westminster Bridge and The Eye is Europe's largest arts complex – the National Theatre, Royal Festival Hall, Queen Elizabeth Hall, Purcell Room, Hayward Gallery and National Film Theatre. Only the Royal Festival Hall survives from the original South Bank complex built in the wake of the 1951 Festival of Britain, and its elegant glass-fronted curves inspire an affection in marked contrast to attitudes towards the grey concrete 'Brutalist' style of the other buildings that followed in the 1960s.

Moving east, Coin Street and the Oxo Tower offers a mix of design shops and restaurants. Historic ships punctuate the walk along the south bank. A reconstruction of Sir Francis Drake's Tudor flagship the *Golden Hinde* sits in a tiny dock near St Mary Overie church. On the other side of London Bridge, HMS *Belfast* is a huge sleek memento of Britain's Second World War navy, playing a key role in the destruction of the German battleship *Scharnhorst* as well as in the Normandy landings.

Between the two ships, Borough Market is a colourful rendezvous (best on Friday and Saturday mornings) for anyone in search of good food or people-watching from the market's neighbouring cafés and restaurants.

Keep on, past a mix of old housing and rusting riverbank mementoes of London's heritage, and the soaring masts of the *Cutty Sark* loom above Greenwich. Launched in 1869, this beautiful ship was one of the fastest sailing vessels ever built, speeding tea from China and wool from Australia to London in record times until retired in 1922. In 2007 it was devastated by fire, but is due to re-open in 2012, after extensive renovation. The nearby Royal Naval College is one of the finest buildings in London, built on the site of the Tudor palace where Henry VIII was born by two of Britain's finest architects, Sir Christopher Wren and his pupil Nicholas Hawkmoor.

Rising behind the College, Greenwich Park offers superb views of the city. Landscaped in 1662 by the designer of the legendary gardens at Versailles, the park boasts several historic buildings – the National Maritime Museum, the Ranger's House (with its fine collection of musical instruments) and the Queen's House, built for the wife of James I. The Greenwich Observatory, meanwhile, is the place from which the world's time (Greenwich Meantime) is measured. This is the place where, by standing astride the meridian line, visitors can say they have a foot in two different hemispheres.

Blackheath, to the south of Greenwich, is one of London's most historic open spaces – a rallying point in 1381 when Wat Tyler's peasant army almost overthrew the king, and the place where Henry V was greeted on his return from the famous victory at Agincourt in 1415. Bordered by the pretty streets of Blackheath Village, the heath is now a rival to Parliament Hill in north London as the city's kite-flying mecca.

Dinosaurs stalk the undergrowth as you sweep through south-east London to Crystal Palace Park. These full-sized stone models were created during the nineteenth century by Benjamin Watkins, a testament to the Victorian obsession with paleontology as well as a complement to the Crystal Palace that was moved here from Hyde Park (and which later burned down in 1936). The park is also home to one of London's few mazes.

A westward arc brings us back to the river via Battersea – home to Britain's most famous dog sanctuary – a pleasant Victorian park whose Pagoda is one of the more unusual landmarks on the Thames, and Battersea Power Station. Its quartet of giant chimneys make the power station one of London's most recognisable buildings (even more so after it featured on the cover of Pink Floyd's *Animals* album).

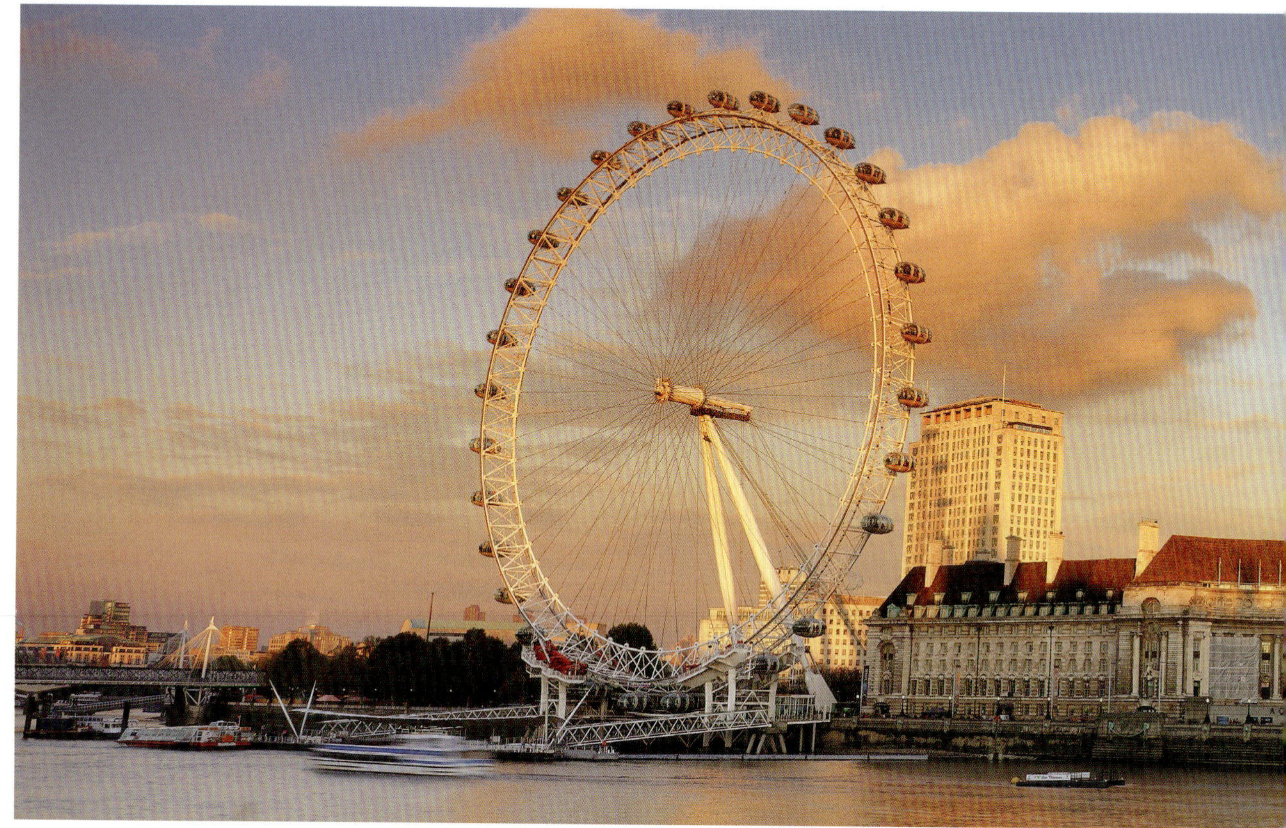

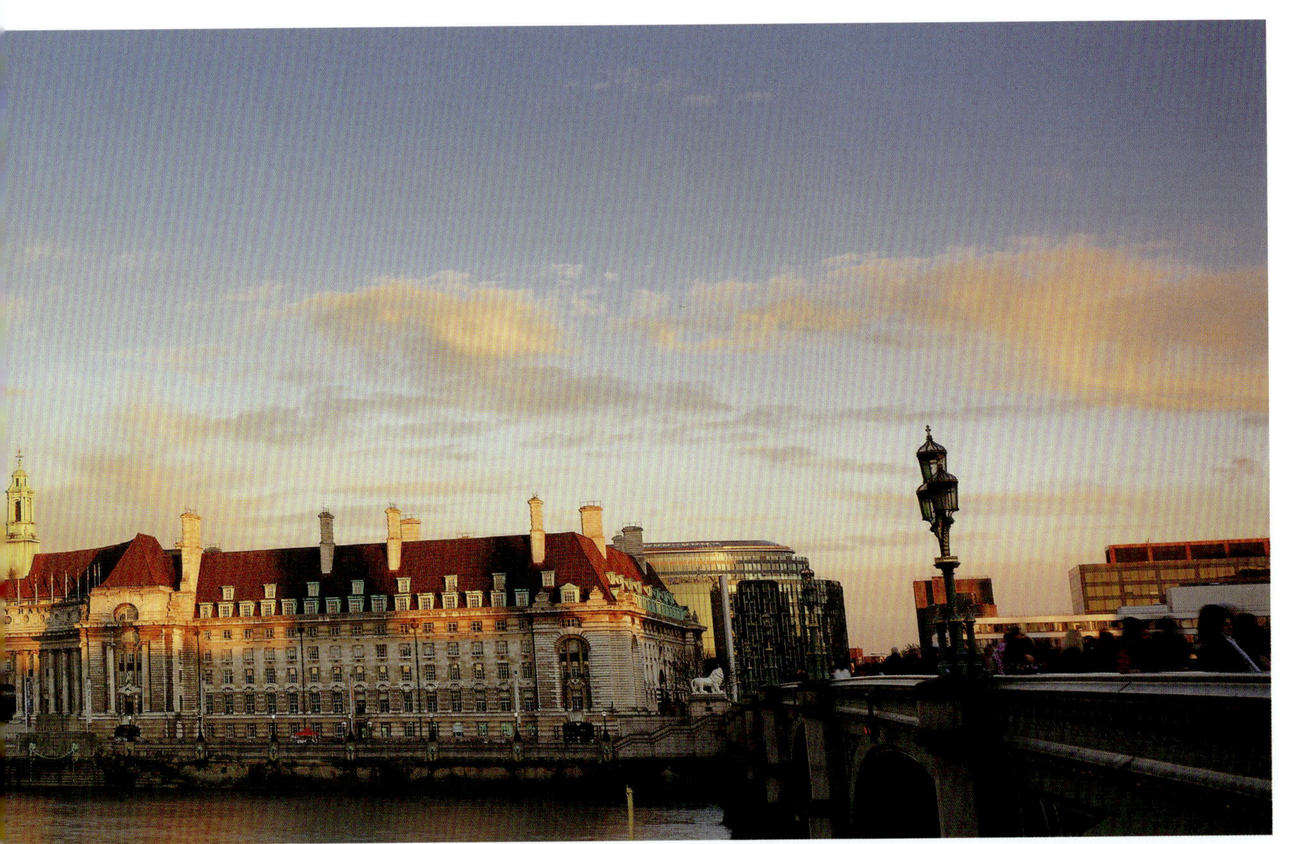

FINE LIGHT ON THE LONDON EYE

PUTNEY BRIDGE DISAPPEARS IN MIST

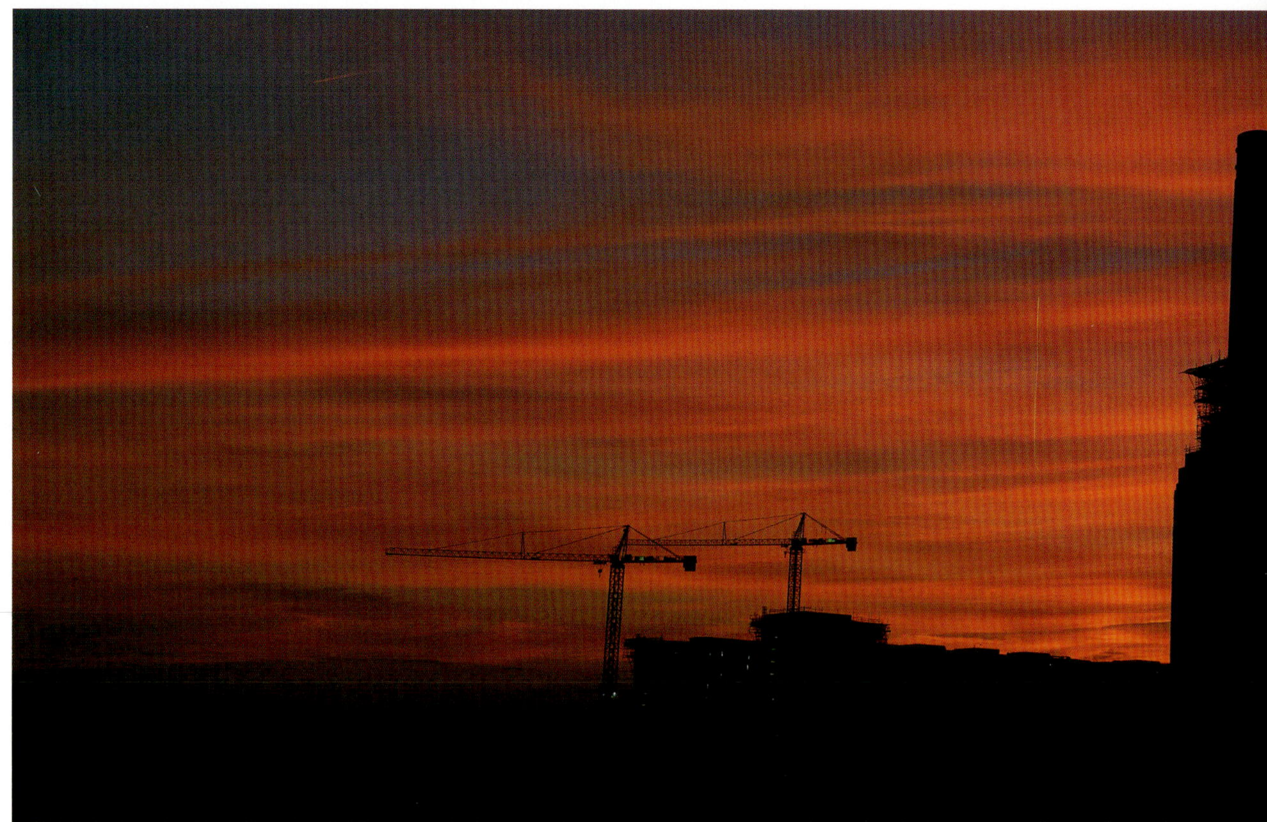

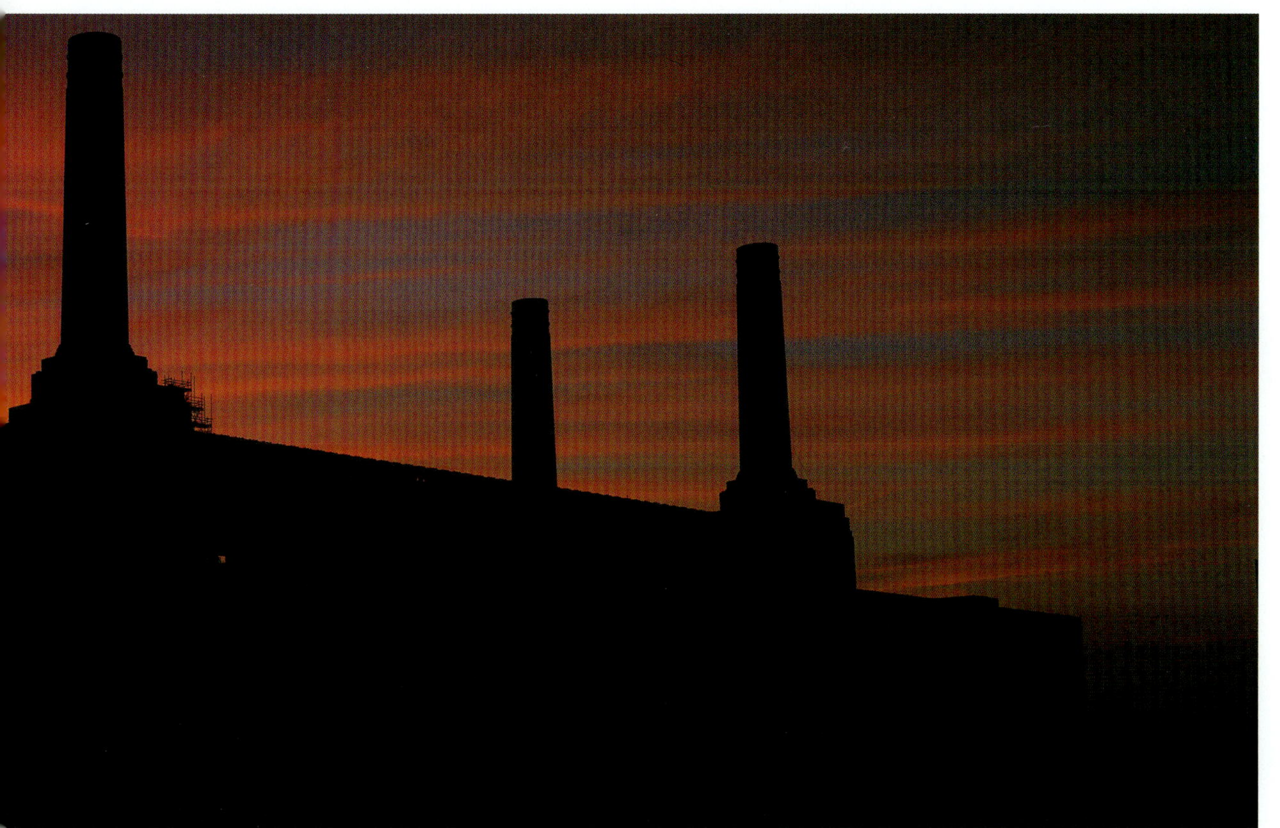

BATTERSEA POWER STATION

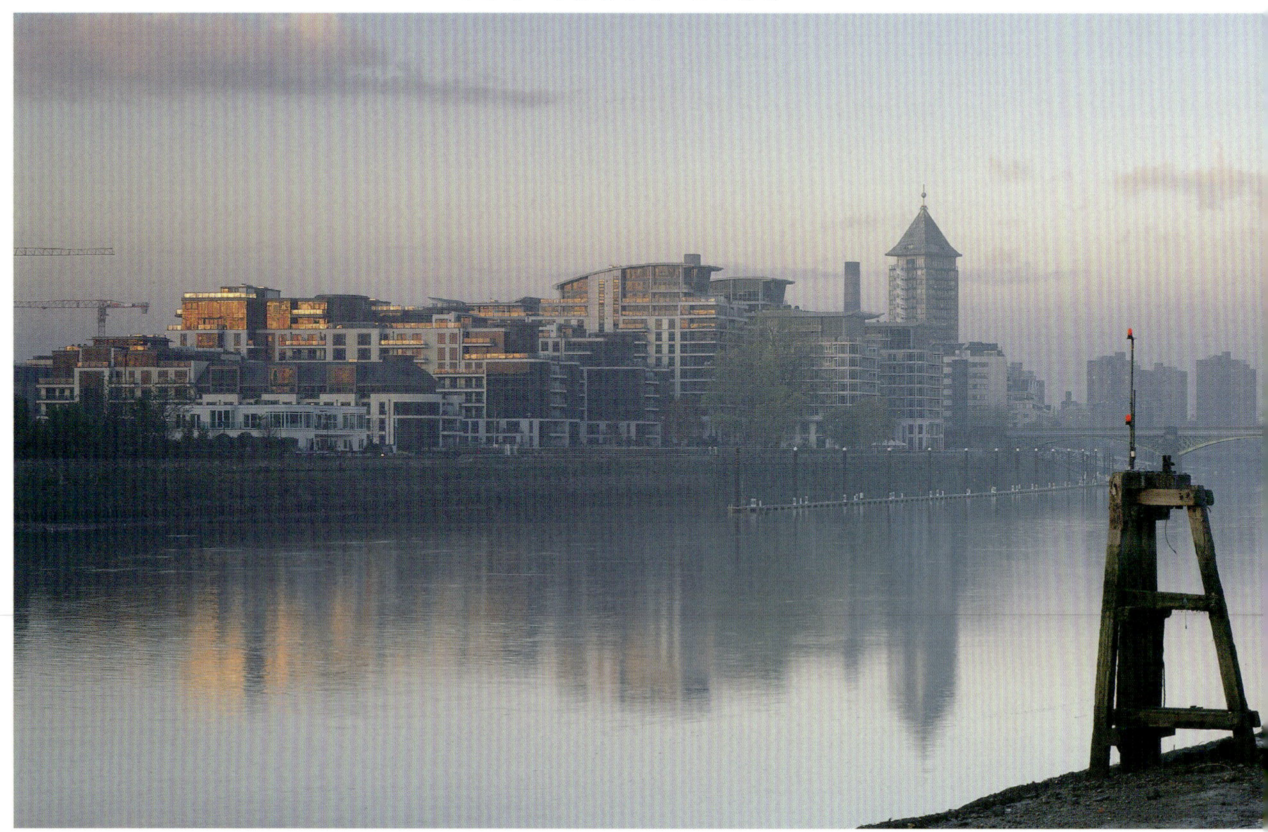

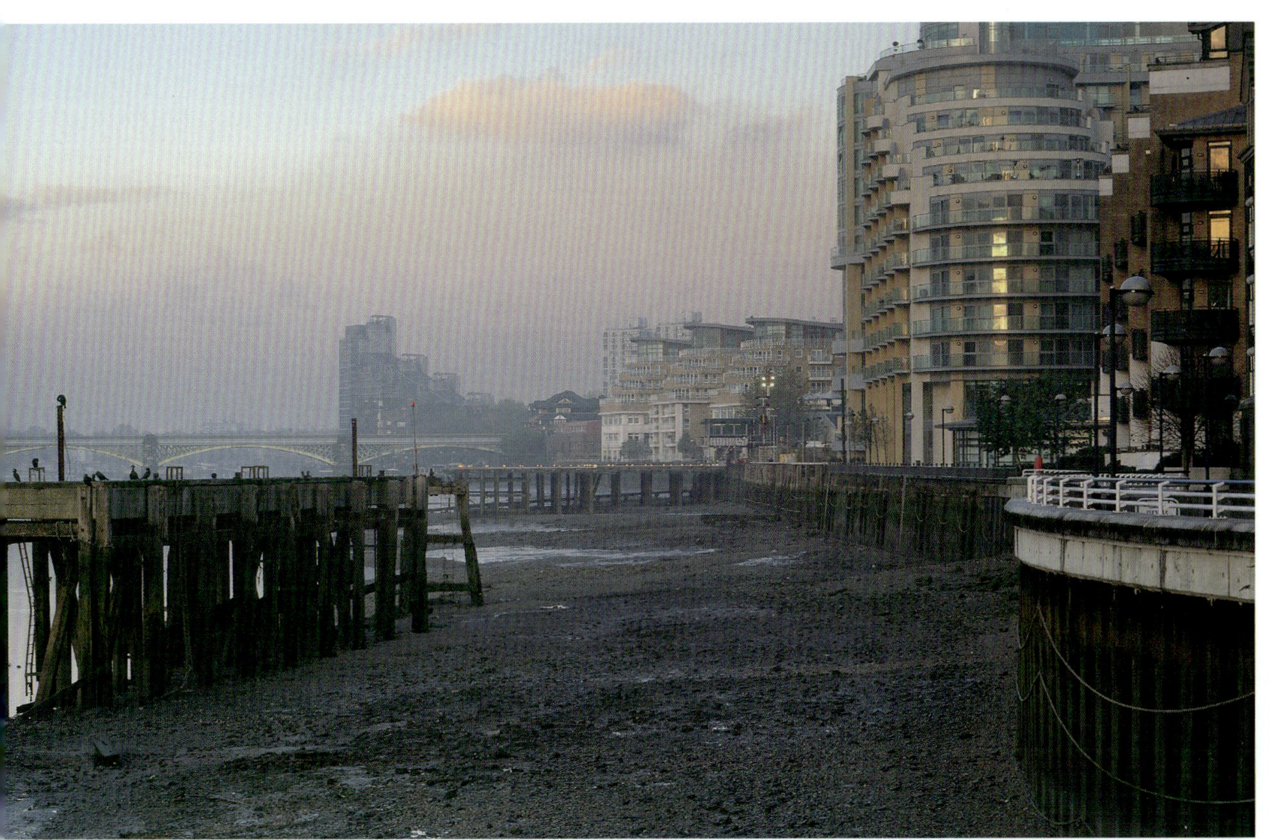

WOODEN JETTY AT BATTERSEA, THAMES

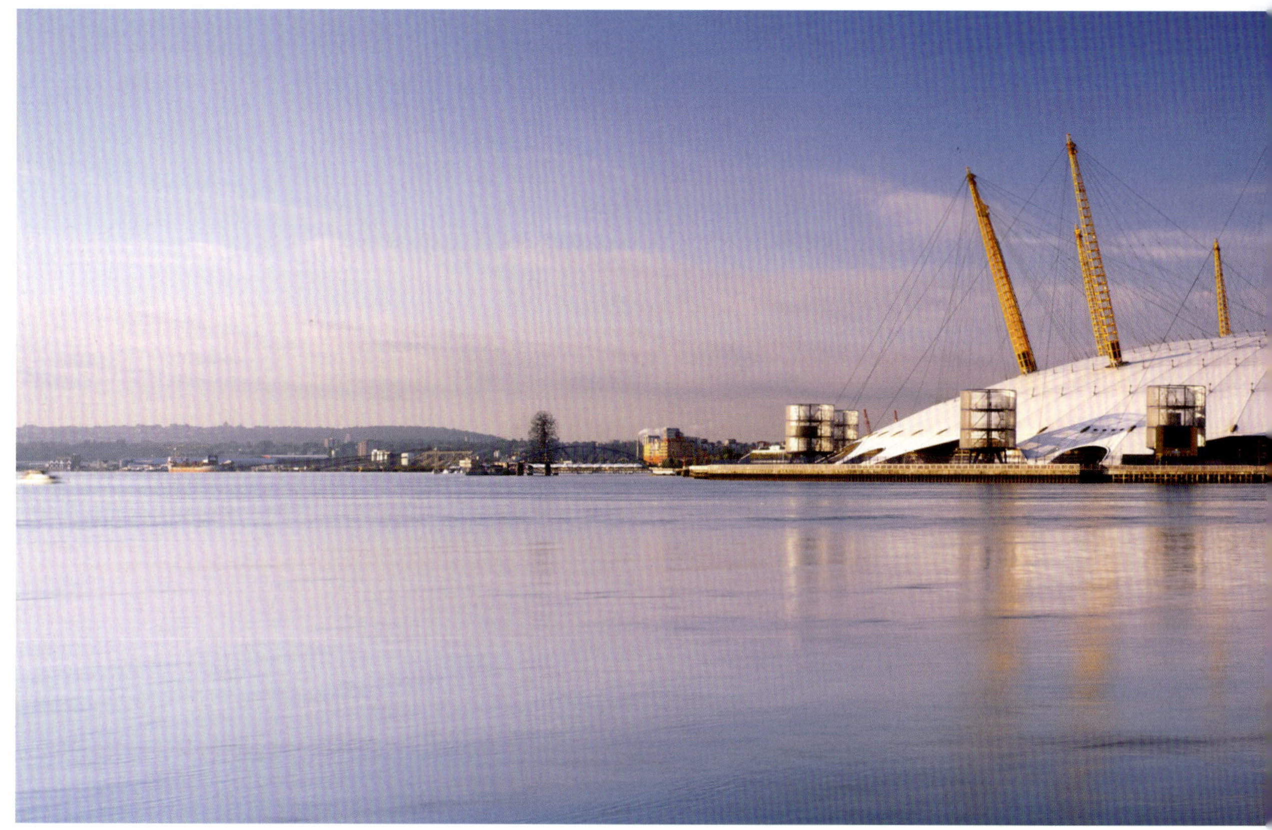

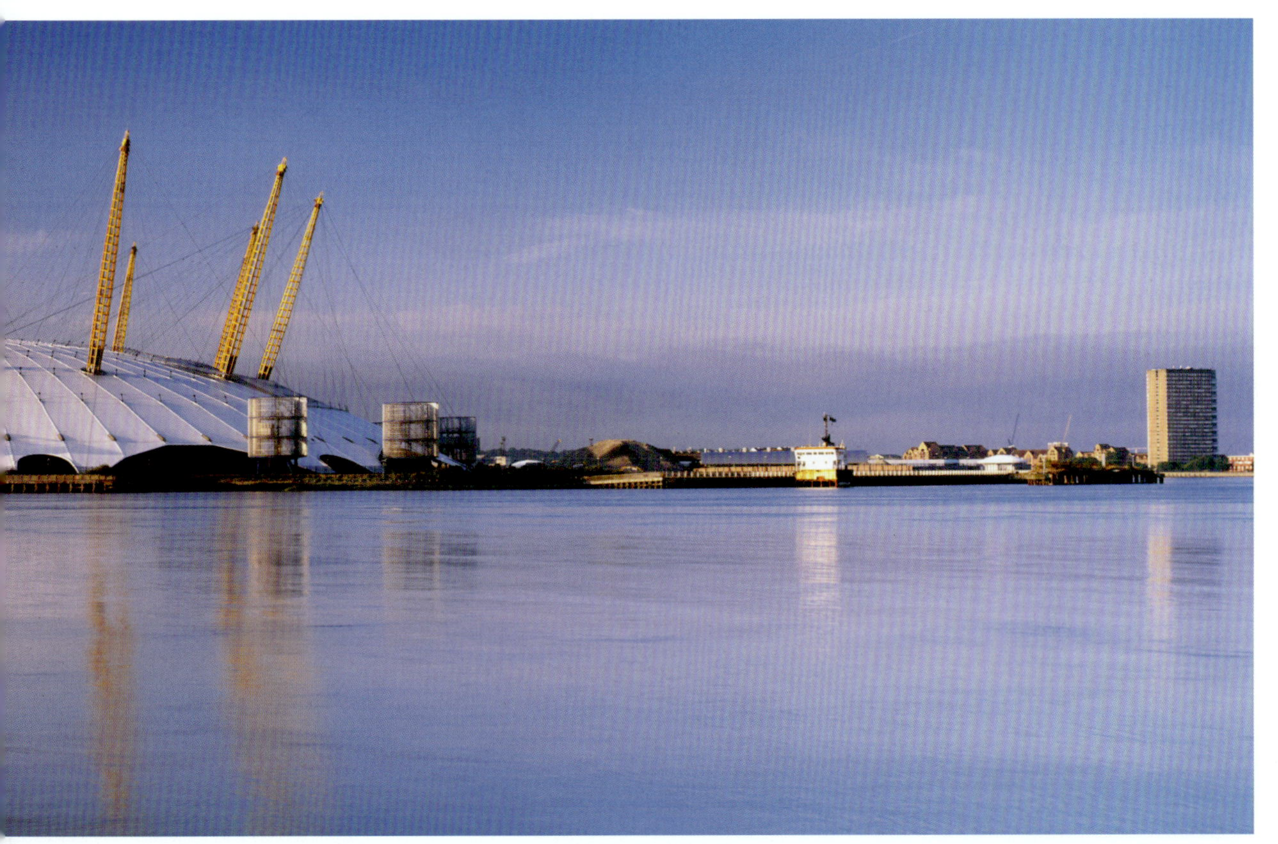

O2 ARENA AT DAWN

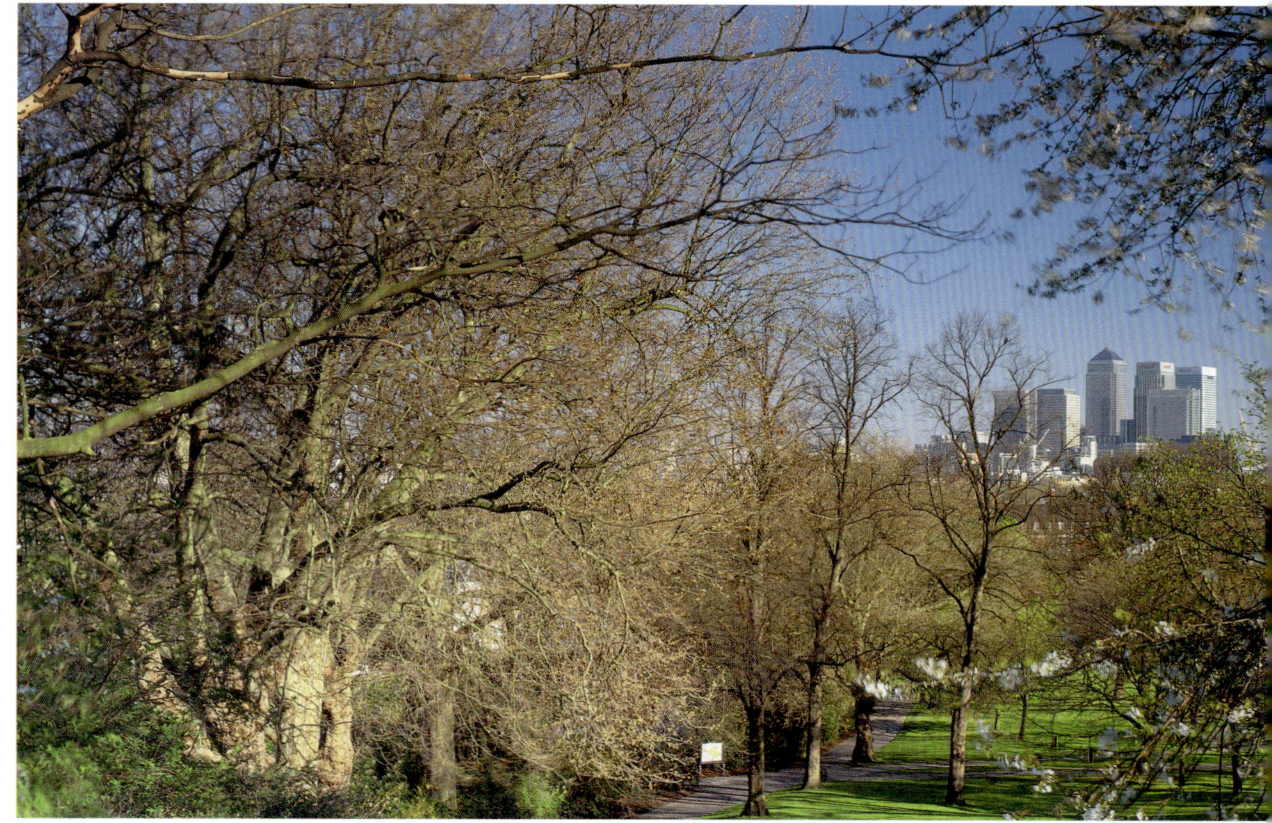

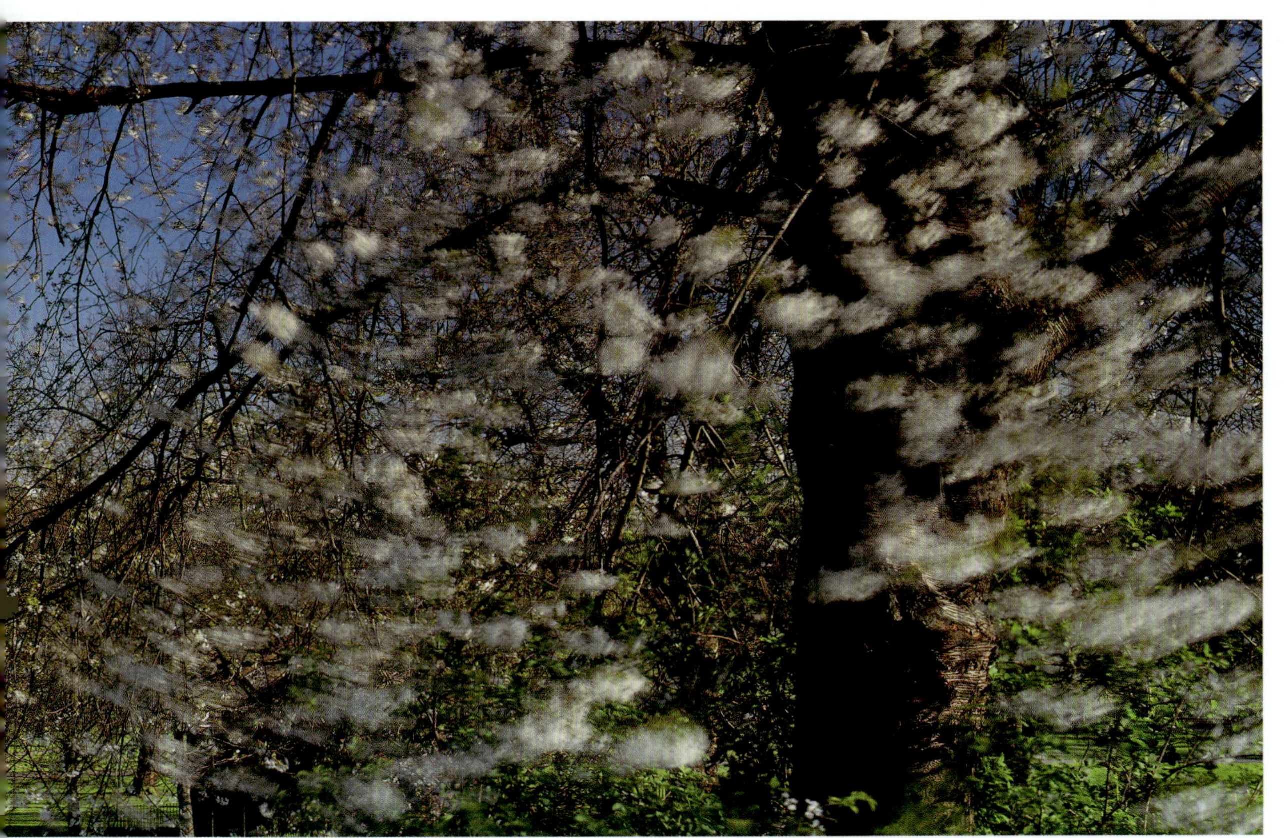

APRIL BLOSSOM AND CANARY WHARF, FROM GREENWICH PARK

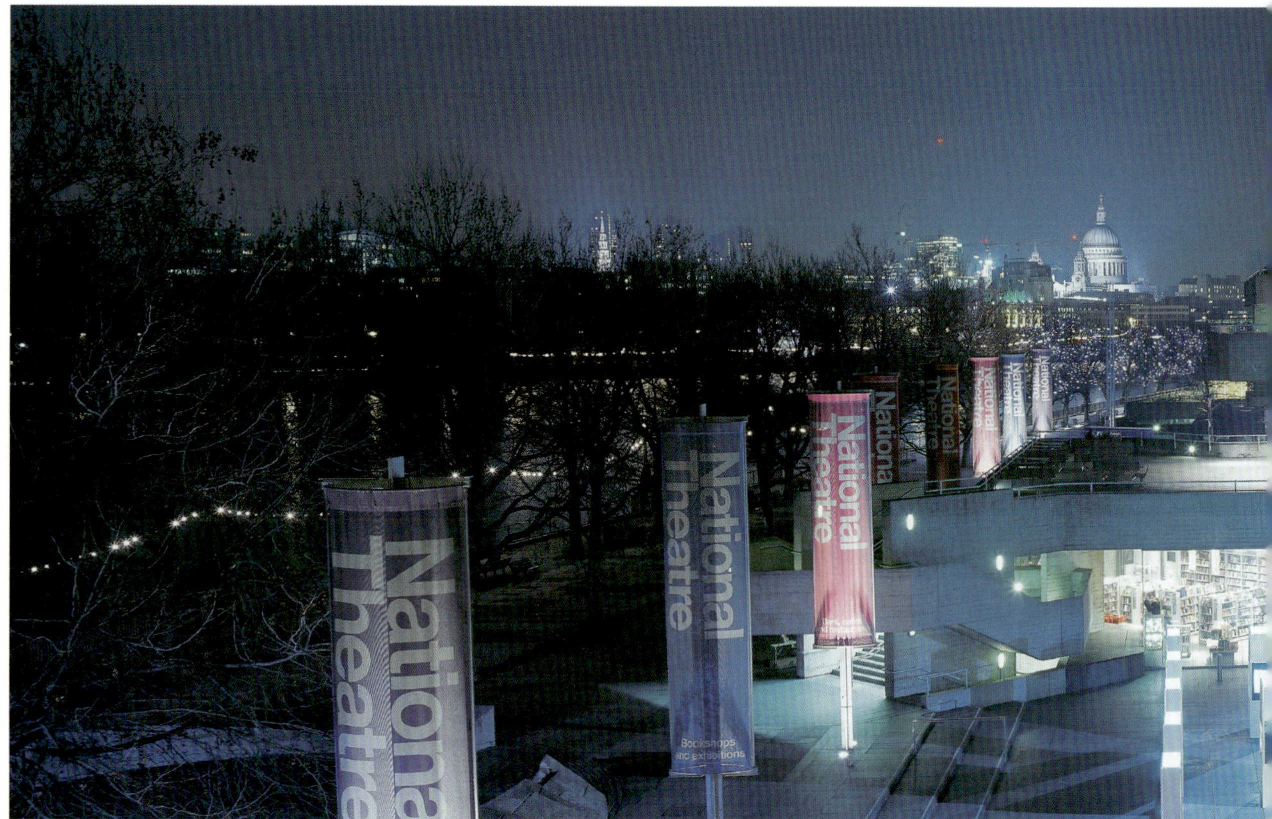
National Theatre
National Theatre
Bookshops and exhibitions
National Theatre
National
National Theatre
National Theatre
National Theatre
National Theatre

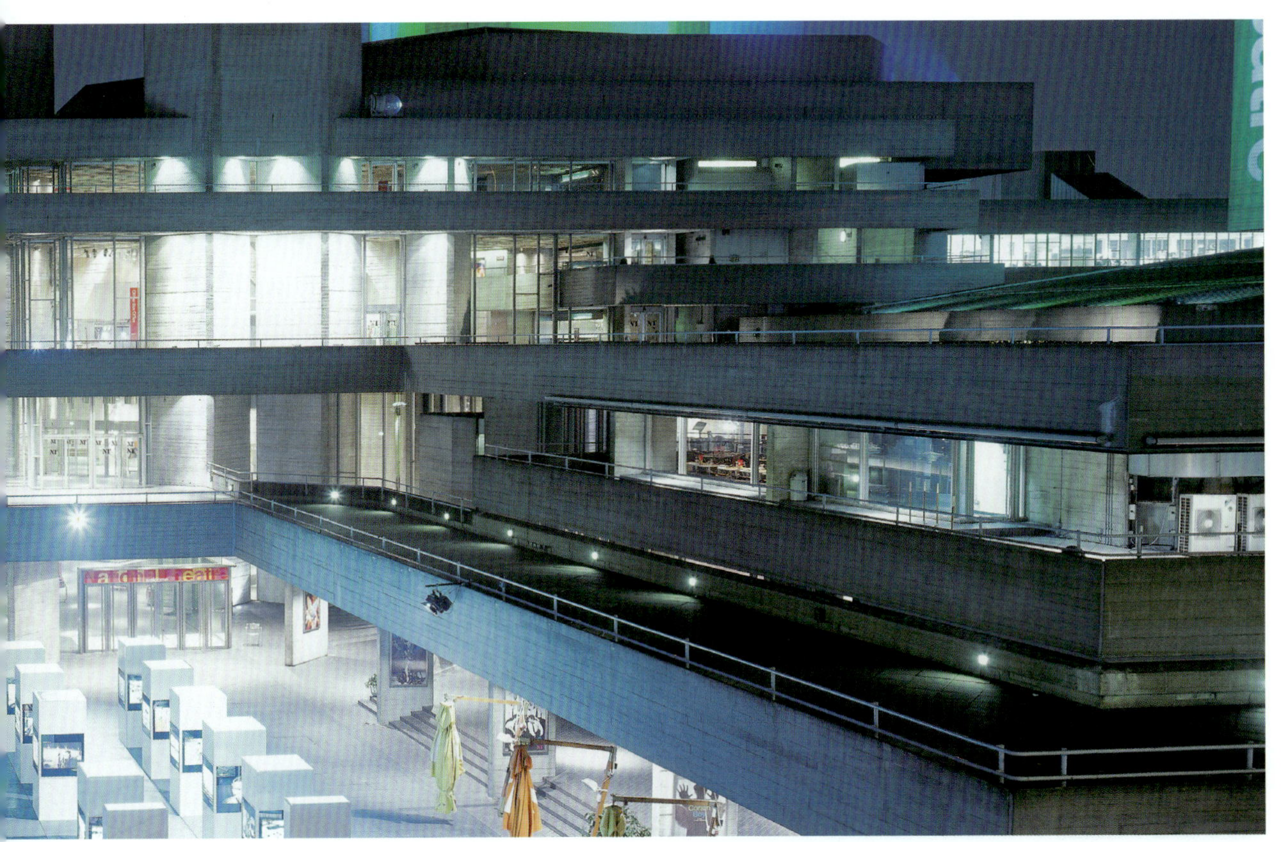

NATIONAL THEATRE AND ST PAUL'S BY NIGHT

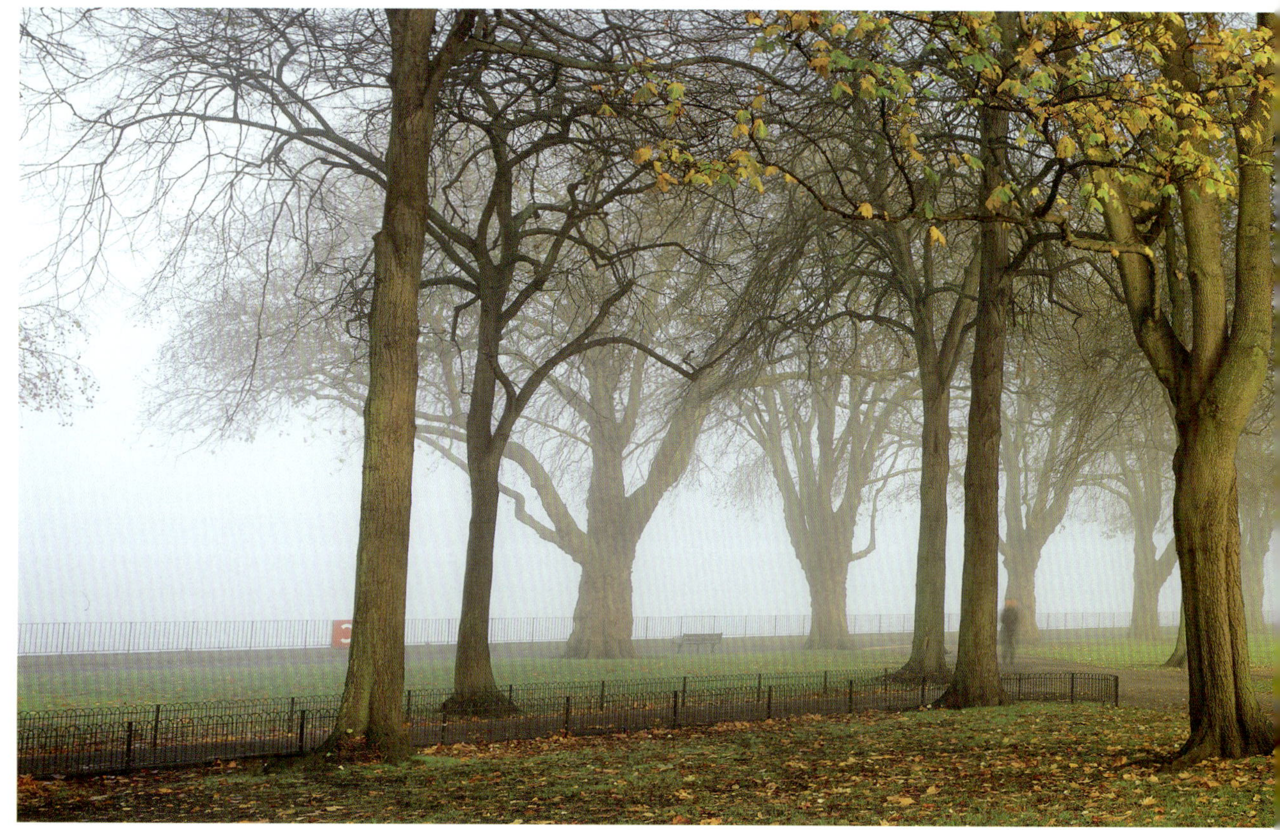

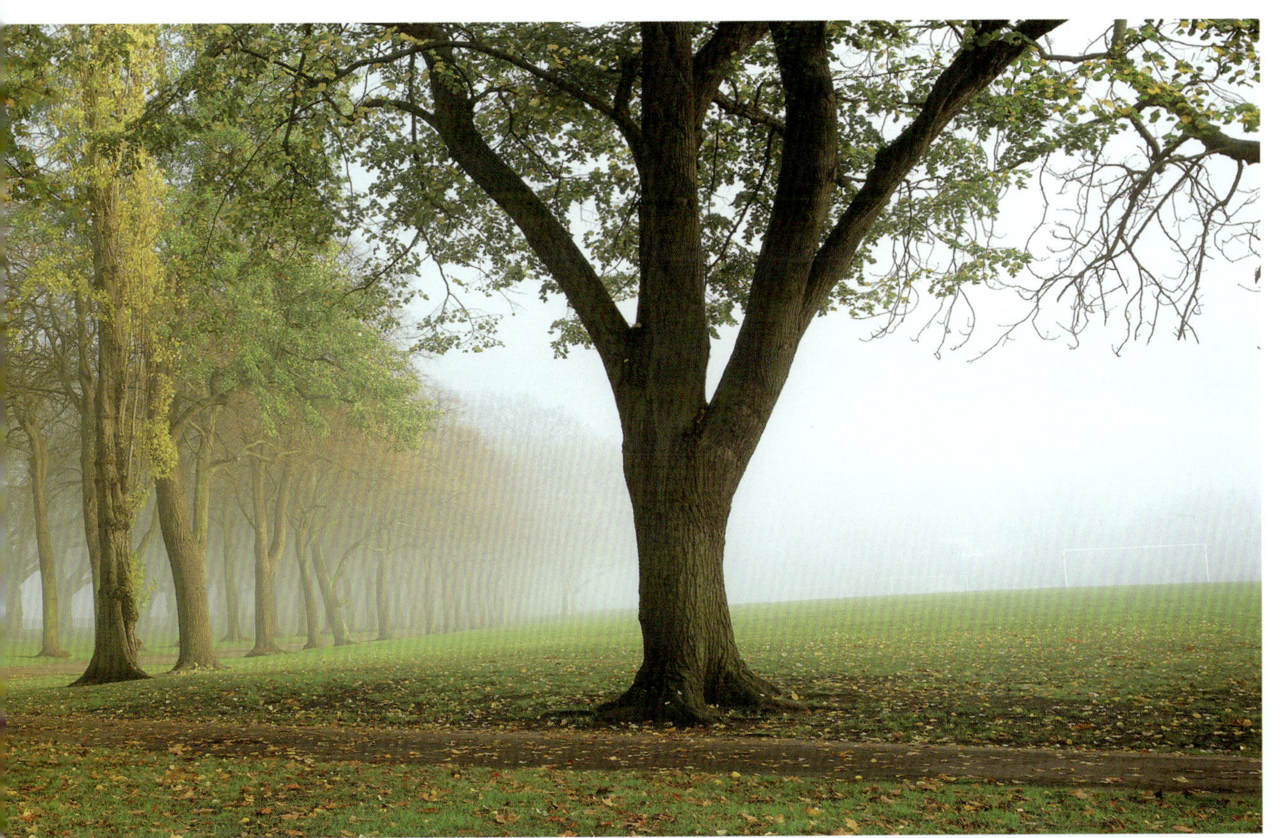

TREES IN THE MIST, WANDSWORTH PARK, RIVER THAMES

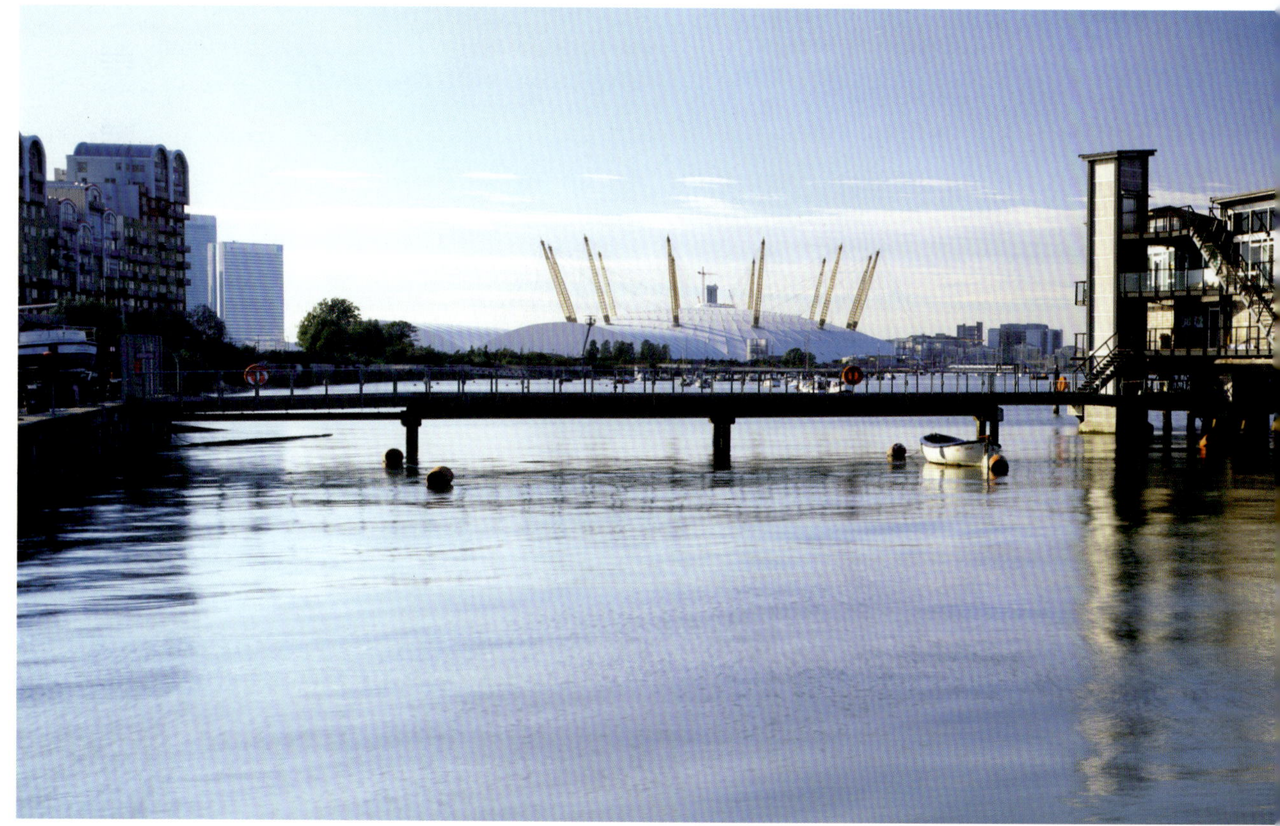

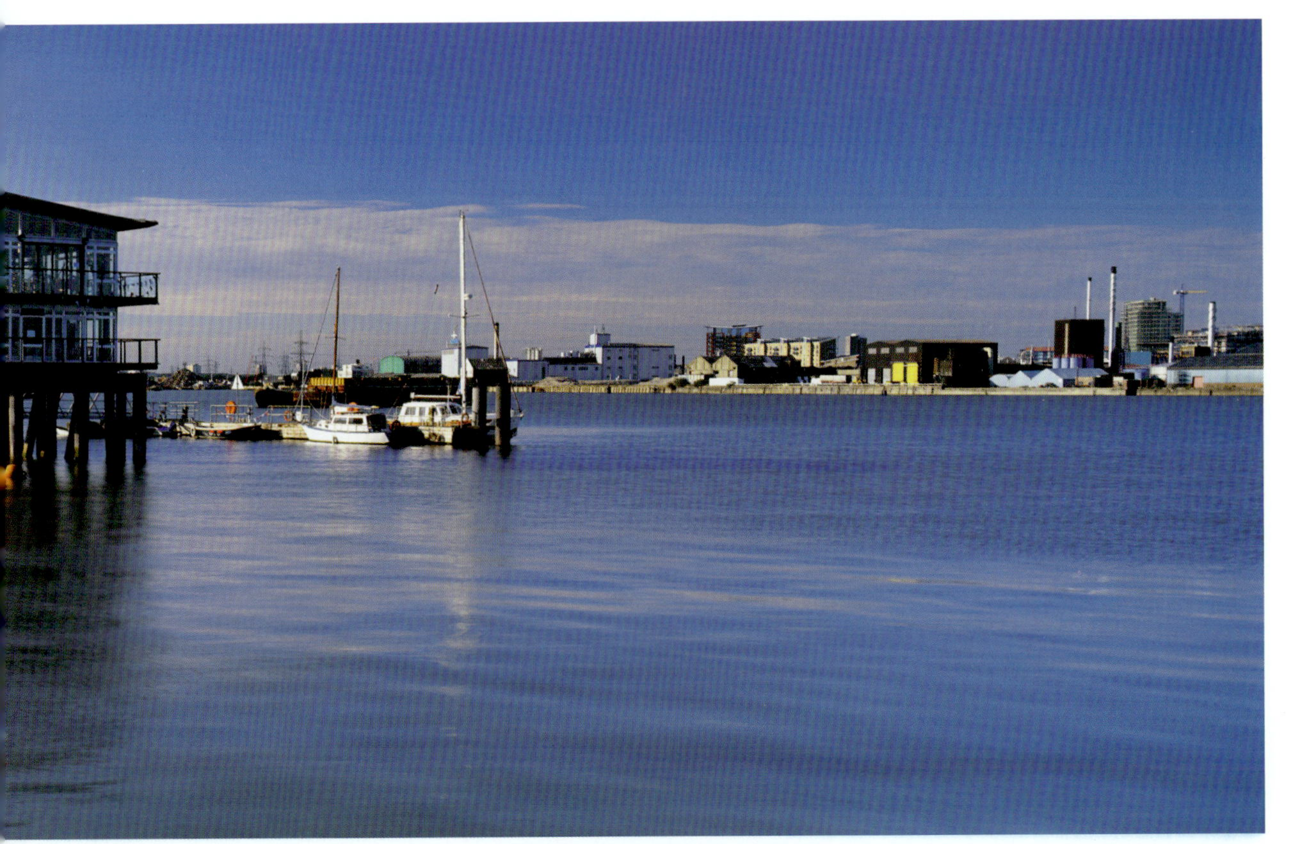

GREENWICH YACHT CLUB

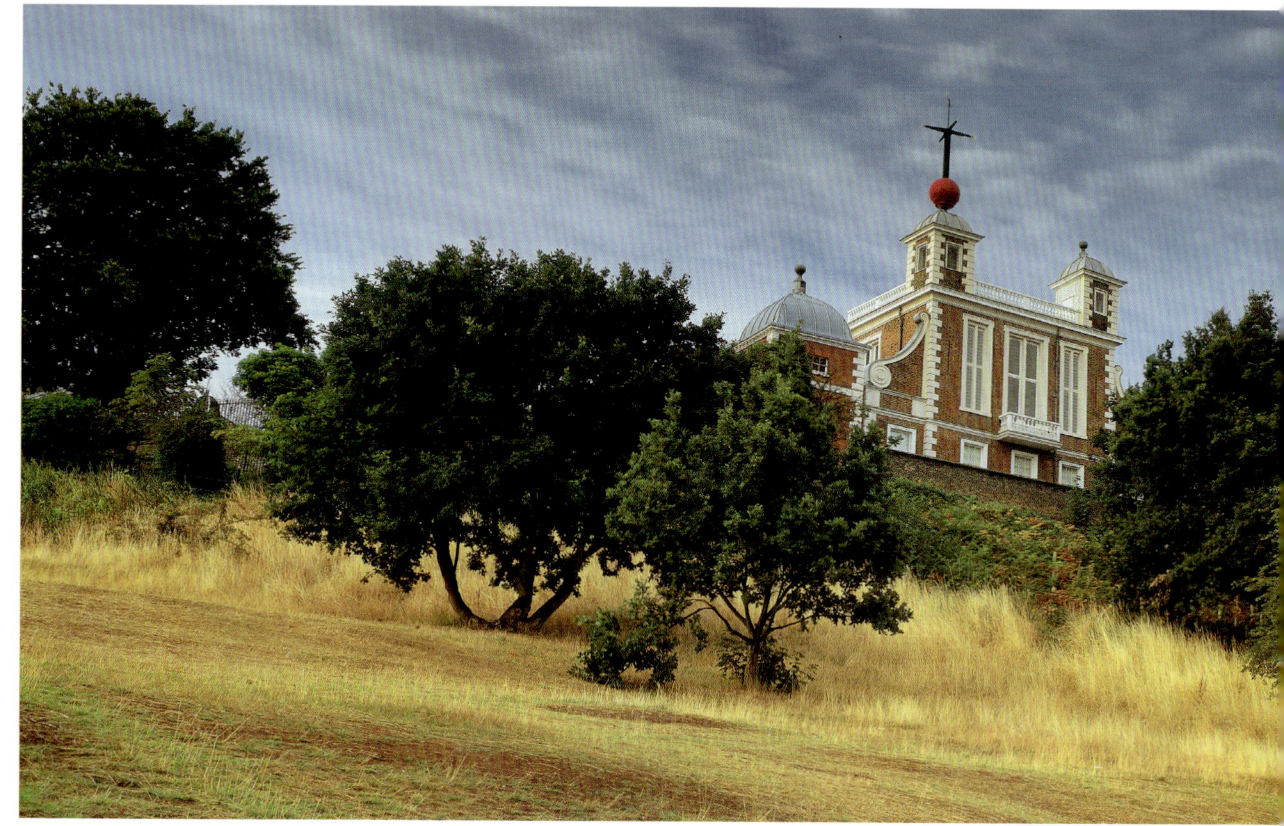

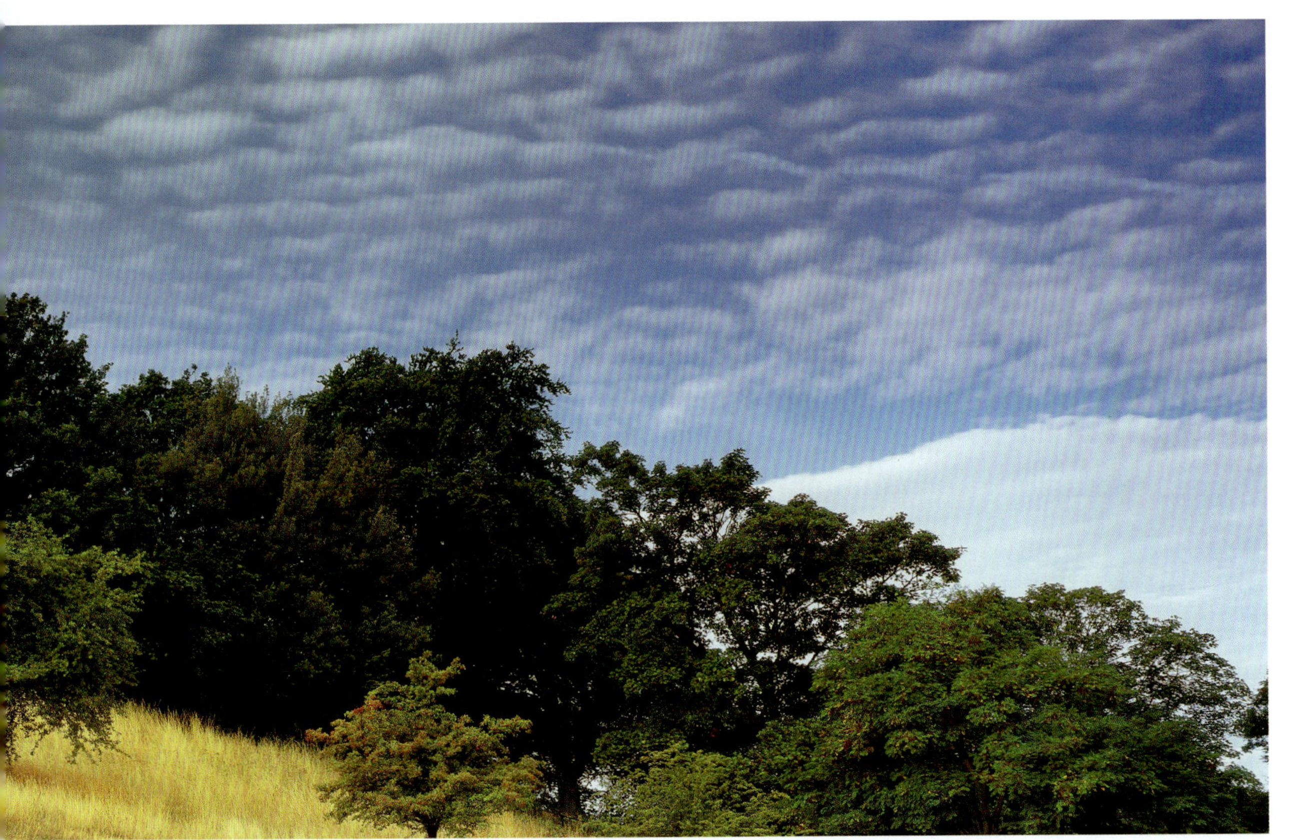

BROKEN CLOUD OVER THE ROYAL OBSERVATORY, GREENWICH PARK

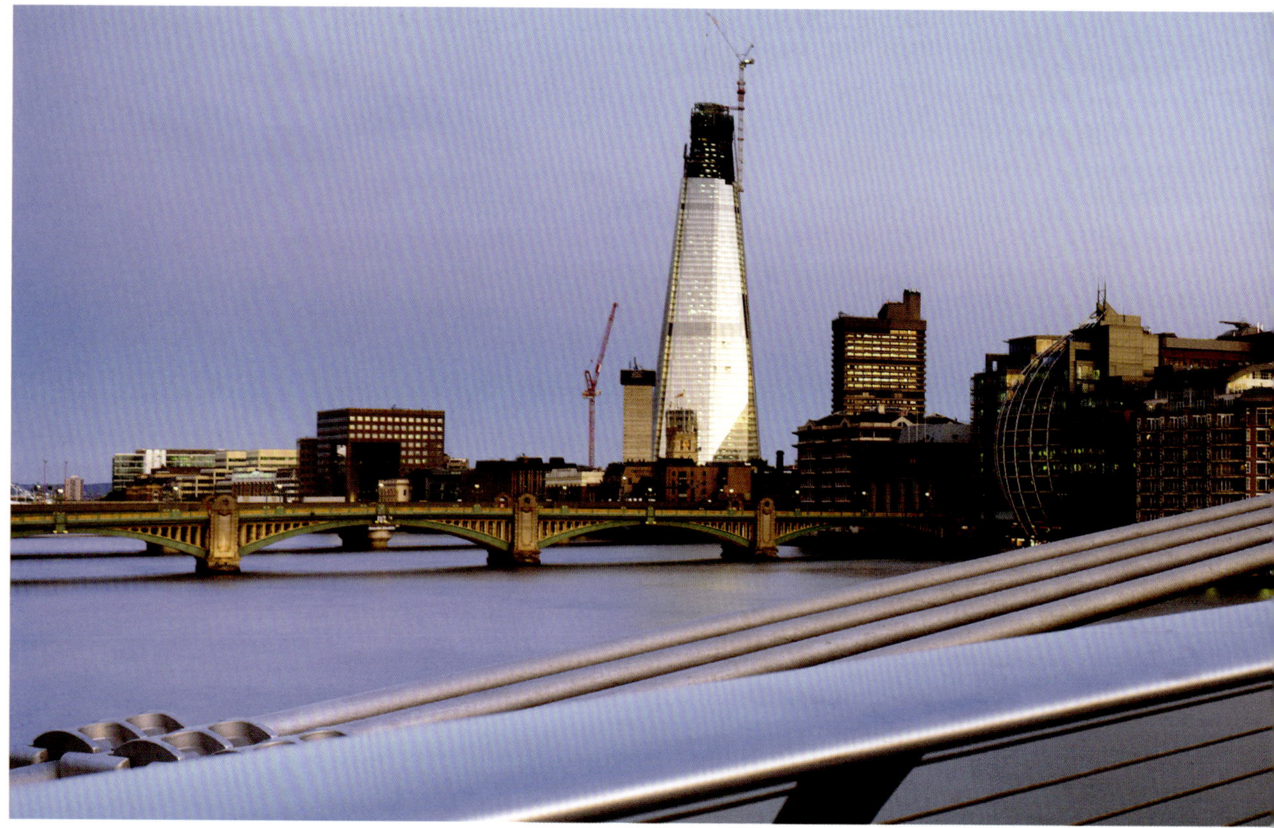

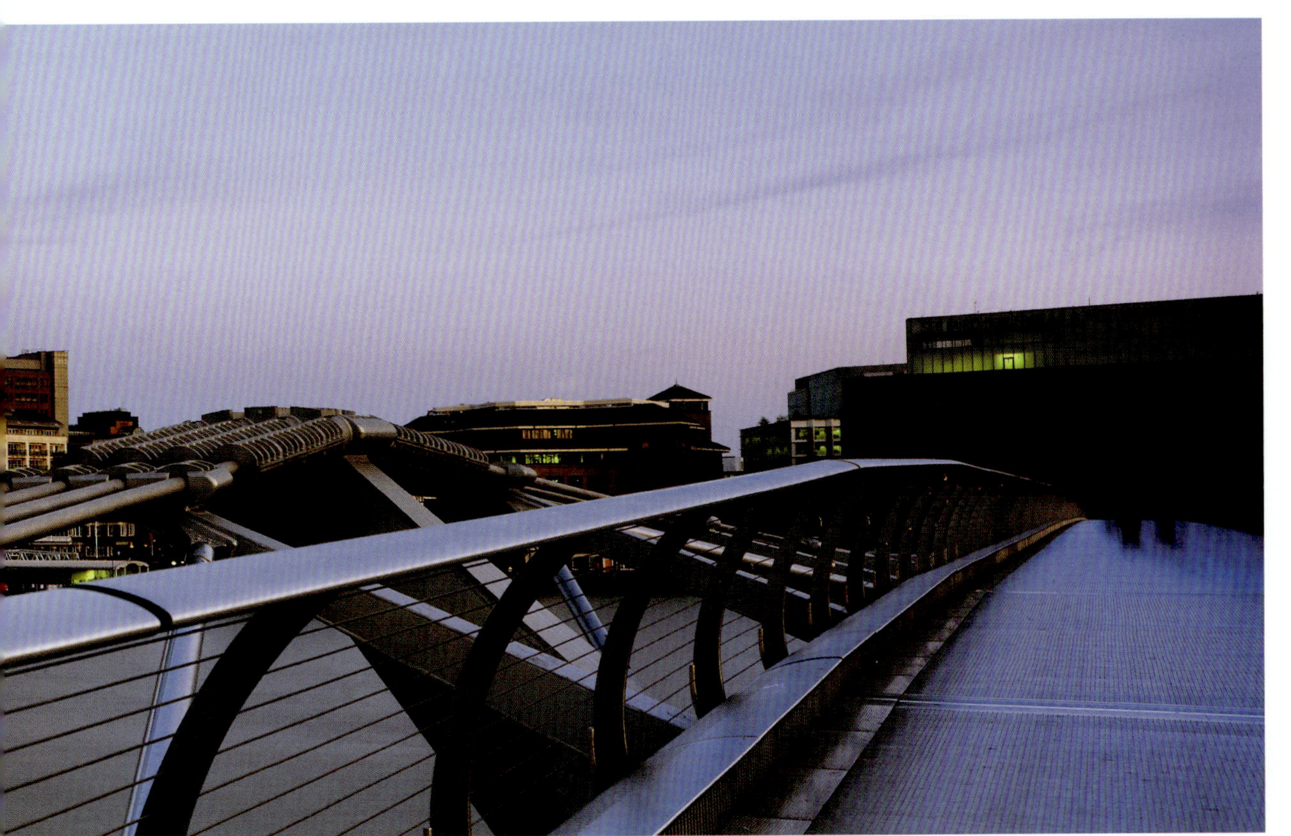

THE SHARD GLOWS, MILLENNIUM BRIDGE

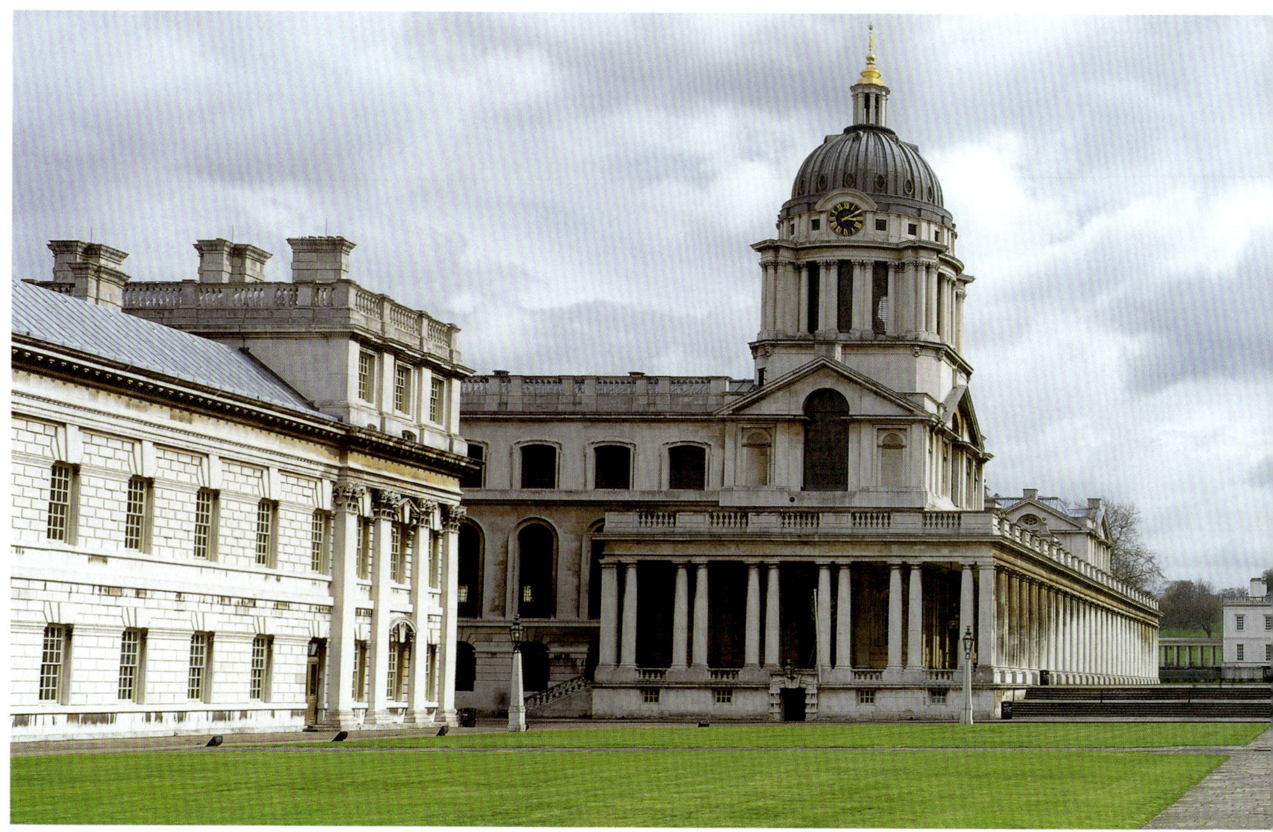

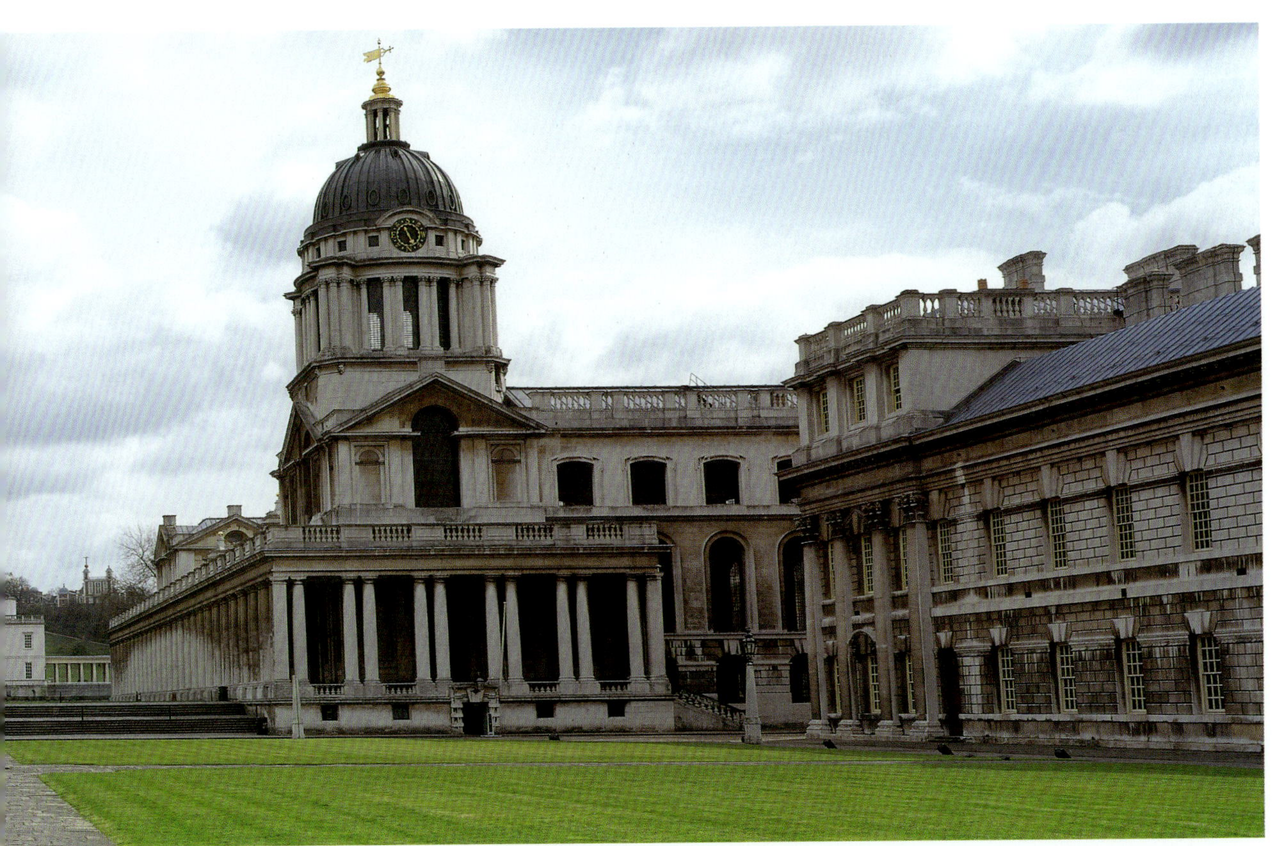

ROYAL NAVAL COLLEGE, GREENWICH

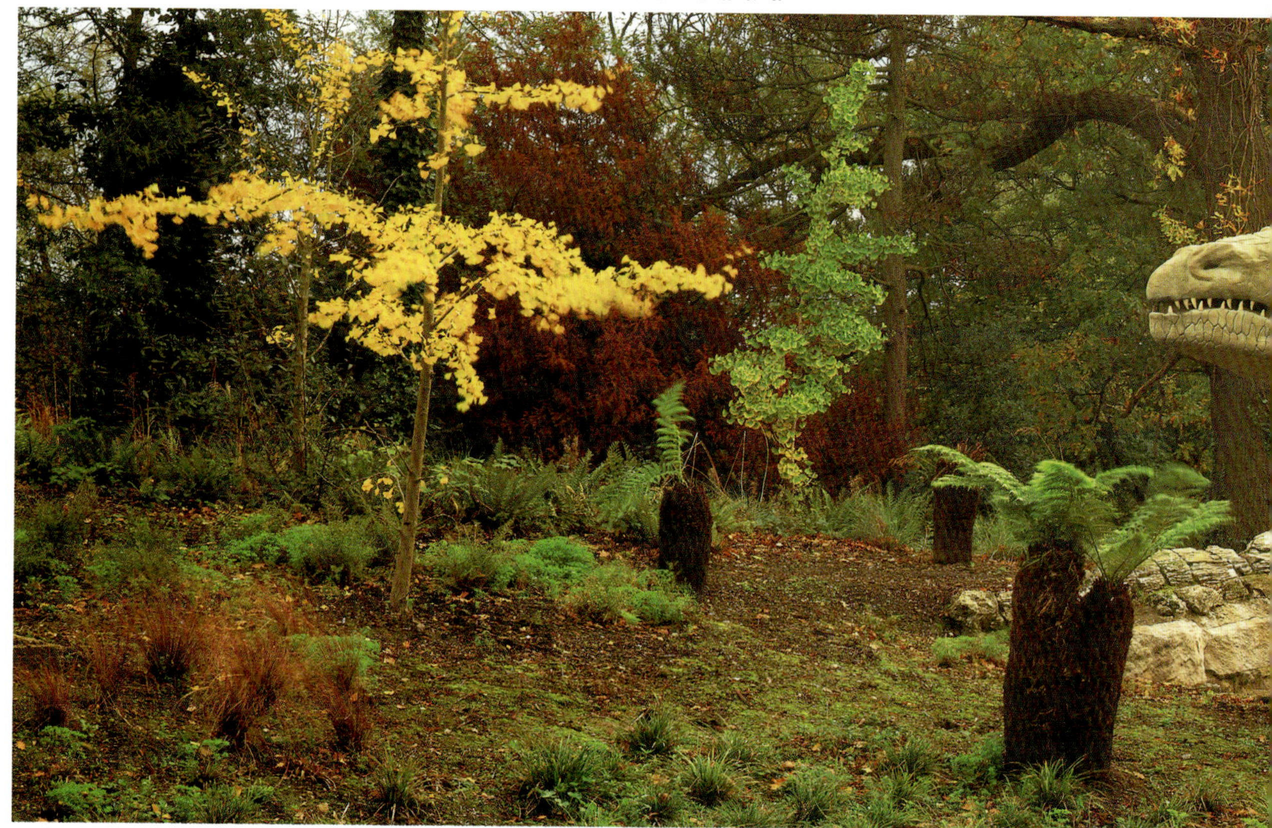

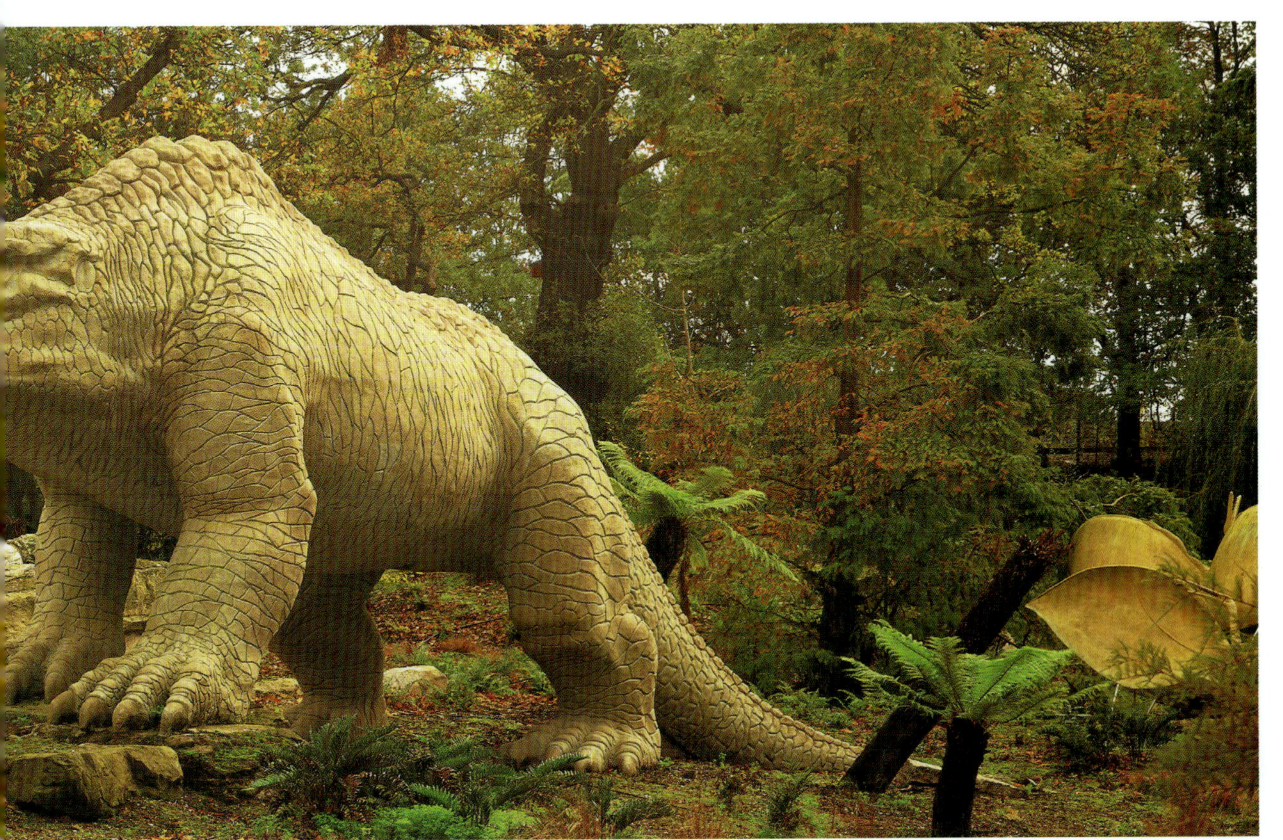

DINOSAUR LAKE, CRYSTAL PALACE PARK

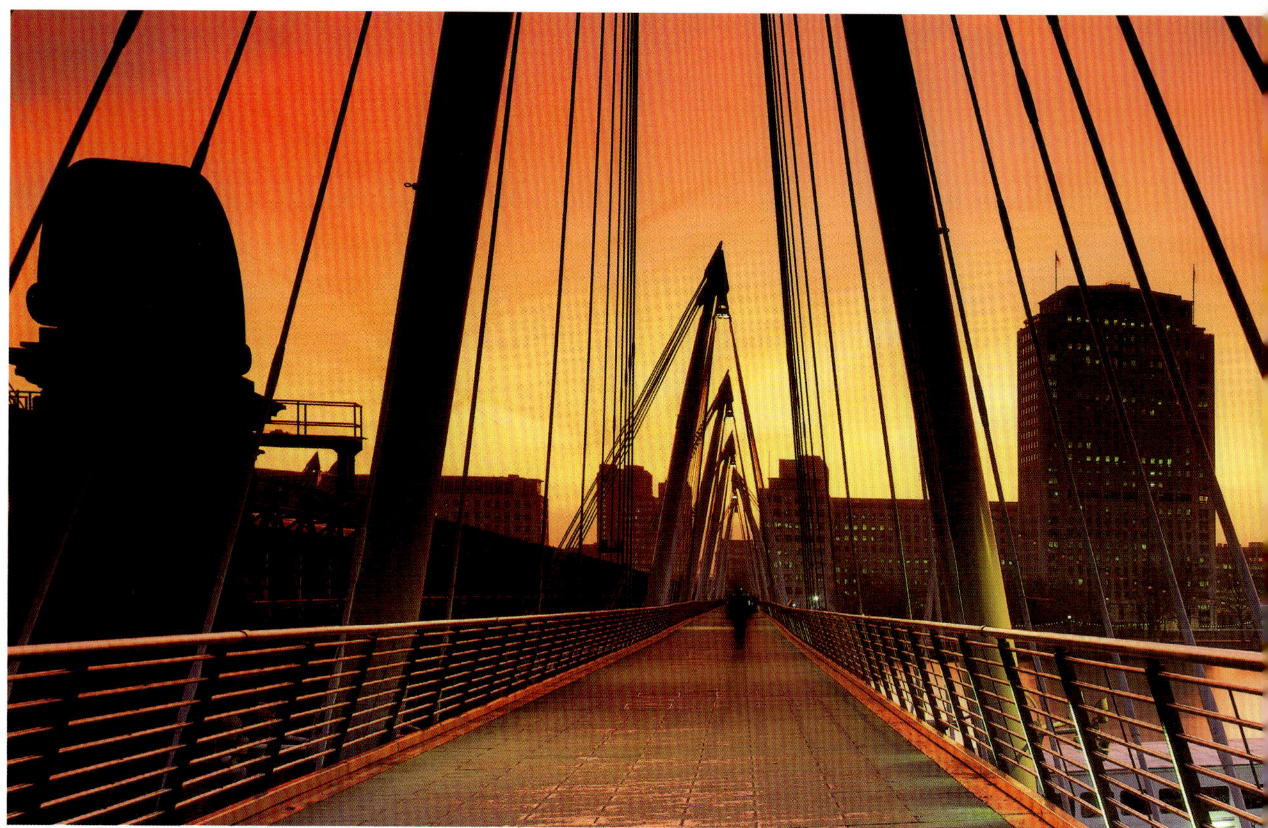

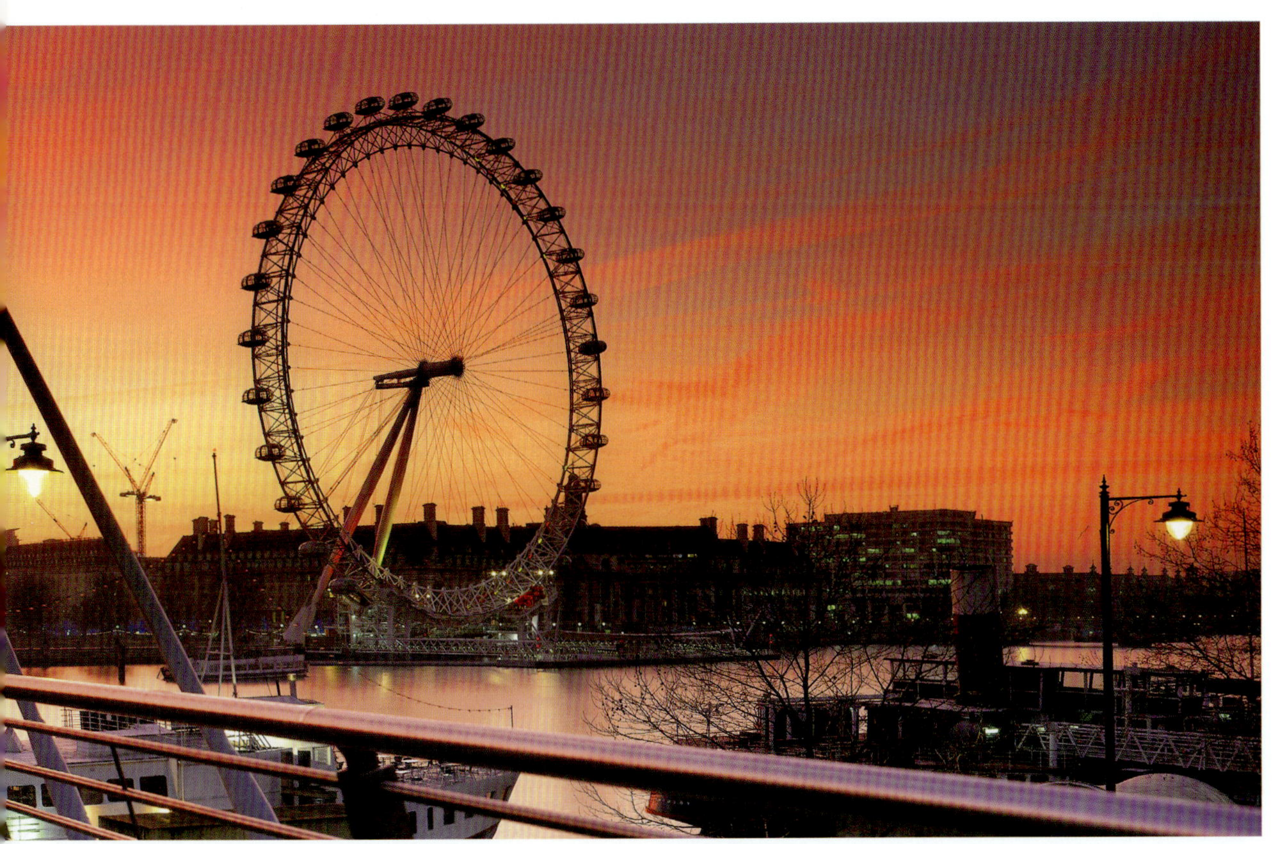

FIERY DAWN, JUBILEE BRIDGE

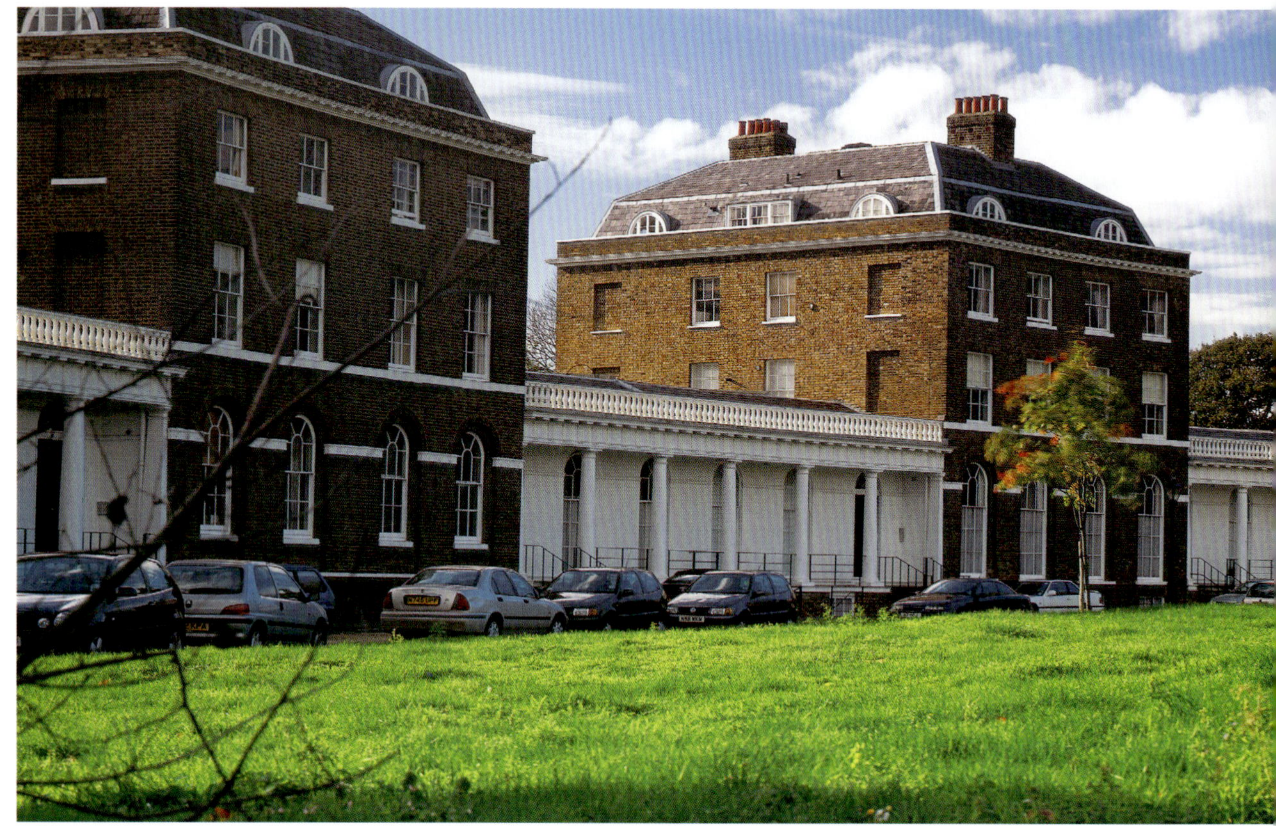

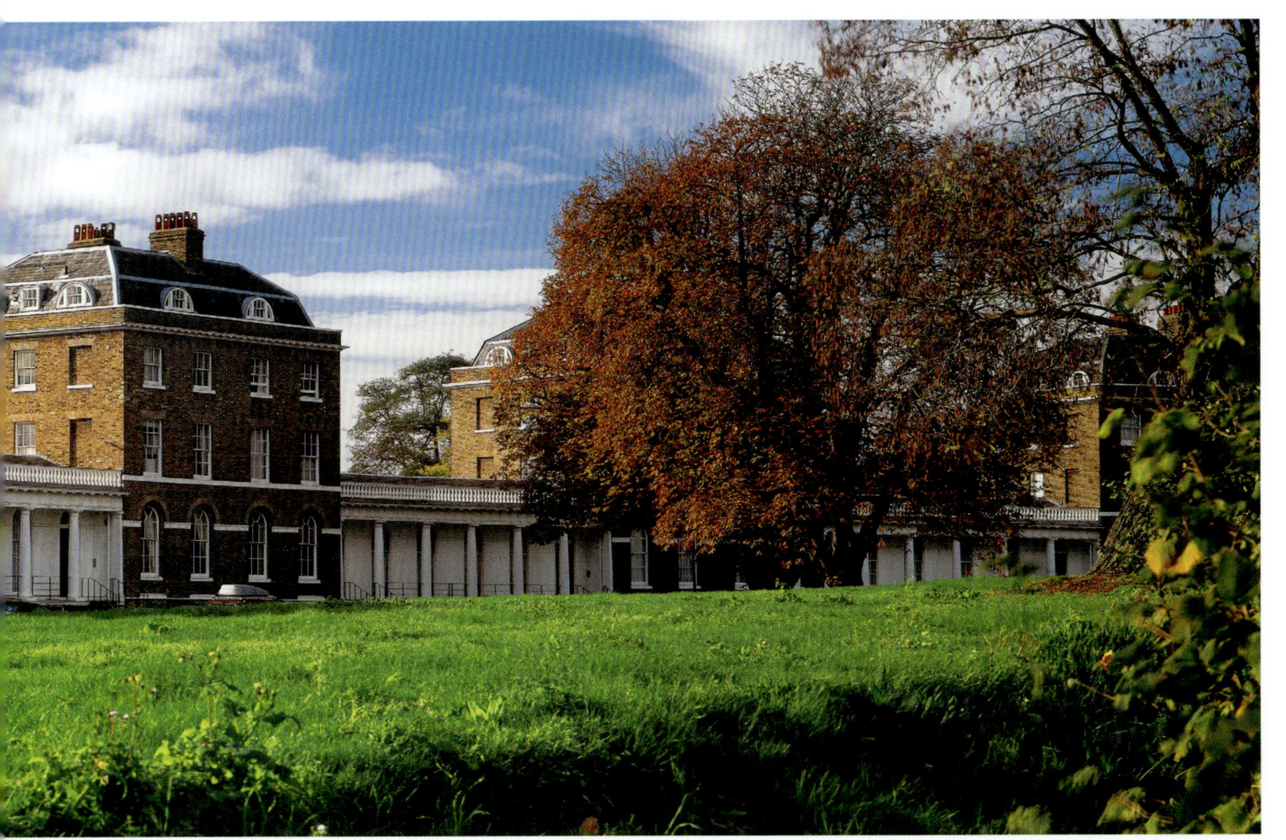

THE PARAGON, BLACKHEATH

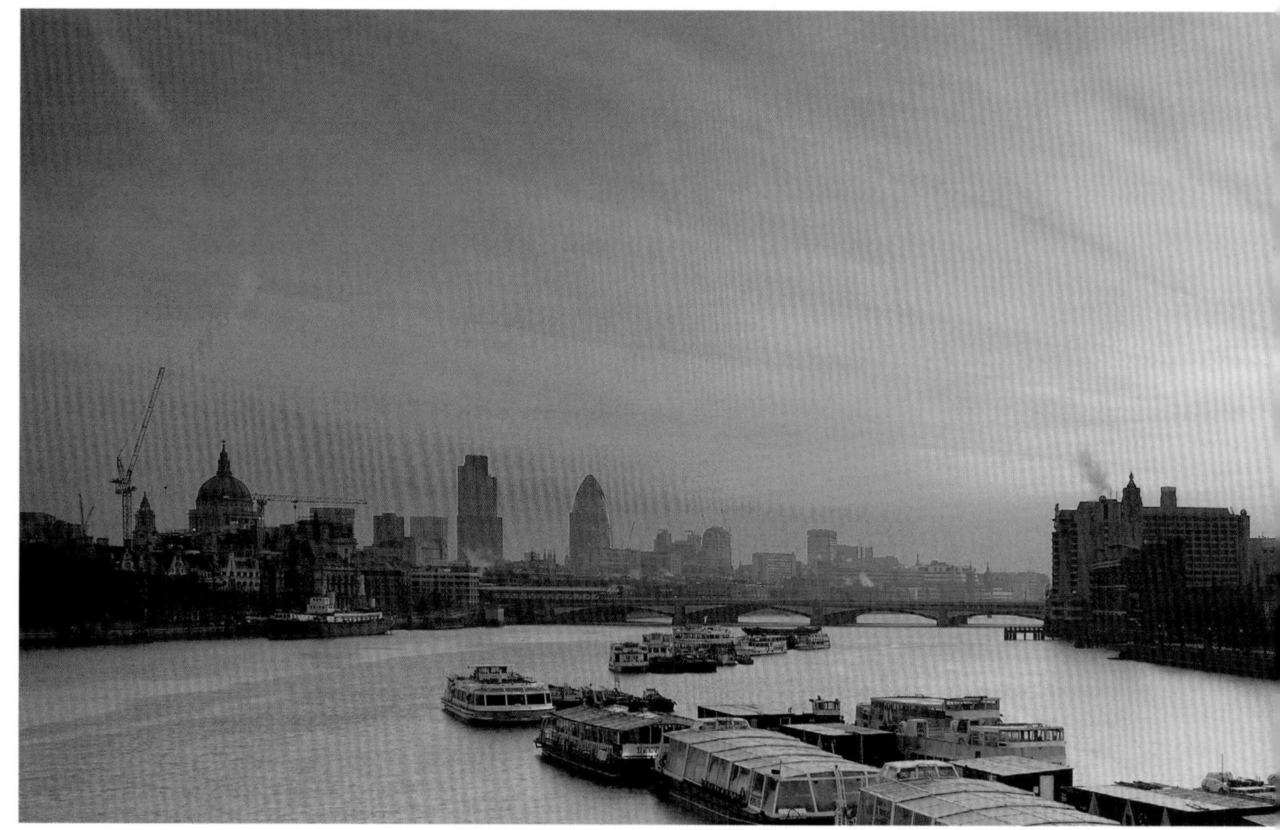

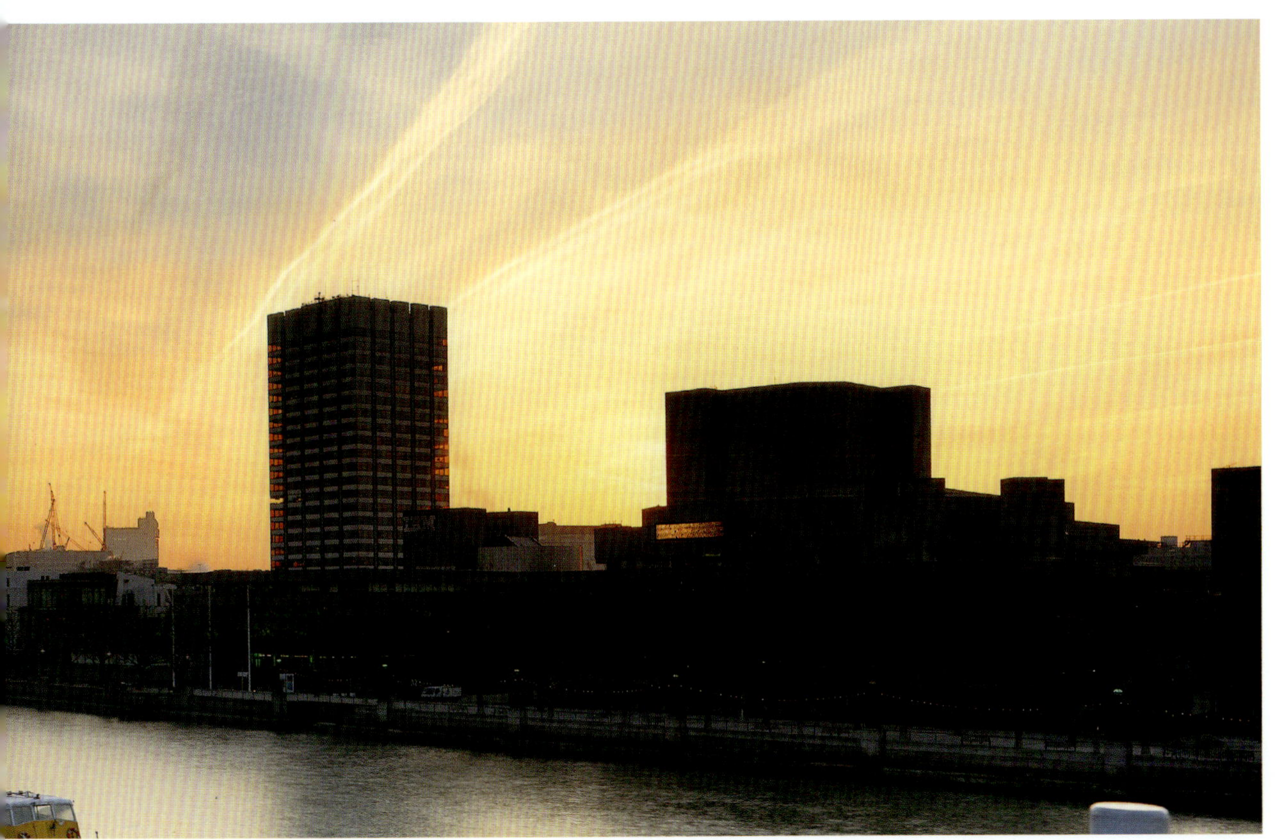

DAWN FROM WATERLOO BRIDGE

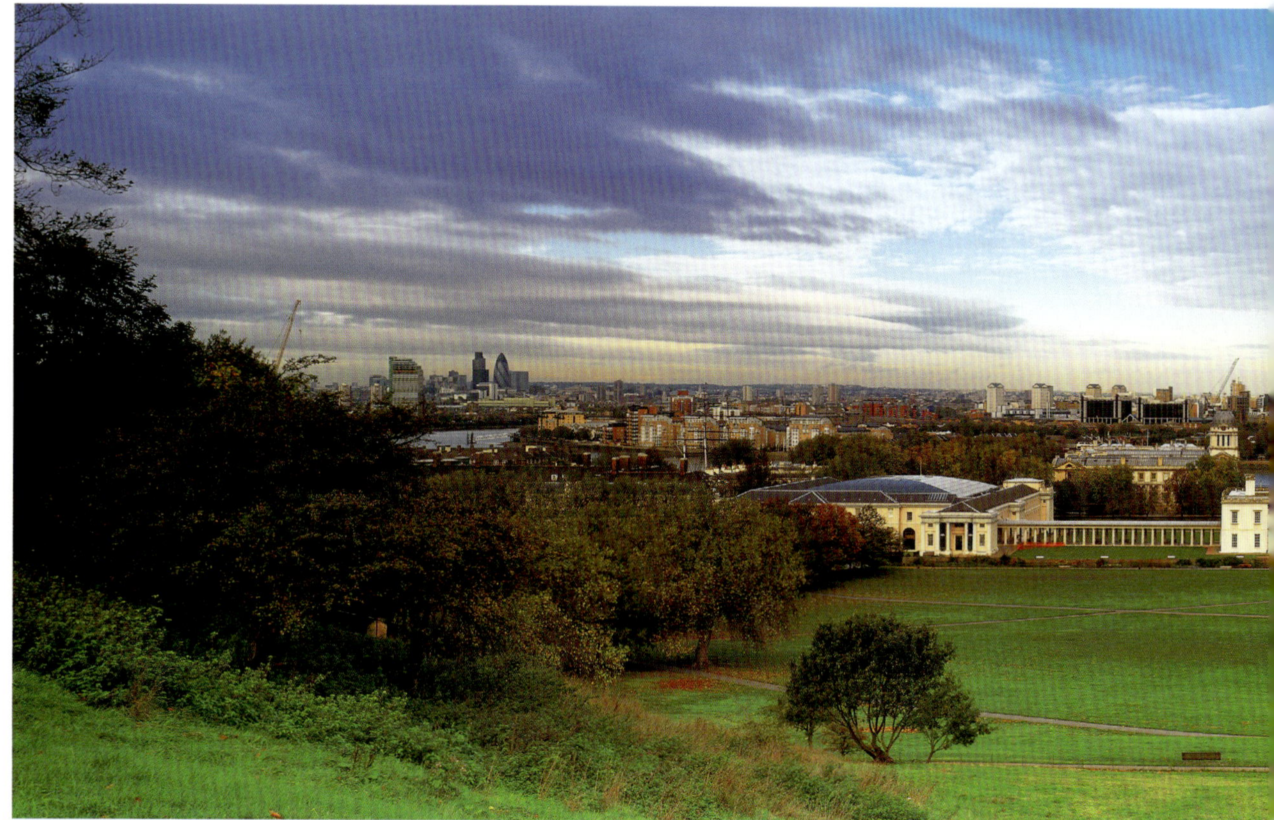

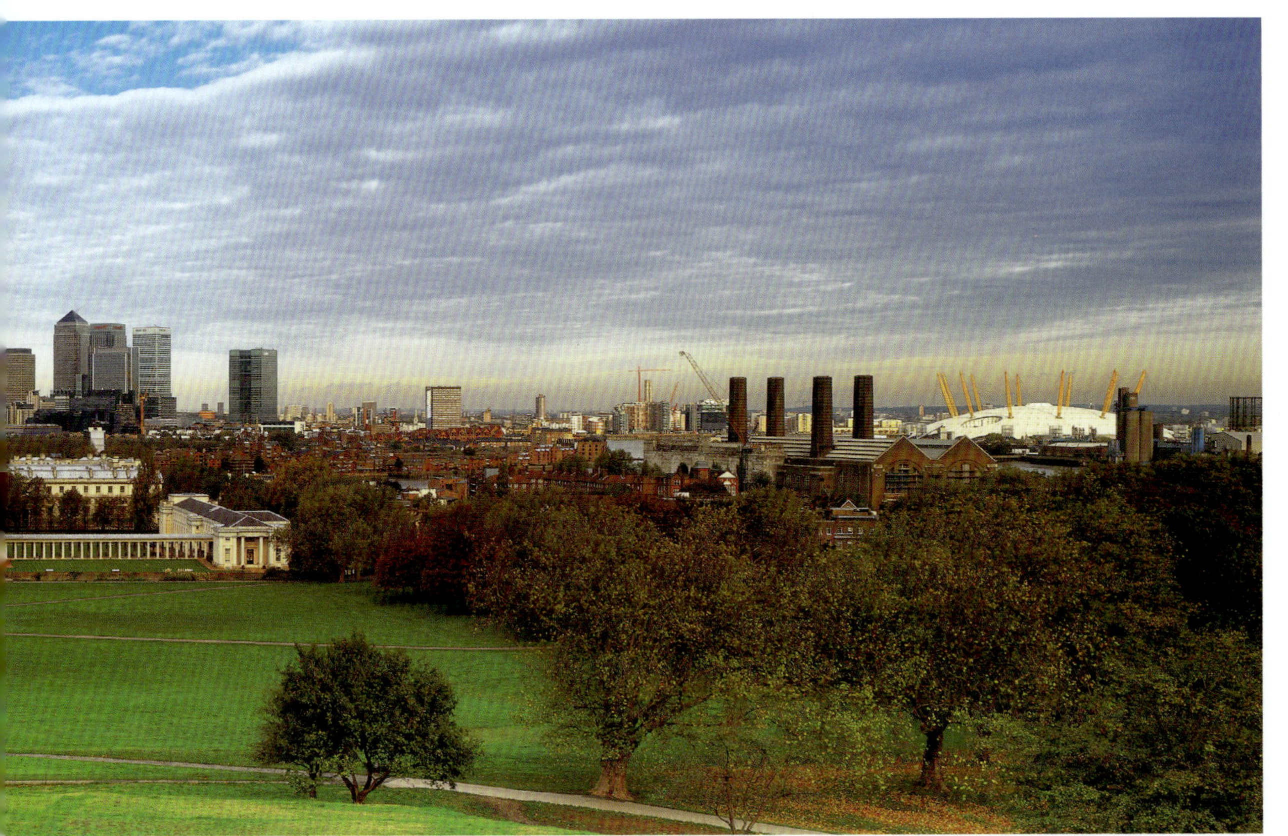

CLOUD BANKS FROM GREENWICH PARK

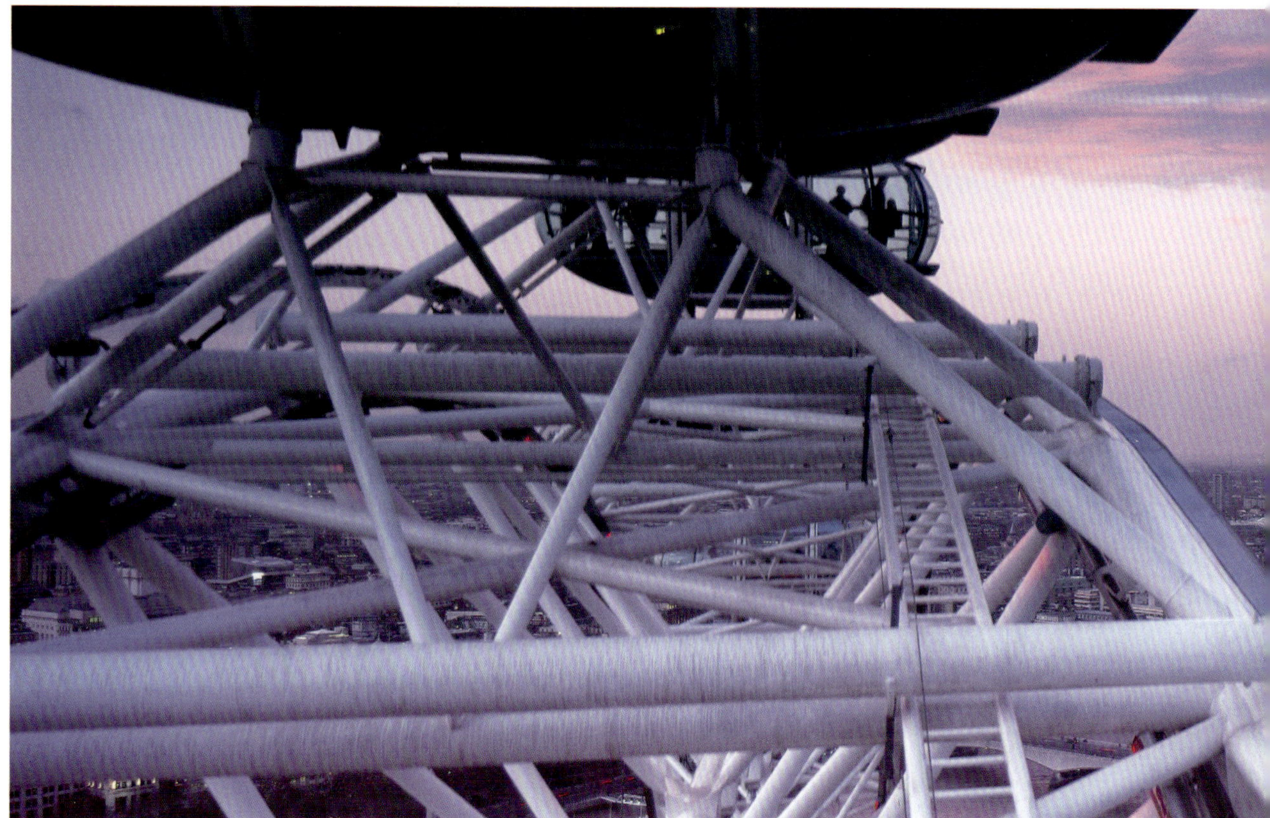

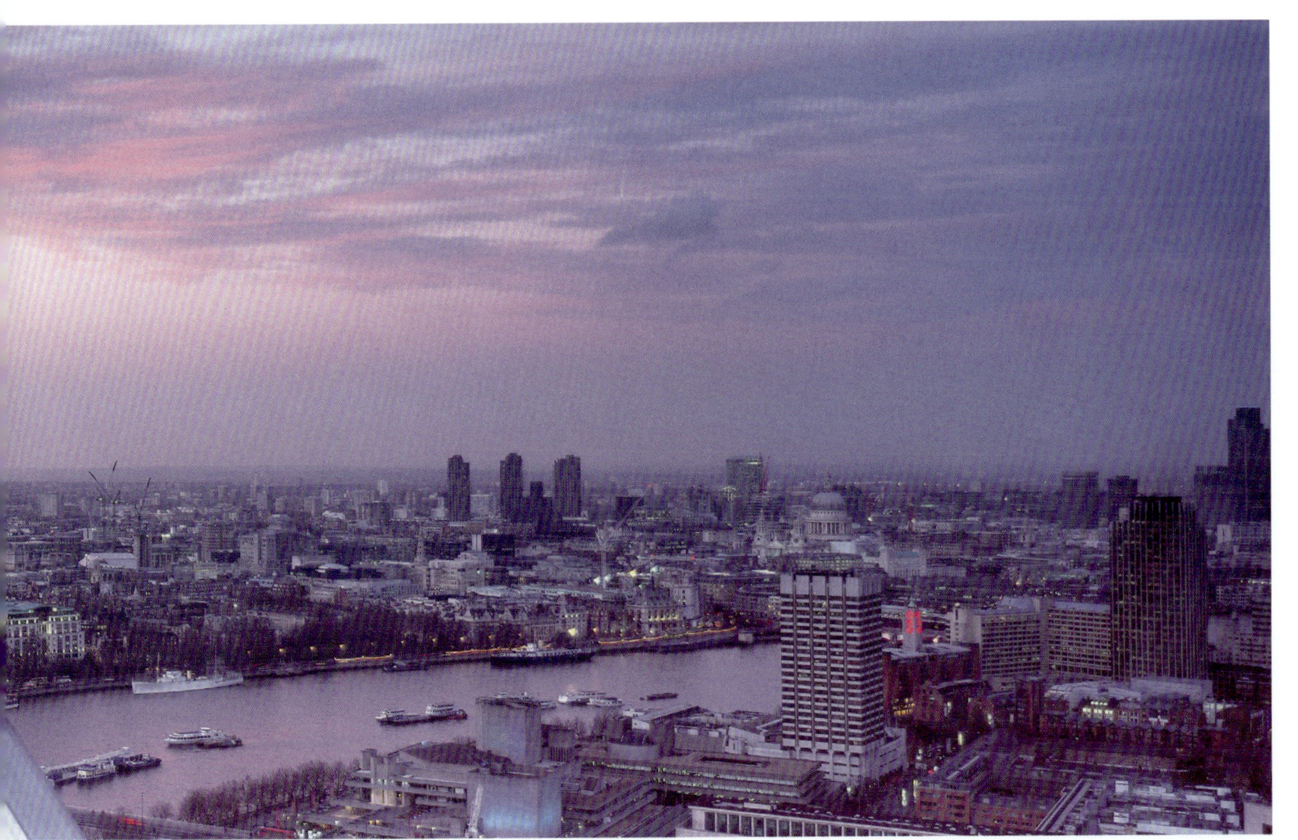

LOOKING EAST, LONDON EYE

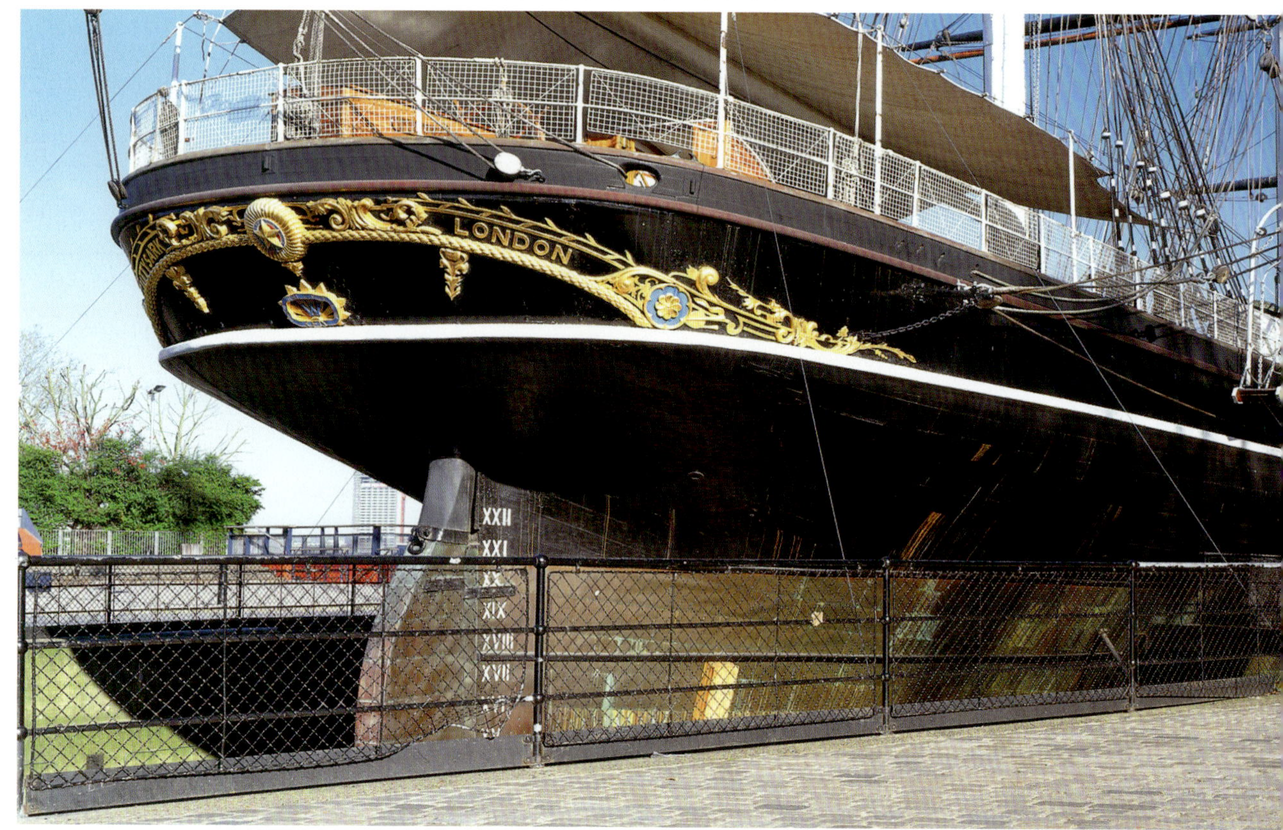
LONDON
XXII
XXI
XX
XIX
XVIII
XVII

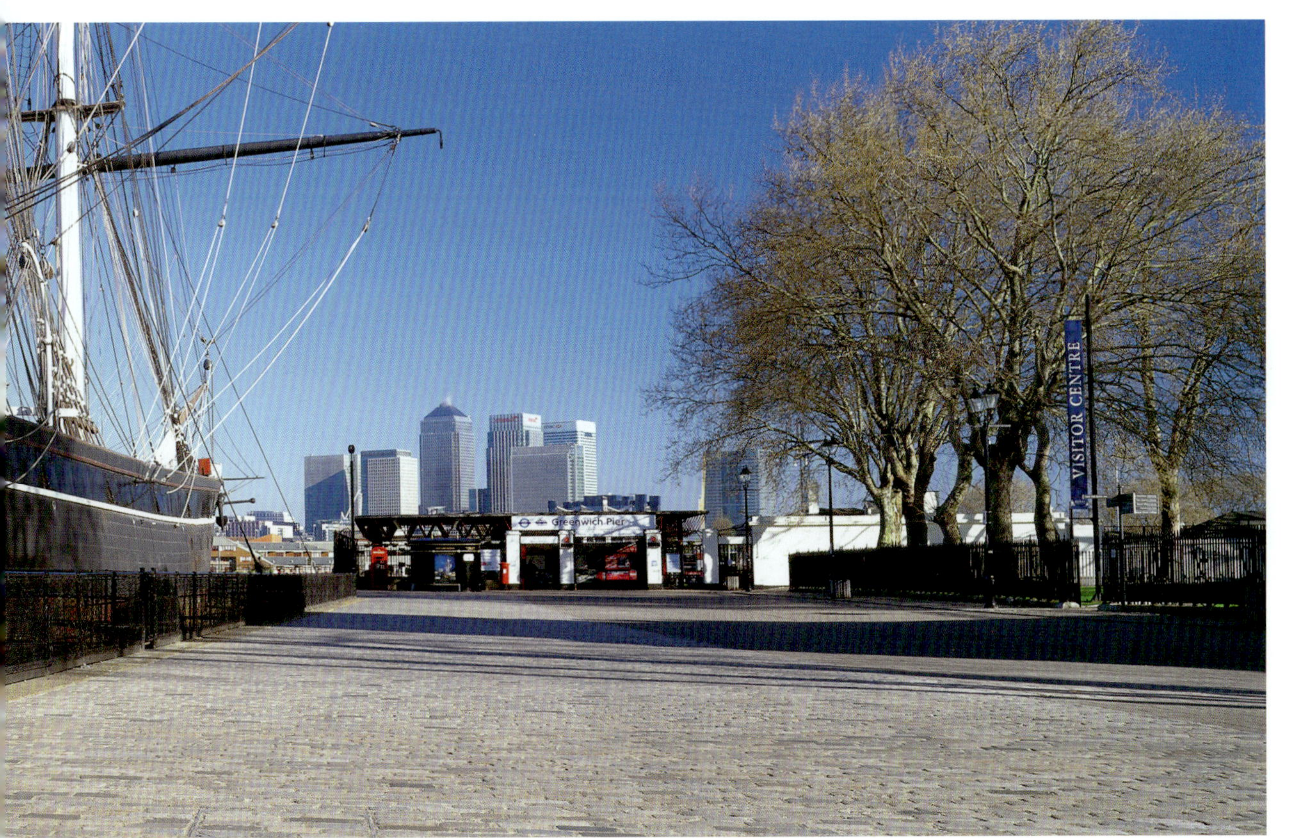

CUTTY SARK, SPRING MORNING

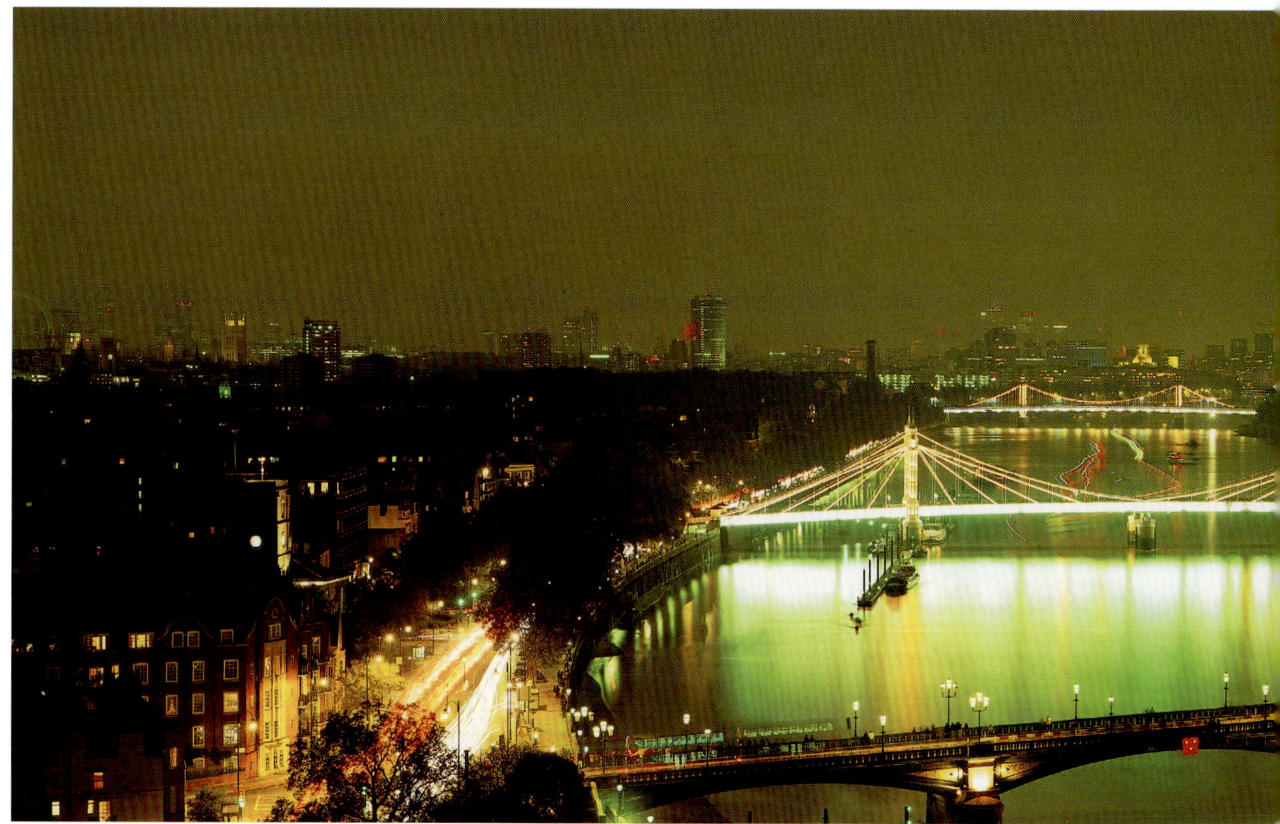

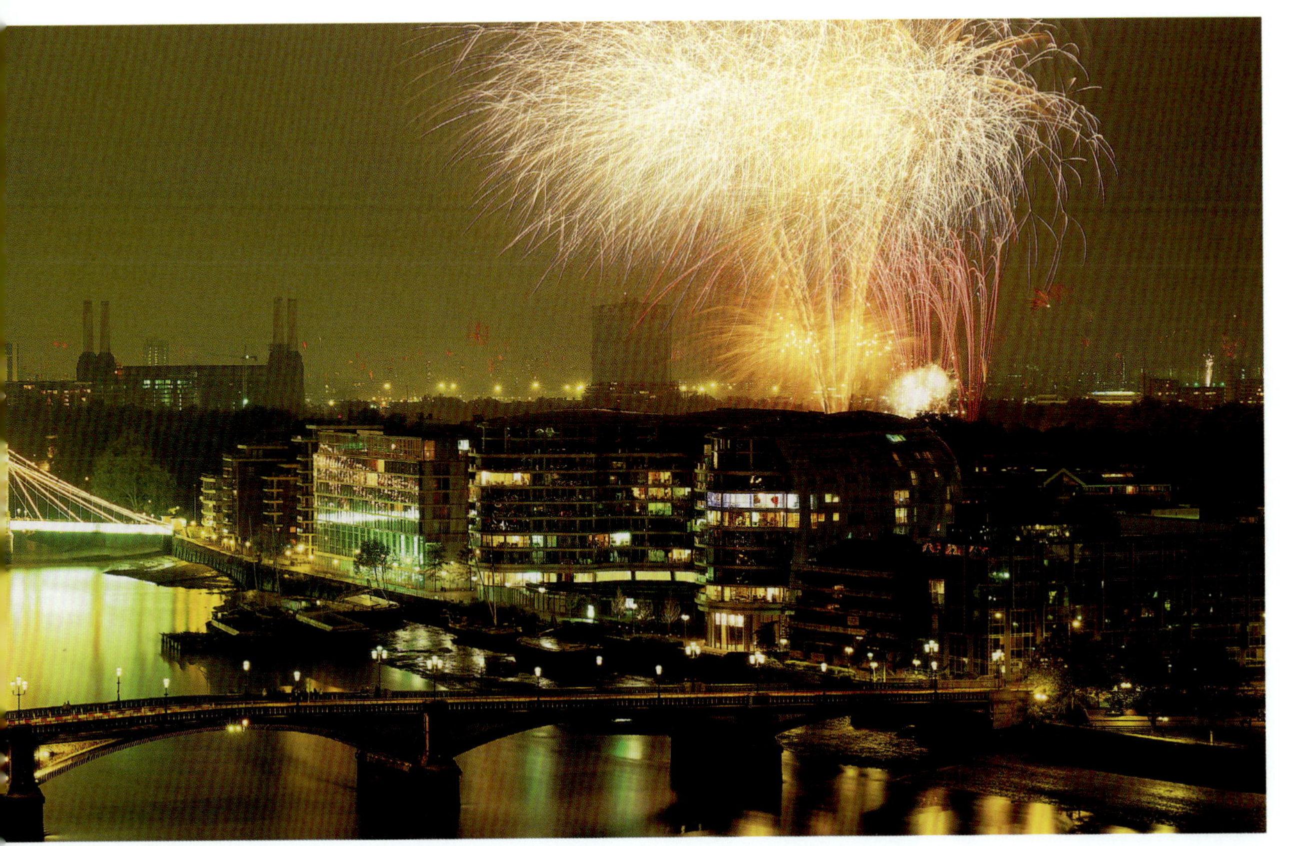

FIREWORKS IN BATTERSEA PARK, ACROSS THE THAMES

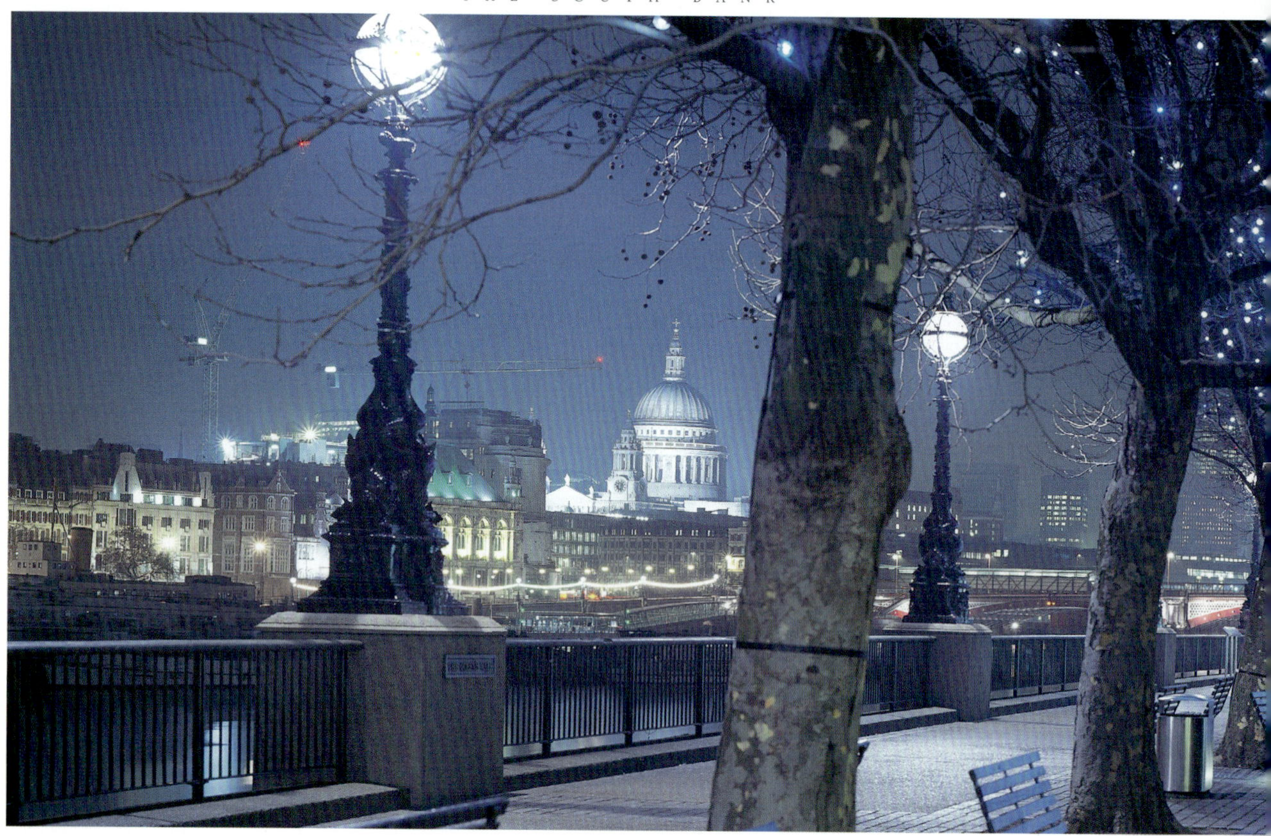

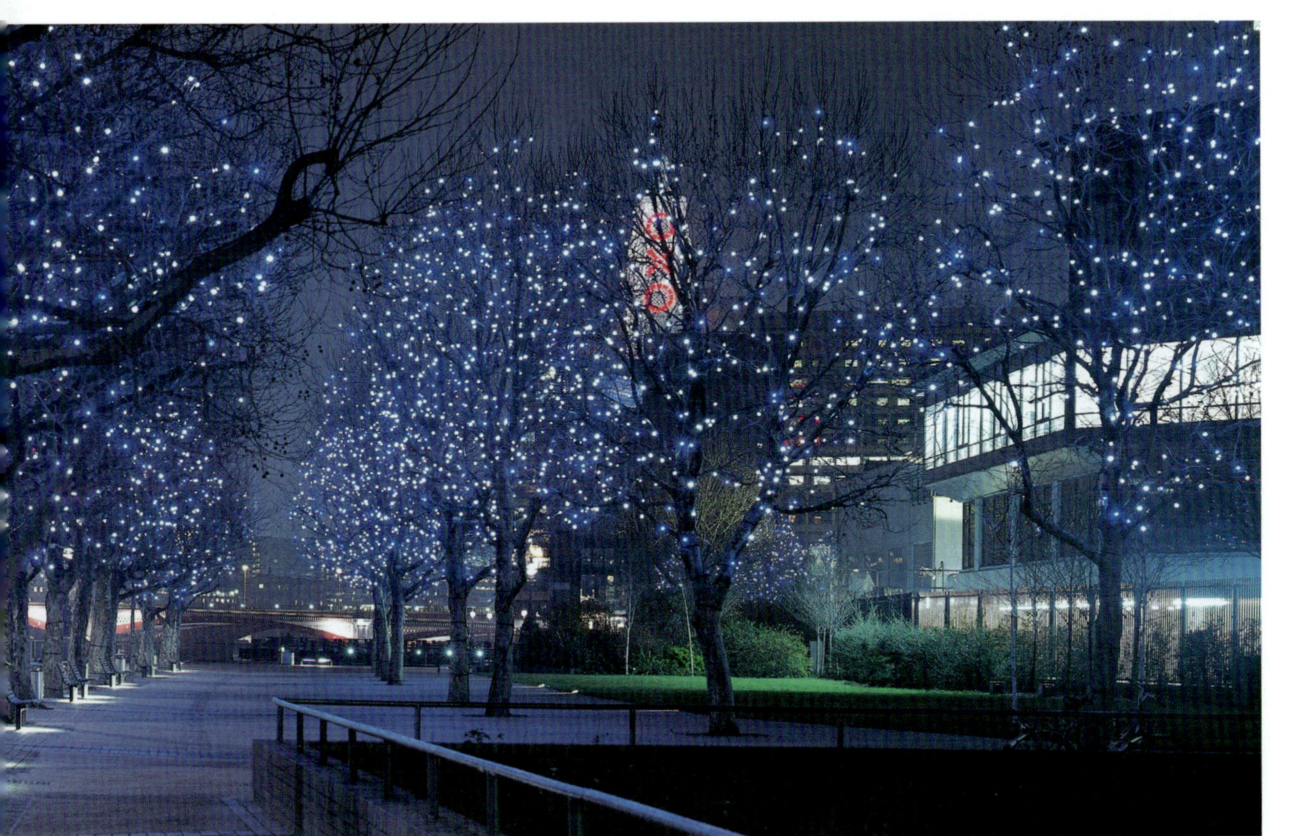

CHRISTMAS LIGHTS, SOUTH BANK

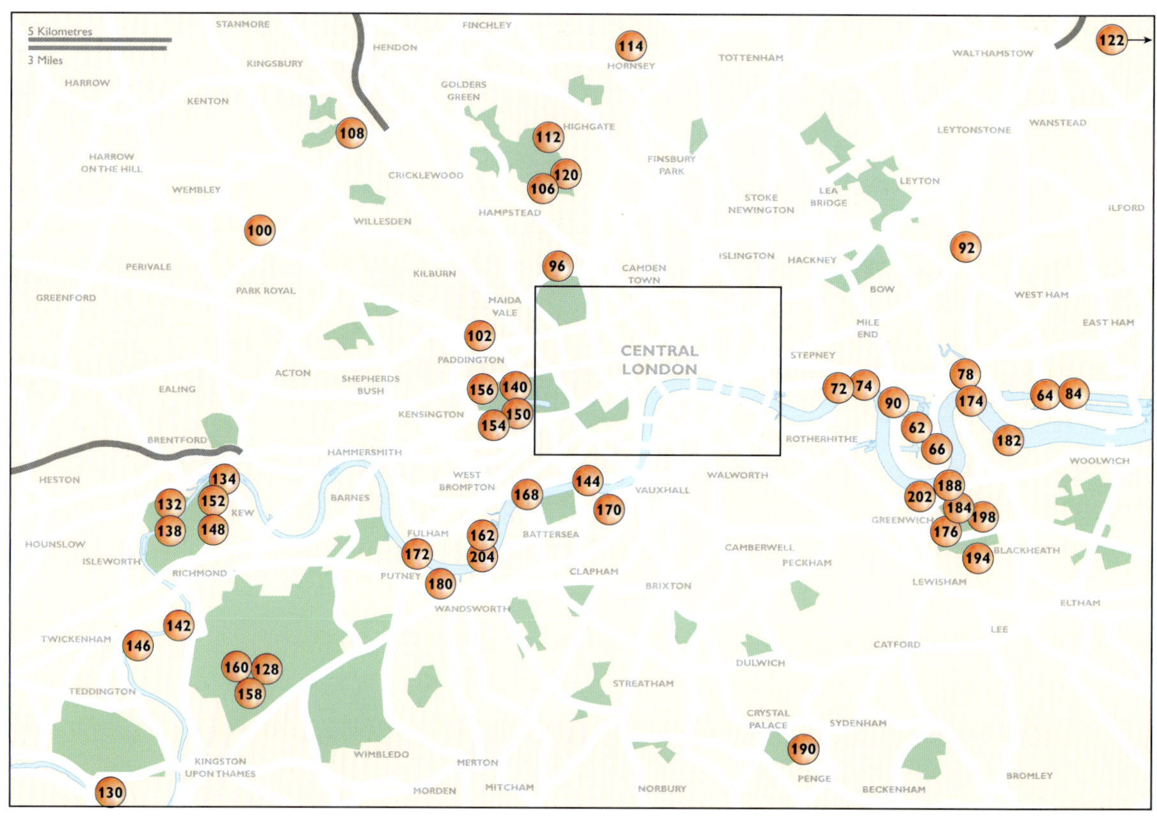
5 Kilometres
3 Miles
STANMORE
FINCHLEY
HENDON
KINGSBURY
HARROW
KENTON
GOLDERS GREEN
HORNSEY
TOTTENHAM
WALTHAMSTOW
HIGHGATE
LEYTONSTONE
WANSTEAD
HARROW ON THE HILL
CRICKLEWOOD
FINSBURY PARK
LEYTON
WEMBLEY
HAMPSTEAD
STOKE NEWINGTON
LEA BRIDGE
ILFORD
WILLESDEN
PERIVALE
KILBURN
ISLINGTON
HACKNEY
CAMDEN TOWN
BOW
WEST HAM
GREENFORD
PARK ROYAL
MAIDA VALE
MILE END
EAST HAM
PADDINGTON
CENTRAL LONDON
STEPNEY
ACTON
SHEPHERDS BUSH
EALING
KENSINGTON
BRENTFORD
ROTHERHITHE
HAMMERSMITH
WOOLWICH
HESTON
WEST BROMPTON
WALWORTH
VAUXHALL
BARNES
KEW
GREENWICH
FULHAM
BATTERSEA
HOUNSLOW
ISLEWORTH
CAMBERWELL
PECKHAM
BLACKHEATH
RICHMOND
PUTNEY
CLAPHAM
LEWISHAM
BRIXTON
WANDSWORTH
ELTHAM
LEE
TWICKENHAM
CATFORD
DULWICH
STREATHAM
TEDDINGTON
CRYSTAL PALACE
SYDENHAM
WIMBLEDO
KINGSTON UPON THAMES
MERTON
BROMLEY
PENGE
MORDEN
MITCHAM
NORBURY
BECKENHAM
114
122
108
112
120
106
100
96
92
102
156
140
150
154
72
74
90
78
174
64
84
62
66
182
134
132
152
138
148
168
144
170
188
202
184
198
176
162
204
172
180
194
142
146
160
128
158
190
130

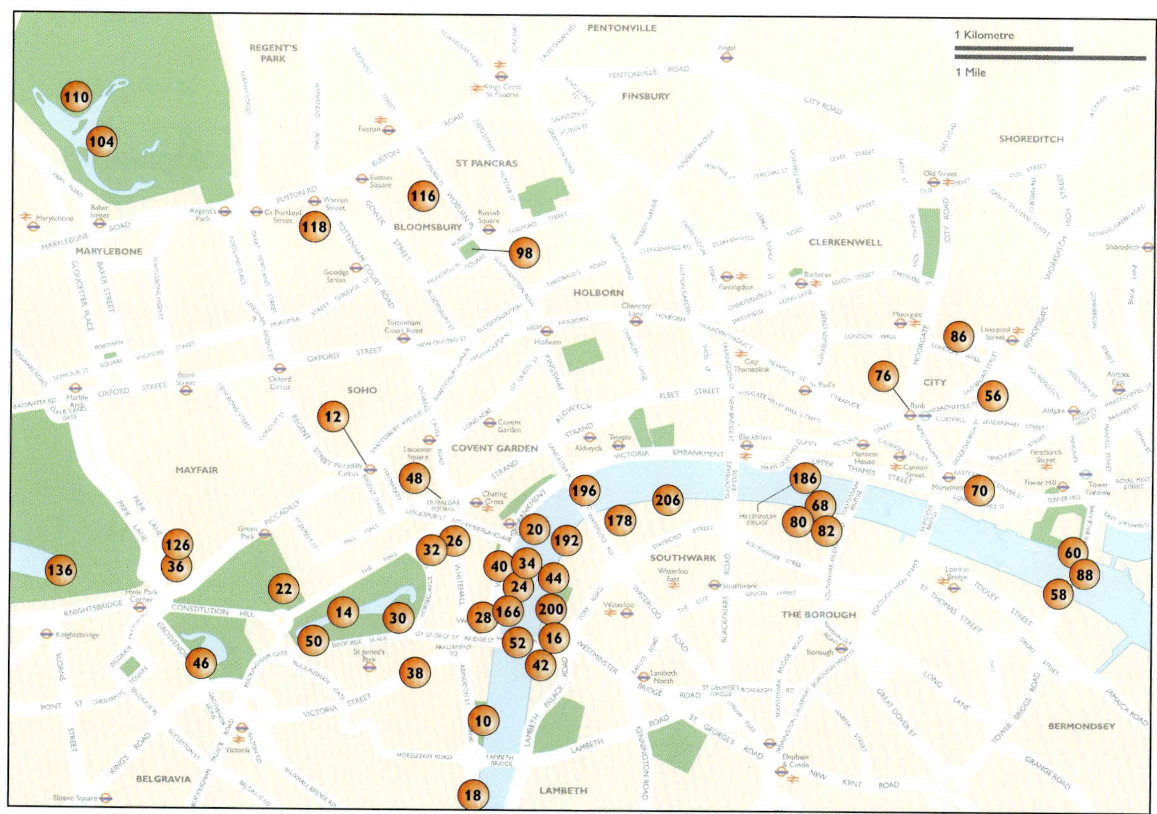
1 Kilometre
1 Mile
PENTONVILLE
REGENT'S PARK
FINSBURY
SHOREDITCH
ST PANCRAS
BLOOMSBURY
CLERKENWELL
MARYLEBONE
HOLBORN
SOHO
CITY
COVENT GARDEN
MAYFAIR
SOUTHWARK
THE BOROUGH
BERMONDSEY
BELGRAVIA
LAMBETH
Angel
Euston
Kings Cross St Pancras
Euston Square
Warren Street
Russell Square
Marylebone
Baker Street
Regent's Park
Gt Portland Street
Goodge Street
Farringdon
Barbican
Old Street
Shoreditch
Moorgate
Liverpool Street
Tottenham Court Road
Holborn
Chancery Lane
Oxford Circus
Bond Street
Marble Arch
Covent Garden
Temple
Blackfriars
St Paul's
Bank
Aldgate
Aldgate East
Mansion House
Cannon Street
Monument
Tower Hill
Tower Gateway
Fenchurch Street
Leicester Square
Piccadilly Circus
Charing Cross
Green Park
Hyde Park Corner
Knightsbridge
Waterloo
Waterloo East
Southwark
London Bridge
Lambeth North
Borough
Elephant & Castle
Victoria
Sloane Square
St James's Park
TRAFALGAR SQUARE
MILLENNIUM BRIDGE
LAMBETH BRIDGE
OXFORD STREET
PICCADILLY
CONSTITUTION HILL
KNIGHTSBRIDGE
VICTORIA STREET
FLEET STREET
EMBANKMENT
110
104
116
118
98
86
76
56
12
48
196
206
186
68
80
82
70
178
20
192
126
36
136
32
26
40
34
24
44
22
14
30
28
166
200
16
52
42
50
46
38
10
18
60
88
58

NOTES ON THE PHOTOGRAPHS

I principally employed two panoramic film cameras, the Fuji G617 and Fotoman 617. 617 refers to the size of the image captured on the film which is roughly 6 x17 cm, or more precisely 4 exposures of 56 x 168 mm on 120 roll film. This is around 11 times the size of a 35mm slide and consequently delivers fantastic image quality. I have four lenses available for these cameras – a fixed 105mm lens on the Fuji G617, which remains my favourite and 90mm, 180mm and 300mm for the Fotoman system.

Balancing light is the principal technical concern when I am shooting landscapes. The slide film I most often used, Fuji Velvia, is highly sensitive and will easily burn out or black out if improperly exposed. To get the best results I measure light with a Pentax Digital Spotmeter, and then use Lee neutral density filters to balance areas of light and shadow.

Why not digital, I hear people ask? The answers at the moment are the huge expense for a similar level of quality to film, the necessity of stitching (cropping on even a 40 megapixel digital back does not deliver the sharpness), and also that composition is very fiddly and rather slow using a sliding digital back. Digital may come…but not yet. Even when it does for me, looking at a beautiful 617 slide will be hard to surpass.

Mark Denton Sept 2011

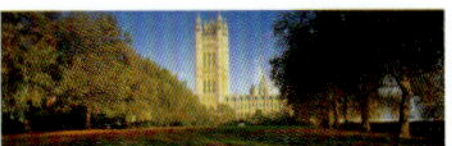

pages 10-11
Victoria Tower in autumn, Palace of Westminster
Nov 2010, Fuji G617, Lee 0.6 ND grad, 81b, Velvia 50 asa
My previous shot was a rather murky effort, so on this grandest of autumn days it was easy to improve. The mist that clung to the Thames became central to my day of shooting in the capital, and here can just be detected.

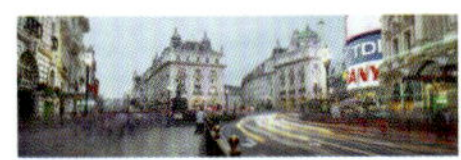

pages 12-13
Traffic trails, Piccadilly Circus
Sept 2005; Fuji G617 105mm, Lee 0.9 ND grad, Velvia 50 asa
After an extended period of scouting I positioned myself near the traffic lights for a 30-second exposure, and was cheered by a passing cabbie stopping there. 'That's a big camera,' he remarked, not unreasonably.

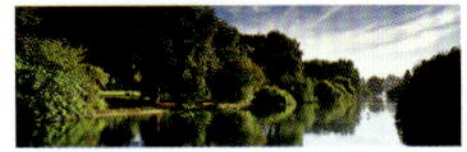

pages 14-15
Dawn, St James's Park
Sept 2005; Fuji G617 105mm, Lee 0.6 ND grad & polarizer, Velvia 50 asa
It didn't seem that dawn was the ideal time to shoot, with strong sunlight coming from behind Horse Guards Parade. Use of a polarizer and an angled grad made all the difference, giving strong colour and pleasing skies.

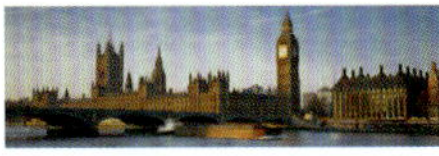

pages 16-17
Morning sunshine, Palace of Westminster
Jan 2006; Fotoman 617 180mm Rodenstock, Lee 0.6 ND grad, Velvia 50 asa
A sparkling winter morning on the South Bank. The barge totally escaped my attention, displaced by two policemen approaching. The 180mm lens could pass for a rocket launcher, so it was unsurprising that they had to investigate.

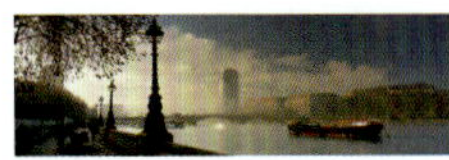

pages 18-19
Millbank Tower in mist
Nov 2010, Fuji G617, Lee 0.3 ND grad, Polarizer, 81b, Velvia 50 asa
It's usually the boundary between a fog bank and clear air that make the best shots. I wasn't able to shoot directly into the sun as I would have liked, but Millbank Tower looked unusually appealing for a bland 1960's tower block.

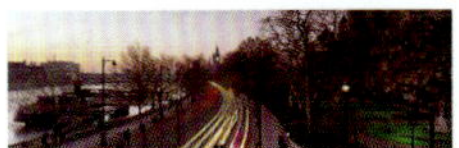

pages 20-21
Morning dash, Victoria Embankment
Jan 2006; Fuji G617 105mm, Lee 0.6 ND grad, Velvia 50 asa
The early morning race of expensive vehicles on the Embankment contrasted harshly with the homeless sleeping on the stairs and in the lift of Jubilee Bridge. I felt most fortunate being somewhere in between.

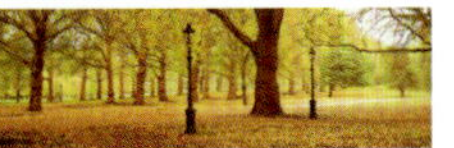

pages 22-23
Narnia lamps, Green Park
Oct 2005; Fotoman 617 180mm Rodenstock, Lee 81d, Velvia 50 asa
I hadn't expected to find inspiration in Green Park but I was immediately struck by the elegant avenues and ornate lighting. f32 was used to lengthen the exposure to 25 seconds, removing any trace of the suited procession marching to work.

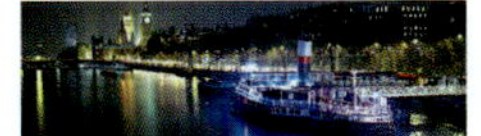

pages 24-25
***Tattershall Castle* and Westminster from Thames**
Jan 2006; Fotoman 617 180mm Rodenstock unfiltered, Fuji RTP 64
The paddle steamer *Tattershall Castle* now serves as a riverside bar, facing the Palace of Westminster. These sightlines proved irresistible, and the foreshortening effect of the 180mm lens helped to stress its wonderful location.

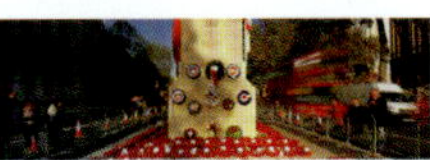

pages 26-27
The Glorious Dead, The Cenotaph, Whitehall
Nov 2010, Fuji G617, Lee 0.9ND grad, 81b, Velvia 50 asa
I paid my own small tribute the day after Remembrance Day with a simple shot of the memorials, while a few members of the public take time out to view the wreaths. The sun smiled on the heroes on that day.

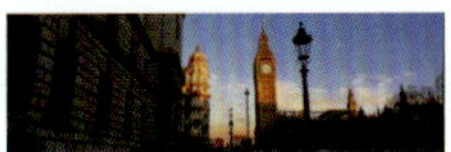

pages 28-29
The moon beyond Big Ben
Nov 2010, Fuji G617, Lee 0.45ND grad, Velvia 50 asa
Rushing to be by the river once again I was stopped in my tracks by glorious light falling on Big Ben, and I was putting the camera up in the middle of the pavement, as work-leavers dodged around me.

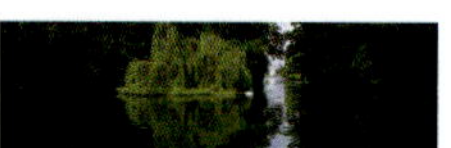

pages 30-31
Lone swan, St James's Park
June 2005; Fuji G617 105mm, Lee 0.6 ND grad, Velvia 50 asa
I'm no wildlife photographer. Distant shots of slow-moving swans are within my capabilities though, and when this obliging creature sailed gracefully towards Horse Guards, I was ready with a short exposure.

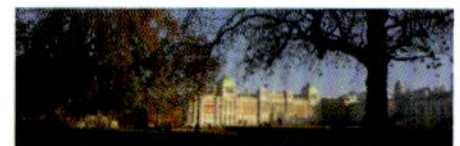

pages 32-33
The Old Admiralty Building, Horse Guards Parade
Nov 2010, Fuji G617, Lee 0.3ND grad, 81b, Velvia 50 asa
I used the trees at the edge of St James's Park to break up the flat sky, and an 81b warm-up filter to tone down the blue light. Positioning the important features of buildings between tree branches is a well-rehearsed technique of mine!

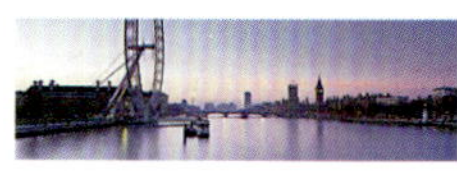

pages 34-35
Crescent moon at dawn, Thames
Jan 2006; Fuji G617 105mm, Lee 0.6 ND grad, Velvia 50 asa
A simple shot of the crescent moon setting. Exposure times need to be kept down when photographing the moon; its motion will lead to blurring on the image if the shutter is open too long.

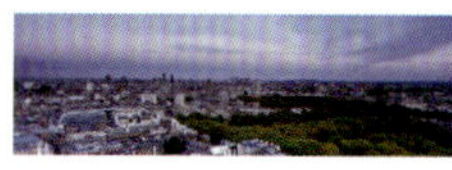

pages 36-37
View east, Park Lane Hilton
Nov 2005; Fuji G617 105mm, Lee 0.6 ND grad, Velvia 50 asa
This view from the top floor of the Hilton Park Lane compacts many landmarks into a curiously small channel, but what I particularly noticed were the trees of Green Park defiantly holding their leaves despite the impending winter.

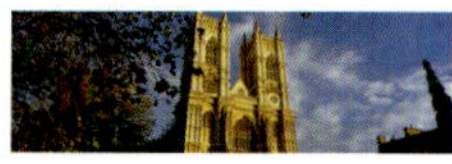

pages 38-39
Westminster Abbey, autumn light
Oct 2010, Fuji G617, polarizer, Velvia 50 asa
The cramped Abbey is possibly the most difficult subject in the city for my lenses. This was more successful than some attempts – a simplistic treatment of the fine towers, glowing in late afternoon light.

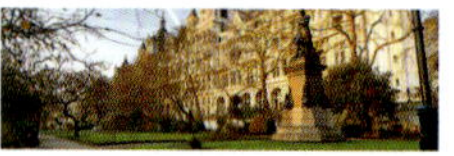

pages 40-41
Victoria Embankment, dawn
Jan 2006; Fuji G617 105mm, Lee 0.6 ND grad & polarizer, Velvia 50 asa
A winter dawn: the sun illuminates Northumberland Avenue, bringing out detail and reflecting subtle colour in the stone. London can make such architectural masterpieces seem commonplace.

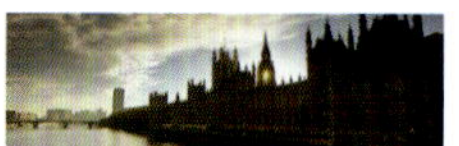

pages 42-43
Light in the tower, Palace of Westminster
Nov 2010, Fuji G617, Lee 0.9ND, Lee 0.3ND grad, Velvia 50 asa
A moment of serendipity on Westminster Bridge, as the dipping sun lights the intricately designed central tower like a beacon. The delicate cloud hanging over the Thames completed the scene in fine style. I reacted quickly.

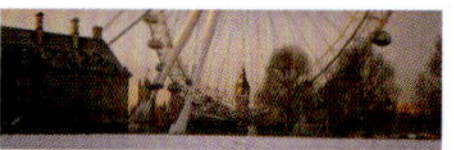

pages 44-45
Big Ben through the Eye, December
Dec 2010, Fotoman 617, 180mm, Lee 0.6ND grad, 81b, Velvia 50 asa
I spent much of the week before Christmas skating around on pavement ice, in contrast to the deserts of Jordan I'd recently returned from. I shot this image and the cover within ten minutes of each other as the sun gradually rose.

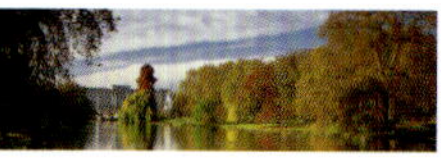

pages 46-47
Buckingham Palace in autumn, from St James's Park
Nov 2010, Fotoman 617, 180mm, Lee 0.6ND grad, 81b, Velvia 50 asa
Conscious of the lack of a good shot of the palace in the first London work, the challenge was how best to represent it in a new volume. Autumn in St James's was the obvious choice. The buck stops here, you could say.

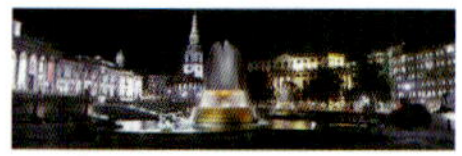

pages 48-49
Trafalgar Square by night
Nov 2005; Fotoman 617 180mm Rodenstock, RTP 64 asa
I spent a hours scouting in Trafalgar Square trying to find an ideal angle, with no ultimate satisfaction. Finally, I stepped backwards and settled on this overview, using a ground glass with the Fotoman for precise positioning. Simple is often best.

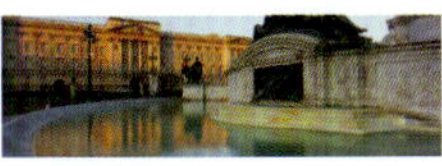

pages 50-51
Fountain reflections at Buckingham Palace
Dec 2010, Fuji G617, Lee 0.3ND grad, 81b, Velvia 50 asa
Just a month after my first shot of Buckingham Palace I returned on a freezing morning in December; so cold that the fountain pools were frozen. The sun arrived however, and added a welcome red warmth to the cold white stone.

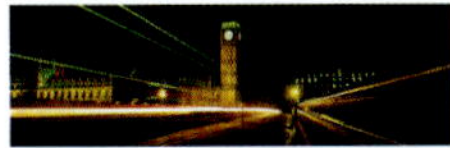

pages 52-53
Big Ben and traffic trails
Feb 2006; Fuji G617 105mm, Velvia 50 asa
I don't keep precise timings on my shots, but Big Ben helps here. The only worry after that was to prevent pedestrians from crashing into the tripod in the darkness, as the bridge was still busy.

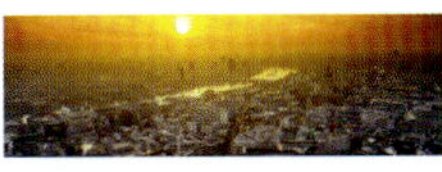

pages 56-57
Dying sun from Tower 42
Jan 2006; Fuji G617 105mm, Lee 0.3 & 0.9 ND grads, Velvia 50 asa
Open windows at Vertigo Bar are generally discouraged, so I was alerted to the risk of reflections from the glass. Despite several unwanted layers of filtration from the window, the results were pleasing, as the winter sun fell into a dense haze.

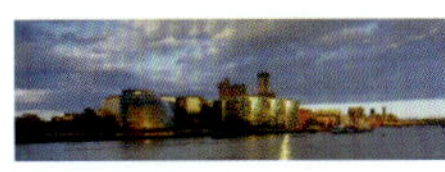

pages 58-59
City Hall and the beginnings of the Shard, from Tower Bridge
Aug 2010, Fuji G617, Lee 0.6ND grad, 81b, Velvia 50 asa
The tallest free-standing building in Britain begins to take shape. At the time I'm not even sure I knew what the significance of this pile of concrete was. By the time I finished it was already an elegant spire of glass – sadly still with a crane on the top!

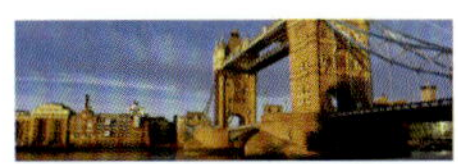

page 60-61
Morning light on Tower Bridge
Aug 2010, Fuji G617, Lee 0.6ND grad, polarizer, Velvia 50 asa
Finding a good perspective on Tower Bridge I always found surprisingly tricky. Things improved when I realised that including the tops of both towers was not entirely essential. This enabled me to get closer to the impressive structure and bring out more detail.

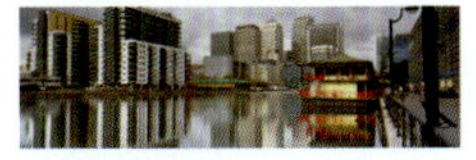

pages 62-63
Chinese barge, Canary Wharf
Feb 2006; Fuji G617 105mm, Lee 0.3 ND grad, Velvia 50 asa
My single shot this day proved to me once again that you shouldn't always write off grey conditions. The restaurant barge and the Canary towers juxtaposed give a sense of East meets West, Hong Kong or Singapore in miniature.

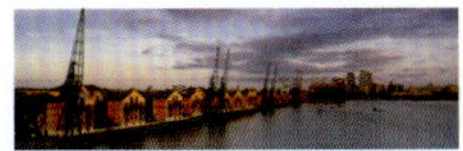

pages 64-65
Royal Victoria Dock at dawn
Jun 2005; Fuji G617 105mm, Lee 0.6 ND grad, Velvia 50 asa
Things have changed dramatically since my first visit to the Royal Victoria Dock in 1987, but the iconic steel forms of the cranes remain exactly as they were. My exposure here was simply a question of timing as the June sun lit the south of the dock.

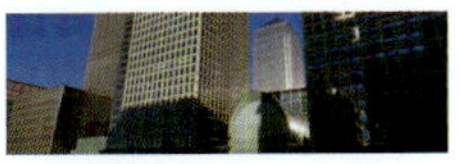

pages 66-67
Canary Wharf towers at Heron Quays
Jan 2011, Fotoman 617, 180mm, 81b, Velvia 50 asa
It's hard not to be impressed by the overload of architecture that greets you when disembarking at DLR stops such as South Quay. By walking miles and checking the viewfinder a few glimpses of the heart of this frenzy emerge.

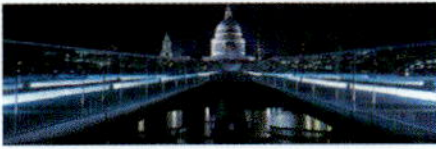

pages 68-69
Misty Night, Millennium View
Nov 2005, Fotoman 617, 180mm, RTP 64 asa
In September 2011 I visited to shoot at night with the 300mm lens for the first time. Sadly the St Paul's floodlights were switched off, making any attempt pointless. So it was time to dig out an old friend of an image, shot on a freezing evening, with mist swirling up the Thames.

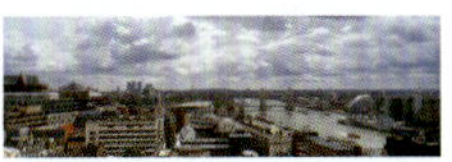

pages 70-71
View east from the Monument
Jun 2005; Fuji G617 105mm, Lee 0.3 ND grad, Velvia 50 asa
When the Monument was built to commemorate the Great Fire, an observer from it must have felt like a king. Today, surrounded by mundane office blocks, the view is less commanding, but remains impressive, particularly towards the Tower in the east.

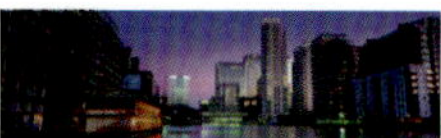

pages 72-73
Chinese Barge revisited, Canary Wharf
Jan 2011, Fuji G617, Lee 0.6ND grad, 81b, Velvia 50 asa
Reaching the point where I shot the Chinese restaurant barge in 2005 it was fascinating to gauge how things have moved on since then. A very rare shot with my better half in tow; she's normally got far better things to do!

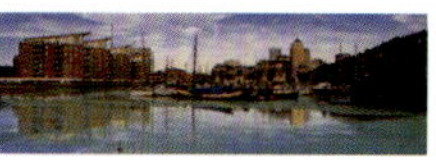

pages 74-75
Evening, Limehouse Basin
Jun 2005; Fuji G617 105mm, Lee 0.9 ND grad, Velvia 50 asa
Limehouse Basin was a surprise location for the project. After randomly stepping off the Docklands Light Railway, I found inspiration in the spacious dock and fine vista towards Canary Wharf. Not a shock to locals, I'm sure, but certainly to an ignorant Northerner.

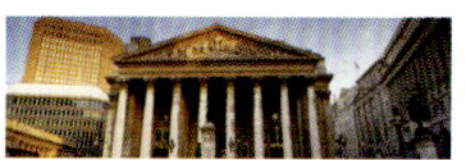

pages 76-77
Royal Exchange, the City
Jan 2006; Fuji G617 105mm, Lee 0.6 ND grad, Velvia 50 asa
The Royal Exchange and the Bank of England still feel like the fiscal heart of the nation. This small arena proved difficult to encapsulate when standing back, so I closed in on the Corinthian columns of the Exchange, to give them back their grandeur.

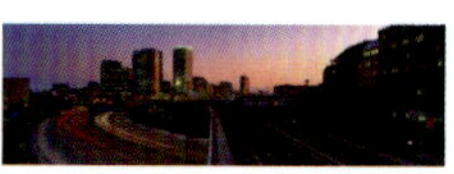

pages 78-79
New city from East India
Jun 2005; Fuji G617 105mm, Lee 0.9 ND grad, Velvia 50 asa
There was never any question as to whether I should photograph Canary Wharf, only where from. I found the opportunity late on a June evening after sundown. The unclouded afterglow proved an ideal backdrop for the dynamic lines of the foreground.

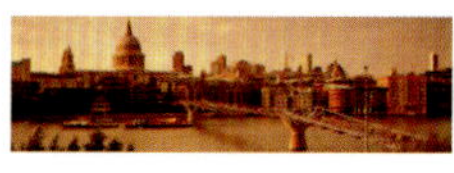

pages 80-81
Evening light on St Paul's, River Thames
Sept 2011, Fotoman 617, 180mm, Lee 0.6ND grad, 81d, Velvia 50 asa
The Tate Modern is a fabulous addition to the London cultural scene, not least because nobody complains when you whip out a large camera on their balcony. I'd taken this view before but been rather disappointed with the result. Not this time.

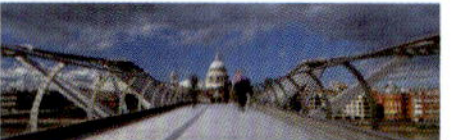

pages 82-83
St Paul's from Millennium Bridge
Apr 2005; Fuji G617 105mm, Lee 0.3 ND grad & polarizer, Velvia 50 asa
Using a polarizer had the side effect of softening the impact of the walkers by giving them motion blur, but exposure had to be kept down to retain detail in the cloud and avoid vibration from those walking past me.

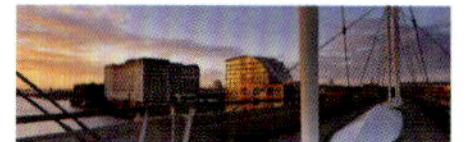

pages 84-85
Millennium Mill, Royal Victoria Dock
Jun 2005; Fuji G617 105mm, Lee 0.6 ND grad, Velvia 50 asa
The Millennium Mill is a remarkable hulk of a building that appears to have slipped into the same planning black hole that Battersea Power Station inhabits: too good to demolish, but apparently too difficult to develop.

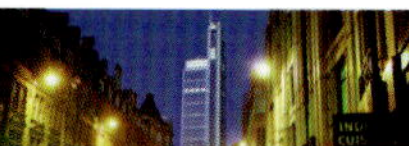

pages 86-87
Heron Tower from London Wall
Sept 2011, Fuji G617, Lee 0.75ND grad, 81b, Velvia 50 asa
The Heron Tower did not make much impression on me until I happened to be walking down London Wall. The sign for an Indian restaurant made for a curious juxtaposition. My tribute to the excellent curry houses of London perhaps!

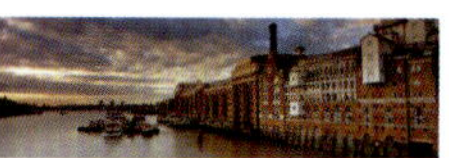

pages 88-89
Butler's Wharf at dawn, from Tower Bridge
Aug 2010, Fuji G617, Lee 0.9ND grad, 81b, Velvia 50 asa
One of my favourite riverside buildings, I thought Butler's Wharf deserved top billing for once, and not just be a backdrop. My choice for a bijou London pad I think, when funds allow. Don't think I'll be troubling the estate agents soon though.

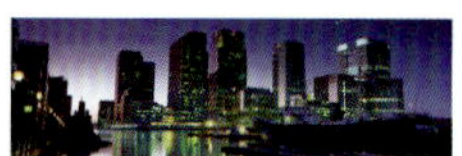

pages 90-91
Canary Wharf from West India Docks
Jan 2011, Fuji G617, Lee 0.9ND grad, 81b, Velvia 50 asa
One of the best viewpoints from where to capture the Isle of Dogs. Conforming to the recent photographic trend I bought a powerful torch and flicked it across the *Lord Amory* and jetties to add a little extra light during the 2-minute shot.

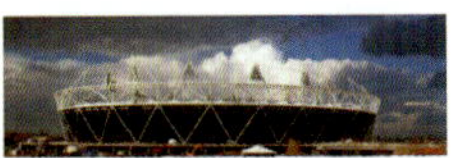

pages 92-93
Storm clouds beyond the Olympic Stadium, Stratford
Feb 2011, Fotoman 617, 180mm, 0.6ND grad, 81b, Velvia 50 asa
Access to Olympic buildings was impossible for the purposes of this book. Fortunately there was at least the 'Vue Tube' café. I shot this with stormy skies blowing in from the west. The tight lens emphasised the new structure against a powerful sky.

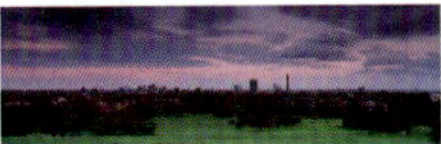

pages 96-97
Evening skies from Primrose Hill
Apr 2005; Fuji G617 105mm, Lee 0.6 ND grad, Velvia 50 asa
An April evening with a choice of exposure time that produced an improved result. The second attempt, going up to 40 seconds, meant that the wind had time to stretch the cloud into more attractive patterns in the sky.

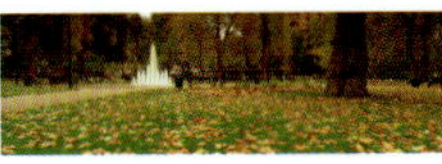

pages 98-99
Leaves, Russell Square
Nov 2005; Fuji G617 105mm, Lee 81c grad & 0.6 ND grad, Velvia 50 asa
I had to be sharp and run the gauntlet of an eager council worker raking the autumn leaves into huge mounds to scoop up later. When I explained my task, he kindly diverted to equally important rakings elsewhere.

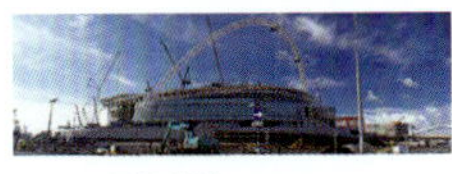

pages 100-101
Cranes, new Wembley Stadium
Feb 2006; Fuji G617 105mm, Lee 0.6 ND grad, Velvia 50 asa
Wembley Stadium is now finished and looks rather magnificent, worthy of the aspirations of the country. As a fan of Sunderland AFC though, I'm not sure I'll be rushing back. My three previous visits have all coincided with personal tragedy!

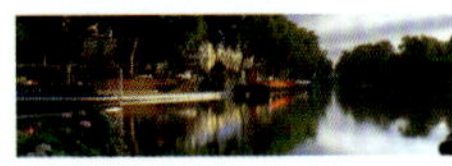

page 102-103
Dawn colours, Little Venice
Sep 2005; Fuji G617 105mm, Lee 0.3 ND grad, Velvia 50 asa
A tranquil oasis, Little Venice shows what was achieved in a less frantic era of transport. The few sleepy barge dwellers I encountered seemed entirely at odds with the suited folk dashing to work down the towpath at Paddington.

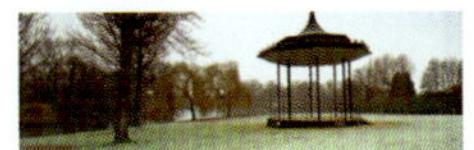

pages 104-105
Bandstand in winter, Regent's Park
Jan 2006; Fuji G617 105mm, Lee 81c & 0.6 ND grad, Velvia 50 asa
The 'coldest night in the capital for many years', and twin willows and the deserted bandstand reflect the mood of still hibernation in Regent's Park. A warm-up filter was employed but it did little to warm up the frozen photographer.

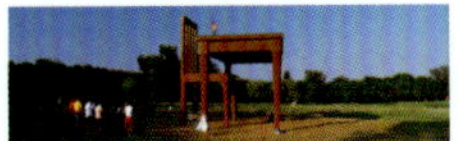

pages 106-107
Gary climbs The Writer, Parliament Hill
Jul 2005; Fuji G617 105mm, Lee 0.6 ND grad, Velvia 50 asa
Alerted to the commotion at the table and chair, which I was composing from a distance, I closed in to find Gary shinning up the chair leg and delighting all onlookers except his horrified girlfriend (seen as a white blur).

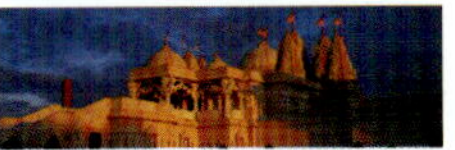

page 108-109
Neasden Hindu Temple, evening light
Aug 2010, Fotoman 617, 180mm, Lee 0.6ND grad, Velvia 50 asa
An astonishing building, found not in the exotic climes of Uttar Pradesh, but in relatively dowdy North London. Shots were possible thanks to the most charming security men I have met, and through the barriers with a long lens after closing time.

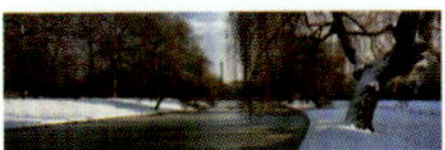

page 110-111
Thick snow in Regent's Park
Dec 2010, Fuji G617, 81b, Velvia 50 asa
I drove through terrible conditions to reach London for my urgently needed snow scenes, but it was well worth the effort. I spent the lunchtime hours using the frozen waterway in Regent's Park. Willow trees are great subjects, and in deep winter the quality of light remains high even at midday.

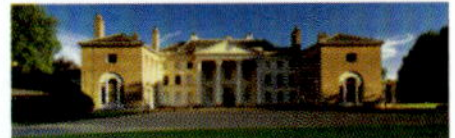

pages 112-113
Kenwood House, Hampstead Heath
Jun 2005; Fuji G617 105mm, Lee 0.6 ND grad & polarizer, Velvia 50 asa
Kenwood House is more normally photographed from the south. However, on a late June evening the sun has moved around to bathe the northern façade with light.

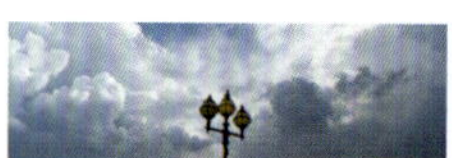

pages 114-115
Lamps, Alexandra Palace
Sep 2005; Fuji G617 105mm unfiltered, Velvia 50 asa
I did not travel to Alexandra Palace with the intention of avoiding images of the building, but under ominous skies there was no light cast on it. Instead, I was unable to resist the dramas occurring in the skies to the south as a thunderstorm crossed Highgate.

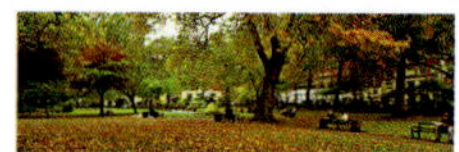

pages 116-117
Autumn, Tavistock Square
Oct 2005; Fuji G617 105mm, Lee 81c, Velvia 50 asa
A trip to Tavistock Square to pay my respects to those who died on 7 July. I found that the scene was one of peaceful normality. Only the quickening breeze and buildings shrouded in plastic gave a reminder of the disturbing events three months previously.

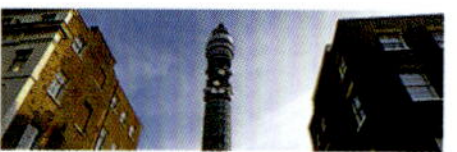

pages 118-119
BT Tower from Capper Street
Jan 2006; Fuji G617 105mm unfiltered, Velvia 50 asa
I elected to shoot the BT Tower from Fitzroy Square, using the convergence of the Fuji lens to bring together the gable ends of the buildings. The set-up had to be speedy and portable, as the best position proved to be in the middle of the road.

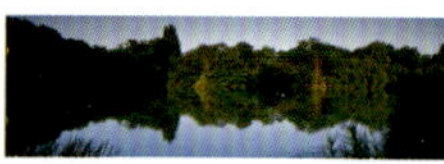

pages 120-121
Swans, Hampstead Heath
Jul 2005; Fuji G617 105mm, Lee 0.6 ND grad, Velvia 50 asa
A summer evening on one of the Highgate ponds, and a pair of swans go about their business in a relaxed fashion. Hampstead Heath is the stamping ground of Bill Oddie, and it would have surprised me little to run into him, binoculars in hand.

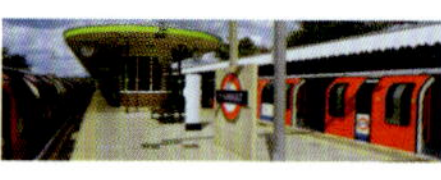

pages 122-123
Art Deco waiting room at Hainault, Central line
Sept 2011, Fuji G617, Velvia 50 asa
I was always looking for a photograph to nicely represent the London Underground. By its nature, the Tube is frenetically busy, and dark in the central areas. Finally, on effectively my last day of shooting, I found an opportunity while changing Central Line trains at Hainault.

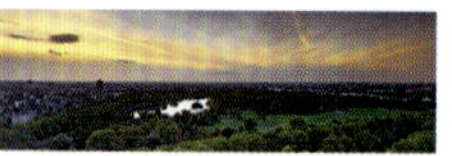

pages 126-127
View west, Park Lane Hilton
Nov 2005; Fuji G617 105mm, Lee 0.9 ND grad, Velvia 50 asa
With only two afternoons to capture the view from the Park Lane Hilton, it was going to require a little good fortune to gain workable conditions. The first evening was flat and grey. The second, however, brought a sublime fading sunset.

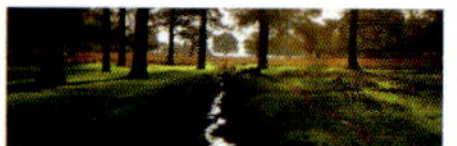

pages 128-129
Stream, Richmond Park
Nov 2005; Fotoman 617 180mm Rodenstock, Lee 0.9 ND grad, Velvia 50 asa
This view had many themes I look for in a panorama: strong lead-in lines, a distinct central feature, good symmetry and nice light to boot. To ensure accuracy, I used the Fotoman and ground glass, and positioned the central tree precisely.

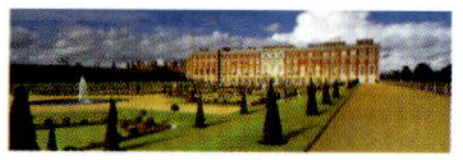

pages 130-131
Fluffy cloud, Hampton Court Palace
Jan 2006; Fuji G617 105mm, Lee 0.6 ND grad, Velvia 50 asa
Richmond photographer Joanna Jackson was an invaluable guide to Hampton Court Palace and its grounds. As I prepared another all-encompassing panorama, she was happily rummaging in the undergrowth somewhere.

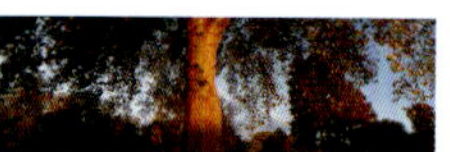

pages 132-133
Leaf shower, Kew
Nov 2005; Fuji G617 105mm unfiltered, Velvia 50 asa
A rather experimental moment in Kew Gardens under the canopy of an autumnal tree. This was a sparkling November afternoon, and my heart was warmed by the opportunities for shooting, as well as by the friendly staff at Kew.

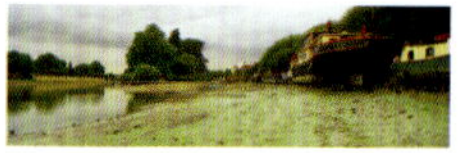

pages 134-135
Houseboats, Kew Bridge
Sep 2005; Fuji G617 105mm, Lee 0.6 ND grad & 81c, Velvia 50 asa
Floating homes line the river between here and Chelsea, and give respite from traffic noise, as well as being safe from the threat of increased flooding. At low tide the green algae in the river is revealed, and by the time shooting was over I was covered in mud.

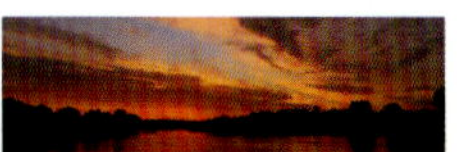

pages 136-137
Serpentine sunset, Hyde Park
Sep 2005; Fuji G617 105mm, Lee 0.3 ND grad, Velvia 50 asa
A gaudy September sunset in Hyde Park, captured from the eastern end of the Serpentine. I don't go seeking out glorious sunsets, and when they come another point of interest such as a striking silhouette is advantageous.

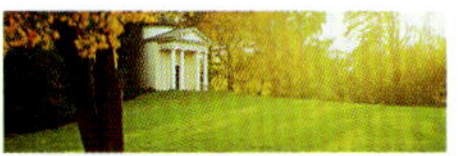

pages 138-139
Temple, Kew Gardens
Nov 2005; Fuji G617 105mm, Lee 0.9 ND grad, Velvia 50 asa
Firing into the sun is a hit-and-miss practice especially when you're trying to retain foreground detail it is especially difficult. Here, shooting at Kew, I just about got away with it, avoiding damaging flare by a whisker.

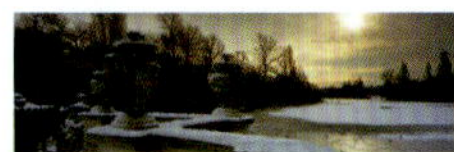

pages 140-141
Italian Gardens, Serpentine, Hyde Park
Dec 2010, Fuji G617, Lee 0.6ND grad, 81b, Velvia 50 asa
The country remained gripped by the big freeze. I walked from Waterloo at dawn and finally ended on Parliament Hill. On the way I made the best use of the frozen Serpentine in Hyde Park, while warming myself with a cup of coffee.

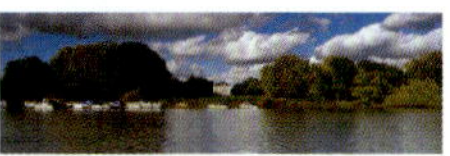

pages 142-143
Marble Hill House, River Thames
Oct 2005; Fuji G617 105mm, Lee 0.6 ND grad, Velvia 50 asa
There are always opportunities for shooting with fast-moving fluffy cumulus, and Marble Hill House provided a good setting. I was rewarded with a life-saving cup of tea and selection of cream cakes by the wonderful staff at Ham House.

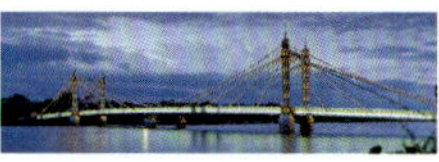

pages 144-145
Blue dusk, Albert Bridge
Jun 2005; Fuji G617 105mm, Lee 0.6 grad, Velvia 50 asa
I came to the Albert Bridge late on an evening in high summer, and waited for what seemed like an age for the bulbs to illuminate. Finally I looked down to check my exposure, looked up again and the bridge was lit, with pallid blue cloud in the background.

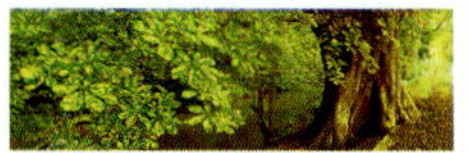

pages 146-147
Horsechestnut, Thames path
Sep 2005; Fuji G617 105mm, Lee 81c, Velvia 50 asa
Autumn is always my favourite time to shoot, but I was taken by surprise by this magnificent horse-chestnut on the Thames Path near Chiswick. This was early September and the tree seemed to be making premature contingency plans for winter.

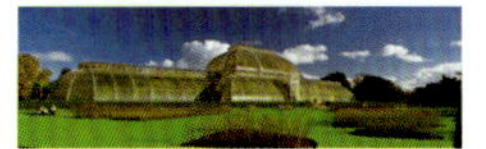

pages 148-149
Fluffy clouds, Palm House, Kew Gardens
Nov 2005, Fuji G617, Lee 0.6ND grad, polarizer, Velvia 50 asa
I have resurrected this older shot of the Palm House as it represents the building better than the shot in volume one. It was a beautifully clear late autumn day and you could have imagined it was the height of summer, as could the walkers enjoying the sunshine.

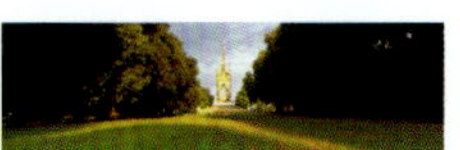

pages 150-151
Albert Memorial, Hyde Park
Sep 2005; Fuji G617 105mm, Lee 0.6 ND grad, Velvia 50 asa
The Albert Memorial was a classic subject for a panoramic camera, but this proved a difficult location in which to gauge exposure, thanks to the small gap of light between the trees and the dazzling sunlight on the gilded statue.

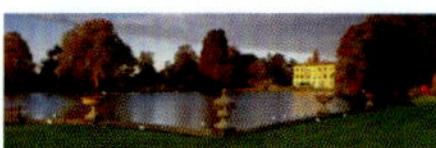

pages 152-153
Lake at Kew Gardens
Nov 2005; Fuji G617 105mm, Lee 0.6 ND grad, Velvia 50 asa
At the end of a beautiful November afternoon, the falling sun brings intense colour to the lake and surrounding trees. Adding to the colour are the floating globules of Chihuly glass and the extravagant rowing boat commandeered by the sculptor.

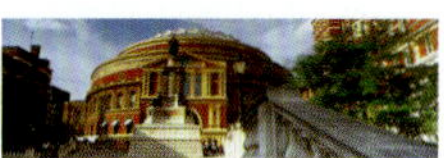

pages 154-155
Royal Albert Hall, afternoon sun
Sep 2005; Fuji G617 105mm, Lee 0.6 ND grad & polarizer, Velvia 50 asa
The Royal Albert Hall required some thought over timing and conditions, given its cramped location. The steps and forecourt were occupied by extras from a feature film on location at the Science Museum behind me.

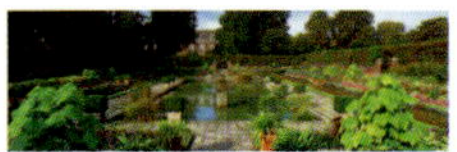

pages 156-157
Gardens, Kensington Palace
Jun 2005; Fuji G617 105mm, Lee 0.6 ND grad, Velvia 50 asa
Intense greens of late spring give a lush appearance to the Italianate gardens of Kensington Palace in Hyde Park. The magnificent gilded gates of the palace were obscured by hundreds of personal memorials to Lady Diana, which made for its own panorama.

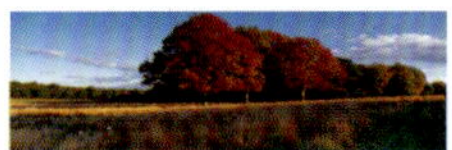

pages 158-159
Autumn trees, Richmond Park
Nov 2005; Fuji G617 105mm, Lee 0.6 ND grad, Velvia 50 asa
Walking into Richmond Park at dawn for the first time was a revelation. A lone stag grazed 50 metres to the left of shot, but I knew my lenses would not allow me to pick it up in detail, and stalking is not one of my specialities.

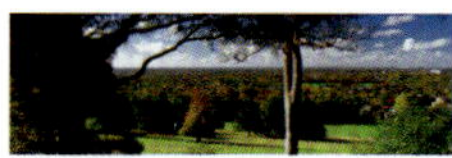

pages 160-161
View from Henry VIII's Mound, Richmond Park
Nov 2005; Fuji G617 105mm, Lee 0.3 ND grad & polarizer, Velvia 50 asa
I had heard that this particular view from Henry VIII's mound in Richmond was 'the most painted view in England'. The new Wembley arch, far to the north-west, is barely a dot on the horizon.

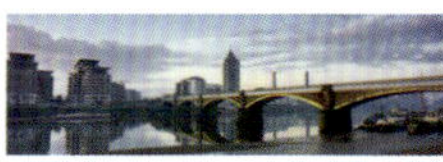

pages 162-163
Belvedere Tower, Chelsea Harbour
Nov 2010, Fuji G617, Lee 0.6ND grad, 81b, Velvia 50 asa
An epic day. I began shooting in St James's Park, then Westminster, rode the tube to Putney Bridge, then walked to town on the Thames Path south of the river. The subtle skies combined well with Belvedere Tower, home to some of the rich and famous.

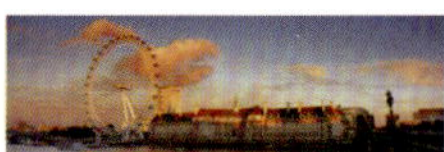

pages 166-167
Fine light on the London Eye
Nov 2010, Fuji G617, Lee 0.45ND grad, 81b, Velvia 50 asa
I made it to the riverside, to witness terrific late sunlight catching County Hall. There wasn't much space, as crowds seemed to gather around me to watch the scene, and Westminster Bridge bustled with activity. I just had time to get my shot before the sublime light faded out.

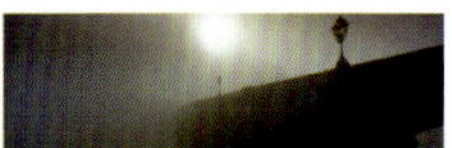

pages 168-169
Putney Bridge disappears in mist
Nov 2010, Fuji G617, Lee 0.9ND grad, Velvia 50 asa
Putney Bridge is architecturally satisfying, but I'd not really imagined it making it into this volume. My ideas changed when I viewed it as a dense bank of fog moved up and down the river. The result was very atmospheric, as was the whole day.

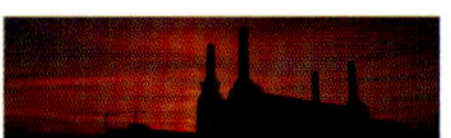

pages 170-171
Battersea Power Station
Jun 2005; Fuji G617 105mm unfiltered, Velvia 50 asa
After a frustrating hour of scouting I found myself running down Nine Elms Lane, to catch a vivid red sky behind the world's most famous chimneys. Strange that the derelict industrial hulk of Battersea Power Station should provoke such admiration.

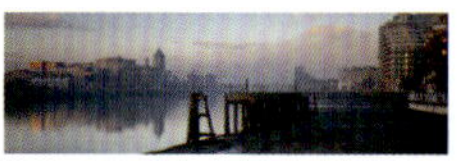

pages 172-173
Wooden jetty at Battersea, Thames
Nov 2010, Fotoman 617, 180mm, Lee 0.45, 81b, Velvia 50 asa
Another shot from the November 'mist' day, this time an old wooden jetty next to the new housing developments of Battersea. Seabirds perched enticingly on the structure, and I tried to shoot with the 300mm but the wider angle proved more satisfying.

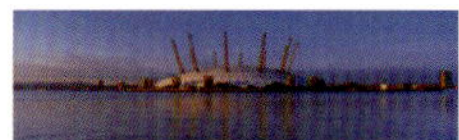

pages 174-175
O2 Arena at dawn
Jun 2005; Fuji G617 105mm, Lee 0.3 ND grad, Velvia 50 asa
I appreciate the Dome for what it is now, a quite beautiful folly that catches the light delightfully at dawn in June. I mused whether a polarizer added or detracted, and on this occasion was happier with the non-polarized version.

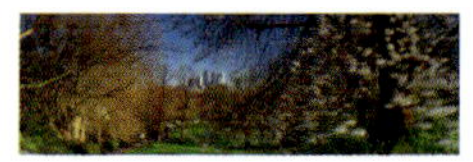

pages 176-177
April blossom and Canary Wharf, from Greenwich Park
Apr 2005; Fuji G617 105mm, Lee 0.3 ND grad & polarizer, Velvia 50 asa
Strolling downhill in Greenwich Park I had one of those moments that you long for in this line of work: sighting the distant Docklands towers perfectly framed by a gap in the trees.

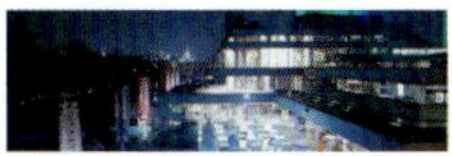

page 178-179

National Theatre and St Paul's by night

Jan 2006, Fotoman 617, 180mm, RTP 64 asa

The National Theatre is a seventies concrete monstrosity or a brave statement. Famously described by Prince Charles as a 'nuclear power station in the middle of London', I'd rather see it as supplying cultural and artistic power to the city.

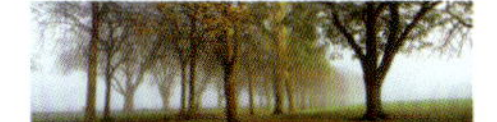

page 180-181

Trees in the mist, Wandsworth Park, River Thames

Nov 2010, Fuji G617, Lee 0.6ND grad, 81b, Velvia 50 asa

Not a shot I'd planned for, but that is the beauty of exploring London by foot. The slender trees fading out into the mist and the monochromatic tones reminded me somewhat of a shot by the Parisian master Cartier-Bresson.

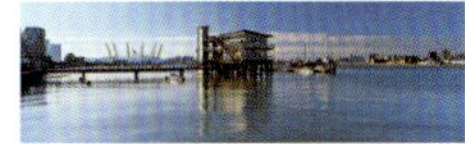

pages 182-183

Greenwich Yacht Club

Sep 2005; Fuji G617 105mm, Lee 0.6 ND grad, Velvia 50 asa

Intending to shoot the Thames Barrier, I discovered the curious building on stilts: the Greenwich Yacht Club. Using a nearby building to narrowly shield myself from the sun, I balanced the blues of sky and river with a ND grad.

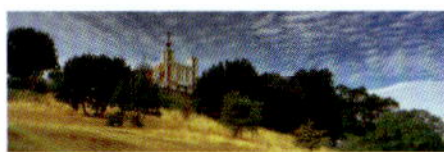

pages 184-185

Broken cloud over the Royal Observatory, Greenwich Park

Aug 2010, Fotoman 617, 180mm, Lee 0.6ND grad, 81b, Velvia 50 asa

The morning was bright and warm in Greenwich, although early cloud meant that the sun didn't emerge until after 7am. It was when a fractured cloud bank rolled in and without direct sunlight that the scene looked its best.

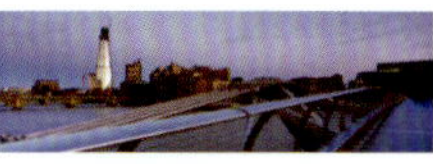

pages 186-187

The Shard glows, Millennium Bridge

Sept 2011, Fuji G617, Lee 0.75ND grad, 81b, Velvia 50 asa

The almost-completed Shard proved a fine sight. The wobbling Millennium bridge proved an issue, with my first shot suffering from camera-shake, but my second managed to avoid the vibration of passing feet for the 40-second duration.

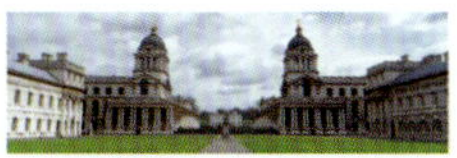

pages 188-189

Royal Naval College, Greenwich

Apr 2005; Fuji G617 105mm, Lee 0.3 ND grad, Velvia 50 asa

Long one of my favourite buildings in London, the Royal Naval College posed the problem of where to shoot from. The answer was to approach from the bank of the Thames. There was just about enough in the sky to give a point of reference.

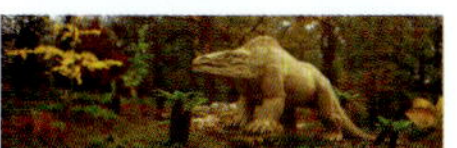

pages 190-191

Dinosaur lake, Crystal Palace Park

Nov 2005; Fotoman G617 180mm Rodenstock, Lee 81ef, Velvia 50 asa

Pedantic complaints have persisted that the designs fail to follow the fossil record with any accuracy – but I can't help imagining that this chap once strode out in south London and chewed on passing photographers.

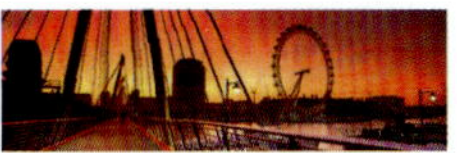

pages 192-193

Fiery dawn, Jubilee Bridge

Jan 2006; Fuji G617 105mm, Lee 0.6 ND grad, Velvia 50 asa

A fiercely burning dawn sky, shot from the western Jubilee Bridge. Frosting on the pavement gives an indication of the temperature of the morning. A medium ND grad was needed to balance the sky and foreground.

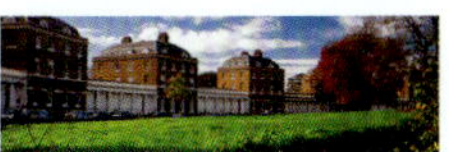

pages 194-195

The Paragon, Blackheath

Nov 2005; Fotoman 617 180mm Rodenstock, Lee 0.3 ND grad & polarizer, Velvia 50 asa

A short walk from Greenwich Park is the Paragon at Blackheath. Quite why all houses weren't made this way, I've no idea. The only thing liable to spoil the scene was the row of cars, so I took a low vantage point behind a grass verge.

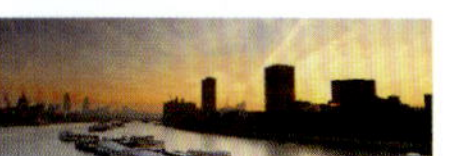

pages 196-197

Dawn from Waterloo Bridge

Jan 2006; Fuji G617 105mm, Lee 0.6 ND grad, Velvia 50 asa

The January rising sun highlights strange linear forms in the cloud, and steam rises from the vents of various buildings. Waterloo was probably the only accessible bridge I'd not crossed by this time, and I heard that the views from here could be special.

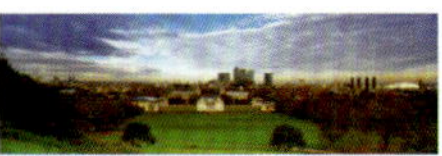

pages 198-199
Cloud banks from Greenwich Park
Nov 2005; Fuji G617 105mm, Lee 0.9 ND grad, Velvia 50 asa
I was delighted to see such interesting cloud forms from the Observatory hill. Two separate weather systems seemed to be meeting for my benefit, and although the sunlight was intermittent and weak, there was just enough.

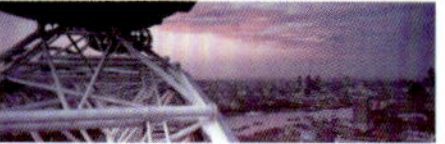

pages 200-201
Looking east, London Eye
Feb 2006; Fuji G617 105mm, Lee 0.6 ND grad, Provia 400 asa
The London Eye was conceived and designed by Marks Barfield Architects. The wheel is constantly moving, so my usual 50 asa film had to be replaced with Provia 400. A combination of polarization and getting as close to the glass as possible was the best compromise I could find.

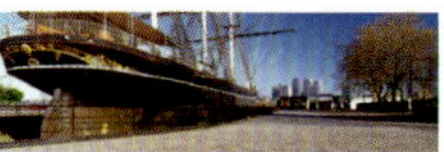

pages 202-203
***Cutty Sark*, spring morning**
Apr 2005; Fuji G617 105mm, Lee 0.3 ND grad & polarizer, Velvia 50 asa
Bright sunlight strikes the venerable timbers of the *Cutty Sark*, on a pristine morning in April. Using diagonals, here formed by the ship and the trees on the right, is a classic technique but in the panoramic format is particularly important.

pages 204-205
Fireworks over Battersea Park
Nov 2005; Fotoman 617 180mm Rodenstock unfiltered, Velvia 100f
The 400th anniversary of Guy Fawkes' attempt to blow up the Houses of Parliament is celebrated with fireworks. I was at the safe distance of a flat in Chelsea, where I had gatecrashed a party to capture this two minutes exposure from the balcony.

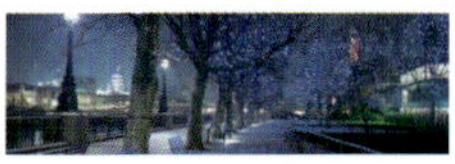

pages 206-207
Christmas lights, South Bank
Jan 2006; Fotoman 617 180mm Rodenstock unfiltered, RTP 64 asa
I often think of myself as somewhat lucky with the conditions I find, but this particular stroke of luck owed nothing to the weather. Finding these Christmas lights still switched on in late January made for a wonderful foreground for a vista of St Paul's.

ACKNOWLEDGEMENTS

Mark Denton would like to thank Anthony Mortimer for his help and support when shooting this updated volume. And Rachel, Lucy and Sam for bearing with him. xx

Mapping on pages 208-209 (© ML Design 2006) based originally on the 1939 Bartholomew Atlas, revised with the assistance of copyright free material provided by Alan Collinson Design and checked extensively on foot. Subsequent revisions courtesy of Lovell Johns Ltd, Oxford and David Haslam Publishing, Glos.

Mark Denton recommends Lee Filters (www.leefilters.co.uk)
Film processing was by the incomparable Bob Harvey at NPS Media, Middlesbrough (www.npsmedia.com) and Positive Images, Richmond on Thames (www.positive-images.co.uk)

Mark Denton's images are distributed by Panoramic Images, Inc. (Chicago) at www.panoramicimages.com and by www.markdentonphotographic.co.uk.
Some images are used with kind permission of Panoramic Images Inc.

Limited edition prints of images from this book are available from www.markdentonphotographic.co.uk
For prints, postcards, commissions, photo & camera sales and any other enquiries see www.markdentonphotographic.co.uk

Email: markdentonphotographic@gmail.com
Tel: 07709 905639
Twitter: @markdentonphoto

CONSTABLE

This edition first published in Great Britain in 2012 by Constable, an imprint of Constable & Robinson Ltd

3 5 7 9 10 8 6 4 2

A CIP catalogue record for this book
is available from the British Library.

ISBN: 978-1-84901-971-2

Printed and bound in China by C&C Joint Printing Co.

Constable
An imprint of
Little, Brown Book Group
Carmelite House
50 Victoria Embankment
London EC4Y 0DZ

An Hachette UK Company
www.hachette.co.uk

www.littlebrown.co.uk

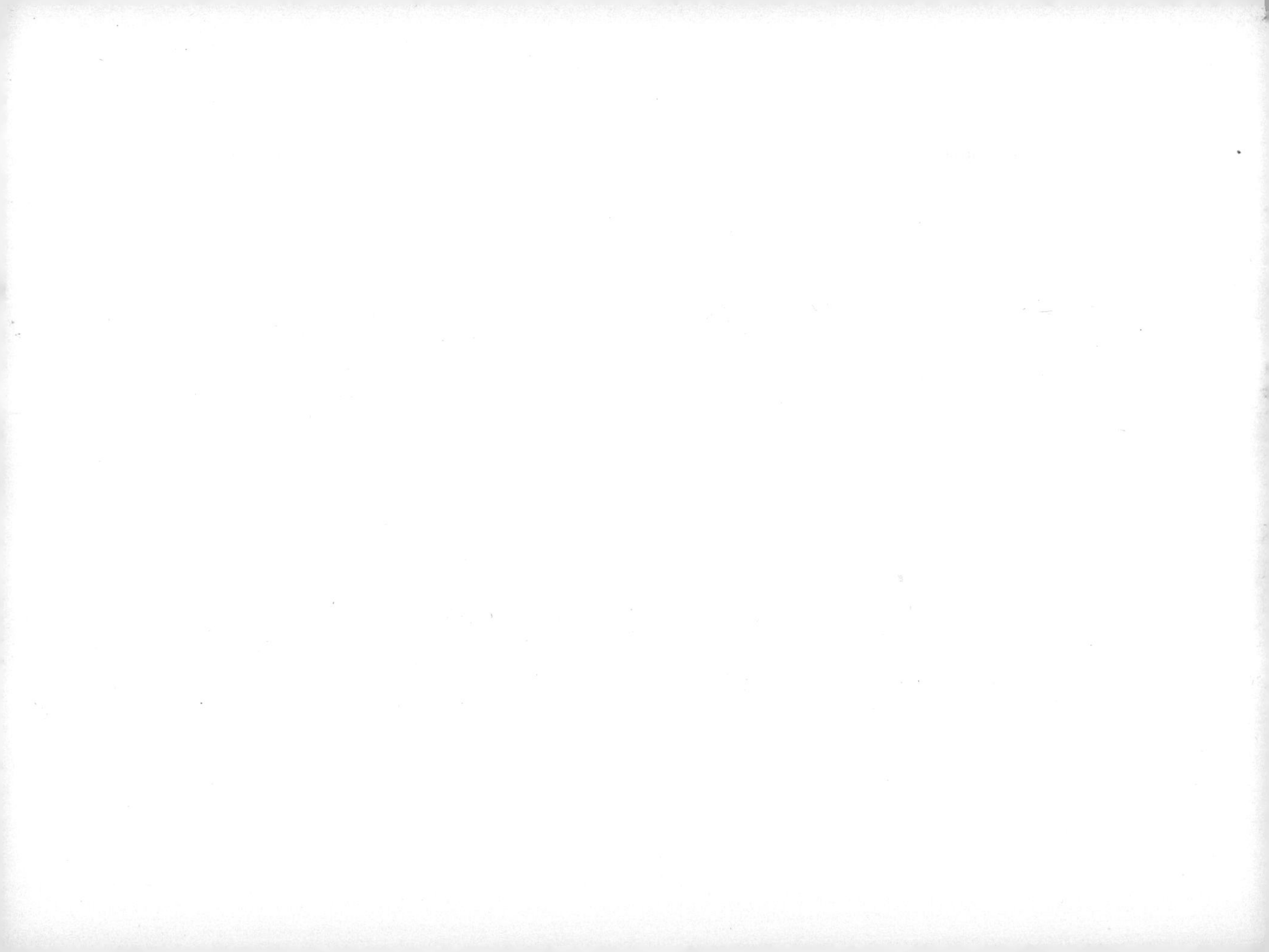